AMERICA AND
THE PATTERNS OF CHIVALRY

AMERICA AND THE
PATTERNS OF CHIVALRY

John Fraser

Cambridge University Press

CAMBRIDGE

LONDON   NEW YORK   NEW ROCHELLE

MELBOURNE   SYDNEY

Published by the Press Syndicate of the University of Cambridge
The Pitt Building, Trumpington Street, Cambridge CB2 1RP
32 East 57th Street, New York, NY 10022, USA
296 Beaconsfield Parade, Middle Park, Melbourne 3206, Australia

First Published 1982

Printed in the United States of America

Library of Congress Cataloging in Publication Data
Fraser, John.
America and the patterns of chivalry.
Includes bibliographical references and
index.
1. American literature – 19th century –
History and criticism.   2. American literature
– 20th century – History and criticism.
3. Chivalry in literature.   4. United States –
Intellecutal life.   I. Title.
PS217.C48F7   810'.9'353   81-6180
ISBN 0 521 24183 9   AACR2

For Tom and Betty Roberts

Contents

Preface

This book grew out of an earlier book of mine called *Violence in the Arts* (1974). While I was working on that one, I became increasingly interested in a couple of paradoxes: Certain attitudes that on the face of it were very reasonable and enlightened appeared to increase the likelihood of violence at times or to aggravate it when it occurred; and others that ostensibly encouraged violence appeared able to reduce it or even prevent it altogether. These paradoxes seemed to be linked to some further ones about freedom and form, and about American dealings with European cultural patterns. I was particularly curious as to the political implications of a fondness for chivalric values, especially as embodied in works of more or less romantic fiction. By the time I had finished the new book – and the task was more complicated than I had anticipated and took me down some historical paths that I had not foreseen – I had made sense of a number of things that had puzzled me. I had also found, to my pleasure, how seemingly unconnected phenomena that had lodged themselves in my consciousness over the years, such as the enduring charm of *The Great Gatsby* and *Huckleberry Finn*, or the fascination of Israel in its early days, or a political exile's radiant singing of "Joe Hill" at a Dublin party in the McCarran-McCarthy years, belonged together in a meaningful configuration.

Since I started work on the book some years ago, there has been a conspicuous increase of interest in chivalric matters. I have resisted the temptation to be up-to-the-minute, because up-to-the-minute examples have a habit of fading fast. But I can bring to mind several dozen movies from recent years that would have fitted in very comfortably, along with assorted novels, biographies, plays, magazine articles, and so forth. The significance of this interest seems to me as complicated now in some ways as it was during the period with which I am chiefly concerned. So do some of the shifts in American politics.

I would like to express my gratitude to the following: to Michael Black of the Cambridge University Press, who encouraged me to write the book and patiently endured my delays; to James W. Clark and Barbara Clark, for their extraordinarily helpful reading of the penultimate draft; to Thomas J. Roberts and James C. White, whose informed, civilized, and gently skeptical scrutiny I knew the finished work would have to face; to Michael and Norma Zwerin, as they then were, without whose generous friendship

Preface

almost thirty years ago the book and much else would not have been possible; to Aubrey M. Shane, whom it was always a pleasure talking with about what I was up to; to Hubert Morgan, for his lucid answers to my various questions; to the English Department of Dalhousie University, for being a place in which it was possible to get a lot of work done; to Donald and Greta Hogan, Herschel Shohan, Roland Dille, Edward Coleman, David Hansen, and Ronald and Ruth Hafter, who in various ways and in various places, but chiefly at the University of Minnesota, contributed to my understanding of my subject before I knew that it *was* my subject; and above all, to my wife Carol, who bore the brunt of my anxieties and continued to sustain me during a period in which questions of professional honor and dishonor were acutely relevant to her.

August, 1981   JOHN FRASER
Dalhousie University
Halifax, Nova Scotia

Part I

FROM CAVALIERS TO COWBOYS:
CHIVALRY IN HISTORY AND IMAGINATION

1

Introduction: Twain and the chivalry business

"Camelot – Camelot," said I to myself. "I don't seem to remember hearing of it before. Name of the asylum, likely."

Mark Twain, *A Connecticut Yankee in King Arthur's Court* (1889)

Call the shapes from the mist,
Call the dead men out of the mist and watch them ride.
Tall the first rider, tall with a laughing mouth,
His long black beard is combed like a beauty's hair,
His slouch hat plumed with a curled black ostrich feather,
He wears gold spurs and sits his horse with the seat
Of a horseman born.

Stephen Vincent Benét, *John Brown's Body* (1928)

The War Corps...The trumpet summoned America's knights and squires to the battlements of Camelot...Enlistment posters appealed not to greed or avarice, but to high purpose. To chivalry.

Grand Fifth Term Inaugural Issue, *National Lampoon* (1977)[1]

THE CHAMPION OF COMMON SENSE

TOWARD THE END of Mark Twain's *A Connecticut Yankee in King Arthur's Court*, there is a conveniently symbolic tournament. Clad in "the simplest and comfortablest of gymnast costumes – flesh-colored tights from neck to heel, with blue silk puffings about my loins, and bareheaded" – and equipped with a lariat and a couple of concealed dragoon revolvers, Twain's time-warped engineer hero takes on the massively armed and armored Sir Sagramor, who is aided by a battery of spells cast by his backer Merlin. While he waits for the affray to begin, The Boss, who has been at odds with Merlin from the outset, reflects that

the world thought there was a vast matter at stake here, and the world was right, but it was not the one they had in their minds. No, a far vaster one was upon the cast of this die: *the life of knight-errantry*. I was a champion, it was true, but not the champion of the frivolous black arts, I was the champion of hard unsentimental common sense and reason. I was entering the lists to either destroy knight-errantry or be its victim.

3

Naturally he does not become its victim – not then, at least. The bone-headed Sir Sagramor and other assorted opponents, including Galahad and Lancelot, "the very sun of their shining system," go crashing down to the lasso before a standing-room-only crowd of twenty thousand. Sir Sagramor, persisting in his folly, is tidily dispatched with a revolver. So are nine of the knights who are foolhardy enough to take up The Boss's challenge when he announces, "Here I stand and dare the chivalry of England to come against me – not by individuals, but in mass." After that salutary demonstration, reports the hero, "the day was mine. Knight-errantry was a doomed institution. The march of civilization was begun." Next day he reveals to the kingdom the network of schools, mines, factories, and workshops that he has been clandestinely building up as part of his enterprise of turning "groping and grubbing automata into *men*."[2] Civilization, the "genuine and wholesome civilization of the nineteenth century," has arrived.[3]

Though everyone remembers such episodes, if only from the movie versions, *A Connecticut Yankee* is not an endearing work. Its satire is too often ham-fisted, its tone uncertain, its would-be hilarious violences unfunny ("During the next fifteen minutes we stood under a steady drizzle of microscopic fragments of knights and hardware and horse-flesh"[4]). And the culminating holocaust that leaves The Boss and his fifty-three young technocrats the masters of England in the midst of twenty-five-thousand slaughtered knights is by common consent one of the bleakest nightmares in literature. But the novel is a deeply felt one and stands ideologically at the center of Twain's writings. It is the central work of Twain considered as America's Cervantes – central with respect to what he called "absurd chivalry business." Appearing in 1889, it was the fullest articulation of attitudes that he had displayed earlier in the decade in *The Prince and the Pauper* (1882), *Life on the Mississippi* (1883), and *Huckleberry Finn* (1884) and that he would display in *Pudd'nhead Wilson* (1894) and in his lambasting of Fenimore Cooper's Leatherstocking novels. And the aspirations symbolized in the tournament episode were manifestly his own at the time. He was obviously bent on destroying the chivalry business and exorcising what in *Life on the Mississippi* he called "dreams and phantoms," the "sillinesses and emptinesses, sham grandeurs, sham gauds, and sham chivalries of a brainless and worthless long vanished society."[5]

The novel's depressing features testify not only to the strength of Twain's feelings but to the strength of the difficulties that he experienced. When he began it, he was at the height of his creative powers and, like his hero jauntily lassoing knights or getting them to wear top hats and carry bulletin boards, he obviously felt that it should be possible to "extinguish" chivalry – or, more precisely, an excessive contemporary fondness for it – by exposing it to the clear light of republican common sense and making it ludicrous. As he wrote in his notebook at the time, "no church, no nobility, no royalty or other fraud, can face ridicule in a fair field and live."[6] But, also like his hero, he found his subtler weapons failing him and was drawn more and more into figurative and literal violence – the violence of invective, the violence of exposed medieval horrors, the violence of dynamite. And the novel's Armageddon, wiping out not only the attacking army of knights but all the comfort- and enlightenment-bearing institutions of the newly created civilization, was a baffled and bitter acknowledgement of intellectual failure. Despite all The Boss's ridicule, cunning, and technological resourcefulness, all the demonstrated benefits of modernity, all the palpable follies and horrors of medievalism, he had in fact ended up with the whole kingdom against him. And his situation resembled Twain's own with respect to chivalry.

It was a very odd situation. On the face of things, what Twain was saying in his capacity as a Connecticut Cervantes was eminently orthodox. In his rational republican egalitarianism, he was squarely in the tradition that had been described by Alexis de Tocqueville in *Democracy in America*. America, he not unreasonably felt, was committed to the belief that "there is plenty good enough material for a republic in the most degraded people that ever existed,"[7] and to a total rejection of the idea of aristocracy, with its mysterious innate inequalities, its logical invitations to dominance, and its destruction of the manhood of the dominated. When he pointed out how "the blunting effects of slavery upon the slaveholder's moral perceptions are known and conceded the world over; and a privileged class, an aristocracy, is but a band of slaveholders under another name,"[8] he was simply displaying sturdy republican good sense. It was perfectly obvious, as Andrew Carnegie declared in *Triumphant Democracy* (1886), that "the Republic honors her children at birth with equality; the Monarchy stamps hers with a brand of inferiority".[9] And Carnegie's own career testified to the glories of an egalitarian America in which poor but worthy immigrant lads such as himself could soar like Twain's Boss to positions of unprecedented technological might. The pacific verities – what Edgar Allan Poe in 1850 called "our modern and altogether rational ideas of the absurdity and impiety of warfare"[10] – were no less obvious. As the poet Joel Barlow announced at the start of the century, America had a duty to ensure that "true and useful ideas of glory" replace "the false and destructive ones that have degraded the species in other countries"; and in *Triumphant Democracy* Carnegie explained how:

5

Part I From cavaliers to cowboys

Instead of making conquests over nature, [Europeans] strive for conquests over each other, incited thereto by selfish and conceited kings and self-styled noblemen. But the end is near. It is probable that it is by an industrial conquest feudalism and standing armies in Europe are to be overcome; and that has already begun. America, blessed land of peace, is inundating the world...with her gospel of the equality of man as man.[11]

From any rational point of view, the "medieval," the structures and spirit of what the popular illustrator and children's writer Howard Pyle described in a novel in 1888 as "a great black gulf in human history, a gulf of ignorance, of superstition, of cruelty and of wickedness,"[12] was the prime American enemy.

These considerations had been of the liveliest practical relevance in America. Not only had Americans fought a long war, both physically and mentally, to liberate themselves from the mystifying and tyrannical claims of royalty and aristocracy. Within recent memory, they had fought a far bigger and bloodier defensive war of liberation against the chivalric, aristocratic, and fire-eating South. And the antebellum South, the South whose psyche Twain analyzed in the books that I have mentioned, had abundantly demonstrated what "medieval" unreason looked like. It had been the land of the slaver's whip and chains, the branding iron, the mutilating knife, the burning of offending slaves alive, and all the other amply documented infamies.[13] It had been a society, as Twain noted in *Pudd'nhead Wilson*, in which a Junoesque white-skinned brunette could be a "nigger" because of a sixteenth part of colored blood – and hence a potential victim of those infamies – and in which deciding which of two equally white youths was a slave and could be sold down the river was simply a problem of terminology. It had disgraced itself with feuds like the one between the Grangerfords and Shepherdsons that nauseated Huck Finn, and killings like the one in the same novel in which the gentlemanly Colonel Sherburn coldly gunned down an unarmed and terrified old man who had insulted him, and the plethora of Bowie-knives-and-buckshot duels and affrays reported in the antebellum Southern press.[14] It had disfigured American politics with the episode in the Fifties in which Congressman Preston Brooks of South Carolina had thrashed Senator Charles Sumner of Massachusetts with his cane in the Senate chamber on behalf of Southern honor. The incident elicited from the *Richmond Enquirer* the unendearing reflection that "these vulgar abolitionists in the Senate are getting above themselves. They have grown saucy, and dare to be impudent to gentlemen... They must be lashed into submission. Sumner, in particular, ought to have nine and thirty every morning. He is a great strapping fellow, and could stand the cowhide beautifully."[15]

Introduction: Twain and the chivalry business

Nor was Twain being naive in his concern about the shaping power of romantic fiction. Admittedly, the growth of Southern nationalism in the decades before the Civil War had been caused by more than a too enthusiastic reading of Scott's Waverley novels. As articulated by political thinkers like John C. Calhoun, George Fitzhugh, and others, Southern nationalism had involved a complex striving after a cultural self-definition that would permit the slaveowning South to see itself as governed by historical principles and patterns different from, and as worthy as, those of the industrializing and abolitionist North. And the growing Southern belligerence during those decades testified to the tensions of a war of ideas in which it was increasingly inescapable that, as a Mississippian acknowledged in 1851, "whether right or wrong, the opinions and sympathies of the whole civilized world are against us."[16] But Twain's famous attack on Sir Walter Scott in *Life on the Mississippi* was a response to major energies. Scott was not only the first great imaginative recreator of the Middle Ages, with a keen sociological eye for representative types, a poetic feeling for meaning-charged settings –the castle, the greensward, the banqueting hall, the torture chamber – and a remarkable ability to build up major episodes, such as the tournament in *Ivanhoe* and the fraternizing of Crusaders and Saracens at the oasis in *The Talisman*. He also provided a conveniently cleaned-up set of values and virtues – honor, generosity, hospitality, and so forth –that could be incorporated into the South's new cultural self-definition. And he made vividly plausible the possibility of legitimate cultural pluralism, an idea essential to the South in its ideological struggle against the monistic North. The South could see itself mirrored in the culture of the Saxons in *Ivanhoe* (1820), the culture of a supposedly primitive but in fact proud, sturdy, and morally admirable slaveowning people who rightly refused to acknowledge any inferiority to the ostensibly more sophisticated Normans who shared the country with them and were seeking to dominate them. And in *The Talisman* (1825), the culture of the Saracens, as embodied in the nobly chivalrous Saladin, was in no way inferior to that of the Crusaders who faced them across the ideological divide, any more than Scotland's culture was inferior to England's. Scott's influence had been reinforced, too, by the works of British, American, and French novelists, including Cooper and Alexandre Dumas, who were creatively in his debt; by Scott-inspired histories of chivalry like those of Charles Mills and G. P. R. James; and by books like Thomas Johnes's much-reprinted translation of Froissart's *Chronicles* (1803–10), his translation of Jean de Joinville's memoirs of the crusading Louis IX (1807; reprinted 1848), and William Gilmore Simms's life of the Chevalier Bayard

7

(1847), whose name, as he put it, had "grown into proverbial identification, in modern times, with all that is pure and noble in mankind, and all that is great and excellent in a soldier."[17]

Hence, as Twain saw, an American fondness for the absurd chivalry business was not simply a laughing matter. A sham-medieval state capitol in Baton Rouge; newspaper gush about "the beauty and the chivalry" of Southern gentry at a mule race;[18] the literary offenses of a novelist like Fenimore Cooper in his romanticizing of frontiersmen and Indians – all, even if richly deserving to be made fun of, formed part of a system of deception and self-deception too serious in its consequences to be merely funny. When Twain described in *The Prince and the Pauper* some of the cruelties and squalors of the picturesque doublet-and-hose Tudor world, dissected Southern romanticism in *Life on the Mississippi*, and showed up the absurdities of the code of honor in *Huckleberry Finn*, he was going after real game. And he was going after real game in *A Connecticut Yankee* when he tried to debunk Arthurianism and force his readers, especially Northern readers, to confront what he saw as the actual medieval awfulness – the brutish ignorance and compulsive belligerence of the knights; the discomforts of daily life; the wretchedness of the lower orders; the pervasive superstitiousness and unreason; the absurdity of a court that was "just a sort of polished-up court of Comanches";[19] the overwhelming preposterousness of a social order dominated by "a king, nobility and gentry, idle, unproductive, acquainted mainly with the arts of wasting and destroying, and of no sort of use or value in any rationally constructed world";[20] the whole gallimaufry supported by the systematized unreason and intellectual tyranny of the Church. Romantic nostalgia had flesh-and-blood consequences. A day or two before his thrashing, Charles Sumner had remarked scornfully of a relative of his assailant that "the Senator from South Carolina has read many books of chivalry, and believes himself a chivalrous knight, with sentiments of honor and courage."[21] The chivalric ideology that left Sumner a cripple contributed to the outbreak of the war five years later, and afterwards assisted the South to bring to a standstill the process of Reconstruction and go on brazenly affirming its doctrine of innate inequalities.

But if the signposts of reason all pointed in one direction, where people actually went in their cultural preferences was another matter. From a rational point of view, in fact, the history of nineteenth-century America could be seen as a progressive overlaying of Enlightenment common sense by chivalric romanticism. The process had been most obvious in the antebellum South, with its enthusiasm for the duelling code disseminated by European officers during the War of Independence, and its appetite for ring tournaments, such as the one in Virginia

8

in 1845 in which knights in full armor, among them Ivanhoe and Don Quixote, performed in front of heralds and trumpeters, or the one in South Carolina five years later in which, as a gratified spectator noted, "Mr. Mazyck Porcher was the King at Arms very handsomely dressed in Sir Walter Raleigh style."[22] (Twain's comments on Mr. Porcher might have been worth having.) But Scott and his imitators were popular in the antebellum North too, as were Arthurian works like the first group of Tennyson's *Idylls of the King*, and after a postwar interregnum the romanticization of Northern taste began in earnest. By the time *A Connecticut Yankee* appeared – a year after the final version of the *Idylls* – it was gaining an irresistible momentum.[23]

As the author of *Chivalric Days: and the Boys and Girls who Helped to Make Them* assured his readers in 1886,

all days may be chivalric, however barren they may seem of opportunity for heroic action. For, as truth and honor, courtesy and gentleness, purity and faith can never grow old; as valor and courage, kindliness of heart and knightliness of soul, are ever the highest orders of nobility; so all days may be full of chivalry, all deeds may be instinct with that earnestness of purpose that lives in the heart of every well-regulated girl or boy.[24]

Well-regulated readers of all ages were being given an increasingly broad range of reminders of the values and virtues of chivalry. The Arthurianism that would become a torrent a little later was available not only in the prestigious pages of Tennyson but in works like the lastingly popular abridgment of Malory, *The Boy's King Arthur* (1880), by the poet and former Confederate officer Sidney Lanier.[25] The historical basis of chivalry was being fortified in books like Lanier's *The Boy's Froissart* (1879), new editions of Johnes's translation of Froissart, and biographical celebrations of heroes like the Black Prince, Henry V, Sir Walter Raleigh, and of course those two nonpareils, the Chevalier Bayard and Sir Philip Sidney. Above all, romantic fiction was becoming increasingly enticing as the appeal of respectable American writers like Hawthorne, Irving, and Longfellow waned. In his admirable reminiscences about his youth in a small Maryland town, more Northern than Southern, Henry Seidel Canby recalls how in the Eighties and Nineties "what we fell upon, read besottedly, thought about, and were moulded by, were... most of all the novels of Sir Walter Scott."[26] The influence of Scott and of writers like Dumas and R. D. Blackmore, the author of the glorious *Lorna Doone* (1869), was being reinforced by irresistible contemporary imports like *Treasure Island* (1882), *Kidnapped* (1886), and Conan Doyle's *The White Company* (1890). In the Nineties, according to Canby, British and American historical romances became "a landslide, millions of copies circulating among all classes except the proletariat... so that each season it was certain that virtually every literate American had read one such book." He comments that, "I am sure that Scott and the near-Scotts and the school-of-Scotts were such real determinants of inner life for readers brought up in the eighties and nineties that no one will ever understand the America of that day without reading and pondering upon" *Ivanhoe* and novels like Winston Churchill's *Richard Carvel* (about the period of the War of Independence), Stanley Weyman's *Under the Red Robe* (about Richelieu's France), and Booth Tarkington's *Monsieur Beaucaire* (about eighteenth-century England).[27]

The Northern appetite for romance extended to Southern matters. Even before the Civil War, Northern readers had enjoyed the evocations of Southern life in novels like John Pendleton Kennedy's *Swallow Barn*, G. P. R. James's *The Old Dominion*, and James Hungerford's *The Old Plantation*, with their glimpses of what William Alexander Carruthers, in *The Cavaliers of Virginia*, called "that generous, fox-hunting, wine-drinking, duelling and reckless race of men, which gives so distinct a character to Virginians wherever they may be found."[28] But in the postwar decades the South really came into its own. By the end of the Seventies, enterprising new magazines like *Lippincott's*, venerable established ones like *Harper's*, and the larger publishing houses had opened their doors to Southern writers, and Northern readers were displaying a hearty appetite for the vision of plantation life purveyed by writers like George Eggleston and Thomas Nelson Page, with their gallant and graceful gentry, their idyllic settings, their happy and well-cared-for darkies. By the end of the Eighties, the Northern novelist Albion W. Tourgée reported that American literature had become "not only Southern in type but distinctly Confederate in sympathy" and that "a foreigner studying our current literature...and judging our civilization by our fiction, would undoubtedly conclude that the South was the seat of intellectual empire in America."[29] As the century closed, the distinguished South Carolinian Greek scholar Basil S. Gildersleeve could speak casually in the *Atlantic* of "the Virginian planter whom all have agreed to make the one national hero."[30] There had been a good deal of prescience in the diary entry of a young Georgia girl, Eliza Frances Andrews, near the close of the war:

Time brings its revenges, though it may move but slowly. Some future Motley or Macaulay will tell the truth about our cause, and some unborn Walter Scott will spread the halo of romance around it. In all the poems and romances that shall be written about the war, I prophesy that the heroes will all be rebels, or if Yankees, from some loyal Southern state.[31]

These changes, moreover, were accompanied by other manifestations of a fascination with chivalric, aristocratic, and neomedieval structures. In the early Seventies, as the radical cartoonist Art Young said of his boyhood years, "kings and dukes were still jokes. Nor did newspapers

10

dare to glorify a man just because he was wellborn or rich. Any one who boasted of a family tree would have been laughed at."[32] But by the Eighties the new rich were putting up what H. L. Mencken called their "elegantly hand-tooled"[33] chateaux and castles on Fifth Avenue, the Chicago Gold Coast, and San Francisco's Nob Hill, and filling them with entertainments like the Vanderbilts' colossal fancy dress ball in 1883 (at which the host appeared as the Duc de Guise and the hostess as a Venetian princess), and marrying into the European aristocracy, and buying country estates in Britain, including the vast Scottish estate purchased by that champion of democracy Andrew Carnegie.[34] At a somewhat more modest level, in Canby's words, "all through the eighties and early nineties Gothic adornments clustered thicker and thicker on our red-brick houses and every established family began... its long and often very expensive search for a genealogy, to find usually dubious ancestors of impeccable nobility in England, and to acquire at still more expense a still more dubious coat of arms."[35] The prestige Eastern universities and colleges, as Thorstein Veblen caustically noted, were likewise buying into glamor, by means of academic costumes, exclusive student societies, and the enthusiasm of well-heeled alumni and other benefactors for pseudo-Gothic architecture. The expanding network of eastern prep schools was demonstrating what one of John P. Marquand's proper Bostonians would call "the advantages of the Arnold and Rugby idea,"[36] an idea in which sports played, as they did in the colleges and universities, a major part. In the larger cities, exclusive men's clubs were welcoming the gentlemanly products of the changing educational system, which would itself, as in Gilbert Patten's Frank Merriwell stories and Owen Johnson's immortal *Stover at Yale*, become a terrain for romantic fiction.[37] By the end of the Nineties, the gentleman hero of Charles Dana Gibson's drawings had provided the period with one of its most potent icons – broad shouldered, clean cut, steady eyed, and a fit mate for Gibson's even more memorably patrician young Amazon, with her proudly upsurging bosom, her soaring neck and emphatic chin, her piled masses of hair. It is not surprising that the Eighties and Nineties witnessed a growing fascination with the idea of class, and that by 1902 the socialist W. J. Ghent was complaining of "the fervid praise of inequality of condition which in recent years is so often heard."[38]

Furthermore, in the twentieth century the Twainian paradox – the powerlessness of a masterly would-be debunker in a country with a rich tradition of debunking – would grow worse. If one were to judge by the strength of the antichivalric and antimartial sentiments of a host of educators, psychologists, sociologists, intellectual journalists, ironical novelists, and others, equipped with much more sophisticated weap-

11

onry than was available to Twain, a fondness for the chivalric should
have been extinct years ago, at least outside of realms of darkness like
the South, with its good old boys, and Faulknerian gentry, and what a
Mississippian calls the "curious...appositon...of courtliness and extraordinary kindliness on the one hand and sudden violence on the other."[39]
But despite the numerous obituary notices – some gloating, some
regretful – the chivalric would continue to prosper.

TWENTIETH-CENTURY CAVALIERS

The family of chivalric heroes has been by far the largest and most
popular one in twentieth-century American culture, and its members, in
whole or in part, have entered into virtually everyone's consciousness.
They include, naturally, the legion of knightly Westerners in print and
celluloid sired by Owen Wister's *The Virginian* and their Indian counterparts. They include Robin Hood, Errol Flynn's especially, and Zorro, and
the Scarlet Pimpernel, and gentlemen buccaneers like Rafael Sabatini's
Captain Peter Blood, "a slim, tall fellow with light-blue eyes in a tawny
face, eyes in which glinted the light of a wicked humour."[40] They include
the officers and gentlemen of *Lives of a Bengal Lancer*, and the gentlemen
rankers of *Beau Geste*, and the First World War aviators of *Dawn Patrol*,
and clean-cut American fly-boys like Steve Canyon. They include honest
cops like Dick Tracy, and fearless investigative reporters, and incorruptible district attorneys, and upstanding young doctors like Doctor Kildare.
They include battered but romantic private eyes like Raymond Chandler's Philip Marlowe, buoyant ones like Jonathan Latimer's Bill Crane and
Richard S. Prather's Shell Scott, efficient ones like Alex Raymond's Rip
Kirby, depressive ones like Ross Macdonald's Lew Archer. They include
John D. MacDonald's battered, rangy knight errant Travis McGee. They
include gentlemen knights like Prince Valiant, and Nature's gentlemen
like Tarzan and Joe Palooka, and miscellaneous *samurai*, and the martial-
arts experts of Bruce Lee. They include Superman and Buck Rogers. They
include men about town like Philo Vance, the Saint, and Dashiell
Hammett's Nick Charles, and the figures played by Fred Astaire –
"society's hoofer and the world's," as Hemingway called him.[41] They
include gentlemanly English actors like Ronald Colman and George
Sanders, and gentlemanly American ones like Douglas Fairbanks, Jr. and
William Powell, and all those immortals, Gary Cooper, Spencer Tracy,
and the rest, who have epitomized native American gallantry and grace.
They include their female partners or adversaries like Katharine Hepburn, Rosalind Russell, Myrna Loy, Ava Gardner, and Lauren Bacall.
They include the bowler-hatted Oliver Hardy endeavoring to charm the
ladies with ponderous Southern courtesies, and the self-sacrificing figure

of the Tramp in Chaplin's more sentimental movies, and the Battle of Britain pilot incarnated so unforgettably by Danny Kaye in *The Secret Life of Walter Mitty*, and Snoopy in his "Curse you, Red Baron" phase.

And if everyone knows the players, everyone knows the games. In the science-fiction movie *Westworld* (1973), two of the three locales in which well-heeled romantics were enabled to act out their fantasy lives were a simulated Western township and a simulated medieval castle, with all the customary trimmings. The promoters could as profitably have added the private eye world of trench coats, enigmatic blondes, and bourbon in the desk drawer, the plantation world of juleps and sexy octaroons, the cloak-and-rapier Three Musketeers world, the sweaty, stubble-chinned explorer world of sun helmets, long-barreled revolvers, and ominous native drumming, and the pirate world of creaking rigging, duels on the poop deck, and the rescuing of governors' daughters from fates much much worse than death. Everyone knows, too, that one's strength is as the strength of ten because one's heart is pure, and that it's how one plays the game that counts, not whether one wins or loses, and that one gives it the old college try, and that a man's gotta do what a man's gotta do. Everyone recognizes the codes and conventions in a passage like the following:

"The first plane out of here is at ten fifteen this evening," I said. 'You'd both better catch it. The deal's gone sour."

Knight sat up and swung his feet to the floor. "God, St. Ives, when you get noble, you're awful."

"I liked him better when he was a shit like us," Wisdom said. "I don't care much for him when he's Carstairs."

"Carstairs?" Knight said.

"Carstairs the magnificent. You know Carstairs. When they come to the edge of the desert he's the one who always turns to his two buddies and says, 'If you don't hear from me in three weeks, tell Mary...' Then he breaks off and goddamned near blushes and says, 'But you know what to tell her,' and then one of his buddies, the stupid one, like you, Knight, says, 'But that's fifteen hundred miles of burning sand, Carstairs,' and Carstairs, the prick, shades his eyes with his hand and says, 'Isn't that what all life is?' "[42]

Moreover, in a culminating paradox, the Arthurianism that Twain tried so hard to debunk and deglamorize would become established at the center of liberal America's political imagery as the gleaming towers of Camelot aspired above the Washington mists, and youth and beauty and gallantry came into their own at last, and the arts and graces mingled in a shining throng. And when, after all too short a reign, the young ruler was struck down, John Steinbeck was obviously speaking for many other mourners when he quoted in a letter to his widow the words of Sir Ector upon the death of Lancelot:

Ah Launcelot, he said, thou were head of all Christian knights, and now I dare say, said Sir Ector, thou Sir Launcelot, there thou liest, that thou were never matched of earthly knight's hand. And thou were the courteoust knight that ever bare shield. And thou were the truest friend to thy lover that ever bestrad horse. And thou were the truest lover of a sinful man that ever loved woman. And thou were the kindest man that ever struck with sword. And thou were the goodliest person that ever came among press of knights. And thou was the meekest man and the gentlest that ever ate in hall among ladies. And thou were the sternest knight to thy mortal foe that ever put spear in the rest.[43]

Thirteen years later, the author of a letter in *Time* was likewise obviously speaking for a good many people when he asked yearningly:

Where are the men of heroic proportions, soul-stirring, uniquely gifted, magnetic in inspiration, who can truly personify the leadership necessary to keep the U.S. strong and worthy of world esteem?

There must be a "knight in shining armour" waiting in the wings of the political arena to truly inspire the American people.[44]

The chivalry business had prospered in America with a vengeance.

In the rest of this book, I shall try to account for the phenomena that I have described in this chapter and to define more precisely how and why chivalric patterns were incorporated into American life during the later nineteenth and early twentieth centuries and what some of the consequences were. America has not, of course, been *sui generis* in its dealings with the chivalric. Nineteenth-century Britain, for example, witnessed the counterpointing of utilitarianism and neo-Darwinism with the celebrations of medievalism by writers like Carlyle, Ruskin, and Morris, and the emergence of the imperialist romanticism that I have already touched on; and the conflicts in American liberalism that I deal with were also present in late nineteenth and early twentieth century British liberalism. But the dichotomies and antitheses have been much sharper and the paradoxes more interesting in America, so that to examine the relevant American attitudes toward concepts like violence, order, freedom, competition, and peace is an economical way of exploring issues that are more than merely American. It is also, of course, a convenient way of exploring and testing out the chivalric patterns and attitudes themselves, given the strength of American hostility to them and the aspiration to annihilate them by exposing them to the light of rational analysis. In Chapters 2 and 3 I shall look principally at the seeming vulnerability of the chivalric to such analysis. In Chapters 4 and 5 I shall offer some reasons for its stubborn resistance to it. I shall then, in Part II (Chapters 6 through 10), examine various assimilations, transpositions, and metamorphoses of chivalric patterns that occurred in education, business, and politics. Finally, in Part III (Chapters 11 and 12) I shall sketch some broader social implications of what I have been describing, with particular reference to the problematic concept of honor.

2

Violence

It is astonishing what a demoralizing influence association with horses seems to exercise over the human race. Put a man on horseback and his next idea is to play the bully or steal something.

> Eliza Frances Andrews (1864), *The War-Time Journal of a Georgia Girl*

The whole pleasure of [it] standeth in open manslaughter and bold bawdry – in which book those be counted the noblest knights that do kill most men without any quarrel, and commit the foulest adulteries by subtlest shifts.

> Roger Ascham on Malory's *Le Morte d'Arthur*

> I should like
> – Who wouldn't? – to shoot beautifully and be obeyed.

> W. H. Auden[1]

DREAMS OF LOVE AND GLORY

IN SOME RESPECTS, there is no mystery about why Americans should have found the chivalric attractive, and to ignore them would be like discussing Twain without ever mentioning that he was funny. It is not mysterious that the quintessential glamorous foreign correspondent Richard Harding Davis, as a boy in the 1870s, "was forever leading his little band over the pass," or that one of the popular fiction writer Owen Johnson's prep-school boys, around 1890, "would read The Count of Monte Cristo, and follow The Three Musketeers through a thousand far-off adventures," or that F. Scott Fitzgerald's Amory Blaine, at prep school, wallowed in books like Conan Doyle's *The White Company*.[2] No great critical acumen is needed to explain why young readers in the early 1900s were charmed by how Booth Tarkington's Monsieur Beaucaire, "with perfect ease...ran Captain Rohrer through the left shoulder – after which he sent a basket of red roses to the Duke of Winterset," or why in Charles Dana Gibson's drawing, "The Seed of Ambition," a delivery girl is pausing in front of a billboard to gaze yearningly at a haughty eighteenth-century belle behind whom a gallant swordfight rages.[3] Every reader – every male reader, at least – can project himself into the boyhood dreams of glory of Fitzgerald's Basil Lee around 1910:

All eyes were now fixed upon the masked but well-groomed man in the dress suit and opera hat who stood nonchalantly in the door.

"Don't move, please," he said, in a well-bred, cultivated voice that had, nevertheless, a ring of steel in it. "This thing in my hand might – go off."[4]

15

Part I From cavaliers to cowboys

As Charles Mills had exclaimed in his *History of Chivalry* in 1825, "baronial pomp, knightly gallantry, women's beauty, gay caparisons, rich attire, and feudal pageantry, throng the mind in wild and splendid confusion, when we hear the herald's trumpet clang summoning the knights to achievement."[5] The chivalric was the magical kingdom of castles and greensward, and twisting cobbled streets at midnight, and sun-baked islands and jostling wharves, and graceful Southern plantations, and velvet tropical skies, and the majestic spaces of the Western landscape, an enchanted composite realm of the imagination in which picturesquely garbed figures coped with the ever-changing configurations of warfare, or cattle drives, or the intricate rituals and plottings of aristocratic society. It was a world of freedom in which a stripling sea captain, in E. S. Brooks's *Chivalric Days: and the Boys and Girls Who Helped to Make Them*, could calmly face down haughty aristocrats:

"But at least, good Jean," said the Chevalier d'Harcourt, swallowing his alarm and wrath and striving to speak calmly, "at least, good Jean, you will explain to us – "
The boy straightened himself proudly.
"No, sir, I will explain nothing," he said. "At sea I answer only to my superiors and on this deck I have none. *I* am captain of the caravel!"[6]

It was a world whose allure was displayed three years after the appearance of *A Connecticut Yankee* when the hero and heroine of the Midwestern realist Hamlin Garland's first novel went to the theater:

The curtain rose upon the fair at Nottinghamshire; and with the sweet imaginative music as solvent and setting, the gay lads and lassies of far romance sang and danced under the trees in garments upon which the rain had never fallen, and unflecked with dust. Knights in splendid dress of silver and green, with graceful swords and sashes, came and went, while the merry peasant youths circled and flourished their gay scarfs and sang task-free and sin-free.
The scene changed to Sherwood Forest; and there, in the land of Robin Hood, where snow never falls, where rains never slant through the shuddering leaves, the jocund foresters met to sing and drink October ale. There came Little John and Will Scarlet and Alan-a-Dale in glittering garments, with care-free brows and tuneful voices, to circle and sing. Fadeless and untarnished was each magnificent cloak and doublet slashed with green or purple; straight and fair and supple was every back and limb. No marks of toil anywhere, no lines of care, no hopeless hunger, no threatening task; nothing to do but to sing and dance and drink after the hunt among the delightfully dry and commodious forest wilds – a glorious, free life![7]

The knight errants, and cavaliers, and cowboys, and men about town, and all the other heroes were lively, and graceful, and free spirited. They had strong and healthy bodies and were masters of enviable physical skills. They lived and fought in the spirit of Thomas Osbert Mordaunt's clarion proclamation that "One crowded hour of glorious

16

Violence

life / Is worth an age without a name," the spirit that moved Alexis de Tocqueville to remark that "there is something in the adventurous life of hunting people which seizes the heart of man and carries him away in spite of reason and experience."[8] They were insouciant and imperturbable, whether robbing a bank or mounting a scaffold, and grew old, if they did grow old, without becoming withered or lumpish. Like Sabatini's Scaramouche, who was "born with a gift of laughter and a sense that the world was mad," and who had the "philosophic outlook and mercurial temperament which are the stock-in-trade of your adventurer of all ages," they were men who never had to "stoop to a mechanical / Or servile shape at others' beck and call."[9] Nor were their charms confined to fiction. The Mississippi politician Sargent Prentice, as described by Joseph G. Baldwin in 1842, "bet thousands on the turn of a card and witnessed the success or failure of the wager with the *nonchalance* of a Mexican monte-player, or, as was most usual, with the light humor of a Spanish muleteer," and, "starting to fight a duel... laid down his hand at poker, to resume it with a smile when he returned, and went on the field laughing with his friends, as to a picnic."[10] The Civil War had been graced by cavaliers like Jeb Stuart,

> Reckless, merry, religious, theatrical,
> Lover of gesture, lover of panache,
> With all the actor's grace and the quick, light charm
> That makes the women adore him.[11]

Ernest Hemingway, who had cut his boyhood teeth on romances, would write in 1932 of the American bull fighter Sidney Franklin that he "has the ability in languages, the cold courage and the ability to command of the typical soldier of fortune, he is a charming companion, one of the best story tellers I have ever heard, has enormous and omniverous curiosity about everything."

Furthermore, the chivalric patterns were satisfying with respect to social relationships. Hemingway speaks of how a special "degree of bravery, which comes with exhilaration, is the ability not to give a damn for possible consequences; not only to ignore them but to despise them."[12] A great many youthful readers, including Hemingway, were obviously thrilled by bravery of that sort in works like Richard Harding Davis's enormously popular Cuban novel, *Soldiers of Fortune* (1897):

> "They're shooting better," said MacWilliams. "They'll reach us in a minute."
> "They've reached me already, I think," Langham answered, with suppressed satisfaction, "in the shoulder. It's nothing." His unconcern was quite sincere; to a young man who had galloped through two long halves of a football match on a strained tendon, a scratched shoulder was not important, except as an unsought honor.[13]

17

The courage and self-possession of chivalric heroes were made considerably easier by the relationships they enjoyed with peers and superiors. They had available to them the kind of fraternal bonding shown in *The Three Musketeers* when Athos asks, "Are you not aware that we are never seen one without the others, and that we are called among the Musketeers and the Guards, at court and in the city...the Three Inseparables?",[14] the bonding of men (or boys) who had passed through rituals of initiation and acceptance and had a common code. If they were lucky, as they usually were, they also shared the code with authority figures who, like the various noblemen rewarding Conan Doyle's youthful Nigel Loring in *Sir Nigel*, recognized courage and prowess when brought to their attention and were often agreeably permissive to boot. The protective relationship between an authority figure like M. de Tréville and the obstreperous but still servants-of-right Musketeers would be repeated in numerous friendships between intelligent teachers and high-spirited boys in school stories, tolerant lawmen and decent gunslingers in Westerns, and blind-eye-turning police officers and law-bending private detectives in thrillers.

Relations with members of the opposite sex were also made more enjoyable. Henry Seidel Canby recalls "the chivalrous attitude (it was more than a pose) toward girls, which reached its height just about the turn of the century and was literary in its origin. The decorous familiarity of the eighties was too stiff for us...We tried to see our girls as romantic beauties and ourselves as gentlemen who lived by honor."[15] A chivalric hero could be thoroughly masculine – hunting, duelling, drinking, card playing, fighting – and yet behave gracefully toward women, to the latter's benefit. As Scott had explained in *The Talisman*, and as had been affirmed over and over in one way or another, the true knight thought of his lady

as of a deity, who, having deigned to show herself for an instant to her devoted worshipper, had again returned to the darkness of her sanctuary – or as an influential planet, which, having darted in some auspicious minute one favourable ray, wrapped itself again in its veil of mist. The motions of the lady of his love were to him those of a superior being, who was to move without watch or control, rejoice him by her appearance, or depress him by her absence, animate him by her kindness, or drive him to despair by her cruelty – all at her own free-will, and without other importunity or remonstrance than that expressed by the most devoted services of the heart and sword of the champion, whose sole object in life was to fulfil her commands, and, by the splendour of his own achievement, to exalt her fame.[16]

The hero got plenty in return for his gallantry too. In one of Richard Harding Davis's stories, for example, the heroine called the hero "her knight-errant, and gave him her chain and locket to wear, and told him whether he failed or succeeded it meant nothing to her, and that her life

18

was his while it lasted, and her soul as well."[17] And things became peppier at times, such as when one of the royal heroes in the Virginia-born James Branch Cabell's *Chivalry* (1910) "smiled whimsically, and presently one arm swept beneath [the princess's] knees, so that presently he held her as one dandles a baby; and presently his stiff and yellow beard caressed her burning cheek. Masterfully he said...."[18] At times, too, the heroines of costume romances and of novels like *Soldiers of Fortune* behaved with admirable courage and spirit themselves. The radical writer Floyd Dell remembered how, "out of books and not out of life, I formed an ideal of a jolly and exciting relationship with a girl. In books, a boy and a girl *did* play and talk together." The "Glorious Playfellow" of his and his contemporaries' imaginings was "more with us, and more like us; she took the shock and jostle of life's incident more bravely, more candidly, and more lightly" than the traditional American young lady.[19] If Scott Fitzgerald's youths understandably yearned to become Gibson men, there were obvious advantages for girls in becoming Gibson women, just as there were in the idea of the Knight in Shining Armor coming to carry a girl off from the dull world that stifled her and ignored her true virtues. All of this was very different from the classic American pattern described by Hamlin Garland in the early Nineties when he spoke of small-town women, "in their starched neatness, leading rebellious boys in torturing suits of winter thickness topped with collars, stiff as sauce pans; while the little girls walked as upright as dolls, looking disdainfully at their sulking brothers."[20]

The kinds of appeals that I have been describing were relatively innocent ones, at least when considered in isolation. They did not automatically entail fantasies of dominance and brutality or the idea of intrinsic social hierarchies and the pleasures of caste and class. They answered to cravings for fuller and more colorful ways of life than most people normally enjoyed, cravings for vitality, spontaneity, fullness of being, gusto. They answered to desires that young Northerners had felt even before the Civil War, when Dickens had noted the "prevailing seriousness and melancholy air of business" in America.[21] The Northern novelist John William De Forest, for example, who referred scornfully to "what can be done with youthful blood, muscle, mind and feeling by the studious severities of a Puritan university," had reported in a letter from Italy in the Fifties how "I felt as if my northern stiffness jarred harshly with the flexile movement and power of personification intuitive in these southern natures."[22] And the wellborn Bostonian abolitionist Thomas Wentworth Higginson remembered at the end of the century how no one had so aroused his envy at Harvard in the early Forties as did "a reckless Southern law student" rescuing people in a fire.[23] In the later nineteenth century the craving for fullness of being was intensify-

19

ing, particularly among the more or less well-to-do young, who were experiencing, in Canby's words, "the needs of an industrial society distressed by its own prosaicness and not knowing just what it wanted except that it must be gayer and more emotional,"[24] and who were conscious that the glamor of the Civil War years was slipping ever further into the past.

It was perfectly understandable that the young were turning away from the official cult of niceness and decorousness and rational pacificity and that, as Canby says, "we yearned after heartiness, and found it in romances." Looking back to his Maryland youth, he recalls how

our small-town culture was drying up, and its genial friendliness was an end product of a great gusto for eating, quarrelling, worshipping, and money-making that our grandparents remembered. My two grandfathers...would shake their beards for hours...over men, women, and experiences that seemed, and I believe were, much richer and heartier than anything or anyone in our parents' generation. They still savored the age of the frontier. The eccentrics, the temperamentals, and the powerful living people I knew were nearly all old in the nineties, and the stories they told were paralleled in what I read in Scott, with only a romantic difference.[25]

The official line of goods was *dull*. Owen Wister noted that in Harvard in the early Eighties, "senior and sophomore set small store upon most *literary* literature, perfectly nice, well behaved prose and verse." John Reed, the author of *Ten Days that Shook the World*, recalled the school-room boredom of the Nineties—"the flawless purity of Washington, Lincoln's humdrum chivalry, our dull and virtuous history."[26] In contrast, the romances, as Thomas Beer says of Kipling, "met the unspoken, half conscious wish of Americans for an entertainment that would reverse the formulas of Louisa May Alcott."[27] And in the light of the romances, middle-class business culture looked all the more prosaic. Even John P. Marquand's Henry Pulham saw that his father "was not like Dumas...or like the romances of Robert W. Chambers where girls sometimes appeared in the hero's bedroom in negligee. He was not contemporary or sprightly."[28]

THE RIGHT SORT: A SLIGHT CASE OF IMMATURITY

But if the yearnings that I have described are peculiarly appropriate to the young and have been felt by a great many of them, this fact has, of course, been a central theme in the rational American indictment of the chivalric, whether voiced by wives exasperated at their husbands' fixation on baseball and poker, or by *Newsweek* writers complaining that "literature from Homer to Hemingway has exalted the male rites of passage on the battlefield, in the sports

Violence

arena and in the boudoir. Hemingway virtually wrote the code of behavior for modern machismo. His protagonists did whatever is expected of a man – fought wars, bedded women, hunted lions – with a minimum of fuss."[29] In terms of the tradition of enlightenment, American culture, at least in the North, has been committed to leaving behind the older and more primitive patterns and structures of Europe, so that ultimately, as the historian Oscar Handlin puts it, the New World would be peopled by "a New Man, no mere derivative of any extant stock, but different from and superior to all."[30] Likewise, a growing and maturing person was supposed to leave behind more primitive attitudes. Hence the intellectual New Englander was several stages farther along the evolutionary road than Southerners like the antebellum Harvard undergraduate, Robert E. Lee's son Roony, of whom Henry Adams recalled that, "strictly, the Southerner had no mind; he had temperament. He was not a scholar; he had no intellectual training; he could not analyze an idea, and he could not even conceive of admitting two."[31] And to progress into maturity, whether cultural or individual, meant ceasing to admire physical force or want to settle issues by force when they could be settled by reason.

The general case against the chivalric in such terms was made with characteristic trenchancy by Thorstein Veblen, contemplating the emergence of a leisure class in America and the adjustment of the educational system to its needs. His diagnosis has been operative in American liberal thinking ever since, and goes back via the Enlightenment to the Renaissance Humanists – to figures like Erasmus, Roger Ascham, and the writer who, when the eighteen-year-old Sir Philip Sidney wished to go off and fight the Spanish in the Low Countries, complained that "you and your fellows, I mean men of noble birth, consider that nothing brings you more honour than wholesale slaughter."[32] For Veblen, the aristocratic was the primitive and archaic. As he said of the South, "offenses of an archaic character...are and have been relatively more prevalent and are less deprecated than they are elsewhere; as, for example, duels, brawls, feuds, drunkenness, horse-racing, cock-fighting, gambling, male sexual incontinence." This primitivism was characterized by superstitiousness, both in "the gambling propensity [which] is another subsidiary trait of the barbarian temperament" and in the belief in certain kinds of supernatural sanctions, such as in "the well-accredited maxim, 'Thrice is he armed who knows his quarrel just'." It was also characterized by, and inseparable from, the kind of predatoriness that results in "a prevalence of sharp practice and callous disregard of the interests of others, individually and collectively." Noting "the essential immaturity of the fighting temperament," Veblen observed that "the traits that distinguish the swaggering delinquent and the punctilious gentleman of leisure from the

21

common crowd are, in some measure, marks of an arrested spiritual development. They mark an immature phase, as compared with the stage of development attained by the average of the adults in the modern industrial community."[33]

Moreover, in the later nineteenth century this kind of primitivism and regressivism had political implications beyond those that I have touched on already. As Canby recalls, "in our town, where the past and the future seemed to become romantic together at the turn of the century, I cannot separate in my own memory the bands and cheering of '98, Hobson, Dewey, and manifest destiny in an expectant world, from the extravagant romanticism of the shallow, unphilosophical, unpsychological novels we had all been reading." And he notes how "we, like our period, were hot for expansion, with no more analysis than Scott's as to what the uttermost was in living or what expansion meant in its next stages."[34] Among the consequences of the new spirit of expansiveness were the jolly little war of 1898 against what the historians Charles and Mary Beard call "the most decrepit and powerless imperial nation in all Europe,"[35] the seizing of Cuba and the Philippines, the genocidal suppression of the Filipino guerrillas, which infuriated Twain, and a more aggressive Latin American policy. And certain features of the new, romantic imperialism differentiated it from earlier waves of imperialism such as that of the 1840s, which had permitted Americans to fulfill their manifest destiny by acquiring Texas, the Southwest territories, and California in the Mexican War.

At the center of this new imperialism was the highly visible and controversial figure of Theodore Roosevelt – the Roosevelt of the big stick, the Roosevelt who, according to one contemporary, "fifteen years before the Spanish war... painted to me in glorious colours the glory of going to war with a regiment of cowboys from the plains," the Roosevelt of whom a Veblenesque observer wrote in the radical journal the *Masses* in 1917 that

he goes in for the strenuous life, and becomes our main apostle of virility. When occasion offers, he naturally assumes the role of the cowboy, because the cowboy is highly symbolic of the vital type he once fell short of. Next, in the Spanish War, he appears as a rough rider; a distinct promotion in the scale of virility, the rough rider being in essence the cowboy plus the added feature of participation in the virile game of war. Later on, as an explorer, playing with jungles and living among wild men and beasts, he approaches still nearer to the primitive male.[36]

With Roosevelt, whom Harry Truman remembered being on his return from Cuba "about the most popular hero since Andy Jackson won the Battle of New Orleans" and whom a recent unenchanted commentator characterized as "action without direction, purpose without belief, energy without thoroughness, activity without consequence,"[37] the idea of imperial expansion became intertwined ideologically with ideas of masculine self-worth. The figure of the real-life hero was celebrated in Roosevelt's enthusiastic account of his Rough Riders – men such as "Micah Jenkins, the captain of Troop K, a gentle and courteous South Carolinian, on whom danger acted like wine," and R. P. Jones, "tall and lithe, a remarkable boxer and walker, a first-class rider and shot, with yellow hair and piercing blue eyes, [who] looked like what he was, the archetype of the fighting man." All of them, "Easterners and Westerners, Northerners and Southerners...cow-boys and college graduates," shared "the traits of hardihood and a thirst for adventure. They were to a man born adventurers, in the old sense of the word" – as was, of course, Colonel Roosevelt himself.[38] And along with red-blooded adventurousness came the importance of "character" and focused social effectiveness, as noted in the reference in Owen Johnson's *Stover at Yale* to "a dozen fellows, clean-cut, steady of head and eye, carrying a certain unmistakable quiet assurance" and derided when one of Marquand's Harvard alumni sarcastically quotes Sir Henry Newbolt's "The voice of a schoolboy rallies the ranks: /'Play up, play up, and play the game.' "[39] A prime specimen of the right sort of fellow would be offered to the admiring American gaze in the obituary pamphlet published in New York in 1917 about a British army captain:

He was good to look on. He was big and tall, and held himself upright. His eyes looked his own height. He moved with the grace of an athlete. His skin was tanned by a wholesome outdoor life. Physically he was a prince among men... He had a kind of innate nobility which marked him out as above us. He was not democratic. He was rather the justification for aristocracy. We all knew instinctively that he was our superior – a man of finer temper than ourselves, a "toff" in his own right.[40]

Moreover, this new Northern machismo was accompanied by other manifestations of an admiration for force and strength. The Nineties witnessed an immense enthusiasm for Napoleon (its impress, according to the historian Theodore P. Greene, was everywhere apparent among the leaders of that generation), and the first decade of the new century was the heyday of the worship of the Strong Man, as displayed in 1913 toward the just-departed quintessential Captain of Industry, J. Pierpont Morgan:

> With no uncertainty of fate
> He brushed aside the angel throng
> And strode through the emblazoned gate
> Into the Heaven of the Strong.[41]

For the Strong Man, as described by Owen Johnson in his society novel *The Sixty-First Second* (1913), only two classes existed, the strong and the weak. The strong was that brutal race which could not be held down by the restraints of society, who must rise, acquire power, dominate, obeying the natural instinct within them; the weak those who aided them in their upward progress, who served them when they had arrived, and who committed crimes in their name. It was not a moral view of life so much as it was a perception of the persisting law of all animal nature.

As a tycoon in that novel remarks to his fellow dinner guests, the strong are "a few, a handful, who create something – an empire, like Rhodes, invent a locomotive or a system of electric production, add something to human history. What if they steal, or grind out the lives of others? They are the only ones who count." And he goes on:

"Look at the sympathy a murderer gets on trial – look at the respect a great manipulator gets. Why? Because to murder and steal are natural human instincts. A couple of thousand years ago, it was a praiseworthy act for one ancestor, who coveted a hide or a cave that another ancestor had, to go out and kill him. All animals steal by instinct. We are only badly educated animals, and we admire in others what we don't dare do ourselves. Only succeed – succeed. Ah, there is the whole of it."[42]

The would-be successful young businessman, the strong-jawed, unsmiling hero of Gibson's drawings, took to his heart the imperative to cultivate and demonstrate his "will power." Below him, the working-class young Irishman like James T. Farrell's Studs Lonigan aspired to be a tough-guy hero in a world in which, as a historian of Irish America explains, "to be manly [came] to mean simply to be exploitative in sexual relations with women and always ready for a fight with other men."[43] Above both of them William James was looking questioningly at pacificism and Roosevelt's friend Justice Oliver Wendell Holmes was affirming in various ways his conviction that "now, at least, and perhaps as long as man dwells upon the globe, his destiny is battle, and he has to take the chances of war."[44] And that rising young intellectual star H. L. Mencken was enthusiastically propounding the doctrines of Nietzsche, such as his implacable opposition to the "demand for peace and the demand for equality," and his conviction that "the aristocratic individualist...must seek every possible opportunity to increase and exalt his own sense of efficiency, of success, of mastery, of power."[45]

Seen in such contexts, the literary phenomena that I talked about earlier look considerably less innocent, of course. So does the enormous popularity of a writer like Richard Harding Davis, of whom Booth Tarkington said in an obituary notice in 1917 that "to the college boy of the early nineties [he] was the 'beau ideal of *jeunesse dorée*'...His stalwart good looks were as familiar to us as were those of our own football captain...Of all the great people of every continent, this was the one we most desired to see."[46] The new American romanticism, including the literary romanticism, was obviously inseparable from the British imperialism of writers like Haggard, Doyle, and, above all, Kipling, whose "world predominance" in the mid-Nineties was noted by H. G. Wells,[47] and who addressed his "The White Man's Burden" to Americans at the time of the Philippine affair, after having charmed them with his Soldiers Three and gentlemen rankers and the Road to Mandalay and all the rest of it. Obviously, too, several of the locales that figured prominently in romances – Latin America, Africa, the Caribbean, the South Seas – were areas of imperial expansion, and a good deal of smash and grab went on in them, whether by bearded pirates or square-jawed, pith-helmeted treasure-seekers. Naturally, one clean-cut white man was worth a dozen blacks or dagos, especially in Latin America. At one point in Davis's *Soldiers of Fortune*, for example,

the Englishman...began to descend the stairs slowly, a step at a time, staring at the mob so fiercely that they shrank back before the look of wounded pride and anger in his eyes. Those in the rear raised and levelled their rifles. Without taking his eyes from them, Stuart drew his revolver, and with his sword swinging from its wrist-strap, pointed his weapon at the mass below him.[48] "What does this mean?" he demanded. "Is this a mutiny?"

And for all the talk about knightly homage to the fair sex, the chivalrous male, as Henry James noted of the ambitious young Mississippian Basil Ransom in *The Bostonians*, was prone to have "most definite notions" about the place of women in society.[49] When it came to political power, women too were a species of subject race.

In the development of the new romanticism, furthermore, a suspiciously large part was played by the well bred. Roosevelt, for example, who did so much to popularize the cowboy West, was a New York aristocrat, whose Southern mother remained "entirely 'unreconstructed' to the day of her death."[50] His friend Owen Wister, who in the words of one Western writer "traced the code of the cowboy back to Middle-English Chivalry" and regarded the cowboy as "a knight-at-arms, the 'Anglo-Saxon' tradition come to flower again,"[51] was a well-born Philadelphian and numbered a Southern plantation owner among his grandparents. So was Richard Harding Davis, whose author mother was yet another Southerner. Even Edgar Rice Burroughs, whose first novel about the athletic Lord Greystoke appeared in 1913, spent a semester at Andover and had been intended for Yale. Naturally, all of them were fans of Kipling. Roosevelt invited him to the White House; Wister said of his own fiction that "a quickening came from the pages of Stevenson; a far stronger shove next from the genius of *Plain Tales From the Hills*";[52] Burroughs cheerfully plundered his *Jungle Books*; Davis, a coeval, yearningly competed with him in his short stories.

THE POLITICS OF ROMANCE

It would appear, then, that Twain's attack upon the chivalric can be expanded into a fuller and more political critique. An unsympathetic analyst might put things as follows.

In a discussion of the appeal of plantation literature, a literary historian spoke in 1925 of "the innate American love of feudalism," and noted the curious fact that "however violent may be our profession of political equality, however we may vaunt our democracy, our imaginative interests are keenly appreciative of social gradations and our romantic hunger is satisfied by some allegory of aristocracy."[53] Rational, pacific, and democratic as was the official Northern ideology, there had in fact always been a strong strain of romantic inegalitarianism on both sides of the Mason-Dixon line. Even in the Jacksonian Thirties, Tocqueville noticed how "from time to time one can see the old aristocratic colors breaking through in the North,"[54] and his perception was amply corroborated by Francis J. Grund in his *Aristocracy in America* at the end of that decade. The Civil War, with its displays of heroism and its celebrations of the heroic values, intensified and popularized aristocratic attitudes, especially the martial, the chivalric, the honorable. And as discrepancies among incomes grew in the postwar decades, so did the attractiveness of the idea of innate inequalities, not least because of the obvious self-flattery involved in what W. J. Ghent described in 1902 as the imported doctrine that all social progress came from an "exceptionally gifted and efficient minority."[55] In those decades, Northern society increasingly made itself over in the light of aristocratic European and Southern patterns, partly as a defense against immigrant groups like the Irish and the Jews, partly to sustain the morale of the wealthy against the working class in general, partly because the older rich wished to preserve distinctions between themselves and the newer rich. Two groups were particularly sympathetic to the changes. Women, those fervent genealogists and devourers of romantic fiction, compensated for their lack of political power by means of the domination attainable through social discriminations and exclusions. (As Finley Peter Dunne's Chicago-Irish saloon keeper Mr. Dooley put it, "ivry free-bor-rn American lady...is a bor-rn aristocrat to her finger tips."[56]) And well-born benevolent masters and mistresses, and its contented, singing darkies, suggested not only that antebellum slavery should not have been interfered with, but that the tacit slavery of the newer South should not be interfered with either, and nor should similar inequalities in the North. The games-playing and gentlemen-making structures of prep schools and prestige colleges also played their ideological part. As C. Wright Mills points out in a Veblenesque analysis, "the one deep young men, pushed toward the margin in a business economy, welcomed affirmations of older and more aristocratic values that served to validate morally their own social positions.

A major ideological role in all this – to continue the hypothetical indictment – was played by the cult of the South, where Jim Crowism had been increasing since the failure of Reconstruction. The romantic image of antebellum plantation life, with its graceful pastoralism, its experience that distinguishes the social rich from the merely rich and those below is their schooling, and with it, all the associations, the sense and sensibility, to which this educational routine leads throughout their lives."[57] With their imitations of the English public school system, and their heavy Episcopalian flavoring, the prep schools encouraged the belief that, in the words of the Bostonian protagonist of Marquand's *The Late George Apley*, "to-day nothing in the world is quite so fine as an English gentleman; there is a politeness, an air and an *esprit* which cannot but make us all a little bit ashamed."[58] And the emphasis on school and college sports also legitimized what Veblen called "impulses of exploit and ferocity" and encouraged "force and fraud," attitudes "similarly present in modern warfare."[59] Again, just as romantic fictions about aristocratic Europe, as Twain contended, helped to accustom people to the idea of the moral rightness of inegalitarian structures, so romantic fictions about swashbuckling and freebooting encouraged an imperialist outlook in the educated young. With their celebrations of the aggressive and often illegal activities of the predatory male, and the happy complicity in them of the kept female, such fictions suggested the naturalness of imperial expansion and defined character types peculiarly fitted for its accomplishment. An additional ideological support for all this unsavoriness was provided by the imported Boy Scout movement, whose best-selling manual, Sir Robert Baden-Powell's *Scouting for Boys* (1908), was described by a contemporary reviewer as a "mixture of all that is best in Chivalry, Red Indianism, Sherlock Holmesism and the Feudal System."[60]

The over-class attitudes that I have been describing spread outwards and downwards to the populace at large. Back in the Seventies the vastly popular dime novels had vulgarized the gentlemanly frontier heroes of Cooper and his imitators with figure like Deadwood Dick and Gentleman Joe, and by the early 1900s pulp magazines like *Munsey's* and *Argosy*, beginning what would become a torrent in the Twenties and Thirties, were likewise vulgarizing and disseminating the types and genres that I have talked about. Gentlemen heroes prospered and proliferated, demonstrating the skills and thrills that could come with money and the right kind of education. Dime novelists like Gilbert Patten ("Burt L. Standish") and the wellborn and grievously downslidden Frederick Marmaduke Van Rensselaer Dey presented working-class youths with prime specimens like the Yale all-rounder Frank Merriwell and the all-round, clean-cut detective Nick Carter; and by the 1930s Carter was living in a house on Fifth Avenue with a Filipino valet, and had been joined by other men-about-town heroes, especially the millionaire playboy Lamont Cranston (The Shadow), the world traveler Richard Wentworth (The Spider), and Clark (Doc) Savage, the "Man of Bronze," with his Ivy League team of world experts.[61] The Kiplingesque notion, amplified in Britain's Four Just Men and Bulldog Drummond, of strong men of virtue operating outside the artificial confines of the letter of the law, was further expanded in Western fiction (published in over twenty magazines by the end of the Twenties) and in the cult of the tough private eye that began in the Twenties with the former preppy John Carroll Daly's Race Williams, was firmed up in the Maryland-born Dashiell Hammett's Continental Op, and reached its notorious apotheosis during the McCarran-McCarthy years in Mickey Spillane's Mike Hammer.[62] Westerns, particularly movie Westerns, also reinforced the idea of ferocious colored peoples interfering with the legitimate expansionist activities of heroic whites, as did works about the Foreign Legion and adventuring in tropical Africa, Latin America, and the South Seas. And in the Thirties, as the imperial interest of America in the Pacific and Latin America intensified, the oblique imperialism and racism of swashbuckling romance passed over into the overt Kiplingism of movies like *Gunga Din* and *The Lives of a Bengal Lancer.*[63]

At the end of the road, as Twain had insisted, lay actual violence, with significant interactions between art and politics. In the Roosevelt period, the kind of over-class machismo that caused W. J. Ghent to complain in 1902 that "fast driving...has become one of the tests of courage, manliness, and skill – what jousting in full armour was in the fifteenth century, or duelling with pistols in the early part of the nineteenth,"[64] was fortified by Kiplingesque calls for military preparedness in the interests of national honor by men like Roosevelt and Davis. And when in 1917 the doughboys left for France to the tune of George M. Cohan's "Over There" ("the best recruiting song of the lot," according to a writer in the *New Masses*[65]), it was only fitting that the principal purveyor of clean-cut, firm-jawed, upper-class young men, Charles Dana Gibson, became, according to Tom Wolfe, "a patriotic figure, as revered as Sir Philip Sidney in England 350 years before, thanks to his role in mobilizing the leading illustrators for martial propaganda."[66] Subsequently, in the Thirties, the Kiplingesque imperialist movies, First World War movies like *Dawn Patrol*, Spanish Main swashbucklers like *Captain Blood*, and Seven Years War movies like *The Last of the Mohicans*, with their displays of honorable combat against powerful foreign

28

enemies, helped to create an atmosphere wherein it seemed morally natural that America should eventually enter the Second World War. And after the war, the Western-type image of what an unsympathetic commentator called the "lonely hero triumphant in a hostile world, perpetuated not only by films and television but by authors ranging from Fenimore Cooper and Ernest Hemingway to Mickey Spillane,"[67] was to serve as a potent epitomization of how America saw itself in world politics. Nor was it only an American statesman like Henry Kissinger who would visualize himself in terms of the Western ("the cowboy who comes into town all alone on his horse," as he put it[68]). Discussing the most aggressive of the Israeli cabinet ministers, a writer in the *New York Review of Books* observed in 1978 that "[Ariel] Sharon's cowboy style both in private on his ranch and in public is in keeping with his treatment of the territories as if this were the Wild West, where land is up for grabs for those with the daring to grab it."[69] A hostile analyst of chivalric transformations might be inclined to argue that in the ultra-violences of the despised and derided Italian Westerns we have a logical culmination of ostensibly nobler chivalric forms, and a disclosure of their innermost natures.

The socially undesirable attitudes that I have discussed came to a head in the 1960s, a decade peculiarly rich in incitements to distrust the chivalric-martial ideology. Not only was there the Vietnam War itself, with its atrocities, its egregious military lying and coverups, and its various reminders of the disproportionately large Southern influence in the army. During the interrelated struggles of the civil rights and antiwar movements, there were abundant displays of what Pauline Kael in a discussion of Clint Eastwood's *Dirty Harry* called "fascist medieval-ism," on the part of Irish cops, redneck Southern sheriffs, and the kinds of "Southern storm troopers" described by John D. MacDonald in one of his thrillers – "big and heavy and young, with leather faces and faded blue eyes and brutal mouths."[70] And presiding over those years were two especially theatrical and chivalric-martial presidents. On the one hand there was the macho pride, coarseness, and touchiness of the president from the Lone Star State, Lyndon Johnson, taking the country deeper and deeper into the white-against-yellow war. On the other, there were the Camelot pretensions, New Frontier rhetoric, and crisis politics of the Boston Irish John F. Kennedy, who got the country into the war in the first place. And if what might be called the John Wayne values were epitomized in Johnson, British imperialist romanticism played its part in the prep-school, locker-room, Establishment ethos of Kennedy and his New Frontiersmen. Kennedy himself reportedly much admired the autobiography of John Buchan, with its glamorous presen-tation of the charmed circle of gifted Oxford youths in the Eighties, the comradeship of Lord Milner's empire-administering young men, the sweet-sad deaths of upper-class young heroes in World War I, the self-congratulatoriness of clubmen walking the corridors of power. And as Henry Fairlie remarks that "it is almost impossible to turn a corner in the literature of the Kennedy administration without bumping into" the OSS of "Wild Bill" Donovan – an organization that, like its offspring the CIA in the early Cold War years, had been, according to Gore Vidal, "manned by fun-loving American nobles."[71] The mystique of the guerrilla for the Kennedy team that Fairlie notes was obviously indebted to the glamorizing of undercover work in books like *Kim*, with its Great Game, Buchan's Richard Hannay novels, and factual-fictional accounts of the career of Lawrence of Arabia and the commandolike trench raiding of the Western Front.

In the kind of history that I have been sketching, an especially regrettable part was played by the cult of honor, of which W. J. Cash, in his analysis of the Southern mind, observes that "one of the notable results of the spread of the idea...was an increase in the tendency to violence throughout the social scale."[72] The Southern preoccupation with honor contributed to the insensate antebellum feuds and affrays, the outbreak of the Civil War, the postwar formation of the Klan, and all the hackles-raising rhetoric about the honor of Southern womanhood. The honorableness of the Irish was on parade in their barroom brawls and criminal gangs, as was the honorableness of later ethnic groups whose gangs were obsessed with courage and loyalty. America's entry into the war of 1898 and into the European war in 1917 took place to a Hallelujah chorus of talk about national honor, like the pronouncement by one of Marquand's Bostonians that "it will be a perpetual blot always on the history of this country that we have not drawn the sword long ago...to defend our national honor in the face of German frightfulness," on behalf of "heroic England and chivalrous France."[73] After World War I, the American Legion thundered to the defense of Americanism and American honor, and moved the psychiatrist Rollo May to say a few years ago that it became for him "a negative conscience – what it was for, I was against, and whatever I was for, it was against."[74] Among the Legion's promoters of nostalgia for the war was, of course, that peppery alumnus of Battery D, Harry S. Truman, the President who took America Lone Rangering into Korea and threatened to punch a music reviewer in the mouth for criticizing his daughter's singing. And the notion of national honor has gone on figuring in American saber-rattling politics. As a letter writer in *Time* remarked acidly, "Now we've got a new resounding slogan, 'Protect human rights everywhere,' that may compel us one day to don our shining silver

Violence

armor, buckle on our nuclear sword, and again ride forth and do battle with the wicked dragon."[75]

When one steps back a little, the picture looks even worse politically. Chivalric-martial attitudes were notoriously active in the various brands of European fascism, whether that of the *Action Française*, which championed the French army in the Dreyfus affair, or Mussolini's version, or that of Hitler, whose pseudo-aristocratic SS, in Hugh Trevor-Roper's words, "made a virtue of 'honour,' and its 'honour' – as its chosen motto declared – was unquestioning loyalty to the Führer."[76] Fascistic possibilities obviously also inhered in some of the American attitudes that I have been describing – martial, racist, Nietzschean, Napoleonic – and were touched on in certain American novels of the turn-of-the-century decades.[77] By the Twenties, liberals had the America Firstism of the American Legion and the revived Klan to cope with, moving the *Nation* to observe in 1922 that "we lack only open and above-board Fascisti, black-shirted and round-capped, and there are those who think that they can be created whenever the...Legion's thirst...becomes a bit greater."[78] By the Thirties there were native American fascists like the good old Louisiana boy Huey Long and the romantic rebel Ezra Pound, the latter having progressed from a predilection for aristocratic troubadours like Bertrans de Born ("Damn it all! all this our South stinks peace"[79]) to a crush on Mussolini, an avowed contempt for pity and softness, and anti-Semitism. And in the aftermath of the Second World War there were McCarthyism and Spillaneism to contend with, a rightism in which the patriotic Irish figured prominently. Moreover, the Second World War not only exhibited the ultimate consequences of chivalric-martial European fascism; the chivalry of martial Japan had also been on display, with its harakiri, kamikaze attacks, and the prison-camp horrors of what a British commentator scornfully dubbed the "Knights of Bushido."[80] And since then, in the Middle East there have been the exasperating activities of Arabs with their own archaic notions of pride and honor. It is hardly surprising that back in the 1920s, according to Robert Ardrey, "certain words almost vanished from the American vocabulary....Honor was one, *glory* another," or that a writer in *Time* should have been able to declare in 1977 that "for a generation the educated young of the U.S. have been taught to deride or satirize the heroic."[81]

31

3

Fictiveness

"You've got to take that back."
"Oh, cut out the prep-school stuff."

Ernest Hemingway, The Sun Also Rises (1926)

When Scarlett was seeing Rhett to the door, she asked indignantly: "If it were you, wouldn't you enlist with the Yankees to keep from dying in that place and then desert?"
"Of course," said Rhett, his teeth gleaming beneath his moustache.
"Then why didn't Ashley do it?"
"He's a gentleman," said Rhett, and Scarlett wondered how it was possible to convey such cynicism and contempt in that one honorable word.

Margaret Mitchell, Gone with the Wind (1937)

It may be taken as axiomatic that any statement of fact about the Middle Ages may (and probably will) be met by a statement of the opposite in a different version.

Barbara W. Tuchman, A Distant Mirror (1978)[1]

CHIVALRY AND IRREALISM

IF MATURITY involves being firmly in touch with reality, then in American terms the chivalric would seem peculiarly to invite the skepticism of the person who wishes to be, like Twain, the undeceivable Man from Missouri. In the course of his classic analysis of the Southern tendency toward romanticism and unreality, W. J. Cash describes how, in the years after the Civil War,

> every boy growing up in this land now had continually before his eyes the vision, and heard always in his ears the clamorous hoofbeats, of a glorious swashbuckler, compounded of Jeb Stuart, the golden-locked Pickett, and the sudden and terrible Forrest (yes, and, in some fashion, of Lord Roland and the douzepers) forever charging the cannon's mouth with the Southern battle flag.[2]

And if an enthusiasm for the chivalric, with its celebration of simpler times and nobler values, appears to make for greater aggressiveness, a complementary indictment is that it can also make for debilitation, a disruption of psychic energy, a weakening of the will to sustained action. When Edwin Arlington Robinson reports of Miniver Cheevy that

> Miniver loved the days of old
> When swords were bright and steeds were prancing;
> The vision of a warrior bold
> Would set him dancing,

we are reminded almost immediately that Cheevy, like Faulkner's Civil War-obsessed Hightower in *Light in August*, "kept on drinking."[3] So, for that matter, did Robinson himself, and Faulkner, and Fitzgerald, and Steinbeck, and Hammett, and Chandler, and Hemingway. And the last-named, the most chivalric-martial of them all, ended up turning his gun upon himself, like Robinson's Richard Cory, that "gentleman from sole to crown,/Clean-favored, and imperially slim."[4] There are obvious difficulties when it comes to chivalry and the reality principle.

For one thing, chivalric romanticism makes the idea of failure insidiously attractive. William James suggested that "the possibility of violent death [is] the soul of all romance"; Bernard Shaw called chivalry "at bottom only romantic suicide."[5] The Lost Cause looms large in the mystique of chivalry – Roland and his rearguard at Roncesvalles; the hopeless charge of Pickett's Virginians at Gettysburg; the whole fore-doomed Confederate enterprise; the Lost Legions and Dawn Patrols; the heroic Irish tradition of military failure. (In a letter to Maxwell Perkins Hemingway blamed Fitzgerald's problems on his "cheap Irish love of defeat."[6]) So do honorable but marginal failures like the lone cowboy and vanishing Indian, the private eye keeping faith with himself in a shabby office, and the type of Southern gentleman described in Walker Percy's novel *Lancelot* as "screwed up by poesy" and "dreaming of Robert E. Lee and...Episcopal chapels in the wildwood."[7] As the narrator of *A Farewell to Arms* remarks of his gallant Catherine,

If people bring so much courage to this world the world has to kill them to break them, so of course it kills them. The world breaks every one and afterward many are strong at the broken places. But those that will not break it kills. It kills the very good and the very gentle and the very brave impartially. If you are none of these you can be sure it will kill you too but there will be no special hurry.[8]

Adolescent male pessimism about sexual relations – a yearning for the perfect woman to serve, and a conviction of the inevitability of failing to find or keep her – encourages the sort of escapism noted in Oscar Handlin's reference to the American fondness for "men able to do things because they were unencumbered: cowboys – Owen Wister's Virginian, offspring of Natty Bumppo and sire of Tom Mix; the detective,...Nick Carter, about to be the Private Eye; the athlete – Merriwell, Dempsey, Ruth; the reporter – scoop."[9]

THE DEBUNKING TRADITION

But beyond that, of course, there are special problems posed for the reflective. They are particularly acute in view of the strength of irony in American intellectual life, whether what Fitzgerald called the "scoffing and mildly ironic attitude" of Princeton men toward Yale machismo, or

33

the "faint, acrid aroma of intellectual irony, cool as pine needles," that the young Communist writer Michael Gold discerned in a number of intellectuals in the Twenties,[10] or the robustly arrogant irony of a Mencken, or the corrosive black irony of works like Hawthorne's "Young Goodman Brown" and Melville's *The Confidence Man*. The ironist perceives the incongruousness of particular energies and enthusiasms, such as the confident gusto with which Twain's Sir Sagramor charged his unarmored and seemingly unarmed Yankee opponent. He perceives people governed by chimeras or mirages, such as images of a beauty or grandeur that does not in fact exist, or models and patterns that cannot be followed, or ends that are unattainable, with disillusionment and Yeats's "desolation of reality" awaiting them,[11] as it does in Gatsby's obsessed pursuit of the grail of an absurdly overidealized Daisy. And the irony can extend to oneself as well as to others, as it did for the Southerner in Walker Percy's *The Last Gentlemen* who "became ironical... In the end he was killed by his own irony and sadness and by the strain of living out an ordinary day in a perfect dance of honor."[12] The trouble with chivalry is not only that a lot of people prefer to play by different rules, like Faulkner's Snopeses, or Margaret Mitchell's Rhett Butler, or the type of person by whom, as reported in *The New York Times* in 1975, "Orwell, like Albert Camus, is regularly attacked in the kneecaps. To be perceived as a good guy, a man of honor, is to invite spite."[13] A major problem is the permeation of the chivalric by fictiveness.

If the debunking approach to the chivalric has been as strong as it has, whether in Twain's works or in more recent ones like Joseph Heller's *Catch-22* and Thomas Berger's *Little Big Man*, this has partly been because so many people, particularly during the period with which I am chiefly concerned, tried to ground their admiration for the chivalric in an unequivocal historical actuality. The America that the correspondent for the London *Times* visited in 1861 had "swarm[ed] with genealogical societies and bodies of antiquaries, who delight[ed] in reading papers about each other's ancestors, and tracing their descent from Norman or Saxon barons and earls."[14] Antebellum Southern writers had assured their readers that "the Southern States were settled and governed, in a great measure... by and under the direction of persons belonging to the blood and race of the reigning family, and belonged to that stock recognized as Cavaliers," and that "the Virginians and Carolinians especially were of direct descent from the 'rufflers' of Hastings and... Agincourt."[15] Writers like Thomas Nelson Page, speaking with the authority of their antebellum Southern birth, confidently proclaimed after the war that "over all [the old South] brooded a softness and beauty, the joint product of Chivalry and Christianity."[16] And of course the Middle Ages – in Cabell's words, "our world's youth when chivalry was regnant, and common-sense and cowardice were still at nurse" – abounded in verray parfit gentil knights and gay cavaliers, like those at the court of Edward I who, as Mills said, "talked and sang of war and love and then merrily returned to their own country."[17] Moreover, America itself, in addition to giving the world that *ne plus ultra*, the Virginian Gentleman, had been graced by figures like the noble woodsman who opened up the savage wilderness without becoming savage himself, and the noble Indian who displayed what Cooper, speaking of him in his best manifestations, called "chivalrous honor," "liberality and candor," "refinement in politeness," the "courtesy of one trained in high society."[18] By the end of the nineteenth century they had been joined by the even nobler cowboy, epitomized by Wister's Virginian. As Twain well knew, powerful emotional energies and vested interests were at work in these historicizings. If people indeed lived more nobly and gracefully in former times, in patterns radically different from those approved of by the official American ideology, it made sense to try to recreate those patterns in the drabber present. Hence, serious doubts about the asserted historicity were all the more consequential.

The antebellum South, so central in these maneuverings, was peculiarly vulnerable to skeptical analysis. In the standard romantic vision of that society, as the historians Charles and Mary Beard observe,

every planting family lived in a stately home of pillared architecture at the end of a long avenue of trees often festooned with hanging vines, set in a luxuriant grove of magnolias. In appointments of furniture, rugs, and silver, in food and drink, in amenities of entertainment, in loyalties and rectitude – in all that made for charm of living – the planting aristocracy had reached the acme of civilization. The lord of the manor was a cavalier, courteous but quick to avenge an insult to his honor even to the point of dueling. His lady was the embodiment of grace, sparkling with social talents. Every planter's mansion had a library well stocked with the classics and belles lettres in which leisure hours were spent cultivating and refining the mind. In the arrangements of this exclusive society, quality, not pecuniary standards as in the North, prevailed. Worth, not wealth, gave entrance to its magic circle. Within it grew men fit to govern and women skilled in the arts of domestic management and hospitality.[19]

Even before the Civil War, however, the debunking process was under way, especially in Frederick Law Olmsted's accounts of his extensive travels through the South in the Fifties, of which Daniel Boorstin comments that "there is no better introduction to Southern life on the brink of the war."[20] The South of those intelligent and persuasive pages, a society "maintained in a frontier condition by the system which is apologized for on the ground that it favours good breeding," was overwhelmingly not only one of discomfort and inconvenience in daily living, slovenliness and poor workmanship, brutality to men and beasts, and intellectual poverty. It was also one in which "the immoral, vulgar, and ignorant newly-rich" bulked larger among the well-to-do than in any other part of the country, the vaunted Southern hospitality proved a pure myth in nine out of ten of the houses visited, and "the Southern gentleman, as we ordinarily conceive him to be, is as rare a phenomenon...at the present day as is the old squire of [Washington Irving] in modern England."[21] There were similar large discrepancies, too, between the asserted and actual roots of the South. In the Nineties Basil Gildersleeve said of the Southerners' pride in being gentlemen that "they have been told in every conceivable tone that it was a foolish pride – foolish in itself, foolish in that it did not have the heraldic backing that was claimed for it."[22] Historians would soon demonstrate how negligible a part was played by aristocrats in the establishment of the colonies, one of them even declaring that, "the cold truth is that the English origins of nearly all of the [Virginian] colonists, even those who founded aristocratic families, are unknown."[23] It would also be shown convincingly that the seventeenth- and early eighteenth-century inhabitants of Virginia, far from being cavalierlike, were hard working, hard trading, and not at all given to duels or the idealization of womanhood.[24]

MEDIEVAL CHIVALRY: WHERE AND WHEN?

The problems posed by the chivalric Middle Ages were even worse. On the face of things, everything was clear as day. Charles Mills, for instance, spoke of "the fair and goodly system of chivalry, which extended itself, as we have seen, over most of the states of Europe, blending with the strongest passions and dearest affections of the heart, influencing the manners of private life, and often determining the character of political events," and Cabell referred to "a world-wide code in consonance with which all estimable people lived and died. Its root was the assumption (uncontested then) that a gentleman will always serve his God, his honor and his lady without any reservation."[25] The complex Arthurian system as presented by Malory and others was foursquare. So was the world of *Ivanhoe*, in which Scott interwove a variety of types and individuals so persuasively that they would become almost inseparable in the popular imagination – the gallant young knight traveling and fighting incognito; the gallant young knight's lady fair; the beautiful, chaste young Jewess and the fierce proud Templar; the robust franklin; the jester and the iron-collared serf; noble King Richard and contemptible Prince John; Robin Hood and his merry men. The knightly code was likewise foursquare. According to Mills, "the highest possible degree of virtue was required of a knight...He was not only to be virtuous, but without reproach." Knights fought chivalrous

Fictiveness

battles, played fair, spared fallen foes, treated prisoners courteously, protected women and orphans. And of course, as Mills said, "if we fancy the knight of chivalry as valiant, noble-minded, and gentle, our imagination pictures to our minds the lady of his love in colours equally fair and pleasing."²⁶ For an inquiring mind, however, the actualities were, and are, somewhat more complicated.

To begin with, there is the nagging problem of where the "real" chivalric world of everyone's imagination was in fact to be found. Twain acted very naturally when he set *A Connecticut Yankee* where he did. It is to Arthur's England that the mind immediately turns for the most vivid embodiments of the chivalric value system – the fellowship of the Round Table, the knightly code, the courteous challenges, the yearning for the Grail, the nobility of the love between Lancelot and Guinevere, the mourning of Arthur for the destruction of his kingdom, Sir Ector's elegy over the dead Lancelot. And T. H. White knew what he was doing when he closed his retelling of the Arthurian cycle, *The Once and Future King*, with the young Thomas Malory serving in Arthur's forces on the eve of the final battle with Mordred. For many readers the marvelous history has obviously felt so real that it must have fitted into actual British history *somewhere*. Hence Steinbeck busied himself in England with trying to discover where the real Camelot had been, and Twain's own satire postulated an actual Camelot awaiting the ministrations of his time-traveling Yankee. Yet the whole Arthurian story as we have it in Malory, so elaborate in its outlines, so memorable in its characterizations, so vivid in its details, was fictitious. The Arthurian section of Geoffrey of Monmouth's twelfth-century *History of the Kings of Britain*, in which the story got its effective start, was, like so much else in that remarkable work, pure fiction, told with the straightfaced and loving attention to detail of the inspired and dedicated liar.²⁷ His Arthur, his Merlin, his Excalibur; his body of noblemen in a festive and trend-setting court under the noblest and most powerful monarch of his time, with mutually supportive relationships between the prowess of the knights in battle and the love of their chaste and gracious ladies; his Queen Guinevere who ends up in a convent; the expedition by Arthur to the Continent, during which the kingdom is taken over by Mordred; the final battle in which Arthur is gravely wounded; the carrying away of Arthur to Avalon – all were fictional. So was the crucial love affair between Lancelot and Guinevere that was featured a little later in the century in the brilliant and beautiful metrical romances of Chrétien de Troyes. Nor were there any actual jousts or quests before that century, or any tournaments before the eleventh century. Moreover, when one looks at the Europe of actuality, one seems to be involved in a long regression of nostalgia. As a literary historian notes, "historians cannot

37

agree on the period of [chivalry's] Golden Age, but are ever setting it farther back in time."²⁸ When William Caxton printed the *Morte d'Arthur* in the fifteenth century, along with works like Ramón Lull's thirteenth-century *Book of the Order of Chivalry* (described by its modern editor as "the most compendious mediaeval treatise on the obligations of knighthood"²⁹), he was avowedly trying to reawaken British interest in the subject and looking back to a period of what he saw as lost virtues. When one turns back to the fourteenth century, which Scott considered the heyday of chivalry, one finds Honoré Bonet in his comprehensive treatise on the rules of chivalrous warfare talking nostalgically about the "*ancient* custom of noble warriors who upheld justice, the widow, the orphan and the poor"³⁰ (italics mine), in contrast to the present grievous mistreatment of poor laboring people. A thirteenth-century writer remarks that "I used to see the barons in beautiful armour following tournaments, and I heard those who had had [sic] given the best blow spoken of for many a day. Now honour lies in stealing cattle, sheep, and oxen, or pillaging churches and travelers."³¹ In the later twelfth century, an indignant archdeacon exclaims, "The knighthood of to-day! Why, it consists of disorderly living!"³² And Chrétien de Troyes, writing in the middle of that century, speaks nostalgically at one point of a time when knights *really* behaved gallantly. Which presumably takes one back toward the nonexistent Camelot.

There are problems, too, about the relationship between the chivalric ideals and the knightly actualities. Faced with the cliché image of brave, loyal, generous, courteous, and just knights in battle with each other, it is natural to inquire, with Twain, how far ideals and actualities coincided. The discrepancies were in fact large. In general, there is obviously no reason to question the statement of a historian that "beneath the high idealism of chivalric honour, war continues much as before, as cruel, atrocious and thoughtless as ever... The occasional feat of arms is a diversion from the more serious business of pillage," or the assertion by another one that "the civilians, and above all the humble, suffered untold hardships in war."³³ In his admiring life of the Black Prince, for example, a fourteenth-century writer reports how, on one occasion, the English entertained themselves by laying waste a whole region, and Froissart in his *Chronicles* talks of episodes like the sacking of Limoges, in which over three thousand persons had their throats cut, and of Edward III ordering the whole population of Caen to be put to the sword. And things were even nastier in the fifteenth century, the century that saw the burning of Joan of Arc. Moreover, from the outset the chivalry business was indeed a business. A knight could make his fortune in war by the unabashed plundering of conquered towns and from ransoms and the sale of safe conducts, especially during the

Hundred Years' War. The tournament, too, had become quite early an enterprise in which a skillful knight, riding the circuit like a modern golf professional, could make a very comfortable living for himself, as did William Marshall in the thirteenth century for his first twenty years as a knight.

The evidence itself is curiously slippery as well. One scholar, for instance, speaks of "the obscurity that shrouds most phases of the history of the early Middle Ages" and the scarcity of documents giving the opinions of actual French noblemen of that period, while another suggests that "the three most lucid accounts of the varying ideals of knighthood in medieval England" are the thirteenth-century *Song of William the Marshall*, the fourteenth-century *Life of the Black Prince,* and the lament of Sir Ector over Lancelot.[34] Because the other most frequently cited text is the account of the Knight in the Prologue to *The Canterbury Tales*, that would make it two nominally factual works and two plainly fictional ones. And even with supposedly factual documents there are problems. As another writer points out, the fifteenth-century French biographies of chivalric figures like the Chevalier *sans peur et sans reproche* are in fact "chronicles written in a romantic idiom," and the "pretence that fiction was not fiction at all was beloved of medieval writers, and particularly of writers on chivalric subjects... The borderline between the romantic dreamworld and the military reality was always indistinct."[35] Jacques de Mailles's *Life of Bayard* contains extended dialogues as obviously fictive as any to be found in "true-life" novels. And prose treatises on the chivalric virtues like Lull's and Bonet's are obviously at least as much prescriptive as descriptive. Furthermore, the activities of knights and literary men – troubadours spreading the doctrines of courtly love, minstrels celebrating the knightly generosity on which they themselves were so dependent, clerics trying to soften the martial fierceness, and the various authors of the Arthurian mythos – were so interwoven from the outset that a historian can suggest that "chivalry owes more to the pen than to the sword."[36]

Indeed, in one sense fictions lay at the very center of the chivalric. Not only was the whole system, as a structure of ideas, inseparable from the Arthurian mythos. The whole aristocratic culture revolved around the elaborate game of the tournament – a game whose history was full of play acting, pageantry, and revivals, all harking back to the splendid Arthurian tournament described by Chrétien de Troyes, who according to one historian, almost created by himself the concept of knight errantry. The literariness was at its most flagrant in relatively late tournaments like the mid-fifteenth-century Burgundian one in which the presiding duke was handed

a letter from the princess of an unknown isle, in which she proffers her favour to any knight who would deliver a certain giant from captivity, whom she had placed under the guardianship of her dwarf. The dwarf, gaily dressed in crimson and white satin, now entered the arena, leading in the giant by a chain, and, binding him to [a] golden tree, took up a position on a flight of steps, with a trumpet and sand-glass in his hands. The dwarf then sounded a note on his trumpet....[37]

But as early as 1280 there had been a tournament with a damsel in distress, an insolent dwarf, a knight playing Sir Kay, and the like;[38] and things went on from there. It was entirely appropriate that the preposterous Southern ring tournaments had been sparked by a tournament staged in England in 1839 at great cost by a few romantic aristocrats; and that that tournament had been based on the tournament at Ashby-de-la-Zouche in *Ivanhoe*; and that Scott's description was anachronistic by two and a half centuries.[39]

THE MYTHICAL WEST

And the American West, that chivalric landscape of the simple verities that stretches back goldenly decade after decade in everyone's imagination, is of course just as bad when it comes to fictiveness, discrepancies, odd puzzles, romantic nostalgias. As early as 1892 a writer was complaining that, "like the cavalier, the troubadour, the Puritan, and the Forty-niner, the cow-boy and his attendant life have become but figures in history," and reporting that in towns like Dodge and Abilene the tales of saloon killings were "known to but few of the modern inhabitants, so entirely has a new people filled the land in the last decade."[40] But the realer-than-real West of the mind that emerged as the dime novels were supplemented by short stories like Alfred Henry Lewis's and Owen Wister's and by Remington's powerful drawings and paintings, would soon take care of that, especially after Wister introduced in *The Virginian* the classic trio of cowboy knight, genteel lady fair, and bully on the prod. And the firmer the outlines of the Western became, particularly after the movies carried on from writers like Wister and Zane Grey, the stronger would become the curiosity about what the West had "really" been like.

The discrepancies and incongruities were sometimes piquant. In the Seventies and Eighties, for example, indignant commentators described to Eastern readers how the drunken cowboy rampaging in towns like Dodge and Abilene would "deal out death in unbroken doses to such as may be in range of his pistols," and how, "disregarding equally the rights and lives of others, and utterly reckless of his own life; always ready with his weapons and spoiling for a fight, he is the terror of all who come near him, his visits...being regarded as a calamity second only to a western tornado."[41] But according to one scholarly researcher, in the five main Kansas cattle towns there were in fact only forty-five homicides between 1870 and 1885, and no evidence of any *High Noon* kinds of duels, while another remarks that "few incidents of quick-drawing are recorded, and even these are questionable."[42] And the most dramatic of the range wars, the notorious Johnson County War in Wyoming in 1892, which involved more than twenty hired guns and on which numerous novels like Jack Schaefer's *Shane* and Donald Hamilton's *Smoky Valley* would be based, resulted in only four deaths.[43] It is pleasant, too, to discover that for a time Northern cowboys carried their revolvers on their left hips, not their right; that at one point the police in Dodge City wore neat blue uniforms; and that at another the gallant U.S. cavalry, when in full dress, sported spiked helmets with horsehair plumes.[44] As for the emergence of the cowboy hero in the first place, his evolution in the Eighties by way of the dime novels and Buffalo Bill's Wild West Show had entailed so complex an intermingling of personae that it is sometimes difficult to say which is image and which actuality, or where art ends and life begins.[45] The blending of fact and fiction would continue in things like the gunfighter Henry Starr making movies based on his own career, and the honorary cowboy status accorded actors like William S. Boyd and John Wayne.

Given the potency of irony, an admiration for the chivalric would seem particularly vulnerable in view of the kinds of facts that I have been pointing to. Behind the noble facade of chivalrous medieval warfare lay throat-slitting looting. Behind the image of Southern gentlemen dueling like gentlemen on the field of honor lay vendettas and affrays like the one that horrified Huck Finn – "I ain't a-going to tell *all* that happened – it would make me sick again if I was to do that. I wished I hadn't even come ashore that night, to see such things. I ain't ever going to get shut of them – lots of times I dream about them."[46] Behind Southern gush about the sanctity of womanhood lay the unperturbed flogging of women slaves, memorably described by Olmsted.[47] Behind British or Anglophilic World War I talk about martial gallantry, such as in Henry Newbolt's anthology *The Book of the Happy Warrior* (1917), lay the waste, ugliness, and incompetence that disgusted Hemingway and others with the big manipulative words like "honor" and "glory." Behind *High Noon* and *Shane* and Wister's best-known novel lay – well, at any rate evidently not a landscape populated by calm-eyes, soft-spoken Gary Coopers. And there was something else.

CHIVALRY VERSUS THE WORK ETHIC

In terms of the dominant ideology, Americans had long been committed to obtaining the desirable by maximally effective means, and from that point of view not only did fictions and play look like idleness and untruth, weakening the will; rules and forms, too, were deeply suspect. American enterprise had vigorously sought to break with artificial and unnatural constraints. Unfettered technology, which Twain eulogized in *A Connecticut Yankee*, had made possible the triumphant outflowing of national energies after the Civil War – a war that itself had been a large-scale demonstration of untrammeled Northern energies, both in industry and in military operations like Grant's Wilderness campaign and Sherman's unprecedented march to the sea. And in business endeavors rules were only a hindrance. As the author of the Frank Merriwell stories recalled of the businessmen in the small Connecticut town in which he grew up in the Seventies,

with them business was business, which meant that it was legitimate and nowise dishonorable to get the better end of a bargain by hook or by crook.

In fact, they rather prided themselves upon it when they had cunningly deceived and cheated another person, even though he were a near neighbor or close friend. In business matters they were like the poker player who announces that friendship ceases when he gets into a game.[48]

For that matter, Frank Merriwell himself was not above bending a few rules at times.

In contrast, the chivalric flagrantly contained elements of unreality and play. It was pervaded by a liking for conflict not as a byproduct of the rational pursuit of a rational end, as in the railroad and oil wars of the second half of the nineteenth century, but for its own sake, as in the tournament. "Fight on all occasions," D'Artagnan *père* instructed his son. "Fight the more for duels being forbidden; since, consequently, there is twice as much courage in fighting."[49] Chivalric combativeness had resulted in foolish and unnecessary wars, because of the cravings for glory of romantics like Edward III, whose chivalric imaginings contributed to his embarking on the Hundred Years' War. Moreover, conflicts could be deliberately prolonged by a refusal to take certain expedient steps because they were simply not done, such as when French knights declined to attack from battle positions that gave them an "unfair" advantage, or when Lancelot refused to kill his implacable foe Gawain and end the conflict that was wrecking Arthur's kingdom. And the rules of honor bound its votaries to persist in a chosen course even when it was doomed to fail, like the attack of Pickett's Virginians at Gettysburg. The Civil War was typical in the way in which Southerners conceived of war as a species of duel or tournament, waxed indignant about Sherman's brilliantly innovative march through Georgia, and later gave themselves a moral alibi with the myth of the Virginian gentleman doomed by his noble qualities, qualities that made defeat not only admirable but morally superior to victory. And there were other kinds of

Fictiveness

chivalric wastefulness – ornate costume and display; ritualistic games and hunting and gambling; a zealous concern to do things in the "correct" way; the elaborate rituals of the love game. As the great Dutch cultural historian J. Huizinga said of the potlatch culture of West Coast Indians,

a society wholly dominated by those primary impulses and incentives which, in a more cultivated phase, are peculiar to boyhood...will be animated in the highest degree by things like group-honour, admiration for wealth and liberality, trust and friendship; it will lay great stress on challenges, bettings, and "darings" of all kinds, competitions, adventures and the everlasting glorification of the self by displays of studied indifference to material values.[50]

In a number of ways, the chivalric would appear to encourage what W. J. Cash, with the South in mind, called "the tendency toward unreality, towards romanticism, and, in intimate relationship with that, toward hedonism."[51]

Two chivalric paradigms particularly invited, and have continued to invite, mistrust in terms of the reality principle. One was the Quixotic, as derided in the numerous antebellum sneers at Southern chivalry, and in Walter Lippmann's complaint in 1913 that "reform produces its Don Quixotes who never deal with reality," and in a reviewer's assertion in 1979 that "the essential [Evelyn] Waugh hero is a British Don Quixote dejectedly tilting at the 20th century. His troubles begin with a code of honor that is ill suited for campaigns in society or on the battlefield."[52] Not only did Quixote, in his search for heroic action, attack useful windmills, slash valuable wine skins, kill precious sheep, and in general make a pest of himself to merchants, peasants, innkeepers, and others going about their sensible business. He did so because of a persistent, deluded misperception of realities – the result of too much injudicious and fanciful reading. And in his combat with the whole reasonable modern world, he was doomed to acknowledge ultimately the claims of reality and the absurdity of the fictions governing him. He was like the unfortunate real-life cowboy dissected by Jane Kramer in *The Last Cowboy*, of whom Diane Johnson remarks that "she is sorry that [he] totes guns and acts up in barrooms and is so foolish as to believe that a handshake seals a bargain," and that "in the real West, where cattle is big business run by people who live in London or Pasadena, literal trustful people like Henry are destroyed by their naiveté."[53] The other central embodiment of chivalric irrealism was of course Galahad, the quintessential White Knight of countless ironical references. Galahad himself, as presented in Tennyson's *Idylls* and in numerous works addressed to the young, was obviously not ineffectual. He was unbeatable in combat; he attained the Grail; he was the antithesis of the absent-minded, gadget-ridden, well-intentioned, and incompetent

White Knight of Lewis Carroll. But in his humorless rectitude he was the classic type of white-on-white success, the Good Boy held up for emulation by the less-than-good by persons bent on "civilizing" the recalcitrant American male, the paragon recalled by Twain when he said that "the Model Boy of my time – we never had but the one – was perfect: perfect in manners, perfect in dress, perfect in conduct, perfect in filial piety, perfect in exterior godliness; but at the bottom he was a prig."[54] In *H. M. Pulham, Esquire*, John P. Marquand's gentlemanly, ineffective narrator recalls how in his childhood a picture of a praying knight hung over his bed and how his mother told him, "Yes, dear, . . . a knight is always a gentleman, but Sir Galahad was more than that – he could touch the Holy Grail. Do you know what [Tennyson] said in the poem? 'My strength is as the strength of ten because my heart is pure.' And you must be my little knight."[55] The prep-school hero of Edmund Wilson's story "Galahad" similarly learns from a YMCA lecturer how, "without reverence for womanhood, without chivalry and chastity, there can be no clean and enduring love."[56] Moreover, not only was Galahad's virtuousness beyond the reach of normal humanity, but he was the central figure in an obsessive quest – a minicrusade as it were –that ruinously disrupted the Arthurian kingdom. If Quixote epitomized certain aspects of the Confederate South, Galahad epitomized some of those of the abolitionist North. There would be a good many subsequent American crusades, including "vice" crusades and the bogus newspaper crusades of William Randolph Hearst, that would invite a skeptical gaze.

THE ENDURING CHIVALRIC VISION

Yet despite all that I have been saying, the chivalric has in fact proved remarkably resistant to an ironic perception of incongruities and inconsistencies. Froissart and other chroniclers, as Huizinga points out, continued to revere the chivalric system even while describing a great deal of utterly unchivalrous behavior; and chivalric values were able to sustain the analytical attention of minds as fine as those of Chaucer, Shakespeare, the anonymous author of *Sir Gawain and the Green Knight*, and Cervantes. In an ultimate paradox, Cervantes's Quixote was able to maintain an unswerving fidelity to chivalry in the midst of people *none* of whom shared his faith and most of whom behaved ignobly – and to achieve a victory in defeat by virtue of which, as one critic puts it, he "revive[d] the standard of Spanish pride so successfully that he [became] a sort of secular saint."[57] In America, too, the chivalric has not been destroyed by intellectual analysis. The fact is particularly striking when one considers the intellectual mood of the turn-of-the-century years.

On the face of it, that period ought to have been absolutely ruinous for chivalry. The first decade or two of the twentieth century was a vintage time for ironists, as Fitzgerald recalled when he wrote of Anthony Patch, the hero of *The Beautiful and the Damned*, that in 1913 "irony, the Holy Ghost of this later day,...descended upon him." Young men like Patch were discovering Samuel Butler, whose "brisk aphorisms in the note-book seemed...the quintessence of criticism."[58] It was the heyday of Bernard Shaw and of Shaw's American promotor, H. L. Mencken, of whom Hemingway's Jake Barnes later remarked in *The Sun Also Rises* that "so many young men get their likes and dislikes from Mencken."[59] Thorstein Veblen, whose "admirable ironies" H. G. Wells commended in 1906, and whose *Theory of the Leisure Class* the Beards considered "the most consummate piece of academic irony ever produced on this continent,"[60] sardonically uncovered radical discrepancies between persisting archaic forms and the real needs of a modern society. In his *Education*, Henry Adams gazed with mingled fascination and dismay at the chasm between older energizing ideals like religious faith, absolute truth, and political glory, and the reality of political squalor and the mindless energies of a value-free and indifferent cosmos. It was in those years that the young T. S. Eliot received his own Prufrockian education in an ironic perception of the fundamental unreality of human relationships and aspirations.

Yet it was not simply tender-minded romantics who took the chivalric seriously in the turn-of-the-century decades. The period shaped the consciousness of writers like Fitzgerald, Faulkner, and Hemingway, Hammett and Chandler, Steinbeck, Robert Penn Warren, and Allen Tate, whose subsequent investigations of chivalric values would be continued by "serious" novelists like Walker Percy and "popular" ones like John D. MacDonald and Donald Hamilton. And respectful explorations of the chivalric by intelligent older American writers were available. In *The Bostonians* Henry James had sympathetically reconsidered the Southern character, as had Albion W. Tourgée and John William De Forest, the latter of whom loved and frequently reread *Don Quixote*. Stephen Crane had enquired into Western machismo and the phenomenology of battle. William James and the Civil War veteran Oliver Wendell Holmes were proffering their reflections on the martial ethos. And by 1920, Edwin Arlington Robinson had brought out the first two of his three long Arthurian narrative poems, *Merlin* and *Lancelot*.[61] Other writers interested seriously in chivalry will be mentioned from time to time in these pages. Here I will merely note that American scholars have produced some of the most useful accounts of chivalric matters, and that more informal studies like W. J. Cash's *The Mind of the South* and Robert Warshow's essays on the Westerner and the gangster ("the two most successful creations of American movies...: men with guns"[62]) are rightly considered classics.

Furthermore, in a fitting ironical twist, the attitude of America's own Cervantes towards the chivalric was in fact a complex one. If Twain attacked historical chivalry as strongly as he did, it was partly because he himself was incurably fascinated by the chivalric spirit. And despite his voiced esteem for 'the wholesome and practical nineteenth-century smell of cotton factories and locomotives,'[63] his writings are those of someone who adored romance. His two-volume, lightly fictionalized *Life of Joan of Arc*, on which he spent twelve years and which he said he liked the best of all his works ('and it *is* the best'[64]) vibrates with enthusiasm for Joan's 'soldier spirit' and for her martial successes against the occupying English. *The Prince and the Pauper*, though nastier in some of its details than bestsellers like Edwin Caskoden's *When Knighthood Was in Flower* (1898), is every bit as romantic an incursion into Tudor England, the occasional gestures toward period realism in it only serving to underpin the preposterous romantic plot, the pluckiness of the two young heroes, and the loyalty of the out-at-elbows gentleman Miles Hendon, appropriately played in the 1937 movie by Errol Flynn. The earlier chapters of *Life on the Mississippi* are afire with the glory of the great river and those marvelous beings, the riverboat pilots. And *Huckleberry Finn*, that ideal romance of a young hero passing unscathed through a series of physical and moral perils, is the creation of someone as steeped as Tom Sawyer in romantic fiction.[65] Moreover, Twain's presentation of the ceremonious, patriarchal Southern household of the Grangerfords is admiring to the point of hero worship, particularly in the treatment of Colonel Grangerford himself; and he also gazes respectfully through Huck's eyes at that other Southern gentleman, Colonel Sherburn, when he coolly and single-handedly faces down by sheer strength of personality the plebian lynch mob that has come in search of him after his shooting of old Boggs. In general, the comparison of Twain to Cervantes has much more than a surface truth to it. The poet Roy Campbell shrewdly says of Cervantes that "I always feel that he used Quixote to show up the banality and bathos of modern life, which was beginning to settle over Europe as early as the sixteenth century when commerce succeeded to prowess and valour as the chief means of subsistence," and that in another of his works he did "as much to exalt Spanish chivalry and courage as he is supposed to have done to ridicule it in *Don Quixote*."[66] Twain, too, cared passionately for the chivalric values, and in his best writings, *Huckleberry Finn* and the first half of *Life on the Mississippi*, he was transposing them into genuinely American terms.

In sum, what marks the chivalric where America is concerned is a remarkable toughness and resilience. I shall now try to go deeper into its strengths.

4
Fictions and forms

It was a powerful fine sight; I never seen anything so lovely. And then one by one they got up and stood, and went a-weaving around the ring so gentle and wavy and graceful, the men looking ever so tall and airy and straight, with their heads bobbing and skimming along, away up there under the tent-roof, and every lady's rose-leafy dress flapping soft and silky around her hips, and she looking like the most loveliest parasol.

Mark Twain, *Huckleberry Finn* (1884)

General Grant had on a sack coat, a loose fatigue coat, but he had no side arms. He looked as though he had had a pretty hard time. He had been riding and his clothes were somewhat dusty and a little soiled. He walked up to General Lee and Lee recognized him at once. He had known him in the Mexican war. General Grant greeted him in the most cordial way, and talked about the weather and other things in a very friendly way. Then General Grant brought up his officers and introduced them to General Lee.

Colonel Charles Marshall, *An Aide-de-Camp of Lee* (1894)[1]

IF THE COMPULSION in American intellectual life to assail romantic idealism has been perennial, so has an anxiety about what may follow if the assault succeeds. Near the end of *The Great Gatsby*, Nick Carraway reflects that Gatsby, after the flight of Daisy,

must have felt that he had lost the old warm world, paid a high price for living too long with a single dream. He must have looked up at an unfamiliar sky through frightening leaves and shivered as he found what a grotesque thing a rose is and how raw the sunlight was upon the scarcely created grass. A new world, material without being real, where poor ghosts, breathing dreams like air, drifted fortuitously about.[2]

A similar anxiety had sounded, more somberly and disturbingly, in the writings of Melville, and Hawthorne, and Adams, and would continue to sound in those of Hemingway and others. An important aspect of the appeal of the chivalric was precisely that it resisted an ironical or metaphysical undercutting, and that it did so in ways involving more complex relationships between fiction and reality than a simple dichotomizing implies.

As I have indicated, opponents of the chivalric, including Twain, have argued more or less simultaneously both that it is too unreal and that it has been too effective in shaping actual behavior. And once one gets

48

Fictions and forms

beyond the kinds of pseudohistorical exaggerations that indeed cried out to be debunked, it is clear that, despite what I have said about its fictional aspects, the chivalric in America was far from being all fiction. Certain chivalric patterns were not only recreated in America but created more fully and purely at times than they had been in Europe. The transpositions and adaptations went far beyond superficial imitations of European manners by romantic and sentimental persons who had read too much Scott or too many cloak-and-rapier romances too trustingly.

THE REAL THING, SOMETIMES

In the antebellum South, whatever conditions may have been like for the great majority of the inhabitants, it is plain that a minority did indeed enjoy an aristocratic way of life of great charm, the configurations of which I shall return to in Chapter 5. The recollections and eyewitness accounts of a variety of writers are too numerous and circumstantial to be dismissed as a collective delusion;[3] and they are persuasively corroborated by novels like *Huckleberry Finn* and John Pendleton Kennedy's *Swallow Barn* (1832), testimony all the more valuable because of the novelists' skeptical attitude toward romantic chivalric pretensions. Furthermore, the Southern gentleman, and especially the Virginian gentleman, plainly also existed. It was the cool-eyed Frederick Law Olmsted, for example, who said that

to the Southern gentleman...as I have often met him, I wish to pay great respect. The honest and unstudied dignity of character, the generosity and the real nobleness of habitual impulses, and the well-bred, manly courtesy which distinguish him in all the relations and occupations of life, equally in his business, in his family, and in general society, are sadly rare at the North.[4]

It was Twain who wrote of Colonel Grangerford, as seen through Huck's eyes:

He was a gentleman all over; and so was his family. He was well born, as the saying is, and that's worth as much in a man as it is in a horse...There warn't no frivolishness about him, not a bit, and he warn't ever loud. He was as kind as he could be – you could feel that, you know, and so you had confidence. Sometimes he smiled, and it was good to see; but when he straightened himself up like a liberty-pole, and the lightning begun to flicker out from under his eyebrows, you wanted to climb a tree first, and find out what the matter was afterwards. He didn't ever have to tell anybody to mind their manners – everybody was always good-mannered where he was. Everybody loved to have him around, too; he was sunshine most always – I mean he made it seem like good weather.[5]

49

Part I From cavaliers to cowboys

The Civil War would be graced by such flesh-and-blood epitomes of Southern chivalry as Jeb Stuart, Robert E. Lee, and the twenty-three-year old Colonel William Pegram of whom his grieving adjutant wrote in his journal: "Thus died the truest Christian, the most faithful friend and the most superb soldier in all the world. He was, indeed, my Jonathon [sic], pure in heart, brave in deed, chivalric until it bordered on Quixotism, generous and utterly unselfish, he was the Havelock of the Army of Northern Virginia."[6]

Nor should the chivalric aspects of the West be written off quite so lightly as I did in the previous chapter. The writer who complained that *"The Virginian* gave the country for forty years as perniciously false an idea of the West as *Uncle Tom's Cabin* had given it of the South" was perhaps being a little quick on the trigger;[7] Roosevelt was not necessarily in the flood tide of romantic nostalgia when he recalled in his *Autobiography* in 1913 that "one of the men I have mentioned...was in all essentials the Virginian in real life, not only in his force but in his charm."[8] Books as intelligent and richly detailed as Andy Adams's *The Log of a Cowboy* (1905) and Philip Ashton Rollins's *The Cowboy* (1922), both of them drawing on considerable firsthand experience of cowboying during its great days, do much to bear out the assertion by the Western historian Edward Everett Dale – himself a former cowboy – that "there were exceptions, of course, but as a rule the range rider was shy, quiet, and soft spoken. In a region and a society where it is customary to go armed, courtesy is likely to be the rule."[9] Another historian of the West, in support of his assertion that "a man's word on the frontier was in fact as good as his bond," describes how one of the stores in Dodge allegedly "never lost a dime" to customers to whom it extended credit, "even though some of the cowboys often had to ride several hundred miles out of their way to settle their accounts."[10] And Dale recalls how "chivalry, in the original and truest sense of the term, prevailed; for though the range rider was not sworn to protect pure womanhood, he would probably go farther in that direction than did the cavaliers of that older age when 'knighthood was in flower,' " a statement emphatically supported in Rollins's assertion that the cowboys' "adherence to the code regarding women travelling upon the Range transcended punctiliousness and rested on the plane of highest honor. A woman journeying alone upon the open Range was as safe as though in her own house."[11] Irritating as some of Roosevelt's celebrations of individual Westerners in *The Rough Riders* may be, it should be borne in mind that the book appeared only a year after the events described in it and that Roosevelt was presumably not simply fantasizing when he recalled of one of them – Bucky O'Neill, "the iron-nerved, iron-willed fighter from Arizona, the Sheriff whose name was a by-word of terror to every

50

wrong-doer...the gambler who with unmoved face would stake and lose every dollar he had in the world" – that on one occasion he overheard him and the ex-Princetonian regimental surgeon "discussing Aryan word-roots together, and then sliding off into a review of the novels of Balzac, and a discussion as to how far Balzac could be said to be the founder of the modern realistic school of fiction."[12]

In both the South and the West there had in fact been a complex cultural transmission and replication of European patterns, types, and values. In part the replication resulted from a similarity of socioeconomic structures. If the hard-trading Virginian planters of the seventeenth century increasingly took on aristocratic traits in the eighteenth, it was partly because of genuinely aristocratic patterns in their lives – the distance between plantations, the lack of substantial towns, the relative insignificance of the powers of the state, the supreme authority of the equestrian and armed planter over a largely self-sufficient rural domain. Similarly, the ranching West witnessed what Dale justly calls "a curious American feudalism strongly reminiscent of the feudal order of medieval Europe."[13] In the cattle kingdom that had been established by the Eighties in a region as big as Western Europe, the dominant pattern was one of widely spaced ranches, each with its group of armed horsemen and its identifying symbols. It was natural enough that in such a society, with its taxing and often dangerous work and its need for harmonious relationships between those doing that work, a premium should have been put upon central chivalric values like courage, hardihood, prowess, and trustworthiness, and that it should have evolved social codes that were curiously formal at times, such as when cowboys entered a saloon in order of precedence. It was also natural that in a society hungry for entertainment, cowboys should have engaged in formalized tests and displays of professional skills, and that good singers, sometimes moving from ranch to ranch, should have enjoyed a prestige analogous to that of troubadours.

But there was more to it than that. Just as the cowboy's dress, equipment, skills, and terminology had derived largely from the chivalric horsemen of Spanish America, so a number of his basic attitudes –his armed and watchful civility, his sense of honor, his taste for gambling, his generosity, his hospitableness, his contempt for the money making of townspeople and the prudent virtues of smallholders – came essentially from the South, via Texas and via Southerners from other states who had gone into cowboying after the Civil War. Likewise the attitudes and values of Southerners themselves had evolved through a complex transmission and assimilation of ideals. The growing interest in the chivalric in the first half of the nineteenth century had involved much more than an indulgence in ring tournaments and romantic waffle about

51

women. It had entailed a genuine internalization of the values to be found in Scott's novels, the histories of chivalry, Froissart's *Chronicles*, and Simms's life of Bayard. Lee, for example, according to one of his biographers, "believed that he had in his veins the blood of conquerors, crusaders, and cavaliers. That belief contributed to his sense of *noblesse oblige*, and if it was based on fiction it was as influential with him as if it had been sustained by the adjuration of all the heralds of Europe."[14] Moreover, if a good many of the Virginian planters from whom men like Lee were descended may not initially have been gentlemen, the process by which the planters turned into gentlemen had itself been ideological and intellectual as well as economic. As the cultural historian Louis B. Wright observes, "Virginian colonists who had the opportunity of acquiring land and accumulating wealth attempted to duplicate the manner of life led by that most envied of mortals at home, the proud and powerful country squire ... As an aristocratic upper class developed and gained authority and social prestige, its members became increasingly conscious of their inheritance from the English tradition"[15] – a consciousness in which reading played a considerable part.

Furthermore, in making itself over as it did, the planter class was continuing the process wherein, during the Tudor period, the figure of the heroic warrior knight had modulated into that of the gentleman. Amusing or irritating as some of the later stereotypes may be – "the Imperial hero figure...tall, thin, square-jawed, keen-eyed and almost always equipped with pipe and moustache"[16] – the English gentleman, and the idea of the gentleman, were major cultural realities in the life of both England and Europe. And in their inception they were a long way from what Ruth Kelso, in her valuable historical study, calls "the courtesy of Newman's gentleman, who may be said to act rather with the aim of effacing himself to the comfort of his companions, than with the aim of enhancing himself," an attitude summed up in Newman's famous and foolish statement that "it is almost a definition of a gentleman to say he is one who never inflicts pain."[17] If the Tudor gentleman, as was urged by humanists like Thomas Elyot in his *Book of the Governor*, ought to possess such Aristotelian virtues as prudence, justice, temperance, and courtesy, it is plain that he also continued to be, in his ideal outlines, a heroic figure. Courage was as important as ever. So was what Kelso calls

magnanimity, high-mindedness, a sort of sublimation of courage, which belonged peculiarly to the gentleman, directing all his actions, and giving to all his virtues a grace and splendour wanting for the common man. Magnanimity sent a man into high enterprises which taxed to the utmost the powers of mind and body, and before which lesser men would quail; it also enabled a man to throw over his actions [a] fine air of carelessness.[18]

Fictions and forms

The new pattern displayed itself in a variety of forms in the plays of Shakespeare and in figures like the Earl of Essex and Sir Philip Sidney and the first governor of Virginia, Sir Walter Raleigh. It would continue to manifest itself in numerous ways during the next three centuries, including the way described by Hannah Arendt when she said of the Imperialist years that, "As real in England as the tradition of hypocrisy is another less obvious one which one is tempted to call a tradition of dragon-slayers who went enthusiastically into far and curious lands to strange and naïve peoples to slay the numerous dragons that had plagued them for centuries."[19]

The existence of this high-energy pattern testifies to something further about chivalric patterns in general. If it was indebted to Castiglione's *Book of the Courtier*, it diverged from it in its emphasis on a proud and honor-governed independence of spirit and conscience; and in its concern with service to causes beyond mere self-advancement it diverged even more from Machiavelli's image of the power-charged and successful public man in that other major Renaissance handbook, *The Prince*. In so doing it bore witness to the continuing vitality of the chivalric ideals. When Sir Bors in the thirteenth-century *Death of Arthur* referred to "all the virtues through which a man can rise in worldly honour and be called noble – I mean beauty and prowess, valour and chivalry, and gentility,"[20] or when the Bors of Malory's fifteenth-century retelling of the cycle praised Sir Lancelot in the terms that I quoted earlier, they were pointing to important and influential concepts. Barbarous as the treatment of common soldiers and civilians often was, and unlovely as a great many knights may have been, the chivalric code, with its emphasis on dignity, generosity, and honor was not on that account a mere matter of literary chat. In the later fourteenth century, according to a not especially dewy-eyed scholar, "ideals of knighthood and of knightly conduct had a crucial significance. It is probable that for the majority of the ruling class they formed a standard of values at times consciously followed, at times consciously sinned against, but always presupposed."[21] Another suggests that "a nobleman rarely violated his feudal obligations as they were interpreted by his class" and that paroles and solemn promises were very rarely broken.[22] Yet another comments of the knights of the Hundred Years War that "they possessed a code of behaviour – a caste code, certainly, founded largely on mutual self-interest, and in which money played a leading part – which it was the exception not to observe and whose imperatives were backed ultimately by force."[23] Such comments could be multiplied. At its simplest, the code helped to make warfare more tolerable for knights; Froissart, for example, notes approvingly how, when the Scots and English "surrender to each other according to the law of arms, they treat their

53

prisoners well without pressing too hard for money, behaving chivalrously to one another, which the Germans do not."²⁴ At its most complex, as Huizinga says, chivalry was, next to religion, "the strongest of all the ethical conceptions which dominated the mind and heart. It was thought of as the crown of the whole social system." And he observes of it that "the source of the chivalric idea is pride aspiring to beauty, and formalized pride gives rise to a conception of honour, which is the pole of noble life."²⁵ These energies were at work in the books dealing with chivalry that Caxton printed and in the chivalric splendors of the fifteenth-century Burgundian court that helped to shape the consciousness of romantic and noble-minded young Elizabethans like Sidney.²⁶

CHIVALRY AT WORK AND PLAY

It is now possible to be a little clearer about some of the reasons for the American fondness for the chivalric, and its curious resistance to irony. An important reason, paradoxically, is precisely the part played in the chivalric by fictions. The chivalric transcended the simple dichotomy between solid but somehow empty reality and appealing but insubstantial fictions and make believe. And in so doing it also transcended the dichotomy between culture, perceived as effete or marmoreal, and constrictive, and nature, perceived as an affair of raw and probably destructive energies. Appropriately, one of the key chivalric figures, Quixote, is a man who has read a great deal.

In the chivalric transmissions and incarnations, life and letters had interpenetrated from the outset. When Duke Philip the Good in fifteenth-century Burgundy sponsored his extravagant imitations of tournaments and jousts described in the romances, or when the hopelessly romantic Burgundian knight Jacques de Lalaing journeyed from court to court in the hope of finding persons to joust "seriously" with, they were only doing the sort of thing that many others had done before them. In the thirteenth century, Edward I had mounted an Arthurian festival, with appropriate tournaments, to celebrate his wedding, and knights had been accused by unfriendly contemporaries of going off to war dressed like knights going to the Round Table; and the fourteenth century witnessed outbreaks of Arthurianism or quasi-Arthurianism everywhere, such as the chivalric orders initiated when Edward III created the Knights of the Blue Garter. Quixote was only the most extreme of a long line of imitators. Hence, as Baron Kervyn de Lettenhove shrewdly observes,

if Froissart and the other chroniclers or poets of his time admire and exalt chivalry so highly, it is because they perceive that in subjecting kings themselves to the duties of chivalry, and in placing the whole career of a knight between the two extreme limits of the romance which was read to him in his youth, and the chronicle by which his life was judged at its end, they succeeded in giving to letters in the feudal world a more exalted place than that which they had ever attained in Greece and Rome.[27]

Moreover, the relationships between ideals and actualities in the imitating were more complicated than the simple undercuttings of irony would suggest. Some of the imitations were obviously artificial in the sense of there being substantial discrepancies between actors and roles, and by the end of the Middle Ages tournaments and jousts had turned into elaborate pageants in which the ritualization of combat and the massive armor virtually eliminated any risk beyond a bad bruising. But it had not been play acting when the blind young king of Bohemia at Crécy had a group of his knights guide him into the battle so that he could strike a few blows before being killed, or when the Black Prince, after the battle of Poitiers, insisted on serving the captured French king and nobles with his own hands, or when Sir Walter Manny stood up to the enraged Edward III on behalf of the six burghers of Calais. Nor was the career of a professional soldier like Bayard play acting. If the court of Chrétien's Arthurian tales, in Richard Barber's words, became "the paradise of which all secular knights dreamed,"[28] and if knights far tougher than poor Quixote aspired to possess the chivalric virtues, this was because ideals and actual life were not in fact disjoined or disjoinable in the straightforward way that irony implies.

The code of martial honorableness was defined and developed in a variety of ways – in romances, chronicles, clerical treatises about the war, reminiscences, biographies – and in all of them concrete images played a major role. Chivalry, as one commentator puts it, "was fundamentally the imitation of the ideal hero," and Walker Percy's Lancelot Lamar was simply furnishing another example from a long tradition when he said of his father that "Robert E. Lee was his saint; he loved him the way Catholics love St. Francis. If the South were Catholic, we'd have long since had an order of St. Robert E. Lee, a stern military order like the monks of Mont-Saint-Michel."[29]

But more was involved than simply starry-eyed admiration for impossibly ideal types. Obviously actual warriors who, like the fictional Gawain of *Sir Gawain and the Green Knight* and the real Louis IX, combined martial, Christian, and courtly virtues were very few. Conversely, heavy-handed, arrogant, and bone-headed aristocrats of the kind attacked by Twain in *A Connecticut Yankee* must have been many. Nevertheless, a number of individual figures were not absurdly distant from the types of fiction. The oral tradition of martial history was strong.

Part I From cavaliers to cowboys

Froissart, for example, described how at the court of the Count of Foix, where he had stayed for awhile in the 1380s,

one saw knights and squires coming and going in the hall and the rooms and the courtyard, and one heard them talking of arms and love. Every subject of honour was discussed. Reports from every country and kingdom were to be heard, for, because of the reputation of the master of the house, they were brought there in great abundance. At Orthez I was informed of most of the feats of arms which had taken place in Spain, Portugal, Aragon, Navarre, England, Scotland and within the borders of Languedoc, for while staying there I met knights and squires from all those nations who had come to visit the Count.[30]

And a substantial number of actual medieval figures were perceived by their contemporaries and successors as honorable and admirable warriors, brave, loyal, trustworthy, and generous. Froissart reported of the Count of Foix himself that "no contemporary prince could be compared with him for sense, honor, or liberality."[31] The Black Prince, as Barber says, was considered a model knight, and a contemporary reported of him that "those who dwelt about him esteemed and loved him greatly, for largesse sustained him and nobleness governed him, and discretion, temperance and uprightness, reason, justice and moderation."[32] Of Henry V another historian says that "even his opponents admitted that [his] life had been a pattern of chivalrous conduct," a pattern that included trying to safeguard the lives and property of ordinary people in the regions being fought over.[33] And reputations persisted. Caxton spoke of the enduring fame of Richard I, Edward I, Sir John Hawkwoode, Sir John Chandos, Sir Walter Manny, Sir Robert Knolles, the Earl of Salisbury, "and many others."[34]

Moreover, some of the figures as they emerge from the pages of chronicles and biographies, despite the fictive aspects of such works, do so plausibly as flesh-and-blood beings; and obviously it was in such terms that they were talked about from decade to decade by knights and men-at-arms who could distinguish – as antebellum Southerners like Lee could distinguish a Washington from an Ivanhoe – between an Arthur and a Henry V. The shrewd and energetic Count of Foix as described by Froissart is wholly alive in his curiosity, his cheerfulness, his devoutness, his generosity, his skillful management of his estate, his love of music, his humorous brusqueness with his four secretaries ("He did not call them John or Walter or William, but when he had read his letters and wanted to dictate or give them some order, he addressed them without distinction as You Shocking Servant"[35]). The thirteenth-century Crusader Louis IX, as described by his friend Jean de Joinville in his memoir after the king's death, is convincingly likeable and admirable, whether impatiently plunging into a fight with Saracens, or trying to improve Joinville's ways ("At another time King Louis asked me if I

56

washed the feet of the poor on Maundy Thursday. 'Your Majesty,' I exclaimed, 'what a terrible idea! I will never wash the feet of such low fellows!' 'Really,' said he, 'that is a very wrong thing to say' "), or carrying out his civic duties:

I have sometimes seen him, in summer, go to administer justice to his people in the public gardens in Paris, dressed in a plain woollen tunic, a sleeveless surcoat of linsey-woolsey, and a black taffeta cape around his shoulders, with his hair neatly combed, but no cap to cover it, and only a hat of white peacock's feathers on his head. He would have a carpet laid down so that we might sit round him, while all those who had any case to bring before him stood round about. Then he would pass judgment on each case, as I have told you he often used to do in the wood of Vincennes.[36]

Above all, the Chevalier Bayard emerges from the pages of his companion and biographer as a thoroughly solid, admirable, and credible person. On the one hand, he was an extremely skillful professional soldier, whom his biographer called "one of the subtilest, most vigilant warriours that you could meet with"[37] – a thorough professional performing brilliantly in the confused warfare in Italy at the beginning of the sixteenth century, capable of setting efficient ambushes, retreating prudently when outmatched, and on one occasion neatly working the laws of knightly surrender to his own advantage. On the other, he was manifestly a man of great poise and charm, as displayed, for instance, in his good-humored handling of a drunken, duel-seeking confrere; and two of the accounts of his gracious dealings with women – chivalrous in the best sense – are convincing in their essentials, even if obviously fictive in some of their details.

What is significant about all this is that the virtues of such men were in accord with the demands of warfare. As is said of Bayard in Simms's biography, "it was not the smallest merit of Bayard that he knew so well how to infuse, with his own noble and fearless spirit, all who served beneath his banner," and during the Hundred Years' War efforts were made to create a cult of warriors like the Black Prince and Bertrand Du Guesclin who were particularly thought to embody the chivalric virtues. The functional importance of someone like Bayard is brought out especially clearly in Mailles's account of his death:

[There] was much sorrow excited in all the Gentlemen and soldiers, and that on many accounts; for he had ever been wont, when he made military excursions, and took prisoners, to treat them with singular mildness, and was so lenient in regard of their ransoms, that he gave content to every one. They knew that by his death all that was noble would suffer a grievous decline; for without derogating from others, he was a paragon of Knights. And by warring with him the younger Gentlemen of the adverse army were instructed.[38]

Even the more idealized – and simpler – figures of the Arthurian mythos were evidently not sharply separate, in terms of martial effectiveness, from the actual working values of flesh-and-blood knights. Actual warriors would not have gone on taking pleasure decade after decade in the stories of figures whose values and behavior they thought preposterous.

And not only was the chivalric congruent with reality in the ways that I have been describing. In certain respects it appealed precisely because of the elements of artifice in it. As Huizinga points out, the paradigmatic chivalric institution, the tournament, was in some ways like theater and fulfilled some similar needs; and in the chivalric orders, vows, and initiations, reaching back into an archaic past, the play factor was a powerful creative force. The same appeals were at work in the popularity of chivalric patterns in America.

Ostensibly, rational nineteenth-century America was committed to a deep distrust of artifice and play. Play wasted time, artifice was untruth, elaborate codes hampered the energetic in their pursuit of rational success or seduced people into unreason. They were what led to the code-governed butchery of the Grangerford–Shepherdson feud in *Huckleberry Finn*, or Tom Sawyer's fastidious concern to rescue the imprisoned Jim in the "correct" storybook way. But in actuality, of course, Twain himself loved and celebrated the elaborate and fanciful. The circus that enchanted Huck in the run-down, murderous, horrible little Arkansas town vividly displayed admirable human possibilities in its high-energy stylizations and conventions. So did those glorious riverboats that so enchanted Twain himself before the Civil War, with their palatial decorations, their heroic tournamentlike races, their pilots who were "in those days...the only unfettered and entirely independent human being[s] that lived in the earth."[39] And postbellum America in general proved remarkably hospitable to high-energy forms, such as Fourth of July parades, the extravagances of Barnum and Bailey's three-ring circuses, and the rituals of fraternal organizations like the Knights Templar, for which H. L. Mencken's businessman father in the Eighties wore "a uniform resembling that of a rear-admiral," with "a long-tailed blue coat with brass buttons, a velvet chapeau with a black feather, a silk baldric, and a sword."[40] America also, as I said earlier, became increasingly hospitable to literal sports and games.

Some of the reasons for that hospitality are obvious enough. Sports and games, whether the direct physical combat of boxing or football, the more distanced combat of tennis, or the surrogate combat of cards, were the most dramatic entertainments available. They were pervaded by suspense and unpredictability, involved pleasurable risks and tensions, permitted definite and unequivocal conclusions of a sort rarely possible in "real" life, and were frequently accompanied by colorful social rituals. Moreover, their tests of skills and displays of excellence were not simply a wasting of time in terms of the rational business calculus. Working-class youths made their way upwards as baseball players or boxers; Ivy League football stars were welcomed into the higher-level business world upon graduation; and sports and gambling encouraged and rewarded such practical skills as making predictions, estimating probabilities, and cutting down the margin of chance. But a further and more important reason for the popularity of games in America was the recognition that game rules were in fact neither foolish nor unreal nor in essential conflict with reality.

In part this recognition involved a straightforward and important historical continuity. It is not accidental that the image of the tournament, the first major European sport, should come so immediately to mind when one thinks of medieval chivalry. If there was one thing above all others that had contributed to the relative taming and civilizing of the arrogant, bellicose, and dangerously underemployed feudal knights of the eleventh century, it was the invention in France of the tournament. As a historian puts it, "the tournament was the crucible in which the ideas of feudal chivalry took form and remained throughout the Middle Ages the very heart of chivalric practice."[41] Although the tournament ended as almost pure pageant, it began as simply a miniature battle between temporarily unoccupied warriors, with a few basic rules, and for a good while it remained sufficiently martial to invite repeated bannings by peace-loving clerics. As such it had important ethical aspects. The tournament was a combat between equals in which the object was not to destroy or demean opponents but to defeat them on an agreed-upon occasion. Combat had to be face-to-face, without trickery, and without foul blows. The combatants had to be approximately equal in numbers and weapons, and were expected to treat their opponents civilly once they had defeated them. The same rules applied in the joust, the judicial combat, and the *pas d'armes*, the more informal encounter between individual knights out of which the duel mainly developed. In all of these the principles were operative that one sees in the thirteenth-century romance *The Death of King Arthur*, when Lancelot, fighting on behalf of Guinevere's life and honor, dismounts to put himself on equal terms with an unhorsed opponent, and, on one occasion during the civil war, rejects Hector's brusquely practical advice, "My lord, cut off his head, and our war will be over," helps the fallen Arthur back on to his horse, and elicits from him the comment that "today he has conquered my heart more with his gallantry than the whole world could have done by force."[42] In other words, what was being established was the notion of fair play. This had far-reaching consequences.

The concept of fair fighting, as a historian points out, not only forbade foul blows but implied accepting an increasingly elaborate code of war that "if frequently broken was broken knowingly."[43] Although the idea of a law of nations had begun in classical times and been developed in canon law, it was, as Huizinga says, chivalry that made it flower. In principle, according to Maurice Keen in his detailed study of the subject, "no one, in the middle ages, believed that war among Christians ought to be total war. Its extent was limited by its legal purpose, to establish right by appeal to divine judgment, and it should not disrupt the unity of Christian society."[44] And however much they were departed from in the treatment of civilians, the medieval principles of warfare as enunciated in works like Honoré Bonet's *The Tree of Battles* led eventually to what were to become the commonplaces of the idea of civilized war. They led to the conviction voiced in the *U.S. Department of the Army Field Manual* (1956) that "the law of war places limits on the exercise of a belligerent's power...and requires that belligerents refrain from employing any kind or degree of violence which is not actually necessary for military purposes and that they conduct hostilities with regard to the principles of humanity and chivalry."[45] In another line of continuity, the elaborate dueling code that had evolved by the eighteenth century was intended to ensure that those who wished to confront each other upon the field of honor did so on equal terms and had the maximum opportunity to desist honorably from combat when they wished to;[46] and from there it was only a short step to the civilizing of prize fights and fisticuffs in the 1890s by means of the Marquis of Queensberry's rules, and to the dueling code of the Western. Furthermore, the chivalric game rules and the fictions associated with them had an interesting philosophical status.

I have spoken of the American hostility to rules as foolish hindrances to the pursuit of success. A further reason for that hostility was the perception of rules as issuing from individuals who asserted a moral right to give commands, such as clerics, teachers, and parents, figures who usually claimed supernatural sanctions for their authority. Because moral commands were intrinsically restrictive, being made in the first place because of men's natural unruliness, one's manliness was diminished if one obeyed them willingly. Chivalric game rules were different. The moral authorities considered activities like card playing and horse racing and fist fights disreputable, and hence it was precisely by obeying the rules of such activities that one could affirm one's manhood. The same was true of boyhood games of cowboys and Indians, or the pirate-gang games that Tom Sawyer initiated his young coevals into, or the elaborately structured prison-breaking game that Tom and Huck engaged in in order to "rescue" Jim. In such games, the players mimicked violent and often illegal actions, and authority figures like clerics and rulers were conspicuously absent. Yet the games were felt to be charged with moral significance and opportunities for behaving definably well or badly; and implicit in them was the feeling that chivalric values were good in themselves, the feeling that, as Robert B. Parker's private eye Spenser puts it, "honor is behavior for its own reason."[47] These features of the chivalric were fundamental ones.

In some ways, of course, it was natural that the Christian figure of Galahad should have come to be seen as the archetypal knight. "Ideal chivalry," as a literary historian says, "had been born in the fervor of the Crusades, when military supremacy was one with the service of God,"[48] and the creation of such Galahadic orders as the Teutonic Knights and the Knights Templar was of a piece with the subordination of the martial values to the Christian in the thirteenth-century romance *The Quest of the Holy Grail* and in clerical treatises like Bonet's *The Tree of Battles* and Ramón Lull's *The Orders of Chivalry*. Moreover, in *The Creed of the Old South* Basil Gildersleeve commented justly that "the bearing of the Confederates is not to be understood without taking into account the deep religious feeling of the army and its great leaders."[49] The Army of Northern Virginia was, as Stephen Vincent Benét says, a "praying army, / Full of revivals," and figures like Lee and Jackson recalled the devout and sober Knights of Chaucer's Prologue, just as Jeb Stuart, whom Benét describes as

a wild cavalier
Who worships as sober a God as Stonewall Jackson,
A Rupert who seldom drinks, very often prays,

brought to mind the devout and graceful Gawain of *Sir Gawain and the Green Knight*.[50]

Nevertheless, Christianity was only one of the strands in that chivalric Europe on which the South had drawn for authentication. On one side of the Christian knights stood the older pagan warrior described by Tacitus in *On Germany* and dominating the *Niebelungenlied*;[51] on the other, the Provence-derived courtly lover. This triple-stranded nature of chivalry was clearly visible in the pages of Malory in the differences between the Christian-crusading Ector and Galahad, the secular-martial Bors, and the courtly-martial Lancelot. And when it came to choosing between the church-approved figure of Galahad – pristine, humorless, intolerant – and the figure of Lancelot, whose martial prowess, generosity, and capacity for loyalty were inseparable from his adulterous devotion to Guinevere, there is no doubt as to which was the more appealing. It was from the Lancelot side of the spectrum that the popular figure of the cavalier was to derive, by way of the late-medieval chivalric romances, and it would further modulate into the figure of the swordsman, who, even when operating in a context of religious wars, remained largely indifferent to the religious quarrels themselves –

61

essentially the soldier of fortune, the embryo professional. And a Spanish scholar interestingly suggests of the chivalric romances so much condemned by Renaissance moralists that "today we should consider that their fictitious characters act under the guidance of a 'ruling class morality,' as some German thinker would say, or by an ideal approaching the Nietzschean concept of the superman – which evidently has in its basis little connection with Christianity."[52] Nietzsche himself expressed his admiration for "the Provençal knightly poets, those magnificent inventive men of *gai saber* – to whom Europe owes so much, and almost itself."[53]

Furthermore, the end of the nineteenth century and the beginning of the twentieth saw the coming into prominence of images of other chivalric cultures that were rule bound without being Christian. At its simplest, the cowboy ethos was what Eugene Manlove Rhodes, himself a cowboy for twenty-five years, summed up when he said, "It's not the custom to war without fresh offense, openly given. You must not smile and shoot. You must not shoot an unarmed man, and you must not shoot an unwarned man," a code that he called "the rattlesnake's code, to warn before he strikes, no better: a queer, lop-sided, topsy-turvy, jumbled and senseless code – but a code for all that."[54] At its most idealistic, it was what was embodied in Wister's (and Gary Cooper's) Virginian. But either way, the operative codes were not imposed from above or outside, whether through the sermons of ministers or the coercion of courts and law-enforcement officers. And just as the figure of the cowboy recalled the Fenimore Cooper image of Nature's gentlemen living outside the established Christian social order, so did the changing image of the Indian. In the older and grimmer view of them, Indians had been war demons, creatures of darkness, the practitioners of unspeakable tortures (a view still present in Roosevelt's *The Winning of the West* [1889]), and an unfriendly mid-nineteenth-century observer affirmed that "the Indians of our day, besides having a full share of the lower and degrading vices of the Southern negro, such as stealing, lying and filthy tastes, are noted for cowardice, and craft, and meanness of every description."[55] But it was the Cooper image of Indians at their best that was being reinforced in the later nineteenth and early twentieth centuries in books like Charles Eastman's Ojibway reminiscences in *Indian Boyhood* (1902), *Old Indian Days* (1907), and other volumes, and the writings of the naturalist and explorer of Indian life, George Bird Grinnell. And what emerged from them was the picture of a pagan yet strongly code-governed culture whose ritualized warfare, especially among the horseback peoples of the Plains during the bounteous heyday of the buffalo, had made it natural for a witness like the frontier artist George Catlin to speak of "deeds of chivalry and honor."[56] The same was true of the culture of *samurai* Japan as described in Inazo Nitobe's very popular *The Code of Bushido*, published in America in 1900. Nitobe's account of the non-Christian chivalric code that began, like European chivalry, in the twelfth century supported – and perhaps influenced – Huizinga's suggestion that "the fundamental character of [the] whole complex of [chivalric] ideals, manners and institutions is to be seen almost more clearly in the land of the Rising Sun than in Medieval Christendom or Islam."[57]

All this made certain psychological stabilizings easier and helped to allay certain anxieties.

When Tocqueville reported that "one hardly ever meets an American who does not want to claim some connection by birth with the first founders of the colonies, and as for offshoots of great English families, I think America is simply full of them," what he pointed to was more than simply evidence of a craving for inequality and false distinctions.[58] So was the culture buying of the newly rich in the Eighties and Nineties. As the visiting French man of letters Paul Bourget observed in 1894, it was natural for the casual observer to attribute the penchant of the newly rich for old paintings to "a vague and awkward attempt to make a false gallery of ancestors." As he also said, however, such a reaction did not allow for "the sincerity, almost the pathos, of this love of Americans for surrounding themselves with things around which there is an idea of time and of stability... In this country, where everything is of yesterday, they hunger and thirst for the long ago."[59] The chivalric was peculiarly well suited to gratify those cravings and counter the idea that intellectually acceptable human history did not begin until the eighteenth century and that progress consisted of escaping from the past. Not only did the chivalric tradition in Europe go back over seven hundred years. The American relationship to it did not entail getting further and further away in time from the essence of the "real" thing. On the contrary, a paradox of the historical elusiveness of the "real" chivalric period was precisely that the chivalric values grew rather than diminished with the passage of time. Figures like Bayard and Sidney, the two most often mentioned paragons, were from the sixteenth century, not the twelfth; Virginian aristocrats of the eighteenth century, like the second Richard Lee, were, as Louis B. Wright says, living in a manner that Sidney would have approved of; and Twain went so far as to suggest that it was in his own nineteenth century that, "broadly speaking, the earliest samples of the real lady and real gentleman discoverable in English history – or in European history, for that matter – may be said to have made their appearance."[60] Relatedly, forms, rituals, and ceremonies were not simply archaic byproducts of superstition and dominance – that is, of Catholicism and Catholic-supported monarchies and aristocracies – and hence constraints to be escaped from or seductions whose appeal had to be resolutely resisted. And the process of maturation in individuals, as in cultures, need not consist of progressively putting behind oneself the games and rituals that the young, especially the male young, took so much pleasure in.

Likewise, the idea of culture itself was made more stable, particularly for the young. The conventional image of acculturation, as I noted earlier, was the *Huckleberry Finn* one in which authority figures force fed the young with improving but dull information and tried to make them "behave" themselves. In the transmission of chivalric ideas, in contrast, the information came from a variety of sources in a variety of ways. Schoolteachers, YMCA officials, and so forth went on preaching gentlemanliness, and purity, of course, and the young like Tarkington's Penrod, Fitzgerald's Basil Lee, and Johnson's prep-school youngsters went on resisting them. But information also came from romances, and dime novels, and articles about cowboys, soldiers and the like, and from sports reporting, and from sports and games themselves; and to a large extent the rules of chivalry could be assimilated not through the exhortations of the official improvers and civilizers but from the activities and utterances of heroes, whether Mosby, or D'Artagnan, or Wild Bill Hickok. Implicit in those rules was the fundamental notion that conflict and competition need not be a fight to the death and that the agonistic could entail a common language of rules and forms, a language of considerable flexibility and complexity. It was intellectually reasonable for there to be bonding and groups answering to the desires of childhood, with its fondness for games, groups, tests, pledges; it was both possible and desirable for there to be honor and equity in social and business relationships.

The benefits of all this had recently been demonstrated on an unparalleled scale. If the Civil War had acquired an honored place in the American imagination, it was because there was so much in the war that could be remembered with pride. It was a chivalric war, a war in which, in Henry Steele Commager's words, "relations between the two armies were, somehow, good-natured," a war of which he says that "probably no other great civil war was attended by so little bitterness and no other recorded so many acts of kindness and civility between enemies."[61] Even the most problematic episode, Sherman's brilliant march of destruction, was remarkably free of atrocities. And the great commanders on both sides were chivalric figures. In his unfailing honesty, courtesy, compassion, and serenity, Lee, who had loved to read about chivalry when he was young, was, of course, one of the greatest of all examples of the Christian and chivalrous soldier, a figure who has remained invulnerable to irony. But when Sherman said of himself and

Fictions and forms

Grant (who at West Point, according to the British military authority J. F. C. Fuller, had "spent his spare time in reading books of action – Cooper, Marryat, Scott, Washington Irving; he liked romances") that "we both professed to be gentlemen and professional soldiers," he was speaking the truth.[62] And as Fuller notes, though "outwardly it would be impossible to discover men so different as Grant and Lee, . . . inwardly they were very similar in type."[63] General Horace Porter, Grant's aide-de-camp during the Wilderness and Peterburg campaigns, testified persuasively to Grant's "modesty of mien and gentleness of manner which seemed to fit him more for the court than for the camp," to his equanimity of spirit, his unfailing civility to men of all ranks, and his "extreme fondness for taking prisoners" in preference to killing the enemy.[64] And the former Confederate general Richard Taylor, who detested Sherman, acknowledged that "as far as I am aware, [Grant] made war in the true spirit of a soldier, never by deed or word inflicting wrong on non-combatants."[65] But even of Sherman, who declared in one of his orders to his troops that "generosity and benevolence to the poor and distressed are characteristics of good soldiers," a memorialist in *McClure's* in 1894 was able to recall that "gallantry and chivalry were parts of his nature. In peace he was a student, a gracious gentleman. . . I never saw him speak to a young person without smiling; and as to his way toward women, he was a Bayard of Bayards. The term chivalrous belonged to him by birthright."[66] If the term chivalrous seems a paradoxical one to apply to the Sherman of the march to the sea, one has only to compare him with Ben Butler, the Beast of New Orleans, to see what an unchivalrous Northern general really looked like.

And the fact that at the highest military level the war was conducted by men who shared a common language of military decency, and who no doubt rememberd the desert civilities of Richard I and Saladin in *The Talisman*, had the greatest practical consequences for the ending of the war. The great and moving final encounter of Grant and Lee and their attendant officers in the farmhouse parlor at Appomattox was not merely a major example of military civility. The deeply modest respect Grant showed to his senior came from the same moral center that was responsible for his nonrevengeful terms of surrender – "the most magnanimous. . . in history," according to Fuller – and that shortly thereafter permitted Sherman likewise to make the offer to Joe Johnston of which B. H. Liddell Hart comments that, "as a peace treaty its blended wisdom and mercy made it a model for history and humanity."[67] And the existence of this mutual respect, and of the enduring example set by Lee after his surrender, was responsible for the war's ending with so little bitterness and without the lacerating guerrilla warfare that Sherman had feared so strongly.[68] A great deal more than romantic sentimentality was at work in the episode described by the New Englander, General J. L. Chamberlain, who had been in charge of the laying down by the Southern troops of their arms at Appomattox:

The momentous meaning of this occasion impressed me deeply. I resolved to mark it by some token of recognition, which could be no other than a salute of arms. Well aware of the responsibility assumed, and of the criticisms that would follow, as the sequel proved, nothing of that kind could move me in the least...My main reason...was one for which I sought no authority nor asked forgiveness. Before us in proud humility stood the embodiment of manhood: men whom neither toils and sufferings, nor the fact of death, nor disaster, nor hopelessness could bend from their resolve; standing before us now, thin, worn, and famished, but erect, and with eyes looking level into ours, waking memories that bound us together as no other bond; – was not such manhood to be welcomed back into a Union so tested and assured?

Instruction had been given; and when the head of each division column comes opposite our group, our bugle sounds the signal and instantly our whole line from right to left, regiment by regiment in succession, gives the soldier's salutation, from the "order arms" to the old "carry" – the marching salute. Gordon at the head of the column, riding with heavy spirit and downcast face, catches the sound of shifting arms, looks up, and taking the meaning, wheels superbly, making with himself and his horse one uplifted figure, with profound salutation as he drops the point of his sword to the boot toe; then facing to his own command, gives word for his successive brigades to pass us with the same position of the manual, – honor answering honor. On our part not a sound of trumpet more, nor roll of drum; not a cheer, nor word nor whisper of vain-glorying, nor motion of man standing again at the order, but an awed stillness rather, and breath-holding, as if it were the passing of the dead![69]

Ironically, mid-nineteenth-century Americans had put into practice the attitudes celebrated by Scott and summed up in Mills's statement that "we wage our wars [now] not with the cruelty of Romans, but with the gallantry of cavaliers." America, rationalistic America, progressive America, had given the world the greatest of all chivalrous wars.[70]

5

The heroic and the pastoral

Here we have another very important characteristic of play: success readily passes from the individual to the group. But the following feature is still more important: the competitive "instinct" is not in the first place a desire for power or a will to dominate. The primary thing is the desire to excel others, to be the first and to be honoured for that.

Johan Huizinga, *Homo Ludens* (1938)

His bravery was as much celebrated in the mountains as his skill in hunting; but it is characteristic of him that in a country where the rifle is the chief arbiter between man and man, he was very seldom involved in quarrels. Once or twice, indeed, his quiet good nature has been mistaken and presumed upon, but the consequences of this error were such that no one was ever known to repeat it.

Francis Parkman, *The Oregon Trail* (1849)[1]

IT WILL BE PLAIN by now that in *A Connecticut Yankee* Twain was tackling a more formidable adversary than he had realized, and that the forms and fictions of chivalry had not been mere promoters of irrealism and violence. If they had served to intensify aspirations and make for heroic action, they had also helped to control violence and render it less wanton, brutal, and destructive. And there were important implications in how the chivalric values had been disseminated. Medieval chivalry had been sustained by an ideology that, uniquely in the history of Western thought, had been articulated most fully not in expository treatises or dialogues but in works of narrative fiction; and it had not had to be imposed upon people but had been received with enthusiasm. Furthermore, despite all the social changes that had occurred subsequently, its principal fictional carrier was still alive and well in the modern era, as Twain himself testified to when he set out to demolish Camelot. To see what this meant will make it easier to understand what was going on in the turn-of-the-century assimilations and adaptations of chivalric patterns.

When Twain wrote his satire, over seven hundred years had passed since Geoffrey of Monmouth and Chrétien de Troyes between them created the essential configurations of the Arthurian mythos. Inside of seventy years, it had received its definitive shape in the five thirteenth-century French prose romances known as the Vulgate Cycle, of which Malory's *Le Morte d'Arthur* would be substantially a condensation and retelling, not always for the better. And until well into the sixteenth century it remained by far the most popular European mythos, appealing to people at all social levels, generating works in a variety of languages, including Hebrew, and moving William Caxton to exclaim that the adventures of the Knights of the Round Table "occupy so many large volumes that [it] is a...thing incredible to believe."[2] Among later writers who drew on those adventures for subjects were Tennyson, Wagner, Morris, Robinson, Hardy, and, of course, Twain himself. During the Renaissance the mythos was metamorphosed and transposed by writers like Ariosto, Spenser, and the author of the enormously popular *Amadis of Gaul*, which in turn generated the plethora of romances satirized in *Don Quixote*; and a further and major metamorphosis took place in America. The joustlike combat of John Wayne and three adversaries in the movie *True Grit* was a true perception. As John Steinbeck said in the Fifties, "the American Western is not a separate thing but a direct descendant of the Arthurian legend with all the genes intact."[3] The popularity of the Western too has transcended all barriers of nationality, age, degree of intellectuality, and social class; and its generative power, its capacity for assimilations, transpositions, and spin-offs has been one of the most remarkable artistic phenomena of the twentieth century.[4] Steinbeck may not have been exaggerating much when he said that "I don't know any book save only the Bible and perhaps Shakespeare which has had more effect on our morals, our ethics, and our mores than...Malory" – which is to say, the Arthurian mythos as transmitted by Malory.[5]

The fact that the Arthurian mythos took its definitive shape as early as it did, lasted as long as it did, and had such generative power suggests very strongly that the syntheses in it and in the chivalric patterns in general embodied and answered to deep desires and needs. In the rest of this chapter I shall look at some of those syntheses. I shall begin with an aspect of the concept of honor, the concept of which Richard Barber notes in his excellent history of chivalry that "it was this, perhaps more than any other single feature, that distinguished the way of thought of the knight...Honour was the shrine at which the knight worshipped: it implied renown, good conduct, and the world's approval."

THE HONORING OF HONOR

As Barber points out, "the 'word of honour' was the most solemn oath the knight knew...The whole world of romance depends on the convention that a knight's word once given can never be retracted."[6]

68

Hence, for example, Gawain persists in fulfilling his vow to the Green Knight and tells his servant when the latter objects:

> if I turned back now
> Forsook this place for fear, and fled, as you say,
> I were a caitiff coward; I could not be excused.[7]

This honoring of one's word was not confined to fiction. Maurice Keen reports that a knight would keep to contractual arrangements made on the battlefield – especially ones about ransoms – because he had sworn on his honor to do so, so that "if he broke such a promise, he did something much more damnable than simply failing to perform his part of a bargain. He had taken his knighthood in vain, and shown that he was unworthy of his honourable station; he was a 'false knight,' which was as good as no knight at all."[8] And some striking vows, which necessitated a good deal of physical discomfort, were made and carried out by men like Edward I and Sir Walter Manny. The interrelated concepts of the word of honor and the vow carry over into the making of love vows, and into the kind of faithfulness voiced by the fair Elaine, the mother of Galahad, to Lancelot: "Sir, said Dame Elaine, I will live and die with you, and only for your sake; and if my life might not avail you and my death might avail you, wit you will I would die for your sake."[9]

The appeal of the word of honor has been long and strong. There is always a certain solemnity to someone's giving his word, whether in a promise by the kind of old-style merchant whose word was his bond, or a schoolboy saying "Word of honour!" or the signers of the Declaration of Independence pledging "our lives, our fortunes, and our sacred honour." The word giver not only accepts that keeping his word may involve difficulties, discomforts, dangers. In certain situations he may positively invite the dangers of an open-ended situation, like the knight who announces his readiness to fight any challenger in a *pas d'armes* during a specified period or who promises to do whatever his lady commands, thereby putting himself at the mercy of the unpredictable and "unreasonable" female. One of the strongest patterns in the romances is the long-term commitment, whether to a particular end, like the Grail, or to a particular pattern of conduct, such as Lancelot's devotion to Guinevere. Implied in giving one's word is a peculiarly firm sense of one's own identity and confidence in one's capacities.

All this entailed obvious psychological risks. One of the dominant chivalric images, which Dürer epitomized in his "Knight, Death and the Devil," is that of the solitary man – the solitary knight journeying on a quest, the solitary Westerner pacing along the deserted main street toward a showdown or riding toward danger through a hostile or indifferent landscape. And as Shakespeare's histories and tragedies remind us, the desire to comport oneself with maximum honor can subject a man to excessive strains, particularly given the elusiveness at times of the idea of honor and the related problem of determining what the honorable course of action really is. Yet when one turns to the psychological self-sufficiency of the vow-taking knight in the romances, unswayed by rulers, or priests, or womenfolk, or kindred, the general effect is not one of strain.

THE KNIGHTLY FREEDOM

To begin with, the knightly freedom of conscience did not have to be won by a quasi-oedipal revolt against "authority." A knight was not encompassed by figures whose intrinsic superiority to himself must be acknowledged unless resisted by an act of intellect. In Charles Mills's words, "the genius of chivalry was personal, inasmuch as each knight, when not following the banner of his sovereign, was in himself an independent being, acting from his own sense of virtue, and not deriving counsel from, or sharing opprobrium with, others."[10]

The Church, of course, claimed authority over everyone, and clerics attempted to influence knights from the pulpit and through the confessional. But in the Vulgate Cycle, the church of bishops and archbishops and Popes is simply not an operative power system influencing the action. The Galahad-centered *Quest of the Holy Grail* is packed to the point of boredom with sermonizing hermits, monks, and priests, like the one who tells Gawain, "In justice, Sir, were you called a bad and faithless servant. You were not admitted to the order of chivalry to soldier in the devil's cause thenceforward, but in order to serve our Maker, defend Holy Church and render at last to God that treasure which He entrusted to your safekeeping, namely your soul. To this end were you made a knight."[11] But in terms of the cycle as a whole, it is they who are the outsiders, attempting to undermine the much more appealing values embodied in the gallant and adulterous Lancelot or the straightforward battlers; and in man-to-man terms, a valiant knight, a *preux chevalier* who very properly feared no one, was worth a dozen priests or monks any day. Insofar as the higher clerics were seen as worthy, it was to the extent that they themselves had martial characteristics. Even the claims of the highest moral authority of all could be met with the attitude displayed by the French nobleman in Twain's *Joan of Arc* who said, "Fair Sir God, I pray to you to do by La Hire as he would do by you if you were La Hire and he were God."[12]

Moreover, even rulers had no intrinsic moral superiority by virtue of their status. This was partly a matter of historical evolution. As Lewis Mumford, following the French historian Marc Bloch, points out, "in feudal society...vassal homage, however humble, was a genuine contract and a bilateral one; and the right of resistance to unjust or arbitrary authority was not only implied but often specified."[13] The most splendid example of such bilaterality was the oath of fealty of the Aragonese nobles: "We who are as good as you swear to you, who are no better than we, to accept you as our King and sovereign lord, provided you observe all our estates and laws; and if not, no."[14] But the nature of knightly worth was also relevant. Rulers themselves were knights, and worth was a matter of observable action and not a mysterious derivative from birth or money. It came from what one did oneself in combat, whether on the battlefield or in the tournament; it was a matter of the number and worth of the opponents whom one vanquished fairly in hand-to-hand combat, and of one's skill and courage when defending oneself against superior odds. Because tournaments were small and very closely watched, and because battles came to be, in effect, umpired by heralds whose job it was to note how knights performed, it was relatively easy to judge how a combatant did, taking into consideration the reputation and known skills of those against whom he had fought. Hence the worth of a ruler too, qua knight, was not inherent but earned. The virtues of the good king or good nobleman were essentially those of the good knight – courage, generosity, loyalty, skill in combat, firmness and persistence of purpose, wisdom about people. If the Arthur of *Sir Gawain and the Green Knight*, for example, manifestly deserves to be king, it is because of his attractive energy and readiness for combat:

> His life he liked lively – the less he cared
> To be lying for long, or long to sit,
> So busy his young blood, his brain so wild.[15]

Elsewhere in the Arthurian romances, Arthur's authority with his knights, both political and moral, is more like that of a committee chairman than that of a head of state. On one occasion, for instance, Lancelot dismounts to him out of respect, but Ector and Bors refuse; Arthur praises both of them, and Lancelot himself defends the conduct of the other two, saying, "I should not like them to be subservient to anyone."[16] Hence a knight lived within a zone of real moral freedom.

The knightly code itself offered substantial latitude with respect to the correct conduct in particular situations, including such problematic relationships as Lancelot's to Arthur, and Tristram's to King Mark. The range of acceptable ideal types in the romances is broad. It includes Ector the unromantic battler, Lancelot the great warrior serving his mistress, Tristram devoted almost wholly to love, Perceval and Galahad devoted to the quest for the Grail, Kay the skeptic and ironist. And an important coexistence went on. As I have said, there were logical conflicts within the chivalric code between Christian and non-Christian

71

elements. There were conflicts – ultimately unresolvable ones – between the claims of loyalty to one's lord and loyalty to one's mistress, as dramatized in the story of Lancelot and Guinevere. In terms of their dramatic presentation, however, the very different value systems at work in the courtly love *Death of King Arthur* and the churchly *Quest of the Holy Grail* coexist without any overall intimations that the experiences of the characters in the one are any less serious and meaningful than those of the characters in the other. All the knights whom I have mentioned are treated with respect by Arthur and their fellow knights. Even when Lancelot accidentally slays Gawain's brother and starts the feud that destroys the kingdom, there is no implication either that Lancelot should not have stayed faithful to Guinevere or that Gawain should not have sought revenge.

The pattern that I have described has been a very popular one. Scott, for instance, points out in his "Essay on Romance" how in one of the German romances the German ruler Theodorick's "principal followers have each their discriminatory and peculiar aspects."[17] In *The Three Musketeers* Dumas differentiates between the tall, gorgeously costumed, loquacious, swaggering Porthos; the stout, open-faced, mild-eyed, delicately moustached, nongambling, theology-studying Aramis; and the taciturn, noble looking, misanthropic seeming, and enigmatic Athos. Kipling proffers his Yorkshireman, Irishman, and Cockney in *Soldiers Three* and his three differentiated schoolboys in *Stalky and Co.* Thriller writers have given us trios like the three hard-drinking private detectives in Jonathan Latimer's Bill Crane novels in the Thirties. We have had, too, the multiskilled teams like Doc Savage's and the multiethnic army groups in movies, nicely caricatured by the underground cartoonist Gilbert Sheldon: "Zeb Turnipseed – seven foot four of fighting hillbilly from Tennessee...Iggy Schwartz – at age ten he was the toughest kid in Brooklyn...Watermelon Jones – things weren't hot enough for him in Watts...Algernon Truffle – a Ph.D. from Harvard at 16, but he got bored.[18] In numerous robbing-the-bank movies like John Huston's *The Asphalt Jungle* and Stanley Kubrick's *The Killing* diverse criminals who may not even like one another work effectively together for the purposes of a particular operation.

An interesting psychological and moral equilibrium is discernible here. Richard Barber has suggested of the Vulgate Cycle that "each character is in some measure a representative of a particular moral function: Arthur stands for royalty and leadership; Lancelot, human achievement through chivalry; Gawain, human nature which has not come to terms with chivalry."[19] But in the Vulgate Cycle and the other works that I have mentioned, things are not weighted morally in the sense that certain characters are types to which all the others ought to be approximating themselves. The pattern is essentially different from that in a work like *Hamlet*, where every right-minded spectator or reader identifies with Hamlet and not with Horatio or Fortinbras or Laertes, let alone with Polonius or Claudius. Moreover, synthesizings can go on. As Sidney Painter says of the three main strands of chivalry, it is possible to "choose elements from each to form a consistent composite ideal."[20] Considerable overlapping occurs among figures like Lancelot, Ector, and Galahad, and virtues from all three types blend delightfully and credibly in the figure of Gawain (in Britain long the most popular of the Arthurian knights) as presented in *Sir Gawain and the Green Knight*. A similar synthesis is approached in Chaucer's "verray parfit gentil knight," who "loved chivalrye, / Trouthe and honour, freedom and curteisye," and who "nevere yit no vileinye ne saide / In al his lif, unto no manere wight"; his qualities are complemented by those of his son the Squire ("Singing he was, or floiting, al the day; / He was as fressh as is the month of May"), with his graceful clothing, his flair for the arts, his passion as a lover.[21] The poised attractiveness of Gawain and of Chaucer's duo makes clear that most of the character traits that are in the Arthurian pattern can have their place in a healthily functioning psyche. A symbolic representation of this occurs in Dumas's description of his Musketeers as "four men devoted to one another, from their purses to their lives; four men always supporting one another, never yielding, executing singly or together the resolutions formed in common; four arms threatening the four cardinal points, or turning towards a single point."[22]

Futhermore, where personality is concerned, the chivalric is flexible in another way. The ethical and philosophical spectrum extends from the nobly Christian Galahad and the nobly secular Lancelot to the cynical Kay and the unrelievedly sadistic Maleagent of Chrétien's *The Knight of the Cart*, who "found his pleasure in disloyalty, and never wearied of villainy, treason, and felony."[23] Neither Christian idealism nor ethical nihilism negates the less extreme modes of thought and feeling in between; the ordinary secular knightly poise is not the result of ignorance of other possibilities. The range of permissible masculine emotions is likewise broad, including rage, grief to the point of tears or swooning, insouciance, gaiety, and intense eroticism. A knight, in other words, was not constrained into a single stiff mode of feeling and expression. The moral authority of individual passions and commitments is amply acknowledged in the romances, including the passionate self- and world forgetfulness displayed by knights who stay for a year or two in the castles of ladies who have enchanted them, or by Tristram in the famous episode with Isolde in their cave of love.

This flexibility was made easier by the avoidance of certain sharp dichotomies and mutual exclusions. In some respects a knight's life, with its arduous training, its rigors of combat, its journeys like Gawain's when

Part I From cavaliers to cowboys

the birds "peeped most piteously for pain of the cold,"[24] was strongly ascetic and supported William James's characterization of the soldier as the "unencumbered man." But there was legitimate room in it for pleasures, and a knight did not have to choose between hedonism and asceticism. If the proud and unabashedly physical lover Lancelot could display an almost monkish self-denial and abasement when commanded by Guinevere to do so, the chaste Gawain could enjoy the comforts of his host's castle and throw himself into the Christmas fun

> With deft-footed dances and dalliance light,
> As never until now, while the afternoon wore away...
> And all agreed, that day,
> They had never before found him
> So gracious and so gay.[25]

In knightly terms, there was no dichotomy of the ignobly physical and the nobly mental. Physical activities were permeated by thought, forming parts of complex structures of knowledge – the skills and rituals of hunting, combat, and formal socializing; the complexities of *courteoisie* and *fin amour*. And the bodily comforts, the sumptuous clothing and tableware, the luxurious bedding that awaited men after combat or the chase were charged with values, both through their preciousness – their uniqueness, the craftsmanship that had gone into their making, the energy needed to acquire them, their use as ceremonial gifts – and because the pleasures of warmth, and food and drink, and sound sleep had been *earned*. Again, if on the one hand the romances celebrated the rational skills and techniques, the practical mastery, of the warrior, on the other they honored the unexpected, the unknown, the mysterious. Embarking on a quest opened a door into a world of challenges that could not be dealt with simply by force of arms – a world of disguisings, visions, omens, dreams.

FAIR KNIGHTS AND GALLANT LADIES

Above all, inside chivalry violence and love were not antithetical but almost inseparably intertwined. The relationship was a good deal sturdier than is suggested in John Pendleton Kennedy's amused reference to "an age that Sir Walter Scott has rendered so bewitchingly to the fancy of meditative maidens," or Twain's swipe at "girly-girly romance," or the episode in Edmund Wilson's "Galahad" when he describes how at one point, for his preppy hero, "his Barbara was no longer a rowdy wanton, but a noble and passionate woman – a Guinevere. And he, in his illicit love, was still knightly and dignified. Where he had formerly pictured himself as Galahad, he now figured as Lancelot."[26] As Charles Mills puts it, "chivalric love took delight in

74

reconciling and joining the opposites of the world";[27] and, as before, fictions passed over into fact. Initially, in Sidney Painter's words, "the feudal male was chiefly absorbed in war and the chase. His wife bore him sons, his mistress satisfied his momentary lusts. Beyond this women had no place in his life, and he had no interest in them."[28] There were no doubt plenty of contemporary parallels to the domestic boors and tyrants who figured in the twelfth-century Lays of Marie de France, like the one who wrings the neck of his wife's pet nightingale and throws it at her, staining her dress with blood. But at the same time the doctrine of courtly love permeated the romances that for some three centuries were the chief form of verbal entertainment for the nobility, and resulted, as Painter says, in the gradual acceptance of ideas that did not directly conflict with "the traditional prejudices and the environment of the feudal male." These included the ideas that the love of a lady was a worthy motive for fighting, and that some concern to please ladies was desirable in the male. By the end of the fourteenth century, he suggests, they "were generally recognized as an integral part of noble ethics."[29]

This accommodation was psychologically feasible. Just as the romances could not have survived had the bulk of their male hearers thought the conduct and attitudes of Lancelot and the other women-bound heroes absurd, they also could not have survived had those same hearers been outraged by the conduct of the heroines. There may have been occasional twinges of uneasiness about Guinevere's power over Lancelot, especially as described by Chrétien where it is at its most arbitrary and dominative; or about the damsel in one of Marie's Lays who carries away a knight on her palfrey to an enchanted island; or about the insolence of the damsel Linet to Gareth in Malory. But what makes such women disquieting is their energy, their existence as individuals in their own right. The unabashedly physical eroticism in some of the great encounters and relationships in the romances is between equals, often meeting alone in some secluded area of amatory encounter – a cave, a magic castle, a walled and locked garden, a hidden chamber.[30] And the speech of women is memorably self-confident and direct at times, such as when Yvan's wife warns him what to expect from her if he overstays the period of tourneying that he has requested ("I grant you leave until a certain date; but be sure that my love will change to hate if you stay beyond the term that I shall fix. Remember that I shall keep my word; if you break your word I will keep mine"), or when Dame Liones publicly declares to Arthur her love for Gareth:

Most noble King, said Dames Liones, wit you well that my lord, Sir Gareth, is to me more lever to have wedde as my husband, than any king or prince that is christened; and if I may not have him I promise you I will never have none. For, my lord Arthur, said Dame Liones, wit ye well he is my first love, and he shall be the last; and if ye will suffer him to have his will and free choice I dare say he will have me. That is truth, said Sir Gareth; an I have not you and wedde not you as my wife, there shall never lady nor gentlewoman rejoice me.[31]

The confident practicality with which Enid assists Erec on his travels had its parallels in real life, too: Froissart, for example, reports that the Countess of Montfort "possessed the courage of a man, and the heart of a lion" and kept her husband's garrisons in fighting shape after he was taken prisoner.[32] Although the risk of uxoriousness or the drawing of a knight aside from the path of valor is touched on occasionally, the dominant image of women in the romances is of individuals who are challenging to the male without being hostile to the martial ethos.

The point about the courtly love relationship is that it enhanced the vitality and satisfied the desire for power of both parties. It was the antithesis of the pattern described by H. L. Mencken, paraphrasing Nietzsche, in which "woman spent her entire effort in a ceaseless effort to undermine and change the will of man."[33] The woman received the services of the man and was given power over him and over his honor; but she returned his power to him and enabled him to increase his honor more than he could have done unaided, thereby enhancing her own as well. As Gawain tells Yvan, "Whoever has a fair lady as his mistress or his wife should be the better for it." Thus Cligés delights in being able to "display his chivalry and bravery openly before her who is his very life," and Lancelot, having endured defeats in Chrétien's great tournament so as to convince Guinevere of his devotion to her, is allowed by her to put forth his full strength once more, whereupon he sweeps forward to victory under her admiring gaze.[34] The reciprocity was not restricted to fiction, either. The erotic, as Huizinga says, has always been an element in "sportive struggles,"[35] and the pattern in Chrétien's eminently believable tournament, organized by ladies looking out for husbands, and graced by knights lounging with the ladies in the stands and commenting on the combatants, was deep rooted. Moreover, the game of love itself was a contest between equals, in which respect was due on both sides. Huizinga, describing how in the twelfth-century Courts of Love in Languedoc there were imitation lawsuits, and how such forms as the rebuke, the dispute, and the game of question and answer figure in poetic genres, adds that "at the bottom of all there is... the age-old struggle for honor in matters of love."[36] And the rules and procedures of the love game, as set out in a treatise like Andreas Capellanus's *The Art of Courtly Love* and illustrated in the discourses in Chrétien's *Cligés* were sophisticated and subtle. As *Sir*

The heroic and the pastoral

Gawain and the Green Knight demonstrates in the graceful but serious verbal fencing with which Gawain rejects the advances of his hostess without offending her, such ritualizations made honorable relationships psychologically easier on both sides. With their continuation of the esteem accorded women in the early Middle Ages in Celtic and Northern European literature, such attitudes were all the more striking in contrast to the widespread disparagement of women by clerical and bourgeois writers.[37]

In sum, in the patterns that I have been talking about, a number of things that are usually thought of as opposites, sometimes irreconcilable opposites, come together harmoniously. There are "masculine" adventurousness, competitiveness, and glory-seeking, and "feminine" nurturing, loving, and comforting. There are the excitements and challenges of the wild, the unknown, and the mysterious, and the reassurances of the ordered, the humanized, the enclosing. There are the crafts of war and hunting, and the graces of social intercourse. There is the erotic connection noted symbolically in Malory's passing remark that "the book of venery, of hawking and hunting, is called the book of Sir Tristram" – that is, of the Tristram of the Tristram and Isolde story.[38] Such interrelationships are part of broader ones, too. In *Power*, Bertrand de Jouvenel observes that "notable philologists claim... to have found two strata of cults: the terrestrial cults of an agrarian and matriarchal society, later overlaid by the celestial cults of a warrior and patriarchal society."[39] And a great deal of literary culture, as Huizinga points out, has been based on the ancient themes of what he calls the heroic and the bucolic.[40] Those themes are displayed classically in the *Odyssey*, with its occasional shocking violences and its benign images of Mediterranean plenitude, its journeyings among marvels and its yearnings for home, its menacing seas and sheltering courts, its monsters and its comforting women, its tensings and relaxings of the hero's psyche. They are what I shall refer to henceforward as the heroic and the pastoral. As fictional figures like Gawain and historical ones like Louis IX demonstrated, heroic and pastoral attitudes and interests could coexist harmoniously inside a single psyche. Inazo Nitobe described the same pattern when he spoke of the "gentleness... inculcated among the warrior class" of Japan, including the encouragement of such skills as verse writing. "In old warfare," he reported, "it was not at all rare for the parties to a conflict to exchange repartee or to begin a rhetorical contest. Combat was not solely a matter of brute force; it was, as well, an intellectual engagement."[41] As Michael Foss suggests of the troubadours, there was "something magically persuasive" about the "concept of valour blended with delicacy, and activity tempered by thought."[42]

Part I From cavaliers to cowboys

HEROIC AND PASTORAL PATTERNS IN AMERICAN CULTURE

The same patterns have obtained in the American versions of the chivalric. There are the same fusions of the heroic and the pastoral, the same linking of ostensible opposites, the same demonstrations of the possibility of controlled violence that does not necessarily brutalize the employer of it, and that is not inimical to humane values.

As I said earlier, the plantation South was in some ways an unusually high energy culture. In a well-known passage about "the basic Southerner," Cash comments that "the dominant trait of this mind was an intense individualism – in its way, perhaps the most intense individualism the world has seen since the Italian Renaissance and its men of 'terrible fury.' "[43] With its castlelike isolation and self-sufficiency and its induced habit of command, the plantation was preeminently the domain of masculine independence, a domain that helped produce the heroic officers of the Civil War; and its appeal in the North came partly from the "intense respect for virility" and the "air of self-control, and readiness to assume command of whatever matter he may be engaged in" that De Forest and Tourgée respectively noted as distinguishing the chivalrous Southern male.[44] As Henry Adams said of the South, "the life of it all – the vigor – the poetry – was its moral certainty of self. The Southerner could not doubt."[45]

An important feature of that individualism, particularly as viewed from the North, was what Canby calls the "reality of passion freely expressed which fascinated us in the Southern families."[46] The narrator of Walter Hines Page's autobiographical novel The Southerner (1906) remarks of a New England friend and classmate at Harvard that "he had grown up in an atmosphere in which it was not good form to let oneself go," whereas "I had grown up in an atmosphere (a raw atmosphere, no doubt) wherein we permitted our emotions to have free play, till in many cases they had been mistaken for thought, I dare say."[47] And De Forest defines more fully what that free play of the emotions looked like: "Audacity, vehemence, recklessness, passion, sentiment, prejudice, vanity, whimwhams, absurdities, culture, ignorance, courtliness, barbarism! The individual had plenty of elbow room at the South; he kicked out of the traces with a freedom unknown to our steady-pulling society; he was a bull in Mrs. Grundy's china shop."[48] This almost medieval individualism was plainly connected to the pastoral–heroic pattern of plantation life, especially Virginian plantation life.

As a historian of the subject points out, the ideal plantation has stood as "a kind of American embodiment of the golden age,"[49] and when one looks at some of the first-hand descriptions, one can see why. It was an environment of men on horseback, men with guns, an environment of

78

hunting, horse racing, hard drinking, and hard gambling. But the male energies fitted into a nurturing context, an ordered plenitude of inter-relationships. With its blacksmiths' and carpenters' shops, its stables, gardens, and fishponds, its troops of children playing, its constant comings and goings, the plantation of such accounts was a working community of rich variousness, in which the sometimes very lovely central house was not estranged from its surroundings, and in which large symbolic roles were played by the nurturing and prestigious figures of black cook and black nurse. And in keeping with the Virginian tradition of generous hospitality, the household was likely to be engaged in a rich social life of visitings, weddings, club meetings, parties, fox hunts, race meets, and the like. Even when scaled down in a more primitive environment, as in Twain's description of the Granger-ford household, the same outlines of uncoerced gracefulness and plenitude remain. Moreover, as in the medieval romances, the planta-tion was an environment of creative tensions between the surrounding wildness, including the wildness of human beings, and the achieved domestic order and decency, and connected up, via the stories and superstitions of the blacks, with older and deeper patterns of belief and feeling. It was an especially rich environment for children to live in, and one in which they were permitted a great deal of freedom.

Relationships between the sexes were also fortunate, in ways in-debted to the cleaned-up version of chivalric relationships in Scott. Twain observed scornfully that the trouble with Southern journalism was "Women: Women, supplemented by Walter Scott and his knights and beauty and chivalry, and so on."[50] But a good deal more than rhetoric was involved in the Southern cult of womanhood as described by Cash:

She was the South's Palladium, this Southern woman – the shield-bearing Athena gleaming whitely in the clouds, the standard for its rallying, the mystic symbol of its nationality in face of the foe. She was the lily-pure maid of Astolat and the hunting goddess of the Boeotian hill. And – she was the pitiful Mother of God. Merely to mention her was to send strong men into tears – or shouts. . .

"Woman!!! The center and circumference, diameter and periphery, sine, tangent and secant of all our affections!" Such was the toast which brought twenty great cheers from the audience at the celebration of Georgia's one-hundredth anniversary in the 1830's.[51]

A very important adaptation was in fact occurring. The problem, as William R. Taylor points out, was how to endow plantation life with qualities like "moral consciousness, sentimentality, introspection, and benevolence" without emasculating the Southern gentleman. "The Southern answer to this question lay in the cult of chivalry – in having the Cavalier kneel down before the altar of femininity and familial

79

benevolence...Women were projected into the center of the plantation legend."[52]

As the mistress of a plantation, a woman had a good deal of authority, what with managing the house and gardens, keeping an eye on the health of the slaves, and attending to the social side of things. Moreover, unlike the alienated wife of the Northern businessman as described in Francis J. Grund's *Aristocracy in America*, what she did was intimately bound up with the work of her husband. For all the machismo of Southern society, the plantation male was not the restless, hungrily outward-questing business male described by Grund, Tocqueville, and others. He was not even the home leaving and war going knight of medieval actuality, crusader or otherwise, let alone the knight errant of the romances. His place was home on the estate, a hero-in-residence, as it were. And there were also advantages to the new chivalric sexual role of women, with its demonstration that the source of disruption in Arthur's kingdom – the elevation of adultery into an ethical principle – was not in fact an essential part of the chivalric pattern. In the revised chivalric terms of *Ivanhoe*, the woman was a center of power, an energizing principle, someone to be rendered the traditional homage paid by gallant men to fair women, whose approval they courted, and whom she, in her turn, was entitled to charm. But the polarity was one of married love. Not only was there no moral imperative in Scottian terms toward the game of conquest and adultery, such as had persisted in gallantry of the French sort; there was a good deal of emphasis on the heinousness of a man's trying to conquer a woman by force or cunning. Hence Eliza Frances Andrews, looking back to the years before the Civil War, was able to comment that "the exquisite courtesy and deference of the Southern men of that day toward women made the chaperon a person of secondary importance among us."[53] Ideologically, the Southern woman had the best of two worlds. She had romance, sexual romance. At the same time, she was largely free, if she chose to be, of the tyranny of the sexual imperative, the game of physical conquest considered as the prime determinant of a woman's – or a man's – worth.

These factors made possible a combination of sexual vitality, social game playing, and a strong measure of practical good sense, and helped create that much-commented-on figure, the Southern Woman. When Henry Adams wrote wistfully in *The Education* that "The Woman had once been supreme; in France she still seemed potent, not merely as a sentiment, but as a force. Why was she unknown in America?" he cannot have been thinking of the South.[54] In antebellum Washington, the social charms of Southern political hostesses had been formidable. In the Seventies, the protagonist of Walter Hines Page's *The Southerner* remarked the difference between his poised, charming, flattering, seductive Southern cousin and the cooler, more inhibited New England sister of his Harvard roommate. Canby recalled of the role accorded the Southern girl during his youth in the Eighties and Nineties that she "was romantic. She had always known how to respond to chivalry; no Puritan or Quaker inhibitions had kept her from flaunting her sexuality before men."[55] And during the Civil War, many Southern women also displayed the qualities of Stephen Vincent Benét's Mary Lou Wingate:

> The gentlemen killed and the gentlemen died,
> But she was the South's incarnate pride
> That mended the broken gentlemen
> And sent them out to the war again,
> That kept the house with the men away...
> Through four long years of ruin and stress.[56]

As a Louisiana woman commented at the time, "Pshaw! there are *no* women here. We are *all* men!"[57] These interwoven pastoral–heroic strengths, testifying to the deeper emotional strengths of the region, would manifest themselves subsequently in the rich individuality of writers like Elizabeth Madox Roberts, Caroline Gordon, Eudora Welty, Flannery O'Connor, and Katherine Anne Porter.

Similar patterns have contributed to the immense appeal of the classic Western and the fact that the cowboy has been by far the most popular American hero. Again there is individualism. Again a variety of figures occupy the same terrain, sometimes in collaborative relationships – the honest cowpuncher, the duty-oriented lawman, the flamboyant gambler, the good-humored drunkard, the comically self-preserving Sancho Panza, the grim avenger, the incorrigible outlaw. Again pastoral and heroic aspects interweave. Westerners are surrounded by danger, especially when they journey into the mountains and deserts, those haunts of outlaws and Indians. But the ritual campfire, with its communal coffeepot, holds off the darkness and cold, and survivors are able to return to the comforts of the homestead – the kitchen stove, the hot bath in the wooden tub – and the greater pleasures of the small town, centering on the saloon with its ritual miniature tournaments at the card table and its attendant women. Moreover, the relationship between men and women is essentially supportive. The man guards, the woman heals and nurtures, each maintaining self-respect in his or her main role. Civility obtains between them, courtships are ritualized, formality lessens tensions when two near strangers are isolated by accident in cabin or wilderness. One of the agreeable aspects of the classic Western is that men and women do not yell at one another.[58]

Both the Southern and the Western patterns, moreover, exhibit important possibilities with respect to violence. The dominant figure in

81

both is the gentleman, the figure of whom Nitobe says that "fine manners...mean power in repose."[59] In one of his books of reminiscences, Thomas Nelson Page recalls of the old-style Virginian gentleman that "there was the foundation of a certain pride based on self-respect and consciousness of power. There was nearly always the firm mouth with its strong lines, the calm, placid, direct gaze, the quiet speech of one who is accustomed to command and have his command obeyed."[60] Similarly, D. R. Hundley, speaking of "the natural dignity of manners peculiar to the Southern Gentleman," observes that he displayed "on all occasions the utmost self-possession" and was "remarkably easy and natural, never haughty in appearance, or loud of speech – even when angry rarely raising his voice above the ordinary tone of gentlemanly conversation."[61] And Twain gives us the same picture of Colonel Grangerford, who "warn't ever loud. He was as kind as he could be –you could feel that, you know, and so you had confidence." In the classic Western, similarly, the dominant image is that of the nonviolent man of violence, the man who is essentially a guardian, and who uses violence only in order to help peaceful growth – the lawman defending the township, the small rancher defending his homestead, the wandering cowboy defending the household to which for the time being he has given his allegiance. The man of honor may at times be driven to accept a challenge. But he does so reluctantly (like Wister's Virginian), he kills reluctantly, and he only accepts the challenge because if he does not, the challenger will injure the innocent, or because refusing to do so will destroy the public confidence in him that enables him to carry on his protective function peaceably. And what emerges from books of reminiscences like Rollins's *The Cowboy* and Andy Adams's lightly fictionalized *Log of a Cowboy* is a picture of energetic gun-carrying men who were nevertheless civil and nonaggressive in their dealings with one another. Alfred Henry Lewis, reported that, "at work on the range and about his camp...the cowboy is a youth of sober quiet dignity. There is a deal of deep politeness and nothing of epithet, insult or horseplay where everybody wears a gun."[62] Rollins recalled that on the range the cowboys' "nursing was faithful and untiring, however amateurish, for a dangerous life tends to make men womanly; and the average puncher was womanly, though Heaven knows he was in no wise ladylike."[63]

The same character patterns had been observable during the Civil War in unfailingly courteous figures like Lee, Jackson, and Grant. They would be remarked upon by Hemingway when he spoke of the curious gentleness of bullfighters and professional boxers. They would be apparent in a number of the hunter-gatherer communities studied by anthropologists.[64] It was the sensed presence of such patterns, rather than any quasi-Hobbesian notion of the inevitability of violence and dominance, that would eventually be responsible for, among other things, the appeal of Konrad Lorenz's writings in America in the Sixties. I am thinking particularly of his paradox that wolves, those supposedly ferocious and merciless predators, do not in fact fight to a finish, and that they respect the rules of warfare with regard to surrender, in contrast to the supposedly pacific doves who peck their fallen enemies to death.[65] Hemingway pointed to the same kind of paradox in *Death in the Afternoon* when he said that "the bull is a fighting animal and where the fighting strain has been kept pure and all cowardice bred out he becomes often, when not fighting, the quietest and most peaceful acting in repose, of any animal" and that "when they both know how to use the horn the combat usually ends as does a fight between two really skillful boxers, with all dangerous blows stopped, without bloodshed and with mutual respect. They do not have to kill each other for a decision."[66]

Part II

CHIVALRIC PATTERNS IN
INDUSTRIALIZING AMERICA

6

Quality and education

"Most of our rich men were once poor boys," said Rose quietly. "I have a book of biographies at home, and I find that not only rich men, but men distinguished in other ways, generally commenced in poverty."
"I wish you'd lend me that book,"said Ben. "Sometimes I get despondent and that will give me courage."

Horatio Alger, *The Store Boy* (1887)

The task is not to overcome opponents in general, but only those opponents against whom one has to summon all one's strength, one's skill, and one's swordsmanship – in fact, opponents who are one's equals...To be one's enemy's equal – this is the first conditon of an honorable duel. Where one despises, one cannot wage war.

Friedrich Nietzsche, *Ecce Homo* (1888)

Happy, happy, college-days!

Mark Sibley Severance, *Hammersmith: His Harvard Days* (1878)[1]

It is now possible to see more clearly what was going on in those paradoxical turn-of-the-century decades. When the youths in Henry Seidel Canby's boyhood town drew from the romances "an ethics for ideal conduct in emotional stress," and the young Humperdink Stover aspired to become a "gentleman-sport," and the young Jimmy Gatz invented for himself "just the sort of Jay Gatsby that a seventeen-year-old boy would be likely to invent," they were testifying in their various ways to something very important.[2] A complex and morally defensible constellation of values that had been too much rejected and denied in the orthodoxy of enlightenment was becoming operative once more; and far from being merely fanciful and anachronistic, the chivalric patterns were very relevant to a high-energy, urban-industrializing, competitive society. Moreover, their adaptations were considerably broader, more complicated, and more interesting than was allowed for in the indictment that I offered in Chapter 2.

The stereotypes that I talked about in Chapters 1 and 2 are, of course, partly correct. The period was indeed the heyday of the Man in Evening Dress, the type described a little later by that connoisseur of chivalric types, Dashiell Hammett: "He was young, blond, tall, broad, sun-burned, and dressy, with the good-looking unintelligent face of one who would know everything about polo, or shooting, or flying, or

87

something of that sort – maybe even two or three things of that sort – but not much about anything else."³ It was the period of Charles Dana Gibson and J. C. Leyendecker's clean-cut young aristocrats, the period of clubmen like the one in Owen Johnson's *The Sixty-First Second* who "belonged..to that set who live what in England is called a gentleman's life – racing, hunting ...seeking the sensations of big game or big fish, rather courting danger, drinking hard as a matter of pride, on the theory of the survival of the fittest, consuming the night in battles of cunning and physical endurance at the card-table."⁴ Moreover, there was a growing cordiality toward the martial. A Columbia professor could announce in the Nineties that "nothing else in the same degree rouses a people to positive action" like "the unifying and stimulating influence of war."⁵ An undergraduate intellectual in *Stover at Yale* could declare without being shouted or groaned down that

"a war has two positive advantages... It teaches discipline and obedience, which we profoundly need, and it holds up a great ideal, the ideal of heroism, of sacrifice for an ideal. In times of war young men such as we are inspired by the figures of military leaders, and their imaginations are stirred to noble desires by the word 'country.' Nowadays what is held up to us? Go out – succeed – make money."⁶

And the collective pugnacity was indeed embodied in some ways in Teddy Roosevelt. As Richard Hofstadter observes,

Herbert Spencer, whose ideas were supreme in American thinking during Roosevelt's formative years, taught that Western society was passing from a militant phase, dominated by organization for warfare, to an industrial phase, marked by peaceful economic expansion. Roosevelt, whom Spencer would have called atavistic, was determined to reverse this process and restore to the American spirit what he fondly called "the fighting edge."⁷

The "jolly little war" that closed the century was fittingly symbolized by the college men and cowboys of the Rough Riders.

But less than a decade after that war, H. G. Wells was reporting that "the American nation, which a few years ago seemed invincibly wedded to an extreme individualism,...displays itself now alert and questioning."⁸ The early 1900s witnessed what the popular journalist and novelist William Allen White called "that curious insurgence in American politics which afterwards was known as the progressive movement," with its crusading reform spirit that would "surge onward in American life and run for forty years as the dominant note in our political, social and economic thinking."⁹ They also witnessed the insurgence of a new, vigorous, and very interesting radicalism. And in these developments, too, as I shall try to show in Chapters 7 through 10, the chivalric played an indispensable part. Because what was thought and done by the well-educated young was increasingly important

Quality and education

during this period, I shall devote the present chapter to looking more closely at what had been going on in education, particularly as it affected the business ethos.

THE IVY LEAGUE EDUCATION: CLASS FOR SALE

On the surface, as I said in Chapter 1, the changes in education during the Eighties and Nineties, when viewed through Twainian or Veblenesque eyes, were in some ways flagrantly regressive. As Canby reports, "with increasing romanticism through the boom years, the bare and nondescript college of my youth began to transform itself into a romantic alumnus's dream of a proper setting for college life. . . [M]oved by instinct rather than reason, he chose the florid Tudor Gothic style which I have already mentioned as characteristic of our *fin de siècle*." It was a style appropriate to what Canby calls "a glamour of beer, songs, cheers and gaudy nights,"[10] and to rituals like the anxiously awaited accoladelike "tapping" that signified acceptance into Skull and Bones at Yale. In the Nineties, too, according to Frederick Rudolph in his history of American higher education, the athlete hero (epitomized fictionally by the Yale all-rounder Frank Merriwell) achieved "a status surpassing that of any previous undergraduate type, including the student orator in the colleges of the Old South."[11] And the prep schools – Canby again – "soon followed the colleges into the era of loyalty, strenuosity, and sentiment."[12] It was this glamor that was celebrated by writers like Merriwell's creator, Gilbert Patten, who had never been through the system, and Owen Johnson, whose *Stover at Yale* (1912) and Kiplingesque stories about Lawrenceville prep school had the authority of his own experience of both institutions in the Nineties and superseded all previous American college fiction. By 1913, Scott Fitzgerald's young alter ego Basil Lee, who had obviously swallowed Merriwell and Stover whole, was gazing yearningly at Yale as

a sort of gateway to [the] deeper, richer life. . . The name evoked the memory of a heroic team backed up against its own impassable goal in the crisp November twilight, and later, of half a dozen immaculate noblemen with opera hats and canes standing at the Manhattan Hotel bar. And tangled up with its triumphs rewards, its struggles and glories, the vision of the inevitable, incomparable girl.[13]

The general causes of these changes are obvious enough, and not particular creditable. In the Seventies the colleges had started getting their first substantial influx of the scions of the new-rich, and by the Nineties the rich had bought into education as they bought into culture. As successful Americans, their money entitled them not only to give their offspring the education that they themselves had never had, but to give them the best, just as they could, if they wished to, give them spouses from among the European aristocracy. And in terms of international prestige, the best was epitomized in the patterns of Oxford, Cambridge, and the great English public schools, establishments that, among other things, had the good sense not to attempt to turn well-to-do young toughs into intellectuals. When it came to campus architecture and the romantic amenities of undergraduate life, college administrators bent on growth were of course very happy to make the rich and their offspring happy, because the donations of the rich made possible the development of the "serious" – that is, professionalizing –side of the universities. From this point of view, it was just fine that alumni were wild about football and that, in Canby's words, their "romantic enthusiasm for 'our team' [became] a country-wide passion."[14] The popularity of football as a paid and widely reported spectator sport was splendid advertising and helped to create an image of colleges and universities as real-life money-making establishments.

The gentlemanliness being created obviously invited an ironical gaze, as graduates like Johnson and Fitzgerald would note later. One of Fitzgerald's young men in *The Beautiful and the Damned*, "a Scroll and Key man at Yale," displays "the correct reticences of a 'good egg,' the correct notions of chivalry and *noblesse oblige.*"[15] Johnson's "Doc" Macnooder, the Stalky-like fixer at Lawrenceville, reflects drily of a potential sucker, "Now he's off again on that eternal dead game sporting idea of his." And we learn of that idea that

a gentleman-sport was not only a disciple of that magnificent Englishman, Beau Brummel, but of that other distinguished Britisher, the Marquis of Queensbury [sic] ...This ideal was one who never counted his change, never quarrelled over a bill, who played with existence and wagered on the simplest turns of fate with anybody for anything. To be a gentleman-sport, then, was to be magnificent, elegant and racy.[16]

Moreover, if some of the finished products were amusing lightweights like the one in *The Beautiful and the Damned* who, circa 1890, "became an inveterate joiner of clubs, connoisseur of good form, and driver of tandems – at the astonishing age of twenty-six he began his memoirs under the title 'New York Society as I have Seen It' " others were not amusing at all.[17] The changes in education that I am talking about also produced that quintessential Ivy League jock, Fitzgerald's Tom Buchanan, with his surface good manners, his "shiny arrogant eyes," his sexual predatoriness, his ruthless egoism, his menacing physicality: "Not even the effeminate swank of his riding clothes could hide the enormous power of that body – he seemed to fill those glistening boots until he strained the top lacing, and you could see a great pack of muscle shifting when his shoulder moved under his thin coat. It was a body capable of enormous leverage – a cruel body."[18] The network of prep schools, prestige colleges, and exclusive college societies also, of course, helped to set graduates apart by expensively acquired skills and graces and a repertoire of signals unavailable to the socially less fortunate, and encouraged their perception of themselves as a ruling class.

Nevertheless, Thorstein Veblen was too simply dismissive when he defined a "gentleman's college" as "an establishment for the cultivation of the graces of gentility and a suitable place of residence for young men of spendthrift habits," and spoke scornfully of "a certain, highly appreciated, loud tone ('college spirit')."[19] Important ideological issues were involved, and the changes in education resolved or eased some major tension-making contradictions in the official business ethos, contradictions that I shall now examine.

THE BURGEONING OF THE BUSINESS SOCIETY

When the socialist W. J. Ghent spoke in 1902 of "the high professions of morality, the frequent appeal to Christian ideals, the tender solicitude for honesty, integrity, law and order, with which our new magnates gild their worship of 'business,' " or when Veblen suggested three years earlier that "there is a perceptible tendency to deprecate the infliction of pain, as well as to discredit all marauding enterprises," they were describing an outlook that was supported by the moral authority of some thirty or forty years of ostensibly scientific demonstrations.[20] Of its chief proponent, Herbert Spencer, Oliver Wendell Holmes commented that it seemed unlikely that "any writer of English except Darwin has done so much to affect our whole way of thinking about the universe," and Richard Hofstadter calls Spencer's visit to America in 1882 "practically an occasion of state."[21] Between 1872 and 1910, according to Charles and Mary Beard, his principal American disciple, the supremely self-assured sociologist and political economist William Graham Sumner,

trained thousands of undergraduates at Yale in individualism as if it were an exact science... He also trained a small army of graduate students who spread over the country as teachers of the science expounded at Yale by the master ... Few of his academic peers, if any, exerted a more powerful influence, directly and indirectly, on the minds of men especially in high places in education, business, and politics.[22]

The orthodoxy disseminated by Sumner and other prestigious Spencerians, such as E. L. Godkin, the founding editor of the *Nation*, and John William Burgess, whose pupils at Columbia filled most of the chairs in political science in the country for years, included what Andrew Carnegie in 1886 referred to as Spencer's "great law" – namely that "As power is held arbitrarily by king or chief the military type is developed, and wars of dynasties and aggression ensue. As power passes to the people the industrial type is developed, and peace ensues."[23] It also included the belief voiced by Grant in his memoirs in 1882 that "the war has made us a

91

nation of great power and intelligence. We have but little to do to preserve peace, happiness, and prosperity at home, and the respect of other nations."[24] The free, reasonable, and pacific operations of the industrial and commercial processes were bound to result in the maximum development and diffusion of the blessings of civilization. And behind the Spencerians stretched a vista of other commentators affirming the attainable blessings of pacificity and rationality, like the orator who assured his listeners at Yale in 1844 that "the age of *philosophy* has passed, and left few memorials to its existence. That of *glory* has vanished, and nothing but a painful tradition of human suffering remains. That of *utility* has commenced, and it requires little warmth of imagination to anticipate for it a reign lasting as time, and radiant with the wonders of unveiled nature."[25] Such attitudes were reinforced by the many images of pastoral harmony in literature and art – in Virgil's *Georgics*, in the Eden of *Paradise Lost*, in Claude Lorrain's golden landscapes, in the paintings of the Hudson River school, in the sun-warmed, grassy, rural scenes of Winslow Homer, in the generalized image of the clean, wholesome, innocent life of the American village or small town – outside of the South, that is.

To be sure, some atavisms persisted after the Civil War. The Spanish-American was unfortunately still around, of whom an observer had reported around 1850 that "the 'Greaser' has all of the characteristic vices of the Spaniard; jealous, revengeful and treacherous, with an absorbing passion for gambling; and he has a still greater likeness to the inferior tribes of Indians; the same apathetic indolence; the same lounging, thieving propensity; never caring for the morrow, and alike regardless of the past or the future."[26] The Southerner was, of course, insufficiently reconstructed. The West was disfigured for a time by those lamentable cowboys, of whom the editor of the *Topeka Commonwealth* complained in 1871 that "they drink, swear, and fight, and life with them is a round of boisterous gayety and indulgence in sensual pleasure," and who were put even more firmly in their place by the author of a history of duelling who wrote in 1884 of

a class of Americans known as the "cowboys" of the West, which nothing but the overwhelming approach of civilization and power of empire can effectually obliterate...[The cowboy] is a stealer of horses and cattle, a guzzler of adulterated spirits, and a shooter of men; and it may be said of him, with perfect truthfulness, that he fears neither God, man, nor devil ...He is at once generous, reckless, lawless, dissipated, desperate, and dangerous...His 'code' is to *"always go well heeled and never let an enemy get the drop on him."*[27]

Back East, as an observer noted in 1872, "the 'dangerous classes' of New York are mainly American-born, but the children of Irish and German immigrants...They are far more brutal than the peasantry from whom they descend."[28] And workingmen in general, as another complained, did not always sufficiently "accept the spirit of civilization, which is pacific, constructive, controlled by reason, and slowly ameliorating and progressive."[29]

But such atavisms were doomed to disappear in a period of which the historian Robert H. Wiebe observes that "an age never lent itself more readily to sweeping, uniform description: nationalization, industrialization, mechanization, urbanization"[30] – a period of science, education, professionalism. Willy-nilly, the individual, liberated from the superstitions, hierarchies, and foolishly agonistic structures and patterns of the European past, would be enabled to take full advantage of the benefits of enlightenment.

As I said in Chapter 2, however, growing numbers of the educated young were viewing things differently. In the Eighties and Nineties, they were increasingly conscious of the unsatisfactoriness of a Spencerian environment in which, in Canby's words, "materialism dominated action and governed thought,"; a "tight little Protestant world where industry was god, and imagination was an old devil, romantic and dishonest." Its culture was "emotionally thin and trivial in everything but business and family life," and was personified by figures like the banker in Canby's home town who "was a good business man, and reasonably honest, and constitutionally incapable of a magnanimous action. A business society bred that kind of crustacean. Sir Walter Scott was his antithesis."[31] Such was the atmosphere of the Ohio town in which the Progressive Frederic Howe grew up in the Seventies and Eighties: "Right living was living carefully, avoiding debts of any kind, and husbanding for some distant future when sickness and old age would overtake one...I had no rights as to my own life; danger lurked in doing what I wanted, even though what I wanted was innocent ...The important thing was to live as other men lived, do as other men did, avoid any departure from what other men thought."[32] It was the atmosphere of the intensely conservative Portland, Oregon, in which John Reed grew up in the Nineties and early 1900s – a town that, as one of his biographers said, had "obliterated as quickly as possible all traces of the frontier and cultivated the decorum of a Massachusetts town."[33] In the 1840s, Emerson had complained that "one would like to see Boston and Massachusetts agitated like a wave with some generosity ...; but now it goes like a peddler with its hand ever in its pocket, cautious, calculating."[34] The moral authority of New England persisted. Doors were closing, the range of possibilities narrowing, the psyche thinning out. Speaking of the "instinctive dread" of a business life that would deny the importance of imagination among the youth of his own town, Canby remembers how we were content but never enthusiastic, which was the cause, I believe, of the romantic age of American education whose beginnings must have been not much before the days [in the Nineties] of which I write. The school as I knew it, and the university also, was growing intolerable to active youth. With no emotional outlets, our intellects were being cramped into a routine which we were asked to take on faith.[35]

It was this pattern – "civilization" versus the youthful psyche – that Twain captured so memorably in *Huckleberry Finn*.

THE BUSINESSMAN AS CULTURE HERO

But there is an interesting problem here. Just as in seventeenth-century Europe the simplified pastoralism of the pacific vision had been counterpointed by the high-energy drama of the Baroque, so there had been a good deal more to rational progress in America than the pastoral decencies of a land in which, as a minister remarked approvingly in J. Hector St. John Crèvecoeur's *Letters from an American Farmer*, "every thing is modern, peaceful, and benign."[36] From the outset great energies had been at work, and by the late nineteenth century there should, on the face of things, have been a multitude of heroes for the aspiring young to emulate and challenges aplenty to be excited by. In the Jacksonian Thirties, Tocqueville had remarked that "it is hard to give an impression of the avidity with which the American throws himself on the vast prey offered him by fortune...A passion stronger than love of life goads him on." And he declared that, "I cannot express my thoughts better than by saying that the Americans put something heroic into their way of trading."[37] This sense of the heroic nature of business vastly intensified after the Civil War. As Samuel Eliot Morison and Henry Steele Commager put it, "never before had the American people exhibited greater vitality, never since has their vitality been accompanied by more reckless irresponsibility. To the generation that had saved the Union everything seemed possible... Men hurled themselves upon the continent with ruthless abandon."[38] Increasingly the high-energy businessman, the magnate, the tycoon was perceived nationally as a major hero and associated with another major hero. In an analysis of the extremely influential McGuffey readers of the nineteenth and early twentieth centuries, one investigator reports that the lesson on Napoleon appeared in every edition; by the Nineties, according to another, his name was cropping up everywhere.[39]

Unlike the atavistic chivalric brand, Napoleonic business heroism was ideologically acceptable. Not only was the epithet "Napoleonic" naturally invited by phenomena like Rockefeller's irresistible expansion of Standard Oil and his mastery of the details of operations throughout

94

that industrial empire. When one of the financiers in Johnson's *The Sixty-First Second* exclaimed enthusiastically, "Railroads – a great system – an empire in itself,"[40] it was natural that he should employ the imperial analogy honorifically. The two great energizing analogies for America had both been imperial. One of them came naturally to Herman Melville's pen when he declared in 1850 that "we Americans are the peculiar, chosen people – the Israel of our time; we bear the ark of the liberties of the world."[41] The Children of Israel had demonstrated that a small group could escape from the bondage of a much larger and ostensibly much more civilized country; endure long years of hardships successfully without giving way to despair and crippling divisions; take deserved possession finally of a land of milk and honey in the face of vigorous opposition by morally inferior groups; and go on from there to exercise an enormous moral influence on other peoples. Likewise the other imperial group, the Romans – initially a small people looked down upon as barbarians, insofar as they were noticed at all, by the civilized Greeks – had prospered and expanded until they dominated not only the Greeks but the whole culture-saturated area of the Mediterranean, as well as much of the dark interior of their own continent. Neither group, moreover, engaged in expansion because of a simple love of fighting. The Jews, as Rebecca said in *Ivanhoe*, were "a race whose courage was distinguished in the defence of their own land, but who warred not, even while yet a nation, save at the command of the Deity, or in defending their country from oppression."[42] Rome was the bearer of peace and civilization to bellicose primitive tribes like those described by Tacitus. The Napoleonic image combined admirable aspects of each of them. Napoleon's empire had not only greatly extended civil order; it had also, as Twain noted in *Life on the Mississippi*, disseminated throughout Europe those Enlightenment principles of the French Revolution that lay at the bottom of the American enterprise.

The Napoleonic hero possessed further ideological advantages. On the one hand, he was immensely powerful, energetic, potent. As the eminent British historian James Bryce observed in 1892, "the president of a great railroad needs gifts for strategical combinations scarcely inferior to those, if not of a great general, yet of a great war minister."[43] The magnate, whether in railroads, or steel, or oil, deployed vast numbers of men, and engaged in heroic large-scale planning like that of Grant after he took command of the Northern armies, and daring innovations like Sherman's march to the sea. (Carnegie, apropos of Grant, spoke revealingly of "the Scotch blood of that tenacious, self-contained, stubborn force, which kept pegging away, always certain of final victory, because he knew that he could not divert himself, even if he wished, from the task he had undertaken. His very nature forbade

95

retreat. Thus stood the sturdy, moody Scotch-American of steady purpose, fighting through to the finish with no "let go" in his composition."[44]) The Napoleonic hero demonstrated that, as Lord Raglan said, "the power of the god may be for good or for evil, it may be general or particular, but power he always has, and it is this power...which leads to his worship. All the names and attributes of a god are names and attributes of power."[45] The self-made tycoon hero of *The Sixty-First Second* was "a man noticeable anywhere for the overmastering vitality of his carriage and the defiant poise of his head."[46]

But, unlike military conquerors, the magnate was wholly a benefactor. His potency was that of a peaceable, rational bringer of benefits to society by technological means. The empires of the railroads, with their visible embodiments of technological inventiveness and their neo-Roman extension across the continent, were benign empires, and the popular enthusiasm reported by Bryce for the "railway kings," who were "among the greatest men, perhaps I may say are the greatest men, in America,"[47] was a rational enthusiasm appropriate to a pacific country. Furthermore, a magnate like Carnegie did not view his success as resulting from any esoteric and inegalitarian qualities of intellect. On the contrary, if he was successful it was only because, in a Spencerian society in which all persons began equal, he put into practice the universally available principles of hard work, forethought, and self-discipline. And to be flamboyant and idiosyncratic in the fashion of financial buccaneers like Diamond Jim Brady and Bet-a-Million Gates was to be in fact suspect. The magnate simply possessed an uncommon measure of common characteristics. In the Thirties Emerson had discerningly called Napoleon "the idol of common men because he had in transcendent degree the qualities and powers of common men."[48] Like Napoleon, the tycoon was a self-made man; like Napoleon, he demonstrated that once the trammels of aristocracy were removed, every private carried a field marshall's baton in his knapsack.

But in the late nineteenth century, committing oneself wholeheartedly to becoming such a hero posed some difficulties. It is important to see what these were, because – like the concept of Napoleonic greatness – some of them will be relevant to what I shall say about reformism and radicalism.

THE BUSINESS GOSPEL: CONTRADICTIONS AND CONFLICTS

Ostensibly, all should have been well with the gospel of success that reached its apogee in the Nineties and was trumpeted in works like Carnegie's *Triumphant Democracy*, that major prophetic book of the period. The gospel was a natural enough response to the achievements of men like Carnegie and Rockefeller, with their dramatic testimonies to how a poor Scottish immigrant or a humble Ohio bookkeeper could soar to riches beyond the wildest dreams of European avarice. It reinforced the conviction of Americans that they were a new and special people who, liberated from the shackles of the past, were destined to attain grandeur and greatness on a scale transcending that of any previous civilization. And the increasing correlation of success with magnitude had a good deal of emotional logic behind it, as did the fact that, as a writer noted in the *Saturday Evening Post* in 1906, "for years we have taught that money is the one victory in life."[49] In terms of Social Darwinist theory, unfettered free enterprise enabled the fullest advantages to accrue to society by guaranteeing that the best persons – the most industrious, the most enterprising, the most rational – rose to the top, where they maximized the benefits of industrial technology and organization, both in the creation and in the distribution of goods. And money was the most public, the most general, the most objective index of a person's accomplishments, for, by definition, a person who rose to the top financially could not be other than the best. Moreover, above and beyond the feeling, reinforced alike by the imperial analogies and by the doctrines of Social Darwinism, that the large organization was both the fittest and the most virtuous, there was, as Elias Canetti shows in his brilliant *Crowds and Power*, an almost magical aura surrounding great numbers and immense increase.[50] A sense of the marvelous informs the accounts in *Triumphant Democracy* of such phenomena as Chicago's surging from 4,500 people in 1840, to 112,000 in 1860, to over 700,000 by the mid-Eighties, or the mammoth grain crop of 1885:

Built into a solid mass as high as the dome of St. Paul's (three hundred and sixty-five feet), and as wide as the cathedral across the transepts (two hundred and eighty-five feet), it would extend, a solid mass of grain, down Fleet Street and the length of the Strand to Piccadilly, thence on through Knightsbridge, Hammersmith and South Kensington, to a distance of over six miles. Or it would make a pyramid three times as great as that of Cheops.

Obvious analogies with Carnegie's own career were suggested by the fact that the Mississippi, with its "outflow of over two million cubic feet per hour," was

equal in bulk to all the rivers of Europe combined, exclusive of the Volga. It is equal to three Ganges, nine Rhones, twenty-seven Seines, or eighty Tibers. "The mighty Tiber chafing with its flood," says the Master. How would he have described the Mississippi on the rampage after a spring flood, when it pours down its mighty volume of water and overflows the adjacent lowlands! Eighty Tibers in one![51]

But if success was quantifiable, so, unfortunately, was failure. Speaking in 1896 of "the general popular tendency to make the accumulation of wealth the one sign of worldly success, and to estimate men by the size of their income, from whatever source derived," E. L. Godkin pointed out that "there is probably in America today a nearer approach to a literal rendering of the English term 'worth,' as measuring a man's possessions, than ever occurred elsewhere."[52] Logically, if earning a lot of money made a man a glorious success morally as well as financially, then earning little made him a doubly contemptible failure. Because everyone, after the shackles of aristocratic privilege had been removed, started equal, he had failed to use his will power and bring into play the industriousness and self-discipline that would guarantee anyone's rise. And because, in Social Darwinist terms, stronger organizations and organisms won out naturally over weaker ones, he was also contemptible because he lacked vital energy. He was like those "small fry craft," "wretched little farms," and "yellow-faced male miserables" that Twain sneers at in *Life on the Mississippi* from the point of view of the all-powerful riverboat pilot,[53] or like that quintessential loser, George Wilson, the sickly garage keeper in the valley of ashes in *The Great Gatsby*, whom Tom Buchanan cuckolds and whose death he causes. As Rockefeller complacently remarked, "the failures which a man makes in his life are due almost always to some defect in his personality, some weakness of body, or mind, or character, will, or temperament."[54] Hence Frederic Howe could recall of the millionaire political boss Mark Hanna that "his lordship over his associates was scarcely concealed. They were vassals of a system, but vassals of Mark Hanna as well," and Wells reported a friend's saying that J. P. Morgan's manner toward those around him "was Roman...There has been nothing like it since the days of that republic. No living king would dare to do it."[55] Hence, too, as former President Grover Cleveland complained in a magazine article in 1903, "the deference to those who have won great fortunes has grown in many quarters to be so unquestioning and so obsequious as to amount to scandalous servility."[56] For if one committed oneself to the view of success that I have described, there was no logical appeal against the results. As Wells said of the magnates, "people have committed suicide through their operations; but in a game which is bound to bring the losers to despair it is childish to charge the winners with murder."[57]

The tensions created by these dichotomies, insofar as one seriously attempted to achieve success in Social Darwinist terms, were increased by the pattern of business competition. Given the conviction that maximum growth and maximum speed of development would bring about maximum benefits for society; given the feeling voiced by Carnegie that "every enlargement is an improvement";[58] given the equally fundamental idea that the fittest men inevitably rose to the top, where their benefit-bringing skills could be employed with maximum energy, and that the less fit sank downwards and deserved to do so; given these beliefs, the notion of regulating business combat so as to assist the weaker contestants was not only anachronistic but socially vicious. By definition, the rules of the game, insofar as it had any, were those that the most successful devised for themselves and that maximized the possibility of their succeeding. And the ideal businessman was the one who single-mindedly and successfully pursued financial profit. As a banker declares in W. D. Howells's *A Traveller from Altruria* (1894), "in our business battles we don't take off our hats to the other side and say, 'Gentlemen of the French Guard, have the goodness to fire.' That may be war, but it is not business. We seize all the advantages we can."[59]

In practice, such principles did not always obtain. Like other games, the business game partly appealed for its own sake. When Pierpont Morgan died in 1913, his editorial eulogist in the *New York Tribune* was not engaging in empty flattery when he asserted that "his superb energy and intellectual resources easily put him in the first rank of those who do things in the largest way, not so much for self-profit as for the sheer pleasure of doing them."[60] Henry Adams, who remembered of himself around 1870 that "under the excitement of the chase, he was becoming a pirate...and liked it," had said the same sort of thing in more general terms: "That the American... worked to excess, was true...but he never cared much for money or power after he earned them. The amusement of the pursuit was all the amusement he got from it; he had no use for wealth."[61] And what Jay Gould reported of his own activities with the Missouri Pacific Railroad – "I did not care at that time about the mere making of money. It was more to show that I could make a combination and make it a success" – could no doubt have been said by various other tycoons.[62] Moreover, elements of mercantile decency persisted. Mencken, for instance, recalled how

my father and his brother and partner, like most reasonably successful American businessmen of the eighties, always had plenty of time on their hands. The business they were in [i.e., cigar manufacturing] had not yet been demoralized and devoured by the large combinations of capital that were to come later on, and there was room in their field, which was principally in the Southeast, for all the firms in their line in Baltimore. They were thus on peaceful terms with their competitors, and regarded at least some of them with a kind of approval almost verging upon respect.[63]

Even Veblen conceded that "in common with other men, the business man is moved by ideals of serviceability and an aspiration to make the way of life easier for his fellows. Like other men, he has something of the instinct of workmanship...[T]hroughout men's dealings with one another and with the interests of the community there runs a sense of equity, fair dealing, and workmanlike integrity."[64]

99

But as Veblen also drily remarked, the magnate was moved by such attitudes "less urgently" than lesser businessmen, and it was precisely because of that that he *was* successful. The warfare of the magnates was emphatically not chivalrous. As Frederic Howe said of Mark Hanna, in whom "the beliefs of lesser men of his sort were blazoned in unmistakeable colors," "life meant war... War on his business associates, on his employees, on the State itself. And he made war, not to bend men but to break them."[65]

The logic of neoimperial enlargement and expansion, and of what the editor of *Harper's* called in 1902 "the new ideals, the ideals of a pitiless industrialism,"[66] dictated that just as it was natural, logical, inevitable, and beneficial for the Indians and the culturally and economically inferior Spanish and French on the North American continent to be brushed aside or engulfed by the advance of progress, so it was natural and beneficial for the larger business organization to assimilate or put out of operation the smaller one. The official Social Darwinist conception of industrial warfare curiously resembled that of Sir Thomas More's rational and pacific Utopians with respect to literal warfare, which itself curiously resembled that of the official American image of its own expansion in North America. As More explains, "If the natives won't do what they're told, they're expelled from the area marked out for annexation. If they try to resist, the Utopians declare war – for they consider war perfectly justifiable when one country denies another its natural right to derive nourishment from any soil which the original owners are not using themselves, but are merely holding on to as a worthless piece of property."[67]

And not only was it imperative to strive with all one's might to succeed in a world in which, as Carnegie said at the start of the Nineties, "the time has passed when business once established can be considered almost permanently secure. Business methods have changed; good will counts for less and less. Success in business is held by the same tenure, nowadays, as the Premiership of Britain – at the cost of a perpetual challenge to all comers."[68] By means of another turn of the screw of Social Darwinist logic, failure was increasingly likely. When Carnegie exhorted the young to "Say, each to yourself, 'My place is at the top.' *Be king in your dreams*," he was speaking of the top of a company.[69] But insofar as a man's worth was determined in relation to what was possible in American society at large (and Carnegie considered the business career "the exercise of man's highest power"[70]), he might just as well have been talking about the financial top in general. And this was becoming ever higher and narrower. In contrast to the decades before the Civil War when it was still hidden in the mists of futurity, and when the incomes of the great majority of successful businessmen were still relatively modest, the financial peak was now defined by the immense wealth of men like Carnegie himself, who in 1900 became the richest man in the world when he sold what was to become the U.S. Steel Corporation for almost five hundred million dollars. And opportunities to achieve that kind of wealth were fast diminishing. As Carnegie himself acknowledged in 1891, "a few enormous fortunes have been amassed during the present generation..., but under circumstances which no longer exist." It was increasingly inevitable that there should be, as he said, "great inequality of environment; the concentration of business, industrial and commercial, in the hands of a few."[71] It was increasingly inevitable, too, that despite Carnegie's equation of the business hero with the man who "plunges into and tosses upon the waves of human affairs without a life preserver in the shape of salary," and his assertion that "I would not give a fig for the young man who does not already see himself the partner of an important firm," an ever growing number of young men were destined for salaried positions.[72]

The very nature of success and "arrival" was problematical as well. Part of the American promise had been that Americans could obtain anything that Europeans had, if they wanted it. But this raised the question of where in fact a successful American businessman had arrived when he did arrive. In England the rich man could make a qualitative leap and enter the aristocracy; in America, as Wells noted in *Tono-Bungay*, "all he gets is money."[73] The ever more extravagant displays in the Nineties were obviously an attempt to resolve the problem noted by Lord Bryce when he said that "through the country generally there is little to mark out the man with an income of $20,000 a year from the man of $1000, as he is marked out in England by his country house with its park, or in France by the opportunities for display which Paris affords."[74] But despite the Four Hundred, the *Social Register*, the lavish entertaining and theater going, the muckraker David Graham Phillips was able to note in 1905 that "it is still an open and anxious question whether this fashionable society, the growth, as we have seen, of the last two or three decades, constitutes a genuine aristocracy."[75] And the more the older kind of businessman bought or allowed his wife to buy the patterns of housing, clothing, culture, and the like that characterized the European aristocracy, the more he was implicitly acknowledging the desirability and superiority of that despised way of life. The more, too, he was in danger of coming up against all those attributes of aristocratic style and class that he did not possess and that could make him feel like an imposter, such as the fact that whereas the aristocrat was "in" and could never be put out, the businessman was in only by virtue of his money, and could be put out if he lost it. And when it came to display, as Phillips pointed out, it was the ultra-rich who set the pace, to the discomfort of the rest. "There must be no standing still...Each year, more and ever more must be spent, unless one is to fall behind, lose one's rank, be mingled with the crowd that is ever pressing on and trying to catch up."[76]

In Social Darwinist terms, another feature of wealth also presented problems. As a visiting British noblewoman remarked in 1903, the period of the emergence of a leisure class "has arrived, or is arriving, and now Americans are rich and independent enough to spend their life and time as they will."[77] Leisure, traditionally the prerogative of the aristocrat, was in principle both desirable and buyable, unless one were to grant that the European could have things that were unavailable to the American. But as Herbert Croly noted, the businessman of the heroic years of American capitalism "could not conquer except by virtue of a strong, tenacious, adventurous, and unscrupulous will; and after he had conquered, this will had him in complete possession."[78] Leisure would eliminate those very activities that were the source of his self-esteem. And the difficulties increased when it came to his offspring. Traditionally, one of the privileges of wealth was that one could pass on to one's sons the fruits of one's labors. But if those sons did not work, as Horatio Alger pointed out to his innumerable readers, they were not engaged in the prime merit-conferring activity of society; and if they did work, they were patently not beginning equal with others, which both denied them the possibilities of heroism that had been available to their fathers and seriously undermined the Carnegiean image of America as a country where everyone started equal. They were also, of course, faced with one of the catches of Napoleonism, namely, that if glory came from creating an empire, it was a good deal less glorious to manage an empire after it had been established. As one of the well-to-do young undergraduates in *Stover at Yale* sadly remarked, "I wish to blazes I was starting where...my old man did; I might do something worth while."[79]

COLLEGIATE VALUES: QUANTITY INTO QUALITY

But accommodations and adjustments in fact took place, and it was in education that they principally did so. The more prestigious Eastern colleges and prep schools became transformers wherein a number of the difficulties that I have been talking about were ameliorated or resolved. They subtilized the idea of success, refined the rules of competition, and altered the image of maturity so that a man no longer needed, as Hannah Arendt said, "to forget his youth if he wanted to grow up."[80] By 1906, a writer in *Munsey's* was reporting that the new-style businessman must be "a good talker, and many-sided. There must have been more or less of romance and adventure in his life"; and seven years later Owen

Quality and education

Johnson wrote approvingly of the financier hero of *The Sixty-First Second* that his "eyes were a clear blue, the eyes of a boy in mischief who is still sublimely defiant of the tripping obstacles of an ethical code...Life was to him a huge dare, and all the perils of finance the hazards of a monstrous gamble."[81] By means of the ostensibly regressive chivalric patterns, the colleges and prep schools had reintegrated energy, will, and form, and made possible the emergence of what C. Wright Mills later called the power elite.

In their provision of patterns and structures unavailable in a merely quantifying society, the schools and colleges furnished defenses against the open endedness, the indeterminacy, the fragmentation, the emotional insecurity that I have been speaking of. Henry Seidel Canby was looking deeper than Veblen when he described how college gave alumni "a common memory of a vivid and homogeneous experience intelligible to all of them, which, in the restless haphazard life of an American constantly on the move, gave a point of rest and departure."[82] More than anything else in American life, college demonstrated the possibility of patterned growth and change, of structures firm without being static, of meaning-charged symbols, of significant communities and subcommunities. It furnished the young with meaningful groups and groupings – the fraternities, sororities, and other societies, the classroom assemblies, the groupings by year. It provided them with costumes and rituals. It offered them a variety of significant types to take an interest in, such as the Absent-Minded Scholar, the Tyrant Teacher, the Athlete Hero or Strong Silent Man, the Big Man on Campus. It gave them stages and signposts from term to term, season to season, year to year, with increasing codifications as to the proper or expected way to feel and behave at each stage – the freshman innocence, the sophomore knowingness, and so on – and with what Stover quickly perceived as a "graduated system of authority."[83] More generally, it offered what Oscar Handlin speaks of apropos of the young during the Civil War: "To shed routine cares, march in uniform, have an identity in a company, join with others in the disciplined ritual of dedication gave them that sense of belonging they avidly sought. Glory, for the moment, displaced success as the object of the young men's striving."[84]

A central feature of all this was an acceptance of the agonistic as natural, pleasurable, and desirable, as it was for one of Johnson's Lawrenceville boys who "played hard – very hard, but cleanly, because combat was the joy of life to him. He broke other rules, not as a lark, but out of the same fierce desire for battle, to seek out danger wherever he could find it."[85] The agonistic need not be simply a regrettable atavism, leading a discreditable existence among lower species like Irishmen, Indians, cowboys, and whiskey-swilling Southerners. Nor, insofar as it

103

entered into business activities, need it do so only as a logically irrelevant byplay of commercial empire building.

Undergraduate life was permeated by the agonistic, particularly in what Veblen scornfully called "those sports and 'student activities' that make up the chief attractions of college life for a large proportion of the university's young men, and that are, in the apprehension of many, so essential a part in the training of the modern gentleman."[86] Students competed for places in societies, on teams, and on campus newspapers. They debated in debating clubs. They confronted one another in groups, freshmen against sophomores. They fought back in the classroom against teachers who endeavored to catch them out. (In his reminiscences about Yale, Canby recalled how a class, "expert in games, if not in the subject of instruction," would watch the struggle between a professor and an unprepared student, "excited sometimes to the point of groans or applause.") Some of the competition was at so high a pitch that, in Canby's words, apropos of what he calls the "Great Struggle," "there never was a more strenuous preparation for active life anywhere than in the American college of those days."[87] But it was still agonistic rather than simply antagonistic. It was not raw aggressiveness. When Stover enters Lawrenceville like a bellicose Huck Finn, he is soon set straight by a fellow student: "You can't fight your way into being liked... You've got to keep a civil tongue in your head and quit thinking this place was built for your special benefit."[88]

In all this, sports were a major transformer, especially the tournamentlike football rituals that blossomed in the late Seventies after football had replaced rowing as the most prestigious college sport. In his reminiscences of Princeton, Scott Fitzgerald recalled how "football became, back in the 'nineties, a sort of symbol... It became something at first satisfactory, then essential and beautiful... the most intense and dramatic spectacle since the Olympic games."[89] Armored groups, wearing different colors and, after 1915, heraldic numbers, met in physical combat on an agreed-upon ground, under the governance of agreed-upon rules and the supervision of umpires and referees – a miniature warfare that to Stover, as he trod the field at Yale for the first time, felt "more real... than Waterloo or Gettysburg."[90] They did so before cheering, singing, pennant-waving crowds, including members of the fair sex, the latter having first turned up in large numbers in 1885 at the first Yale-Princeton game. And just as the strength, skills, and courage displayed in tournaments related directly to warfare, so football meshed with "real" life. If alumni were intensely interested in their own team, and if college games were reported in big-city newspapers, it was for good business reasons. Making a name for oneself in college football was likely to assist one toward a successful entry into the business world after graduation. Football was thought to demand and display virtues that were required in business – the virtues, in the words of a contemporary observer, of "courage, coolness, steadiness of nerve, quickness of apprehension, resourcefulness, self-knowledge and self-reliance."[91] It focused energy in the way demanded by Stover's captain at Lawrenceville: "When you get in a game get fighting mad, but get cold mad ...Know just what you're doing and know it all the time." It taught Stover "how to use his courage and the control of his impulses."[92] And inseparable from the increased interest in sports was the idea of fair play.

Football, the sport of Fitzgerald's Tom Buchanan, never, of course, became gentlemanly in the British fashion. By the early 1900s, indeed, it was notorious for its violence and for what a *Collier's* writer called "the sordid and contemptible spirit of playing to win at any cost," which he adds was "practically unknown" before the Civil War.[93] The alumni who came to dominate football in the Nineties had no desire to see the worth of their own character-building university years brought into question by a succession of losses by "their" team; coaching accordingly became increasingly purposeful; and by 1902 a writer reported that "recognizing the military aspects of the game, the Americans have developed it farther than any European nation."[94] In his account of Stover's training, Owen Johnson describes how Dink

had never known anything like the fierceness of that first practise. It was not play with the zest he loved, it was a struggle of ambitions, with all the heart-ache that lay underneath. He had gone out to play, and suddenly found himself in a school for character, enslaved to the discipline of the Caesars, where the test lay in stoicism and the victory was built on the broken hopes of a comrade.

And he felt against the opposing practice team "a sort of rage..., a brutal joy, joy in the incessant smarting, grinding shock of the attack of which he was part and the touch of prostrate bodies under his rushing feet."[95] It was not surprising that in 1905 there were eighteen deaths in college football, and that the game had to be cleaned up after Roosevelt threatened to have it banned altogether.

Nevertheless, the idea of fair play in college and prep-school sport was not mere words. As was said in *Collier's* in 1906, "that misused word, chivalry, now too often applied to and appropriated by blatant, noisy, or grotesquely exaggerated incompetency, is still the same good word, meaning, to the clean-minded, the same ideal that died with Arthur."[96] Moral lessons had also been provided for the young by the career of John L. Sullivan, who, in William Shannon's words, found prize fighting in the Seventies "a mean, ill-assorted pastime, half rough-and-tumble wrestling, half eye-gouging, hip-and-knee street fighting" and "left it a modern sport," fighting in 1892 the first American championship bout governed by Queensberry rules and featuring padded gloves.[97] After a dressing down from his football captain, one of Stover's contemporaries at Lawrenceville reflects sadly, back in his room, that, "Yes, he *had* acted like a member of the Seventy-second Street gang! He glanced up at the photograph of... John L., and he thought of Ivanhoe and the Three Musketeers and Sir Nigel of the White Company." Naturally the notion of fair play extended to other kinds of contests, so that, at one point in a duel of wits with a teacher, Stover, "in the part of his soul that was consecrated to fair play, was mightily exercised" about a questionable move that he was trying to bring off.[98]

Moreover, there were broader social dimensions to all this. As a variety of writers noted, there were numerous social inequalities in college life. But in terms of collegiate ideology as articulated in popular fiction – and, like the medieval chivalric ideology, more than merely fictive – it was the inequalities which were the aberrations. Gilbert Patten wrote with an outsider's enthusiasm when he assured his young readers that at Yale when Merriwell entered it in the mid-Nineties "the old democratic spirit still prevailed. The young men were drawn from different social conditions, and in their homes they kept to their own set; but they seemed to leave this aside, and they mingled and submerged their natural differences under that one broad generalization, 'the Yale man.'"[99] But he was not simply gibbering. A year or two earlier the same image had enchanted the young Stover, who as a troubled sophomore would look back nostalgically to

the pride he had felt in the democracy of the [freshman] class, when he had swung amid the torches and the cheers past the magic battlements of the college, one in the class, with the feeling in the ranks of a consecrated army gathered from the plains and the mountains, the cities and villages of the nation, consecrated to four years of mutual understanding that would form an imperishable bond wherever on the face of the globe they should later scatter.[100]

In principle the intensely competitive college life was a fair game in which the best men won by means of their merits, a game in which, as one of Merriwell's mentors observed, "it doesn't make any difference what you have done or what you have been elsewhere, you will have to establish a record by what you do and what you become here."[101] Mere money could not buy a student eminence on the football field, or popularity, or entry into Skull and Bones. A recurring figure in the school stories is the kid from a newly rich home who puts too much confidence in the power of a well-filled billfold and more or less painfully learns better.

Before it could bring any real gain, money had to be transposed back into terms of individual qualities, the possession of certain skills and graces. And those skills and graces were more public and varied than the ones that made a man rich. One could become a multimillionaire and yet, like Jay Gould or John D. Rockefeller, be reclusive, secretive, uninspectable. In contrast, the qualities that brought success in college life, like those in the chivalric romances and tournaments, had to be highly inspectable. And more than one kind of success was possible, none of them involving monetary valuations. One could be good at sports, or shine on the college newspaper, or possess the social skills that gave entry into prestige societies. One could beat the academic system by skillful faking or even, occasionally, by doing some work. Different stages of success were possible – the freshman's, the sophomore's, the junior's, the senior's – with no depreciation of lower ones by higher ones. Group or team success was possible, and with it the achieving of individual distinction by way of the collectivity, not despite it. Larger alternative patterns of success were displayed in the differences noted by Fitzgerald between the top universities – the intellectuality of Harvard, the muscularity of Yale, the irony of Princeton.

Furthermore, the idea of competition became subtilized. In contrast to Napoleonic warfare, winning in college did not mean wiping out rivals and preventing any further competition. On the contrary, pleasurable competition depended on maintaining quasifraternal relationships with them, at least outside of a particular game. In principle, too, game rules were not obstacles to success but conditions for achieving it. A player should not immediately break a rule if he had the chance to do so, and illegitimate moves deserved to be penalized. Nor did failure in one area necessarily undermine one's achievements in others, and even inside a single area a defeat need not imply major defects in one's character. In a game played well, one could respect one's undefeated adversary, and if one fought gallantly oneself but lost, one could retain one's self-respect. Winning was in fact *not* everything. In the great football game in *Stover at Yale*, the Yale team, despite coming within a few feet and a couple of minutes of winning, does not in fact win. In his pep talk immediately afterwards, the Walter Camp-like coach, the "coach of coaches, around whom the traditions of football had been formed," tells his downcast players: "Yale teams take their medicine! No talking, no reasoning, no explanations, no excuses, and no criticism! The thing's over and done. . . . A great Princeton team licked you – licked you well! That's all. You deserved to score. You didn't. Hard luck. But those who saw you try for it won't forget it! We're proud of that second half!" Stover "went out, head erect, back to meet his college, no longer shrinking from the ordeal."[102]

All this helped to bridge the gap between business and gentility. Within the college structure, both brawn and shrewdness, to use Canby's terms, were rewarded, sometimes in the same person. And a graduate with gentlemanly traits could not only go into business, but could be all the more welcome *because* he possessed those traits. The college man was effective and efficient – so much so that a writer went so far as to suggest in 1910 that "the sons of the rough-hewn and the self-made are often spendthrifts, while on the other hand, those who form part of a long, glittering plutocratic chain frequently rival their forebears in their genius for money-making."[103] College increased a person's self-discipline. It helped him to live with complexity, with overlapping games (the business, the social), with hierarchies, with fellow team members, with business rivals encountered on the neutral ground of clubs and alumni organizations. And it did so by transposing, rather than rejecting, the values of adolescents. What had taken place, in effect, was a synthesizing of Northern and Southern values and virtues.

As a consequence, the newer world of business was a pleasanter one to inhabit. In the late Nineties, William James enthusiastically endorsed Robert Louis Stevenson's statement that "to miss the joy is to miss all."[104] The college patterns legitimized enjoyment. As Gilbert Patten exclaimed, with his nose pressed yearningly against the window pane, "Oh, those old college songs! How they linger in the memory! How the sound of them in after years stirs the blood and quickens the pulse! ...Never can other songs seem half as beautiful as those!"[105] Games, song, pageantry, rituals, social graces, were not at odds with reality, and college graduates could enjoy them as legitimate adjuncts to, rather than frivolous distractions from, the life of business. It was possible, too, as Fitzgerald showed in *The Great Gatsby*, for the football hero and the ironic intellectual, both of them covered by the rubric "man-in-business," to get along socially, by virtue of shared codes and manners. Nor did the sexes have to be sharply disjoined socially. The business male could be gallant if he felt like it, and women could be good sports, like Gibson's golf-playing Amazons or the Zelda-like heroine of Fitzgerald's *The Beautiful and the Damned*, with "the British freshness of her complexion and her figure boyish and slim."[106] Moreover, business activities now had more of a moral safety net beneath them. In neo-Darwinist terms, failure was unmitigated, and in the gangster movie that eventually came to symbolize unfettered Napoleonic business warfare, it was logical that, as Robert Warshow said, "when the gangster is killed, his whole life is shown to have been a mistake."[107] A bankrupt businessman could not see himself as "really" a rich man who happened temporarily to be poor. But in chivalric terms, it was not meaningless to see oneself as no less honorable because of having run into financial difficulties. In a short story in *Collier's* in 1904, for example, "Dick Bradford was a gentleman by birth, and consequently he remained a gentleman, even when in later years he was buffeted about,

the victim of circumstances."¹⁰⁸ Such attitudes were reinforced by the
appeal of chivalric figures like the Arthurian knight, the Cavalier, the
Indian, the Virginian gentleman, and the cowboy, all of whom demonstrated that being defeated need not be a mark of weakness of character.

In sum, the changes that I have been describing were practical ones.
Paradoxically, the medievalizing of college life that so exasperated
Veblen was a more effective response to business needs than the
rationalizing and professionalizing of undergraduate education would
have been. By 1910, a well-born observer reported that "a perfect flood"
of rich young men were being

> turned loose each year upon the financial districts of this country...They are
> not working for wages, but they are working for emancipation. They do not
> want to be idlers....These young men are by no means effete dilletanti. They are
> strong, vigorous young men, and they plunge into what they know to be a
> competitive field with a full knowledge that they are not likely to go very far
> unless they earn their way...In the Harvard Club, of a Saturday afternoon in
> winter, you will find groups of [them] sitting around and talking, just as you
> would have found them fifteen years ago. There is one marked difference.
> Fifteen years ago they would have been talking about social events,...sports,
> and various other trivial things...Nowadays many of these groups are earnestly
> discussing finance...in its broader aspect.¹⁰⁹

7

Reform

The Irish do not prosper so well; they love to drink and to quarrel; they are
litigious and soon take to the gun, which is the ruin of everything.

J. Hector St. John Crèvecoeur, *Letters from an
American Farmer* (1782)

"My father, the leader of an industrial trust, is a better man than all of the noisy
reformers that ever lived," she declared. "He makes plans, anyway – makes
them well – millions of them. He doesn't spend his time talking and running his
fingers through his hair."

Sherwood Anderson, *Marching Men* (1917)

How Theodore loves a party!

Edith Kermit Roosevelt.[1]

IF THERE WERE no more to the new gentlemanliness than what I have
described, there would, of course, be ample grounds for disquiet about
the changes that produced it. As Henry Seidel Canby says, the second-
generation rich at Yale considered that "the rest of their lives would be
spent in a Great Struggle for wealth and privilege, where the best
grabbers would win."[2] The college system intensified the power and
energy of the strong, and created tensions and anxieties of its own.
Stover at football practice felt "the weight of the seriousness, the deadly
seriousness of the American spirit, which seizes on everything that is
competitive and transforms it, with the savage fanaticism of its race, for
success," and the tapping for Skull and Bones at the end of the novel
was "like a stampede . . . a sudden shipwreck, when every second was
precious and, once gone, gone for ever; where . . . agony was in the face
of the weak-hearted and a few stoically stood smiling at the waiting
gulf." One of Stover's handful of dissident acquaintances commented
acidly that American colleges were "business colleges purely and
simply, because we as a nation have only one ideal – the business
ideal," and that athletics were "one of the most perfectly organized
business systems for achieving a required result."[3]

What was obviously missing from the pattern that I have described
was any opportunity for civic idealism. Owen Johnson, writing about
the Nineties with the hindsight of the 1900s, nicely explores the
confusions of a well-to-do youth like Stover as he becomes aware of the
discrepancies between college ideals and actualities and compares his

Reform

own shibboleth-ridden self with the freer minds of less well-heeled classmates. As he comments to the judge's daughter who increasingly serves as his chivalric conscience and inspiration, "life's real to those fellows... They're fighting for something. There's nothing real in me."[4] However, a change was coming. Looking back at his representative younger self, William Allen White would remember how, as the present century opened,

I saw the Great Light. Around me in that day scores of young leaders in American politics and public affairs were seeing what I saw, feeling what I felt. Probably they too were converted Pharisees with the zeal of the new faith upon them. All over the land in a score of states and more, young men in both parties were taking leadership by attacking things as they were in that day – notably Mark Hanna's plutocracy and the political machinery that kept it moving.[5]

By 1910, Herbert Croly was able to report that "at the present time average, well-stationed Americans are likely to be reformers of one kind or another, while the more intelligent and disinterested of them are pretty sure to vote a 'reform' ticket."[6] In this chapter I shall be concerned with the upsurge of political activity in the new century, the crucial part that chivalric patterns played in it, and some of the consequences.

POLITICS IN ECLIPSE

In his memoirs, the archetypal liberal Progressive Frederic C. Howe recalled his conviction in the early Nineties that politics ought to be

the business of a gentleman. It should be in the hands of good men – men who had succeeded in business, who observed the conventions of life, who had graduated from universities. Goodness would cure political ills. The scholar in politics was the ultimate ideal, the ideal of Plato, of James Bryce, of Woodrow Wilson. By disinterested service, by not wanting anything for ourselves, the state could be redeemed.[7]

The traditional moral claims of politics as the proper field for a gentleman were strong. Historically politics had been, next to warfare, the great arena of honorable, high-energy, heroic activity in the service of ideals, especially the ideal of liberty. Risking his own liberty or life, the political hero had fought against tyranny in the Roman Senate, in the British Parliament, in the American Congress. The early years of the Republic had been a time of gentleman heroes like Washington, and Jefferson, and John Adams. The Congress of the antebellum decades had been vivified by figures like John C. Calhoun, Daniel Webster, Henry Clay, and Charles Sumner.

But by the Nineties, as one senator remarked, "many think and say that the day of heroic questions [in politics] is past: that it is now too late to make great names by the doing of great deeds... The leaders of the

111

last generation were exceptionally favored in having slavery, the Civil War, reconstruction, and kindred questions to deal with...The souls of men are not stirred by tariff schedules or rates of duty."[8] Hence William Allen White's own undergraduate experience of politics had consisted of "losing five dollars on Blaine in 1884 after which I became, as I think most college boys in midwestern United States were, hermetically sealed to the issues of modern American politics, however we delved into American history. We did not relate history with life. History stopped for us with the Civil War, or at most the panic of '73."[9] During the exceptionally dreary period of the later Seventies and the Eighties, national politics, in the words of Samuel Eliot Morison and Henry Steele Commager, "became little more than a contest for power between rival parties waged on no higher plane than a struggle for traffic between rival railroads,"[10] parties run by directorates of professional politicians concerned to get and keep office, and unwilling to become involved in problematical ideological issues. The politics of ideological confrontation virtually disappeared in Congress. So did political figures like those who had won the public's devotion before the Civil War. In the 1896 election the young William Allen White was struck by McKinley's "statesman's face, unwrinkled, unperturbed: a face without vision but without guile....the mask of a kindly, dull gentleman...a cast most typical to represent American politics; on the whole decent, on the whole dumb, and rarely reaching above the least common multiple of the common intelligence."[11] In the mid-Eighties Carnegie had noted that "one hears more political discussion at a dinner in London than during the whole season in New York or Washington."[12]

In terms of the dominant ideology, these changes were entirely orthodox. The politics of ideological contentiousness had led to the Civil War – the contentiousness, that is, of an atavistic South convinced that politics was the noblest activity for a gentleman, and bent on dominating the North in Congress. It had been a struggle of unreason against reason, a struggle in which, as the abolitionist Wendell Phillips explained at the time, "the North *thinks*, – can appreciate argument, – is the nineteenth century, – hardly any struggle left in it but that between the working class and the money kings. The South dreams, – it is the thirteenth and fourteenth century, – baron and serf, – noble and slave...Our struggle is therefore between barbarism and civilization."[13] With the decisive military refutation of the Southern ideology, there was now only a single system, the "real" American system in relation to which the other had been a mere foolish aberration. And in a society "now governed mainly by ideas about the distribution of commodities," as Godkin said, "any writer or speaker on political subjects [had] to show that his proposition [would] make people more comfortable or

richer."[14] Such improvements, according to the implacable Social Darwinist logic, came about through the operations of the industrial
system, not through law making. As Carnegie announced triumphantly
in *Triumphant Democracy*, "no party in America desires a change in any
of the fundamental laws...The laws are perfect...The 'outs' are left to
insist that they could and would administer existing laws better or more
purely than the 'ins.' "[15] Hence it was an excellent thing that politics
became simply an extension of business interests, a process reaching its
apogee between 1897 and 1903. It was not just bosses like Mark Hanna
who despised old-style agonistic politics, either. Howe remembered
figures like James Bryce and Woodrow Wilson, in their lectures at Johns
Hopkins in the early Nineties, condemning party politics and speaking
of the need to rescue democracy "from the hands of spoilsmen and
politicians."[16]

Hence business and not politics was the field for creative endeavor. In
the absence of great issues, as Carnegie said, able men were "unable to
persuade themselves that attention to the administration of laws already
fixed is the highest field."[17] In Canby's boyhood town

no one ever urged a boy to go into politics. It was the broken men, or the weak
incapables, who found it easier to be genial than to work, that became
politicians. We saw them about the Court House or the City Hall, a shifty-eyed
lot, dribbling tobacco juice, badly dressed, never prosperous and self-respecting. They took care of the necessary but inferior functions of civilization ...Let
those who could not make a living otherwise attend to it, and to all politics. That
was our attitude, and everything we saw bore it out.[18]

When the twenty-three-year-old Roosevelt canvassed friends and acquaintances in 1880 about the idea of his entering the state legislature of
New York, he was assured that politics was out of the question for a
gentleman. As the Rooseveltian hero of Paul Leicester Ford's popular
roman-à-clef, *The Honourable Peter Stirling* (1894), reflected in the
mid-Eighties, "Is it a wonder that our government and office-holding is
left to the foreign element? That the native American should prefer any
other work, rather than run the gauntlet of public opinion and press?"[19]

But the logic of all this went strongly against the deeper American
grain. For liberal-minded persons it went especially against the grain of
the heroic movement that, eschewing traditional power-and-glory seeking, had epitomized the American battle for righteousness, namely, the
abolitionist struggle, the memories of which persisted in the minds of
persons like the teacher who said in the early 1900s that since the Civil
War he had not "had a political thrill, except of disgust."[20] Abolitionism
itself had partly resulted from a hunger for commitment at a time when
business seemed to be displacing politics as the central civic activity. In a
speech in the Fifties, Charles Sumner, who said that he could "see little

else at this time among us which can tempt out on to the exposed steeps of public life an honest man," had reproved those persons, "especially among the young and enthusiastic," who "vainly sigh because they were not born in the age of chivalry, or at least in the days of the revolution, not thinking that in this Enterprise [i.e., abolitionism], there is an opportunity of lofty endeavor such as no Paladin of chivalry, or chief of the revolution enjoyed."[21] In addition to running dramatic physical risks and being part of a dramatic group,[22] abolitionists had chivalrously taken on the whole political establishment and fought against the strong on behalf of the weak. As Emerson commented,

if a humane measure is propounded in behalf of the slave, or of the Irishman, or the Catholic, or for the succour of the poor; that sentiment, that project, will have the homage of the hero. That is his nobility, his oath of knighthood, to succor the helpless and oppressed; always to throw himself on the side of weakness, of youth, of hope; on the literal, on the expansive side, never on the defensive, the conserving, the timorous, the lock-and-bolt system.[23]

When the great war of liberation finally came, the historian John Lothrop Motley wrote to the father of Oliver Wendell Holmes:

I do not regret that Wendell is with the army. It is a noble and healthy symptom that brilliant, intellectual, poetical spirits like his spring to arms when a noble cause like ours inspires them. The race of Philip Sidneys is not yet extinct, and I honestly believe that as much genuine chivalry exists in our Free States at this moment as there is or ever was in any part of the world, from the Crusaders down.[24]

Such images were being lost sight of inside the neo-Roman, power-conscious America of the later nineteenth century, just when Carnegie and others were eulogizing America's unique mission as an agent of liberty.

But strong psychological obstacles lay in the way of repeating the abolitionists' antiofficial politics. True, from early after the Civil War individual reformers, such as the founding editor of the *Nation*, E. L. Godkin, who thought of themselves as successors to the abolitionists insisting on morality in an immoral world, had called unfashionably for Civil Service reform and the abolition of the spoils system. And by the Nineties small reform groups concerned with the problems of civic government existed in a number of major cities. But as William Allen White said in 1903, "heretofore people have laughed at [the honest politician], or have doubted him and sneered at him, and so men of that type have turned to money-making pursuits or wasted their political fragrance on the desert air as Mugwumps or as Populists, or have become Socialists and ceased enjoying their meals."[25] Back in the Thirties, reform had been essentially the work of women, ministers, and other "unmasculine" men – a would-be taming and subduing of energy, whether by Prohibition, or education, or rational diet, or the various other recipes for an enlightened and pacific society. The same alignment characterized reform in the Nineties, with related disadvantages.[26]

Reformers were in the unfortunate position of being nay sayers. They were setting themselves against the lively energies of saloon-based politicos who, as Godkin noted in 1896, were "puzzled by the Mugwump's passion for competitive examinations,"[27] and one of whom, the Boston Irish James Michael Curley, stuck the devastating label "Goo Goos" – almost as devastating as the label "Mugwumps" – on the Good Government Association. (The term "Mugwump," adapted from an Indian word meaning "chief" or "great man," had been used derisively of Republicans who refused on moral grounds to support their party's candidate in the 1884 election, and from there it became extended to gentlemanly and moralistic proponents of "clean government" in general.[28]) Problems were also posed for reformers by figures like Mark Hanna, whom William Allen White in 1896 called "the most powerful man on the American continent."[29] In rational terms, they were as obnoxious as any ward boss: Howe, for instance, recalls how Hanna "enriched himself without compunction, believing that the State was a business man's State. It existed for property. It had no other function," and speaks of Hanna's "feudal" conviction that "the men to do the ruling were the men who owned."[30] But in a curious counterpointing to the official ideology of Carnegie and Rockefeller, the resemblance between the saloon bosses and some of the business bosses went deeper at times. In White's words,

the plutocracy which rose out of the last quarter of the nineteenth century was not greedy and circumspect, not in the least aristocratic. It was the autocracy of boots and whiskers which cavorted, danced and pilfered with a certain fine impudence that was not immoral. It was merely a whimsical bias against the cramping respectability of the Decalogue...I suppose my belief in plutocracy in those first ten years of my emergence from school came from a conviction that it was a diverting frolic to let the public be damned.[31]

In his novel *A Certain Rich Man*, White has his financier hero John Barclay point out around 1880 how "murder for the moment in these piping times has become impolite. But true romance is here. Our heroes rob and plunder, and build cities, and swing gayly around the curves of the railroads they have stolen, and swagger through the cities they have levied upon the people to build."[32] Howe talks about Hanna's physical strength, his "courage, directness, and power of command," his "instinct for monopoly," his temperamental lawlessness; and behind Hanna – Hanna squared or cubed – loomed J. Pierpont Morgan, whom a historian calls the "scion of a brilliant, shrewd, and powerful line, . . . in every sense 'to the manor born.' "[33] Even reformers sometimes looked with surprising sympathy on such figures. A Labour writer recalled how the muckraker Lincoln Steffens "always liked the big crooks more than he did the reformers" and "told epic stories" about the "gigantic lootings and skullduggeries" of the big bosses, with their "immense and powerful personalities; men who had achieved power through their own might, men who won because they packed a wallop."[34]

The deadly thing about late nineteenth-century reformism was that in comparison with both ward politics and tycoonism it was dull. Its causes were those recalled later by the editor of the *Century* when he spoke of how his journal had fought on behalf of "International Copyright, Civil Service Reform, Forest Conservation, Free Art, International Arbitration, Kindergarten Instruction, Tenement House Improvement, the Gold Standard, the Australian Ballot, Art in the Home, More Artistic Coinage."[35] As White perceptively suggested in 1900, "the remedy for Hannaism will [only] be found when Hanna's critics give to the exemplification of high civic ideals the force of unqualified success and the charm of virile personality."[36] Furthermore, reformers were apparently challenging certain fundamental business virtues.

The creative energies that Goo-Gooism aspired to limit were formidable. In big business, as Charles and Mary Beard point out, "from the start, dishonesty, chicane, lying, vulgarity, and a fierce passion for lucre [were] united with an intelligence capable of constructing immense agencies for economic service to the public and a philanthropic spirit that [poured] out money for charitable, religious, educational, and artistic plans and purposes." As they also point out, John D. Rockefeller saw thirteen American Presidents come and go during his Napoleonic career, and

all the giants of his time outlasted at least half a dozen Presidents, and many of them left heirs-apparent...Thus, while political power was being shifted from party to party and dissipated among an ever-changing army of captains and subalterns, most of them nameless in history, the sovereignty of the business empire was kept continuously in the hands of a relatively few dominant figures whose grip was firm, whose experience was cumulative, and whose goal was clear.[37]

The railroad tycoon James J. Hill was not being altogether unreasonable when he thought it outrageous that men like himself had to "fight for our lives against...political adventurers who have never done anything but pose and draw a salary."[38] Nor was it only magnates like Carnegie who were impressed by the size and power of industry, with its testimony to the energy, imagination, and persistence of the minds involved. In 1894, for example, the anonymous author of "Homestead as Seen by One of Its Workmen" spoke of how "a sense of the majesty and glory of the display" of the Bessemer converter "is never absent from your thoughts."[39] And a few years later, a muckraking article about the man-killing Illinois Steel Company described "the diabolical hypnotism exercised over the men in a steel mill, from highest to lowest, by the overwhelming majesty of the instruments with which they work."[40] The industrial world was a world of heroes, not only large-scale ones like Carnegie and Morgan, but lesser ones like the steel-plant superintendent who in one emergency worked a 168-hour shift. It was a world, too, of magical abundance, in which, as a muckraker said in 1906, "the richness of the Butte Hill surpasses the treasure of Monte Cristo, and the story of the crimes and passions which seethed about it makes a narrative almost as romantic as the adventures of Edmund Danton."[41] It was a world possessing an awesome momentum, as exemplified by the engine at the 1878 Centennial Exhibition in Philadelphia that stirred William Dean Howells with its "vast and almost silent grandeur" and ineffable strength – "an athlete of steel and iron with not a superfluous ounce of metal on it"[42] – or by the forty-foot dynamo at the Paris Exposition that so impressed Henry Adams at the end of the century with its impersonal symbolic force. In 1902, Frank Norris said of Chicago that it was Empire, the restless subjugation of all this central world of the lakes and the prairies."[43] His attitude was echoed by the wealthy young New Yorker in Owen Johnson's *The Sixty-First Second*, who exclaimed of Wall Street that "the whole vibrating industry of the nation is here, within a quarter of a mile – the great projects of development, the wars of millions, the future of immense territories to the West and the South."[44]

Hence, paradoxically, reformism was perceived as not only unmanly but immoral. It was natural that people had what Winston Churchill in his popular political novel *Mr. Crewe's Career* (1908) called "a faith in the divine right of Imperial Railroads to rule."[45] It was natural that power and order came together and that the Senate was unabashedly the instrument of business. It was natural and it was moral, and to object to such things was against both order and nature. The system's efficiency was embodied in figures like the political boss of Pennsylvania described by Howe, who linked up railroads, steel, mining and other interests, including saloons and organized vice, into an *"imperium in imperio"* controlling "practically all of the offices of the State."[46] The system's authority was reinforced by the moral certainty of old-style New England men of practical power, like Judge Seton B. Barton in *The Sixty-First Second*, "representative of the great oil interests, . . . the grim Yankee, unrelieved by . . . modifying humor, implacable in small things as well as great, knowing no other interests in life except the passion of acquiring," or George Apley's father, convinced that "affairs will always be controlled by a small group. I, and my group, have controlled them."[47] In consequence, a good deal of weight lay behind the complaint to a young reformer in *Mr. Crewe's Career* that "You don't seem to have any notion of decency or order, or any idea of the principle on which this government was based."[48] And it was really not illogical that, in Howe's words, "the lawyer who took the case of a widow whose husband had been killed in the steel-mills was an 'ambulance-chaser,' while the attorney who represented the corporation responsible for the injury was elected president of the Union Club." Even ward-level politics had its moral ambushes for would-be reformers. In his account of his discovery of that politics in the Nineties in New York, Howe recalled the genuine indignation of a couple of municipal councillors when he voted the wrong way: "They had stuck to their friends, I had betrayed them. They had been faithful to the only political ideals they recognized, which was to keep your word no matter what it cost and to be loyal to those who were loyal to you. From their point of view I had been guilty of the one offense that could not be forgiven."[49]

A reformer like Howe therefore suffered from a double sense of bad faith. As he says of the code of the leading Cleveland businessmen, "industry was war, with the employer and employee on opposite sides of the trenches. The no man's land of this warfare was occupied by liberals and reformers, deserters from their class, entitled, by its pitiless judgment, not even to the rules of humane warfare." But the worst of it was that "I wanted to be part of this herd, even while I hated the things that it did. I wanted wealth, even though I knew that great wealth could only be gotten by means of which I disapproved. I wanted approval from my crowd and from myself as well. That was my conflict."[50] Howe's testimony is all the more revealing because he was an energetic and earnest young man, a prime example of the emergent middle-class professional who was not only morally indignant but had acquired professional credentials, in his case a Ph.D. in political science from the new Johns Hopkins graduate school.

Plainly, a major force was needed to bring about the abrupt change of direction at the start of the new century, the breakthrough that made it possible for many people to challenge confidently the moral authority of business as the supreme embodiment of purposeful energy. The necessary changes in perception had not been produced by a president like Grover Cleveland, who, for all his moral courage and integrity, lacked glamor, had evaded service in the Civil War, and thought of civil-service reform in terms of business principles. Nor could they have been brought about simply by reform politicians like Governors John P. Altgeld of Illinois and

Reform

Robert M. LaFollette of Wisconsin, who, estimable as they were, were too distant from the dominant East.

TEDDY ROOSEVELT – TRANSFORMER

The decisive shift was, of course, effected by "that damn cowboy" Teddy Roosevelt, at forty-two the youngest American president. As one of the editors of Collier's wrote in 1905, Americans "want a moral reality and a moral tone...Theodore Roosevelt is the only statesman, alive or dead, in reading whose speeches you will find the exact note struck which is the note of to-day toward reform, the note which other politicians, all over the country, are beginning to use."[51] A decade later John Reed would report without irony of Roosevelt's supporters at the Progressive Party convention that "Teddy was not Teddy to them; he was Democracy – he was justice and fairness and the cause of the poor...A mighty warrior had risen up to champion the Square Deal."[52] Roosevelt was a transformer, a redefiner of possibilities, both through his political doings and writings and through the extensive media attention given to him. ("The heart of Roosevelt's method was to inspire headlines," Mark Sullivan remarked.[53]) By the end of 1903, according to a Collier's editorial, he had already, in a major symbolic substitution, taken the center of the public stage away from Pierpont Morgan, with whom he was to continue locked in conflict. When he was elected president in his own right in 1906, he would become the most popular president since Andrew Jackson, and the best-known public figure anywhere.

More was involved than simply the Rooseveltian moral strenuousness that Collier's Norman Hapgood called "the central note of American politics to-day, the note of the future, the mark of the new."[54] Looking back to his first meeting with Roosevelt in 1896, William Allen White recalls how "he sounded in my heart the first trumpet call of the new time that was to be," and speaks of "the marvel that I saw in this young man," who "poured into my heart such visions, such ideals, such hopes, such a new attitude toward life and patriotism and the meaning of things, as I had never dreamed men had."[55] It was through Roosevelt that certain chivalric patterns decisively reentered American politics, with lasting consequences.

To begin with, a reintegration of gentlemanliness and civic effectiveness took place. As White noted in 1906, when Roosevelt first entered public life his opponents called him a Mugwump, and he had to fight for his political independence.[56] He was a gentleman, an intellectual, an author, a moralist, a Harvard man of eminently respectable lineage

119

who, like Frank Merriwell as described by an admiring fellow student, "will not drink,...does not smoke, and I never have heard him cuss."[57] When he first joined the New York legislature he was, as an associate recalled, "a joke...a dude [in] the way he combed his hair, the way he talked – the whole thing."[58] Like the Goo-Goos he cared about dreary things like slum housing, and police corruption, and trusts, and impure food, and stock-market manipulations, and income-tax reform, and land conservation. But in fact he was a long way from being one of those Mugwumps he detested; his reformist drive was not a further example of nay-saying, energy-lowering restrictiveness.

For one thing, he was famously pugnacious, whether as a freshman New York state senator challenging the machine system, or as chairman of the New York police board, or as president. Owen Wister said later of his 1902 antitrust suit against Morgan's Northern Securities Corporation that "I doubt if any President since Andrew Jackson... had raised any turmoil such as that which arose around it...I think that to make up his mind to take this first step, to declare this war, on the captains of industry, was a stroke of genius."[59] And he persisted in his outrageousness. During the financial panic of 1907, for example, he had the effrontery to speak of "certain malefactors of great wealth," with particular reference to the railroad magnate Edward H. Harriman,[60] and in the following year he dared to criticize the Supreme Court for being too free with injunctions against strikers. It is beside the point that he was relatively unsuccessful as police commissioner, or that he tacked and veered in his domestic policies, or that his trust busting was less fierce than radicals could wish. What mattered was that he created new possibilities. He was the first president since Jackson to commit serious lèse-majesté against the powers of business, the president under whom, between 1902 and 1907, actions were brought under the Sherman Act against forty corporations, twenty-four of them leading to indictments. The father of John P. Marquand's Henry Pulham considered him a "social menace" whose "attack upon self-respecting men, who had made the nation what it was, broke down confidence."[61]

Furthermore, Roosevelt's pugnaciousness was inseparable from his morally charged physicality. As he said in his autobiography in 1913,

having been a sickly boy, with no natural bodily prowess, and having lived much at home, I was at first quite unable to hold my own when thrown into contact with other boys of rougher antecedents. I was nervous and timid. Yet from reading of the people I admired – ranging from the soldiers of Valley Forge, and Morgan's riflemen, to the heroes of my favorite stories – and from hearing of the feats performed by my Southern forefathers and kinfolk, and from knowing my father, I felt a great admiration for men who were fearless and who could hold their own in the world, and I had a great desire to be like them.[62]

He was a classic example of the potential weakling who turned himself into something very different, mastering his boyhood asthma, building up his body, boxing in college despite his poor sight. During his three years of ranching in the Dakota Badlands in the Eighties, he overcame the drawbacks of being a buck-toothed, squeaky-voiced, college-spoken, glasses-wearing, and clean-living dude who used expletives like "By Godfrey!" and on one memorable occasion exhorted a cowboy to "Hasten forward quickly there!"[63] He risked his life among real bullets in the charge up San Juan Hill, hunted big game in Africa when he was blind in one eye, and gave a campaign speech in Milwaukee in 1912 immediately after having been shot by a would-be assassin. In general, he demonstrated that, as his father had taught him, "a gentleman did not give points to the 'rowdy' on any manly count. He outstripped the rowdy on all scores except his vices. If he did not, he must expect to be thought effeminate, and his code ridiculed."[64]

In all this he enjoyed himself famously and was identified as much with his grin, his infectious laugh, his exclamations of "Bully!" and "*Dee*-lighted!," as with his adage about walking softly and carrying a big stick. As he says of himself during his ranching years, "we felt the beat of hardy life in our veins, and ours was the glory of work and the joy of living."[65] He loved entertaining, and was recalled by Wister characteristically exclaiming during one particularly animated dinner-table conversation in the White House, "Oh, *aren't* we having a good time!"[66] His voracious inquisitiveness moved H. G. Wells to call him "the seeking mind of America displayed" and comment that "any spark may fire the mind of President Roosevelt. His range of reading is amazing; he seems to be echoing with all the thought of the time, he has receptivity to the pitch of genius. And he does not merely receive, he digests and reconstructs; he thinks."[67] He loved combat, controversy, and flamboyant role playing, and, in William Allen White's words, "if he could combine danger with a frolicking intrigue, would get an inner joy out of it that was like the consolation of a great faith."[68] He displayed strong feelings openly, whether courting Alice Hathaway Lee or rushing off to the 1898 war. Even the semiautobiographical hero of Max Eastman's political novel *Venture*, after voicing his general disapproval, acknowledged that "the point is that he enjoys life. There isn't another man in the world that is having as good a time right now, every second, all day long, as Theodore Roosevelt. He's alive – that is why the world loves him. He's the livest kid on earth. That's the only reason why he's famous, and that's a real reason."[69]

In all this, certain important synthesizings were going on.

If Roosevelt appealed to the public as strongly as he did, it was partly because of his persisting youthfulness. As Wells noted, "in his undisciplined hastiness, his limitations, his prejudices, his unfairness, his frequent errors, just as much as in his force, his sustained courage, his integrity, his open intelligence, he stands for his people and his kind."[70] When he was police commissioner, a contemporary remarked that "the peculiarity about him is that he has what is essentially a boy's mind." And William Allen White recalled "the infantile, or perhaps adolescent hunger in his heart" for danger that "rendered him inexplicable [in the White House] to men of solemn and somber maturity."[71] Naturally, his career and personality were peculiarly attractive to the young. As one of his biographers comments, his life – the life of someone who had been among other things a cowboy and deputy sheriff – "was the ultimate dream of every typical American boy: he fought in a war, killed lions, became President, and quarrelled with the Pope."[72] Appropriately, too, he was the first American president to be known almost universally by the boyhood diminutive of his first name. In view of the tension-creating exclusions and narrowings in the post-Civil War Spencerian idea of maturity, this public restoration of continuities between childhood and adulthood was very important.

The range of activities that Roosevelt enjoyed transcended simple dichotomies and antitheses. He unabashedly enjoyed sports, *and* moneymaking (as a rancher), *and* evening-dress entertaining, *and* soldiering, *and* "culture." And he gave himself to both the heroic and the pastoral. If he notoriously adored hunting, he also displayed an abiding interest in conservation, which resulted in the creation of five national parks, fifty-one wildlife refuges, and over sixteen million acres of forest reserves and led the Beards to say that without his "spirited fight the remnants of the public domain already reserved by executive action might have been thrown to the hungry accumulators at the portals."[73] If in the Nineties he cheerfully talked of annexing Canada and informed the cadets at the Naval War College that "no triumph of peace is quite so great as the supreme triumphs of war," by 1906 Wells was able to report of him that "to-day, at any rate, the 'Teddy' legend is untrue. Perhaps it wasn't always quite untrue. There was a time during the world predominance of Mr. Kipling, when I think the caricature must have come close to certain of Mr. Roosevelt's acceptances and attitudes. But that was ten years and more ago."[74] In the same year, he received the Nobel Peace Prize for his peace-making activities in the Russo-Japanese war. Moreover, for Roosevelt the rural was not simply a region of down-on-the-farm, cold-water purity in contrast to the bustle and glamor of the city, but a place where business and sport enjoyably intermingled; and big-city activities, rather than being simply grim and anxious struggles for self-advancement, continued the fun of childhood. Symbolically, too, the much-publicized Rough Riders successfully inter-

Reform

mingled Westerners like Bucky O'Neill and Easterners like Dudley Dean ("perhaps the best quarterback who ever played on a Harvard Eleven,")[75], and the "Roosevelt Familiars" at the White House included such diverse temperaments as Henry and Brooks Adams, Oliver Wendell Holmes, Henry Cabot Lodge, Lincoln Steffens, and the creator of Mr. Dooley, Finley Peter Dunne. Describing Henry Adams bidding farewell to Roosevelt and his family when they left the White House in 1909, Owen Wister reflected that

he could easily have quoted – perhaps in his heart he was quoting – Sir Bedivere to Arthur:
> "But now the whole Round Table is dissolved
> Which was an image of the mighty world."[76]

Roosevelt's White House had, in fact, been a good deal more like Camelot than John F. Kennedy's would be.

All these characteristics bore on Roosevelt's moral authority vis-à-vis business, and the force of his example for the young. As Richard Hofstadter notes, "his popularity was due in large part to the fact that Americans, in the search for money and power that had grown so intense in the Gilded Age, had lost much of their capacity for enjoyment, and that Roosevelt, with his variety and exuberance and his perpetual air of expectation, restored the consciousness of other ends that made life worth living."[77] He vividly demonstrated that even in an urbanizing, industrializing, technological society, one should aspire to more than mere efficiency; that it was not simply the concentrated pursuit of long-term and large-scale goals that counted; that ostensibly small occasions and gestures could also be charged with meaning. He showed, too, that winning was not in fact the only thing, and that how one won and the quality of what one won were no less important. As a writer said in *Collier's* in 1902, he embodied "the spirit of clean, manly sport. The old notion was that sport was mainly a struggle for a prize – a mug or a sum of money. The prize which Roosevelt holds up is the happiness of having been in an honorable struggle and having, in that struggle, strengthened our bodies and freshened our spirits against the mental work of the day."[78] Most significantly, as H. L. Mencken, no fan of Roosevelt's, perceived,

what he stood most clearly in opposition to was the superior pessimism of the three Adams brothers – the notion that the public problems of a democracy are unworthy the thought and effort of a civilized and self-respecting man... Against this suicidal aloofness Roosevelt always hurled himself with brave effort. Enormously sensitive and resilient, almost pathological in his appetite for activity, he made it plain to every one that the most stimulating sort of sport imaginable was to be obtained in fighting, not for mere money, but for ideas.[79]

Part II Chivalric patterns in industrializing America

In sum, it was a new, high-energy – and chivalric – moral pattern that Roosevelt displayed and that gave him a moral weight equal to that of the complacently sermonizing Carnegie, or the insolently imperial Morgan, or the coldly self-righteous Rockefeller. Here too it is irrelevant that in various ways he was strongly probusiness. What mattered was that he could say, and mean, such things as, "I neither respect nor admire the huge moneyed man to whom money is the be-all and end-all of existence; to whom the acquisition of untold millions is the supreme goal of life."[80] As I said, he was a transformer. What one of his biographers calls his "favorite aphorism," as "offered to untold numbers of dazzled small boys," "Don't flinch, don't foul, hit the line hard,"[81] was, of course, one that could encourage the new-style college-business aggressiveness that I described in Chapter 6. But in Theodore P. Greene's words, "As he had removed the curse of idleness from inherited wealth, so Roosevelt had dispelled the dirt and dishonor too often associated with politics";[82] and he had demonstrated that the college graduate not only need not go into business, but could energetically oppose businessmen. William Allen White recalls how reading Roosevelt's *American Ideals and Other Essays* around 1896 "shook my foundations, for it questioned things as they are. It challenged a complacent plutocracy. I did not dream that anyone, save the fly-by-night demagogues of Populism, had any question about the divine right of the well-to-do to rule the world."[83]

"PROUD OF ALL THE IRISH BLOOD THAT'S IN ME"

These new possibilities that Roosevelt displayed were related to another development, without which they would not have had the impact that they did. In the later Nineties, the American-Irish generation born in the Sixties and Seventies were coming to maturity. Roosevelt's potency for the well-bred Protestant young who identified themselves with figures like the Three Musketeers was partly due to his embodying romantic qualities that they perceived in the Irish. And by helping to validate some of the more problematic Irish characteristics he made it easier for the Protestant young to move closer to Irish patterns, and for the Irish young to have more confidence in those patterns.

The well-known pugnaciousness of the "fighting Irish" had presented some obvious difficulties. In romantic fiction, the Irish gentleman-adventurer and soldier of fortune was a charmer, like the Chevalier O'Keefe imagined by one of Fitzgerald's young Wasps, "a semi-fictional Irishman – the wild sort with a genteel brogue and 'reddish hair.' He was exiled from Erin in the late days of chivalry and, of course, crossed over to France."[84] But the flesh-and-blood reality was

124

Reform

something else. Canby, looking back to his Maryland youth, remembered how "the Irish laborers would stagger home drunk on Saturday nights through our street, hugging the maple trees and talking to themselves," and said of the "micks," the "tough boy[s] from the slums or the near slums," with whom "no relations except combat were possible," that they "had no code. They put stones in their snowballs ...They spat in faces and kicked below the belt. I think that for us, with ideals reflected from our elders, they represented the anarchy and lawlessness that ever since the Civil War the country has been trying to subdue...They were the evil, the disorganizing principle, which roused the opposite in us."[85] The Irish had dominated the illegal sport of bare-knuckle prize fighting in the decades before the Civil War, and had figured prominently in the formidable New York gangs of the Seventies and Eighties and in the sometimes equally pugnacious forces of law and order. ("That's the good life – if anyone says boo to him he'd split their skull open with his club," a Donegal youth in one of Joyce Cary's novels says admiringly in the Nineties of a brother in the American police.)[86] The flesh-and-blood fighting Irishman was likely to be the kind to whom, in William V. Shannon's words, "the old-fashioned term 'mucker' used to be applied. Hard-drinking, quick to take offense, carrying a large Irish chip in his shoulder."[87]

Nevertheless, changes both in the facts and in how they were perceived were going on, so that within a few years, according to Shannon, "the phrase 'fighting Irish'...became a proud boast, and the image of the two-fisted, freckle-faced, red-headed Irishman who is twice as brave as anyone else had passed irretrievably into American folklore."[88] In part this resulted from the growing prominence of the Irish in popular sports, and from changes in those sports, changes created partly by the Irish. In boxing especially, the prestige of the great John L. Sullivan, in Shannon's words, "helped give Irish aggressiveness a more popular and genial cast," particularly after the introduction of Queensberry rules in the championship fight in 1892 in which he was beaten by Gentleman Jim Corbett. The Irish image had also been helped by the enthusiastic Irish participation in the war of 1898, in which a group of journalists had taken for granted that the first trooper up San Juan Hill would be found to be "a red-haired Irishman."[89] And the higher educational system saw the emergence of new-style Irish gentlemen and sportsmen, such as the Georgetown- and Oxford-educated, polo-playing editor of *Collier's*, Rob Collier, "handsome, elegantly dressed, with great personal charm, a flair for the dramatic gesture, and a buoyant Irish humor,"[90] or Joseph P. Kennedy, whose all-round prep-school career in the early 1900s later reminded *Fortune* of Frank Merriwell. Subsequently, of course, the

Irish tough guy himself would be glamorized in movie figures like James Cagney and in that virtual Irishman, Scott Fitzgerald's "elegant young rough-neck" the Great Gatsby.

With an increased acceptance of the pugnaciousness – a pugnaciousness like Roosevelt's own – came an increased responsiveness to the Irish insouciance, and theatricality, and stylishness, and charm, the qualities of those "wild, delightful Irish boys" living alongside the Erie Canal with whom the young Frederic Howe had been forbidden to play, the qualities that Max Eastman referred to when he spoke of the "mischievously Irish" light in Isadora Duncan's eyes and her "cult of impulse and impracticality, rapture and abandon," the qualities that T. S. Eliot tipped his hat to in the ur-version of *The Waste Land* when he quoted George M. Cohan's "Proud of all the Irish blood that's in me, / Divil a man can say a word agin me."[91] The appeal of style and flair had been abundantly testified to by Twain, whose own enthusiasm for them was epitomized in Huck's exhilaration at the circus and his statement, apropos of a raft "as long going by as a procession," that "there was a power of style about her. It *amounted* to something being a raftsman on such a craft as that."[92] It would be testified to many times subsequently: Nick Carraway, for example, observed of Gatsby that "if personality is an unbroken series of successful gestures, then there was something gorgeous about him, some heightened sensitivity to the promises of life"; and when Bing Crosby died, a *Newsweek* writer noted that "a great and important presence has departed. He embodied America's aspirations to be carefree, secure and graceful."[93] Style manifested itself at times in theatricality like that of Rafael Sabatini's gentleman-swordsman Scaramouche, who "was the actor always: a man ever calculating the effect he would produce, ever avoiding self-revelation, ever concerned to overlay his real character by an assumed and quite fictitious one."[94]

Irish charm had its political aspects, too. In his recollections of Irish Harlem, to which his family moved in 1914, the novelist Henry Roth remembered how "the Irish didn't want to make a lot of money. Somehow they wanted to express themselves to the fullest and enjoy themselves. They had a different set of values from those regarded as Jewish values."[95] Some of the Irish did indeed make a great deal of money, such as old-style buccaneers like Boss Tweed in the 1860s and new-style ones like Joseph P. Kennedy. For a good many, however, what mattered most was politics. Acording to Shannon, the Irish "had an instinct for power and an understanding that political power exists to be used."[96] And in their pursuit of power, style counted for a good deal, as exemplified in the career of the dandyish Jim Curley, who, in Shannon's words, "kept the greater part of the Boston populace half-drunk with fantasies, invective, and showmanship" for over thirty years."[97] Embodied in style and "class" was the feeling, both validated by and corroborating Roosevelt's activities, that quality mattered as much as quantity, and that winning was not incompatible with humane values. Moreover, far from being machinelike, Irish political life was remarkable for its sociability. The fictive spokesman of the emergent Irish, Finley Peter Dunne's beloved Mr. Dooley, was, appropriately, a saloon keeper. As Frederic Howe had noted, ward politics was basically the politics of the Irish clan transposed to the city: The working man gave his loyalty to chieftans who took his individual problems seriously. And the saloon, so important in ward politics, was a pastoral-heroic locale of drinking and eating, of storytelling and elaborate boasting, of fighting and gambling. It also served as a base for the gangs that had evolved out of the construction gangs of the earlier part of the century; and the Irish gang, as Shannon points out, "put together in an amalgam of its own the precepts of loyalty, obedience, and neighborly cooperation emphasized in the home with the ideals of aggressiveness, daring, and self-help acquired in the school."[98] Significantly, too, Franklin Roosevelt's Secretary of Labor, Frances Perkins, would remember discovering, to her surprise, that at Tammany Hall during the Wilson years "a lady was invariably treated with respect and gallantry and a poor old woman with infinite kindness and courtesy."[99]

THE REBIRTH OF MILITANCY

The new Gestalt that I have been describing had substantial consequences.

As Wells pointed out in 1906, "an increasing number of wealthy young men have followed President Roosevelt into political life," and it was "from the universities that the deliberate invasion of the political machine by independent men of honor and position – of whom President Roosevelt is the type and chief – proceeds."[100] The transformation going on was epitomized in Dink Stover, who, disturbed by the contradictions in college life and the argument that "good government, independent thinking, the love of the fight for the right thing ought to begin here in the enthusiasm of it all,"[101] turned away from his initial commitment to football and club success and, making friends with the "wrong" kinds of college men, became interested in issues demanding a genuine and not merely class-oriented chivalric courage. It was epitomized too in the challenges to the big Republican machine by the young New England hero of Churchill's *Mr. Crewe's Career*, Austin Vane, after his return from a spell out West. What was being demonstrated was the wisdom of the assertion by one of Stover's new friends – perhaps echoing William Allen White – that "the only remedy, the

127

only way to fight the business deal, is to interest young men in politics, to make them feel that there are the new battle-fields."[102]

With Roosevelt in the White House, reformism now appeared an eminently manly activity – agonistic, heroic, gallant. As Theodore P. Greene reports in his study of magazine heroes, "physically the Progressive heroes in all occupations were models of the strenuous life. A clergyman had "the squared shoulders of an athlete, the firm face of a fighter'; a labor leader 'was able-bodied in every sense – stalwart, square-shouldered, powerful.' "[103] The manliness, moreover, was not just a hard aggressiveness. If Roosevelt was the great paradigm of the reformer who *enjoyed* himself, he was not the only one. Frederic Howe remembered affectionately the Falstaffian gusto ("open, frank, and joyous, like a big boy"[104]), the generous hospitality, the fearlessness and love of argument of Tom Johnson, the Kentucky-born businessman who as reform mayor of Cleveland in the early 1900s likewise helped to bring the idealistic young into politics. And the politician-novelist Brand Whitlock spoke similarly of the boyish innocence, the wit and humor, the love of art and music, of the other great Reform mayor of the period, Buffalo's "Golden Rule" Jones, who "was a big Welshman with a sandy complexion and great hands that had worked hard in their time, and he had an eye that looked right into the center of your skull. He wore...a large cream-colored slouch hat, and he had on the flowing cravat which for some inexplicable reason artists and social reformers wear."[105]

Furthermore, the new political activities were perceived in strongly chivalric-martial terms. With an ironic appropriateness, a newspaper editorial in 1901 reported of Mark Twain that "the genial humorist of the earlier days is now a reformer of the vigorous kind, a sort of knight errant who does not hesitate to break a lance with either Church or State."[106] And a growing number of champions were becoming visible and being praised, such as the circuit attorney eulogized in *McClure's* in 1903 "who, single-handed, has brought to bay the bankers, lawyers, corporation managers, and politicians – the boodle ring that robbed St. Louis and rules it yet."[107] Like Roosevelt tackling Morgan's Northern Securities Corporation, the champion was not afraid to take on the large adversary, including those powerful antireform forces that, as a writer complained in 1907, were "unhorsing alike faithful public servant, civic champion, and knight-errant of conscience, and all the while gathering into loathesome captivity the souls of multitudes of young men."[108] And by a natural process of association, the figure of the champion merged with the idea of the crusade. In William Allen White's words, "the insurgents [of the period], who were later called progressives, had the crusaders' ardor and felt for one another the crusaders' fellowship. They sang songs, carried banners, marched in parades, created heroes out of

128

their own ideals."[109] And Howe said of Tom Johnson's "ten-year fight against privilege" that "to the young men in the movement, and to tens of thousands of the poor who gave it their support," it was "a moral crusade rarely paralleled in American politics." Such activities permitted a feeling of being engaged in contests as heroic as those of big business and machine politics. Under Johnson, said Howe, "we were lieutenants, giving unstinted affection to a leader who needed little else from us. He had the resourcefulness of a Napoleon and unwearying courage. He gave us daily adventure, put us in the places where we could do our best work, and we worked under him like players in a football squad."[110] Whitlock compared the enthusiasm of Johnson's young men for their city to "that love which undergraduates have for their university, the *esprit de corps* of the crack regiment."[111]

The images of those on whose behalf the champions fought, and those against whom they did so, were also changing. The standard Social Darwinist picture, as I have said, was of a society in which those at the top were deservedly there because they were strong, and those at the bottom were deservedly there because they were weak, so that to intervene on behalf of the latter and make a fuss about what happened to working-class women and children was to weaken society's moral fiber and interfere with the processes of natural selection. As a millionaire in Robert Herrick's power-fantasy novel *A Life for a Life* (1910) remarked to a would-be reformer, "Think well...Think before you range yourself hopelessly on the other side – with the feeble and the ineffective."[112] But in the new reformist terms, it was as legitimate to intervene on behalf of the innocent at the bottom as it had been in the romances. Furthermore, the strong at the top were no longer sacrosanct. Roosevelt, a historian observes, "destroyed all the rubber-stamp dignity that financial America had labored to build up in its figureheads." And whereas criticism in the nineties, in the words of another, was "phrased in general terms and seldom specified the persons and corporations being attacked,"[113] attacks in the early 1900s were specific and pointed. David Graham Phillips, for example, assailed eminent senators by name in his series of articles "The Treason of the Senate" in 1906, much to their annoyance, and *Collier's* contained editorial comments like, "We observe the following choice quotation from young Mr. Rockefeller: 'Half of the people in the world to-day are on the wrong scent in pursuit of happiness. They seem to think it consists in having and getting and in being served by others'...Dear, dear, dear, in which half does the Rockefeller family belong?"[114] Far from looking strong and heroic and ultramanly in comparison with reformers, a number of power figures now appeared positively contemptible in their business or political conduct, a matter to which I shall return later. Some businessmen, in fact, seemed almost pitiable. Progressive journals emphasized, for example, how there was little or no friendship between magnates, and in *Mr. Crewe's Career* the young reform politician Austin Vane tells his railroad-lawyer New England father, "You never learned how to enjoy life, did you...? I don't believe you ever really had a good time."[115] The same point was made in Gibson's cartoon in *Collier's*, "Mr. A. Merger Hogg is Taking a Few Days' Much-Needed Rest at His Country Home," in which a stiff Rockefeller-like figure in city clothes stands brooding worriedly in front of a ticker-tape mach ne set up on the lawn in front of his chateau, while a frazzled typist slaves away on a rustic seat and a male secretary is busy at a telephone attached to a tree.[116] As the pioneer muckraker Henry Demarest Lloyd said in *Wealth against Commonwealth* (1894), "there is a strong suggestion of moral insanity in the unrelieved sameness of mood and unvarying repetition of one act in the life of the model merchant. Sane minds by an irresistible law alternate one tension with another."[117]

Such attitudes were particularly consequential for journalism. Journalism had, of course, always provided opportunities for the pugnacious, especially in the antebellum years, when, in W. J. Cash's words, "one can almost write the last chapter in the life of a newspaper editor in the Southern country...without making enquiry...The record is rich in entries of 'fatally wounded in a duel,' or 'shot dead in the streets'. "[118] Journalists had tended, too, to be men who did not work regular hours, were catholic in the company they kept, and gathered some of their information in saloons. And their profession had something of the magic of theater about it, in the mysteriousness of its creative processes and the public's uncertainty up until the last minute as to what the finished product would be like. Hence Mencken could recollect of a particular newspaperman in his boyhood that "he was genuinely Somebody in that remote and obscure village, and the fact radiated from him like heat from a stove...He became to me a living symbol of the power and dignity of the press – a walking proof of its romantic puissance."[119] And Howe's daydreams during one phase of his youth in the Eighties "were always of a metropolitan newspaper, of a noisy city office with men rushing in and out."[120] Journalism could sometimes have substantial social consequences, as well. Back in the Seventies, *The New York Times*, *Harper's Magazine*, and the cartoons of Thomas B. Nast had between them brought about the downfall of the Tweed ring in New York, and there had been other campaigns since then in journals like Godkin's *New York Evening Post*, Lloyd's *Chicago News*, and Joseph Pulitzer's *New York World*.

But it was in the early years of the new century, when newspapers had become established as a major industry in every town, and national weeklies and monthlies were prospering, that journalism really came into its own as a glamorous enterprise. Richard Harding Davis, with his Gibson good looks, his impeccable tailoring, his energy, flair, and courage, had exalted the Special Correspondent. The drama of press life had intensified after that aficionado of the scoop, the Harvard-educated William Randolph Hearst, moved in on New York in the mid-Nineties. The corps of war correspondents, with Davis at their head, had further glamorized the profession in 1898, not least because, like Davis and Stephen Crane in Greece the year before, they sometimes came under fire themselves. And when Roosevelt became President, he threw the doors of the White House wide open to reporters. Within two or three years, the muckraking movement was under way, and investigative journalists like Lincoln Steffens, Ida M. Tarbell, Ray Stannard Baker, David Graham Phillips, and others were providing for their readers, in a historian's words, a new "cast of characters for the drama of American society: bosses, professional politicians, reformers, racketeers, captains of industry."[121] Until the end of the Roosevelt years, reform politics and muckraking investigations into things like political corruption, slum housing, adulterated foodstuffs, "vice," and the activities of trusts would be inseparably intertwined.

The influence of turn-of-the-century romanticism was particularly visible in the entry into muckraking of journals like *McClure's* and *Collier's*. After a brief false start with articles like "A Day with Gladstone" and "Where Man Got His Ears," *McClure's* had become in the Nineties a major purveyor of romanticism, inducing in the young William Allen White when he met the editorial team in 1897 the thrilled reflection that "these people knew Rudyard Kipling. They knew Robert Louis Stevenson. They had dealt with Anthony Hope."[122] With the war of 1898 – a key influence on muckraking, according to Ida M. Tarbell –the journal suddenly became, as she put it, "a part of active, public life. Having tasted blood, it could no longer be content with being merely attractive, readable."[123] And with Sam McClure's hero Roosevelt in the White House, it was natural for an interest in white men's burdens to be displaced from foreign to domestic affairs. The chivalric influence was even plainer in *Collier's*, of which Theodore P. Greene remarks that, "if Progressivism was a movement in which the educated took an unusual role in popular leadership, *Collier's*...was the key Progressive journal."[124] Rob Collier himself, who at twenty-eight took over the editor-ownership in 1901 from his father, was remembered by Finley Peter Dunne as "a gay, reckless, laughing Irishman....the Beau Sabreur of journalism in his time."[125] Norman Hapgood, brought in by Rob Collier as editor the following year at the age of thirty-three, came from an old New England family and, after graduating from the Harvard Law

School, had become bored with corporate law and turned to journalism. The third member of the editorial triumvirate, Mark Sullivan, who joined the staff in 1906 at the age of thirty-one, resembled Dink Stover's beau ideal and role model at Yale in that, the son of Irish immigrant parents, he had become self-supporting by managing a country newspaper and paid his own way through Harvard and the Harvard Law School. It was a Musketeer-like group with a strong distaste for commercialization and corruption. The journal it put out was marked by a liking for elegance and fair play, and a Rooseveltian jauntiness.

Moreover, even though the muckraking movement ended in the Wilson years, the muckraking attitudes stayed alive. The *Nation*, after Oswald Garrison Villard revitalized it in 1917, provided a forum for independent-minded journalists and in the Twenties and Thirties ran exposés of such things as the Sacco and Vanzetti case, the Teapot Dome scandal, the activities of the Ku Klux Klan, and the shocking conditions of agricultural workers in California, a fighting tradition continued later under the editorship of Carey McWilliams, and paralleled in the *St. Louis Post-Dispatch*. In the Thirties, Edmund Wilson ventured into investigative reporting in the *New Republic* articles assembled as *The American Jitters* (1932), and Matthew Josephson wrote *The Robber Barons* (1934), and Drew Pearson, the son of a Swarthmore professor and a contributor to the *New Republic*, began his swashbuckling "Washington-Merry-Go-Round" column, which would be carried on after his death by Jack Anderson. Ralph Ingersoll's vigorously liberal New York daily *PM* won itself an honored place in the Forties for its eight years of forceful reporting and its in-depth investigations by journalists like James A. Wechsler (subsequently the editor of the liberal *New York Post*) of topics like slum housing, pro-Axis newspaper chains, and the internal *Realpolitik* of the State Department. In the Fifties, I. F. Stone, who had worked on both *PM* and the *Nation*, started his Washington newsletter *I. F. Stone's Weekly* with the convictions that "every government is run by liars" – "a *prima facie* assumption until proven wrong" – and that "a government always reveals a good deal, if you take the trouble to find what it says";[126] the *Texas Observer* started poking into the rich stew of Texas politics; and the *Village Voice* began its uncovering of political corruption, business rapaciousness, police brutality, and the rest, by writers like Jack Newfield and Nat Hentoff. In the Sixties and early Seventies, of course, muckraking broke out everywhere, on a scale recalling the Roosevelt years, and toppled a president. Throughout, investigative reporting and the activities of researchers like Ralph Nader have been marked by a lack of reverence for the rich and powerful, a conviction of being engaged in heroic enterprises deserving one's full allegiance, and a resolute refusal to be bought off or intimidated.[127]

And just as journalism in the Sixties recalled the Roosevelt years, so did the Kennedyism whose paradoxical nature I mentioned in Chapter 1. In the Kennedy mystique one sees the same continuities and transpositions, the same paradoxical interweavings of fictiveness, factuality, and practical power that I have been tracing in these pages.

In obvious ways, Kennedyism was imbued with fictiveness, especially in the dominant metaphor of Camelot, which was urged upon that chronicler of presidents, Theodore H. White, by John F. Kennedy's widow. In White's words, "She *wanted* Camelot to top the story. Camelot, heroes, fairy tales, legends, were what history was all about ...So the epitaph on the Kennedy Administration became Camelot – a magic moment in American history, when gallant men danced with beautiful women, when great deeds were done, when artists, writers and poets met at the White House, and the barbarians beyond the walls held back"[128] – all this, of course, under the aegis of a brilliant, gay, fearless young ruler aided by a beautiful, charming, intelligent, and adored young consort. The young ruler perished tragically just as he was coming into his prime and was about to transform the rest of the kingdom into a realm of grace and power; and his natural successor, the next of the extraordinary brothers, soon followed him into the shades. Thereafter drabness and darkness lay on the land, except for the intermittently flickering light of the youngest brother. It is the stuff of fairy stories, of course – Arthur and Guinevere, Gatsby and Daisy, Scott and Zelda, and all the other beautiful doomed couples, and it has deservedly invited debunking.[129] It is plain, too, that Kennedy consciously borrowed from not only the structures but the styles and personae of the two Roosevelts, and that only his Scott Fitzgeraldish good looks concealed the fact that he was decidedly the least creative and risk-taking president of the three. Like Jimmy Gatz putting together Jay Gatsby out of the heroes of popular fiction and Gibson's drawings, Jack Kennedy created President John F. Kennedy; and, like Gatsby, he never lost the watchfulness of the self-made man. Among the consequences was that he was less genuinely chivalric than the hopelessly unfashionable Harry Truman.

Yet the progression from Teddy Roosevelt to Franklin Roosevelt to John Kennedy displays a pattern of strengths as well as of ironic discrepancies. The second Roosevelt, born in 1882 and growing up during the new romantic years, was himself a borrower, borrowing from his cousin and namesake who had created and demonstrated new possibilities for the well born and well educated in politics. And if FDR was, in Oscar Handlin's words, "the progressive incarnate, experimental and pragmatic, committed to no general theories or coherent policy, but animated by the impulse to service inspired by Rector Peabody at Groton and by his education as governor of New York,"¹³⁰ he also became as president a romantic figure in his own right, with his courageous surmounting of his physical affliction, his jauntiness and humor, his showman's flair in the use of radio, his metaphor of the New Deal and aphorisms like, "The only thing we have to fear is fear itself," and his more than Irish charm. His greatness as a president was inseparable from his popularity, and the popularity was inseparable from the calculated theatricality and cherished idiosyncracies of his personality, as was the popularity of politicians like Jim Curley and Fiorello La Guardia. Kennedy's strengths were likewise real. Like Teddy Roosevelt he had overcome childhood weaknesses with the assistance of his childhood reading. (White records his widow as saying, "history made Jack what he was...this lonely, little sick boy...scarlet fever ...this little boy sick so much of the time, reading in bed, reading history...reading the Knights of the Round Table."¹³¹) Like FDR he had to contend with physical disabilities as an adult, and endured pain in a way that gave substance to his talk of grace under pressure. And although he would not have arrived where he did without his father's millions to buy victories for him like the one in West Virginia over the real underdog, the archetypal Midwestern Progressive Hubert Humphrey, or without the manipulations of Mayor Daley's organization in Chicago, he could not have become president – the youngest president next to Teddy Roosevelt, and the first Irish president – and overcome the handicaps of his youth and Catholicism, without his strength of will, his shrewdness, his courage, and his charm.

Moreover, if the media gush about Camelot was preposterous and the fawning attitude of many liberals toward the Kennedys dismaying, the strength of Kennedy's popularity testified to real American needs and hungers, and it was natural for Steinbeck, half Irish himself, to quote Ector's lament for Lancelot when Kennedy was killed. With his Gatsby-like air of promise and possibilities, his overcoming of the handicaps of his youthfulness and his wartime injuries, his breaching of the religious barrier that defeated the homely, shrewd, and courageous Al Smith, and his winning of the presidency, Kennedy had demonstrated that exciting possibilities could still be realized, including the possibility of acting upon the promise of American ideals. And the chivalric synthesis of power, will, and the social graces that he displayed was all the more welcome after the Eisenhower decade, with its Doris Day neopastoralism and the cold puritanism of John Foster Dulles. Furthermore, if Robert F. Kennedy was obviously not, as someone said ironically in the *Village Voice*, "a kind of diffident, gentle-souled, rumple-haired young

Reform

Gawain,"[132] the crusading investigative reporter of the *Voice*, Jack Newfield, was pointing to something significant when he spoke of his "coexisting qualities of wanting to do justice and also being very comfortable himself in the application of worldly power," and said that "there was something in him that caused both Tom Hayden and Mayor Richard Daley to weep at his funeral. No other public figure so touched, at the same time, a young radical and an old clubhouse boss."[133] Two other politicians also deserve mention here. If a number of chivalric figures have appealed by virtue of their patrician casualness and humor and their willingness to go up against seemingly undefeatable adversaries as a matter of principle, part of the poignancy of Adlai Stevenson's defeat by Eisenhower and Nixon in 1952 was its massive demonstration that in politics Americans apparently no longer had any use for such qualities. But in 1968 it was exactly that kind of figure, Eugene McCarthy, who in his children's crusade brought down the immensely powerful Lyndon Johnson.

8

Radicalism

"And sing! you never heard anybody sing the way those guys sang!"
James Jones, *From Here to Eternity* (1951)

"He was black Irish, wild, with a reckless kind of poetry in him that drew the men like a magnet. When you were with Johnny, I don't know how to put it, you felt more alive than with anyone else...He had that gift of making you feel larger inside yourself...you felt like a *man*."
Tim Kelly, quoted in Vivian Gornick, *The Romance of American Communism* (1977)

"You big———lug, I'd like to beat the hell out of you with this club."
I returned airy persiflage to his threats.
John Reed, letter to Mabel Dodge (1913)[1]

THE REINTEGRATION OF chivalric patterns into American political life was especially interesting where radicalism was concerned. The changes that helped to create a Dink Stover, an Austin Vane, and the *Collier's* triumvirate also helped to create young radical intellectuals like Max Eastman, Floyd Dell, and John Reed, and that greatest of American radical journals, the *Masses*, which flourished from 1912 until Wilson's government killed it at the end of 1917. And the chivalric radicalism of the *Masses* group was bound up with the chivalric radicalism of what Max Eastman called in 1913 "the only genuinely proletarian organization that ever existed in America – one of the few that ever existed anywhere" – the IWW, the Industrial Workers of the World, the immortal Wobblies.[2] The patterns of the new radicalism were very different from those of Progressivism and of traditional socialism; they threw fresh light on neopastoral pacifism and on the ideas of violence, order, and peace; they would have lasting consequences for American radicalism in general. The next three chapters will explore the nature of that radicalism.

THE GREENWICH VILLAGE RADICALS

Once again, what went on is in some ways obvious. As Floyd Dell observes, 1913 saw the creation of "the Greenwich Village of which all the world has heard – which has become a byword."[3] The young intellectuals who moved into the Washington Square area and effer-

136

vesced in gathering places like the Macdougal Street Liberal Club, Polly Halliday's restaurant below it, and Mabel Dodge's salon a few blocks away on Fifth Avenue sought what David Graham Phillips called "the joy of life in the exaltation that comes through a sense of life lived to the very limit of its possibilities; a life of self-development, self-expression, self-devotion to the emancipation of man."⁴ They had come of age during Teddy Roosevelt's exuberant heyday. They had learned from Nietzsche, as paraphrased by Mencken, that "two things are wanted by the true man: danger and play," and that the true man will see life as "something to be faced gladly and with a laugh."⁵ (Hemingway's Robert Jordan would reflect later in *For Whom the Bell Tolls* that "all the best ones, when you thought it over, were gay. It was much better to be gay and it was a sign of something too. It was like having immortality while you were still alive."⁶) They had learned from Yeats, apropos of the legendary Irish heroes, that

whatever they do...they do for the sake of joy, their joy in one another, or their joy in pride and movement; and even their battles are fought more because of their delight in a good fighter than because of any gain that is in victory. They live always as if they were playing a game; and so far as they have any deliberate purpose at all, it is that they may become great gentlemen and be worthy of the songs of poets. It has been said, and I think the Japanese were the first to say it, that the four essential virtues are to be generous among the weak, and truthful among one's friends, and brave among one's enemies, and courteous at all times.⁷

The young intellectuals thirsted for action, and the *Masses* became, in Irving Howe's words, "the rallying center – as sometimes also a combination of circus, nursery, and boxing ring – for almost everything that was then alive and irreverent in American culture."⁸

Its principal literary triumvirate, all born in the Eighties, were incurably romantic. Max Eastman, described by one of his associates as "a picturesque, slow-moving tall boy with a careless head of hair and a passion for truth, polemics, tennis and swimming," and by another as "handsome as a faun," had been awakened into hero worship as an adolescent by G. A. Henty's novels and one or two daring home-town youths; he spent a "recklessly adventuring, freight-train riding" undergraduate summer out in the Wild West; he loved gusto and the way in which Twain, whom he adored when he met him as a boy, attacked stuffy respectability with "confidence and gay laughter instead of frantic moral anxiety."⁹ Floyd Dell, his mother Irish, his father a pugnacious Civil War veteran who admired Roosevelt and the Rough Riders, had progressed in an exemplary fashion from the *Arabian Nights* and Andrew Lang's fairy tales, via Twain and Frank Merriwell and Nick Carter, to the higher romanticism. Kipling furnished him with "a dream of world-wide adventurous wandering," Wells opened up vistas of "a century of hope and change and adventure," Shaw preferred "a series of delightful vagabond lovers."[10] He had seen himself in some of his early verses as "a young poetic Galahad," and had dreamed of "sometime becoming a Newspaper Man. No other career ever showed itself to my young gaze in which a fellow could actually make a living and have a good time." When he discovered Russian Nihilism in the early 1900s, it had been "located in a kind of Slavic Forest of Arden, or Sherwood Forest, where Robin Hood and Maid Marian robbed and killed the rich and helped the poor."[11] As a Villager, he believed in Free Love and, according to the *Masses* cartoonist Art Young, was addicted to white trousers, Byronic collars, and orange ties.

Above, all, there was John Reed, "adventurer and artist, playboy and propagandist," as Dell called him.[12] If Eastman had grown up in a small New England town under a father "too virtuous to be interesting," Reed had had a Rooseveltian upper-middle-class youth out in Oregon, with a high-spirited grandmother who entertained lavishly in her "lordly gray mansion" in a huge park; a gallant, generous, and witty father whom Reed described as "a great figher, one of the first of the little band of political insurgents . . . to give expression to the new social conscience of the American middle class"; and a favorite uncle, "tanned and bearded," who dabbled in coffee planting and revolutions in Central America. As a boy he read voraciously and loved Twain, Malory, and medieval history, "kings strutting about and the armored ranks of men-at-arms clashing forward in close ranks against a hail of cloth-yard shafts"; and his two years at a New Jersey prep school before he went on to his restless undergraduate years at Harvard were "a period of intense emotion in which I endowed certain girls with the attributes of Guinevere, and had a vision of Galahad and the Sangreal in the sky over the football field."[13] (His Harvard classmate Walter Lippmann remembered him as "the most inspired song and cheer leader that the football crowd had had for many days." Football remained a passion of his.[14]) Like Roosevelt, he was a sickly and timid youth who made himself over, becoming, as the less than perfectly enchanted Lippmann put it in 1914, "one of those people who treat as serious possibilities such stock fantasies as shipping before the mast, rescuing women, hunting lions, or trying to fly around the world in an aeroplane. He is the only fellow I know who gets himself pursued by men with revolvers."[15] His hunger for experience would take him to the great Paterson strike of 1913, to revolutionary Mexico, to wartime Serbia, to Russia in 1917, and ultimately to his tomb in the Kremlin and immortality as, in Daniel Aaron's words, "a Bolshevik Richard Harding Davis."[16]

Radicalism

THE GALLANT AND GLAMOROUS WOBBLIES

And if the romantic young craved for more than Progressivism to identify with, and, like Reed, found the conventional socialism of the Socialist Party "duller than religion," in the IWW they had a group which not only crusaded – one of the Wobblies commented that "we are the modern abolitionists fighting against wage slavery" – but was glamorous as well.[17] The Wobbly leaders and their associates were far more colorful than conventional socialists. There was the massively handsome former miner and cowboy, Big Bill Haywood, with his Western hat, his single piercing eye, his sexual magnetism, a superb orator, the man who reminded Eugene Debs of Patrick Henry and John Brown, and who comported himself with good-humored aplomb among the young lions of Mabel Dodge's salon.[18] There was the Kentucky-born and part-Irish general organizer Vincent St. John, described by Elizabeth Gurley Flynn as "a legendary figure of courage and resourcefulness...broad-shouldered, quick and graceful in his movements,...very companionable, with a lively sense of humor."[19] There was Elizabeth Gurley Flynn herself, written up at the age of seventeen by Theodore Dreiser as an "East Side Joan of Arc" and "a typical Irish beauty," photographed the following year by Alfred Stieglitz, and described as speaking at the Paterson strike so magnificently that "the excitement of the strikers became a visible thing. She stood up there, young, with her Irish blue eyes, her face magnolia white and her cloud of black hair, the very picture of a youthful revolutionary girl leader."[20] There were gallant and charming Italian-American organizers like Joe Ettor, the poet Arturo Giovannitti, and Carlo Tresca, who in the words of a former associate,was a lover of "good food, good friendship, fair women, deviltry and humanity. As a fighter he knew no fear."[21] There was the peripatetic Irish-born Mother Jones, still indomitable in her eighties, dressed always in "an old-fashioned black silk basque, with lace around her neck, a long full skirt and a little bonnet, trimmed with flowers." There were other interesting and admirable figures, among them the troubadour of the IWW, Joe Hill, "tall, slender, very blond, with deep blue eyes," and the poet Ralph Chaplin, the author of "Solidarity Forever."[22]

The Wobblies were genuinely heroic, too, in the risks they ran at the hands of mobs and the forces of law and order. Wobblies who tried to unionize West Coast workers and poured into viciously antiunion cities like San Diego and Spokane in the free-speech fights between 1910 and 1913 were tarred and feathered, beaten with rubber hoses and pick handles, tortured in ad hoc concentration camps. During the great

Part II Chivalric patterns in industrializing America

textile strike of 1912 in Lawrence, Massachusetts, Arturo Giovannitti and Joe Ettor spent ten months in jail on a trumped-up murder charge, a foreshadowing of the Sacco and Vanzetti case. Joe Hill was executed by a Utah firing squad. The charming and courageous Western Wobblies Frank Little and Wesley Everest died in 1917 at the hands of lynchers. (John Dos Passos later described how, when Everest "lay stunned at the bottom of the car a...business man cut his penis and testicles off with a razor. Wesley Everest gave a great scream of pain."[23]) And when Wilson's government set out to smash the organization after America entered the European war, Wobbly leaders like Haywood and Chaplin were given grueling prison sentences, the legal counterparts of the episode at Bisbee, Arizona, when two thousand armed superpatriots of the Loyalty League shipped twelve hundred striking miners out into the August desert in packed, manure-floored cattle cars.[24]

Furthermore, when an observer remarked in 1912 that Wobbly groups that he had seen out West reminded him of "bodies of students at the end of a rather jolly picnic," and that the movement especially attracted the footloose young "free to follow a life of adventure," he was pointing to important aspects of the Wobbly charm.[25] Dell spoke admiringly in the *Masses* of "the friendly recital of his adventures by a sunburned IWW just in from a long spell on the road." And the hobo or bindle stiff acquired an enduring prestige. (In 1961 a sociologist stated proudly that "for twenty years I have carried a card, announcing that I am a 'Knight of the Road,' a member in good standing of 'Hobos of America, Inc.' "[26] The Wobblies demonstrated what the hero of Eastman's *Venture*, a composite of Eastman and Reed, spoke of when he told the Paterson strikers to "fight happy. Don't be gloomy about it. Go in smiling."[27] As one of the Wobblies said in 1913, they were "the men who put a song in the mouth and a sense of solidarity in the heart of the hobo."[28] The Wobbly songs, composed by men like Chaplin and Joe Hill and collected in *The Little Red Song Book*, continued the Irish association of singing with combat, and established the tradition of radical song that ran via Woody Guthrie and the Almanac Singers, through Pete Seeger, to Joan Baez and others. In songs like Hill's "Hallelujah I'm a Bum" and "Pie in the Sky," the cartoons in the *Industrial Worker*, T-Bone Slim's poems, and the tactics of some of the free-speech fights, the Wobblies displayed, too, a sense of humor rare among radical movements. Looking back to his boyhood on a Midwest farm in the Twenties, Thomas McGrath describes how a Wobbly farmworker

> Tried to teach me when to laugh and when to be serious,
> When to laugh at the serious, be serious in my laughter,
> To laugh at myself and be serious with myself.[29]

140

Radicalism

B. Traven's novel *The Death Ship* (1926) was characteristically Wobbly in its narrator's ironic jauntiness in the face of bureaucratic inflexibility and appalling working conditions.

It is not surprising that the Wobblies so strongly attracted the young of the *Masses* group, who, in Dell's words, "believed in fun, truth, beauty, realism, freedom, peace,...revolution."[30] Nor is it surprising that they have figured favorably in numerous strike novels, in Hammett's *Red Harvest*, Dos Passo's *U.S.A.*, and James Jones's *From Here to Eternity*, in several plays, in Bo Weiderberg's *Joe Hill*, and Martin Scorsese's *Boxcar Bertha*, and in a recent movie documentary on them.[31] But more than romanticism and glamor was responsible for their lasting appeal, an appeal not equalled by any other labor group, including their forerunners, the Knights of Labor. In opting for the radicalism of the Wobblies, writers like Eastman, Dell, and Reed were rejecting a complex social and psychological model of rational benevolentism, epitomized in the Wilsonism that was replacing Rooseveltism. They were rejecting the neopastoral vision of what Dell, with reference to Edward Bellamy's immensely popular utopian novel· *Looking Backwards*, later called "a reign of universal peace and order,...a regime of cleanliness, efficiency and common sense, in which...everybody was enlightened, useful and happy."[32] They were rejecting certain contradictions in the reformism that began so confidently at the start of the century but that by 1912 was running out of steam.

THE PROGRESSIVES: BENEVOLENT CONTROLLERS?

On the face of things, Progressive crusading ought to have gone from strength to strength. Its moral authority was nicely conveyed in one of Owen Johnson's Lawrenceville stories when a reformist housemaster, after the headmaster has agreed that "we cannot begin too soon to interest the youth, the intelligent, serious youth of our country in honest government and clean political methods," tells his young charges at the outset of an experiment in self-government:

"Now, boys, I wish you success. You will acquire a taste for public combat and a facility in the necessary art of politics that will nurture in you a desire to enter public life, to take your part in the fight for honest politics, clean methods, independent thinking, and will make you foes of intimidation, bribery, cheating, and that demagoguery that is the despair of our present system."[33]

The new American crusaders were continuing a long and honorable tradition of liberation that included Ivanhoe rescuing Rebecca from the Templars' stake, Don Quixote galloping to the aid of the prisoners of the Inquisition, the blue-clad knights of the Union army, and even the volunteers who sailed off in 1898 to free Cuba from the grasp of the

Part II Chivalric patterns in industrializing America

Spanish tyrants, in those heroic days when, as William Allen White says, "we thought...that the glory we had won and the lands we had taken over had come to us because of the...blessings of liberty which we were showering upon the dark places of the earth."[34] Moreover, the social liberation that was now taking place was doing so by enlightened means. As a graduate student sitting at the feet of James Bryce and Woodrow Wilson at Johns Hopkins, Frederic Howe had learned that

the people were misled, because business men and educated men had not taken the trouble to instruct them. The people were hungry for guidance; of that we are clear – guidance which we, the scholars, alone could provide. To this brotherhood of service I belonged. I was one of the chosen; one of the remnant that Matthew Arnold wrote about. The purple robe of doctor of philosophy dedicated me to this service.[35]

The Johns Hopkins motto, *Veritas Vos Liberavit*, expressed a traditional American wisdom. As Henry Adams said of antebellum New England, "social perfection was...sure, because human nature worked for Good, and three instruments were all she asked – Suffrage, Common Schools, and Press. On these points doubt was forbidden. Education was divine, and man needed only a correct knowledge of facts to reach perfection."[36] These blessings were increased by the spread of the social sciences. Just as schoolteachers, who had earlier liberated Southern blacks during the Reconstruction period, were now liberating immigrants from the tyranny of foreign tongues and alien ways, so medical workers were freeing them from sickness, social workers were loosening the grip of poverty, and the combined forces of enlightenment were saving fearful wives, beaten children, and the drunkard himself from the tyranny of alcohol.

Such attitudes had obvious advantages for those holding them. In an enthusiastic little book on Galahad in 1907, a writer described how Galahad as a young man swore that "he would grapple hand to hand with any misery or misfortune he might come across"; after which he fought "boldly for the right, always conquering and leaving peace and happiness where he had found cruelty and wickedness," and tasting "the joy which comes in giving a loving service to the unfortunate."[37] In this disinterested benevolence, of course, he was simply anticipating the American recognition that, as William Ellery Channing said in 1830, "the lesson of the age is that of sympathy with the suffering, and of devotion to the progress of the whole human race."[38] And Progressivism not only provided the general reassurance about one's own benevolent motives that Grover Cleveland voiced when he spoke admiringly in 1906 of how

an Army of teachers in our schools and colleges are, by their lives of self-sacrificing and continuous devotion to the cause of education, making unremit-

142

ting protest against prevailing selfishness and avarice, and are, by examples as well as precept, teaching the young men of our generation the worth of patriotism and intellectual living, as against the sordidness and soul-blight of conscienceless accumulation.[39]

With the growth of professionalism, the progressive minded could also believe, in Robert H. Wiebe words, that "the process of becoming an expert, of immersing oneself in the scientific method, eradicated petty passions and narrow ambitions, just as it removed faults in reasoning."[40] The Progressive was engaged in bringing about solid improvements in a solid way; and the scientific approach reassured reformers that their activities were essentially nonpartisan politically. Progressives could therefore seemingly enjoy both moral purity and practical power – a legitimate power, because it did not involve martial domination and self-aggrandizement – and could work flat out towards the creation of an efficient, cohesive, and benevolent American state, a morally pure state strong enough to impose permanent peace on the rest of the world.

But the White Knight type has in fact been regarded in America with a good deal of mistrust. Not only, as the hero of Edmund Wilson's "Galahad" reflected, did becoming president of the school YMCA apparently entail "denying the jovial roughhouse, the nonsense and bawdy jokes, of the Fifth Form."[41] As Gawain commented in John Erskine's popular historical novel *Galahad* in the mid-1920s – a work that had obviously been partly stimulated by the career of the quintessential Mr. Clean of American politics, Woodrow Wilson – "these serious youngsters with a high moral purpose always turn out the most dangerous."[42] Moreover, the graduates of Fitzgerald's "clean, flaccid and innocuous preparatory schools" and the better universities who, as Fitzgerald said, "picked up the glorified illusion that certain men were set aside for 'service' "[43] were not even regarded with affection by those whom they set out to serve. Important power relationships were entailed, and disturbing contradictions inhered in the fact, noted by Lippmann, that "the bureaucratic dreams of reform often bear a striking resemblance to the honest fantasies of the utopians. What we are coming to call 'State Socialism' is in fact an attempt to impose a benevolent governing class on humanity" and provide "wise and powerful officials to bring order out of chaos and make men clean, sober and civic-minded."[44] By a slight twist or two, liberative activities and attitudes turned into dominative ones.

As viewed through enlightened eyes, the history of American progress had been, in Michael Novak's words, "a drama of the psyche in which reason and the mild sentiments were to master the dark passions, while, externally, men with their industry and laws mastered a wild, primitive continent. 'The frontier' is the frontier of cool reason, objectivity, pacification. The American destiny is to extend the light."[45] From this point of view, the working classes, particularly in the cities, were liable to figure as creatures of unreason, disorder, and what a Progressive called in 1908 "pigheaded and brutish criminality."[46] The brutishness had manifested itself in the six-day Irish draft riots of 1863 in New York and the large-scale destructiveness of the railroad strike of 1877, during which Ford's Peter Stirling, as a colonel of the militia, braved rifle fire to rescue strike breakers from strikers trying to burn them alive. It was evidenced in a plethora of other labor disturbances and in the "alarming volume of savage crime" committed, as another Progressive said, by the immigrant "European peasant, suddenly freed from the restraints of poverty and of rigid police authority."[47] Working-class people were irrational in other ways, too. As a Progressive, pointed out, "the immigrant lacks the faculty of abstraction. He thinks not of the welfare of the country but only of himself."[48] The working classes drank, gambled, and operated politically on the basis of feudal exchanges of loyalty rather than according to rational sociodemocratic principles. A good many of them, too, accepted the systematized unreason of Catholicism, which, as Roosevelt said, was "in no way suited to this country," and which had understandably produced by the Nineties what the arch Mugwump Godkin called "a dread...which has by now become among all classes of Anglo-Saxons, whether religious or sceptical, an integral part of their mental and moral make-up."[49] All this bore on the Progressive notion of liberation.

When it came to "medieval" attitudes, no debate or compromise was possible. One one side, as in A Connecticut Yankee, lay pacific reasonableness, a belief in human equality, a willingness to experiment, a concern for progress; on the other, hidebound, inegalitarian, aggressive nonsense. Small groups held down large numbers of people by force and fraud; if their grip could be loosened, people's innate intelligence could assert itself, and the benefits of civilization would flow everywhere. But more was needed than simply opening prison doors and knocking off fetters. Intrinsic to "medieval" forms of social injustice was a belief in irrevocably fixed roles and categories and the mystical right of one person or group to give commands to and receive the deference of another. In this respect, the medieval serf with the collar round his neck, the Southern slave, the European peasant doffing his hat to landowner and priest, and the American child of European peasants compelled to submit in perpetuity to the authority of his superstition-bound parents were all victims of bondage. Hence, liberating people meant the destruction of fixed categories, as epitomized in the proclamation by The Boss near the end of A Connecticut Yankee:

The monarchy has lapsed, it no longer exists. By consequence, all political power has reverted to its original source, the people of the nation. With the monarchy, its several adjuncts died also; wherefore there is no longer a nobility, no longer a privileged class, no longer an Established Church; all men are become exactly equal; they are upon one common level, and religion is free. *A Republic is hereby proclaimed.*[50]

Social structures preventing the kind of rational civic government that could save the working classes from illiteracy, bad sanitation, adulterated foodstuffs, fraudulent patent medicines, and the like, had to be broken down. The ethnic American must be liberated from the imprisoning compulsions of archaic emotions, the grip of superstition, the tyranny of atavistic codes, including codes of "honor." He must be set free to govern himself by reason and make enlightened choices that would benefit both himself and society.

These beliefs were reinforced by an intertwining of aesthetic and moral preferences. When Frederic Howe described the fight to make Cleveland an exemplary "City on a Hill" and *Collier's* ran a series of articles "illustrating the progress of cities toward ideal conditions,"[51] it was clear what the ideal conditions would be like. Gleaming white buildings, tidy greenness, and neoclassical symmetry had always figured prominently in American planning, and had achieved an apotheosis in the Chicago Exposition of 1893 and the St. Louis World's Fair of 1904. The joys of coolness, spaciousness, and clarity were celebrated in the drawings by Gibson and others of upper-class vacationers, and would be commended more cerebrally in the aseptic paintings of Precisionists like Charles Sheeler. And the Garden City theorizings of Patrick Geddes spelled out the kinds of aesthetically wholesome environmental conditions that would maximize psychological wholesomeness. In Wiebe's words, "the coarseness, the jagged violence, of city life that so deeply disturbed [reformers] would dissolve into a new urban unity, the progressive version of the old community ideal."[52] It was this period that formed the imagination of Robert Moses, who began his administrative career under the first Roosevelt and who would later so ruthlessly embody his vision of tidy green parks and flowing concrete lines in the bridges and parkways of Manhattan and upper-middle-class Long Island. And the more the actual city life of the Irish, the Italians, the Jews, and others resisted the unifying processes, the more evident was its undesirability. Cleanness of line, sharpness of form, definiteness of demarcation, preciseness of interaction – ultimately, the qualities of the aesthetically and functionally perfect machine – were tokens simultaneously of moral purity and collective power.

The catch, of course, was that this interesting program of amelioration did not depend only on the improvers. As Ford's Peter Sterling had said

145

of the Mugwump's aristocratic craving for government by the "best" men, the underlying assumption was that "the better elements, so-called, shall compel the masses to be good, whether they wish it or no."[53] What Progressivism was after, in effect, was the establishment of a permanent and powerful bureaucracy of liberation, a bureaucracy of enlightenment taking power away from both the dominators *and* the dominated. Like the Southern slave, the urban masses could not simply become free by having chains struck off; in order to become truly free, they must be *taught* how to be free – and prevented from backsliding. Implicit, of course, was the conviction that ethnic groups neither had, nor were capable of creating, any worthwhile culture of their own, and that insofar as their mores differed from those of their self-appointed improvers, it was because they were still immature, which is to say not yet fully adult. It was hardly surprising, therefore, that as Oscar Handlin, himself the child of immigrants, reports, the immigrant's

particular enemies were the officials charged with his special oversight. When misfortune drove him to seek assistance or when government regulations brought them to inspect his home, he encountered the social workers, made ruthless in the disregard of his sentiments by the certainty of their own benevolent intentions. Confident of their personal and social superiority and armed with the ideology of the sociologists who had trained them, the emissaries of the public and private agencies [including the "starched young gentlemen from the settlement house"] were bent on improving the immigrant to the point at which he would no longer recognize himself.[54]

Nor was it surprising that the working-class hero of a later novel should say to a settlement-house worker, "You're not actually suggesting that I become a reformer?...He's as bad down here as an informer, and as cordially hated."[55]

The attempted dominance was liable to be accompanied by a curious animus toward those who were being benefited. The drive toward transformation brought into play the kind of missionary certainty displayed by the Episcopalian bishop who announced near the end of the Nineties that "no difficulties and no anxieties can alter the facts or change the situation or put back the advancing movement of God's will, which tends to the final substitution of the civilization, the liberty, and the religion of English-speaking people for the lost domination of the Latin races and the Latin religion."[56] It also brought into play the craving of professionals or quasiprofessionals, equipped with new techniques and bent on establishing their own indispensability in a power-charged modernizing world, to show that nothing was beyond their capacity to change, and change fast. The irrational resistance to improvement on the part of irrational people was therefore doubly annoying. Speaking out of his experience as mayor of Toledo, Brand Whitlock said in 1914 of certain reformers that "what that type of mind desires is. . .intellectual surrender, the acknowledgment of its infallibility," and that it became resentful when denied that acknowledgment.[57] A good deal of resentment was also possible to the type of sociologist who, in Handlin's words, was "eager to ameliorate the lot of his fellow men by altering the conditions of their lives" and "found the newcomers intractable, slow to change, obstacles in the road to progress"; and even a nice young social worker like Fitzgerald's Frederick E. Paramore could complain that "you have no idea of the amount of poverty in these small Connecticut towns. Italians and other immigrants. Catholics, mostly, so it's very hard to reach them."[58] In the public schools there were teachers for whom, as Handlin puts it, "to admit the least question of the rightness of what they taught would undermine the whole structure of their self-esteem."[59] Later on, another son of immigrants, Lionel Trilling, would suggest that the orthodoxy of progressive child rearing, which began in the Progressive years and was intended to ensure that children would grow up rational, pacific, and cooperative, was "charged with a scarcely concealed animosity to parents and an essential malice toward children which lay hidden under the manifest child-partisanship, an impulse to deprive children of their dignity by underestimating their powers."[60]

It is not really surprising, therefore, that Progressivism ran into difficulties, and that intellectuals like the *Masses* group turned away from it. Insofar as it was pastoral, its ethos was that of the YMCA, the Boy Scouts, the *National Geographic*, an ethos of abstentions and absences, the ethos nicely characterized by a writer who speaks of "a sort of *Saturday Evening Post* American: self-assured, calm, and helpful in a strangely distant way."[61] But the more it aspired to be heroic, as it was driven to be, the more it suffered from psychological strains and disharmonies. As Wilson's career and the attitudes of the Wilsonian *New Republic* made clear, to go wholeheartedly after maximum effectiveness in the Progressive fashion meant throwing one's weight behind, and obtaining a place in, the large organization – ultimately the modernizing and rationalizing state – in a world in which, as Max Weber says, "the most decisive thing. . .is the *leveling of the governed* in opposition to the ruling and bureaucratically articulated group."[62] But the contradiction between ostensible selflessness and actual lively self-interest, and between ostensible benevolence and actual dominativeness, made for an insidious sense of bad faith, particularly given the enlightened conviction that pride and aggressive self-assertion were wrong. And the leveling entailed an emotional stiffness on the part of the levelers. The intense moral compulsion to improve people, with what Brand Whitlock called its "everlasting repressings and denials and negatives," was dependent on perceiving the so-called lower-class

147

Part II Chivalric patterns in industrializing America

patterns as essentially inferior and remaining alienated from working-class vitality and variousness.[63]

WOBBLY PRIDE

A radically different pattern and a much more attractive set of possibilities were furnished by the IWW and incorporated into the new radicalism. Culturally, Progressivism was dominative and homogenizing. It demanded that the Greenwich Village young deny the validity of the dense and rich ethnic cultures that they observed daily in New York. It invited Floyd Dell's questions about "the days when, gloriously confident, we did settlement work or dabbled in 'Charity'. . . Who were we, to undertake the management of others' lives for them? Must the poor, having been robbed of everything else, surrender the direction of their most private affairs to agencies paid by the people who had robbed them?"[64] The IWW pattern, in contrast, emphasized and strengthened identity and asserted the right of working-class people to a different kind of self-definition and self-determination from that prescribed by the improvers. And part of the Wobblies' enduring appeal was that, regardless of whether they won their fights or not, they demonstrated vividly and unforgettably certain working-class possibilities that were more than merely working class. They did so, moreover, in ways that were deeply American and that restored connections with an older American tradition of liberty.

The vitality of the Wobblies was that of a group unabashedly affirming its own working-class characteristics and identity, a group appropriately perceived in terms of the "rough" worker – the miner, the timber beast, the bindle stiff – rather than the upward-bound craftsman. What the Wobblies emphatically rejected was the notion, common to employers, Progressive reformers, and craft unions, of a caste division below which individuals were too uncivilized to merit being attended to in their own terms. They also rejected the notion that workers were merely competing economic units and that a union simply enabled craftsmen to bring about more accurate adjustments of wages relative to productivity and the fluctuations of the market. They denied that the only features of working-class persons that justified collective action by them were the rational skills that enabled them to leave behind their primitive origins. Conversely they affirmed that working-class people, in their manifold cultural differences from the middle and upper classes, constituted groups as worthy of respect as any others. And as a corollary of rejecting the employing classes' idea of "good" Americans and insisting that those classes too were simply groups like any others, with common features and interests, they affirmed likewise that the

148

overclass view of the socioeconomic order was not the only legitimate one. If it was natural for the employing classes to fight for a system of ownership that worked so strongly in their favor, it was no less natural for workers to favor a different one. Hence if one rejected the principle of "respectable" union divisions and the narrow competitive pursuit of, in Handlin's words, "the pure and simple objectives of the larger wage check and the shorter working week"[65] and instead saw all the workers in a mine or factory as a group with a common identity and common interests, it was reasonable to desire the control by workers of their work places.

Furthermore, the Wobblies demonstrated that they were not just talking about a hypothetical future attainable by the abstract worker after having been sufficiently improved. Accompanying their insistence that workers were perfectly capable of managing their own affairs and did not need the assistance of professional supervisors or of professional improvers, was the remarkable democratic openness of their organization. Strong as figures like Haywood, Ettor, and St. John were, the IWW was not the organization of any single one of them in the way that the Knights of Labor had been Terence V. Powderly's or the AFL was that of the "hard-fighting, hard-drinking, hail-fellow-well-met" Samuel Gompers, "bold, relentless, unforgiving, successful," as William Z. Foster described him.[66] Bill Haywood was not simply speaking for the record when he said of the Lawrence strike that "the most significant part of that strike was that it was a democracy. The strikers handled their own affairs."[67] As Ralph Chaplin, no idolator of Haywood, wrote later of Wobbly participatory democracy, "so thoroughly was the rank and file indoctrinated with this creed that we could boast, 'There are no leaders among us – we are all leaders.' "[68] Shortly after the great strike at the Paterson silk mills, Elizabeth Gurley Flynn reported how "we tried to produce among those strikers this feeling: 'Listen to anything, listen to everybody...listen to them all and then take what you think is good for yourselves and reject what is bad. If you are not able to do that then no censorship over your meetings is going to do you any good.' "[69]

In other words, underlying the Wobbly jauntiness and flair for the vivid was an ideological strength that enabled individual Wobblies to act with full commitment, sometimes at great personal cost, without any nagging feeling of being inferior to their adversaries morally or intellectually. They did not, in their own eyes, stand in need of intellectual or cultural liberation. They did not need to be managed by the kind of intellectual described by John Graham Brooks in 1913 as "always on the hunt for power over men." As Brooks said apropos of Georges Sorel's contempt for "educated interlopers," to free people from "this strutting despotism and from all the benumbing 'authority' for which it stands, is one of the great aims of Syndicalism. . . The same attack on 'intellectuals' is incessant in the I.W.W." – an enmity that was reciprocated in the contempt of orthodox socialists for the IWW.[70] Above all, the Wobblies did not need to "earn" their rights. Pervading their activities was the sense of rights not as rewards for good conduct or charitable handouts, but as things to be taken because due. They accepted at face value the American promise of freedom from castes and dominative categorization, and insisted on applying it to America as well as Europe. They implicitly affirmed that liberty was the liberty to be or become what one wanted to be oneself, not what an economic overclass decided it would be good to change one into. They did so in the spirit of the escaped slave Frederick Douglass when he said in the 1840s that "a man without force is without the essential dignity of humanity. Human nature is so constituted that it cannot honor a helpless man, though it can pity him, and even this it cannot do long if signs of power do not arise."[71]

In all this, moreover, the Wobblies were deeply American, playing a major part in the Americanization of the Left that occurred in the early 1900s, and linking up with an older American tradition of radicalism.[72] In 1906, a year after the founding of the IWW, the muckraker Ray Stannard Baker noted that "the East has been increasingly conscious of West winds. The storm in reality began rising years ago, but it is only within a year that it has reached cyclonic proportions as far eastwards as Washington."[73] The Western Federation of Miners, from which the IWW emerged, took its tone, as a labor writer reports, "from adventurous American frontiersmen who suddenly found themselves in the degrading position of workingmen – thousands of feet under the earth."[74] They and the workers in lumber camps were men who were not under any moral compulsion to feel respectful gratitude, like Eastern and Southern European immigrants, for the new-world opportunities offered them by business, or any obligation to adapt themselves to the official American system. They did not have to be made into free individuals. In their own eyes they were free already and the rapidly expanding mining, timber, and agricultural corporations were seeking their enslavement.

ATTRACTION OF OPPOSITES: ARISTO-DEMOCRATIC ALLIANCES

The central and characteristic paradox of the Wobblies' Westernism was expressed in Max Eastman's *Venture* when a character remarked of the Paterson strikers, "They're a sort of aristocrat themselves, in a certain way of speaking," and the hero answered, "The best democrats."[75] The Wobblies' aristo-democracy partly derived from the general aristo-democracy of the West, as displayed above all in the cowboy culture, in which a man's skills and character were central, his previous social

Radicalism

status irrelevant, and money of little importance. In turn, Western
aristo-democracy partly derived from the South, both via the cowboy
culture in which Southerners had figured so prominently, and as
transmitted directly by migrant Southerners forced out of farming.
There was a transmission of what W. J. Cash calls "the old basic feeling
of democracy [which] was preserved practically intact" in the South
after the Civil War, the attitude of which he observes that "prior to the
last ten or fifteen years before Secession, the Old South may be said, in
truth, to have been nearly innocent of the notion of class in any rigid
and complete sense."[76]

This nexus of aristocratic and democratic attitudes had been potent in
American history. As Brand Whitlock put it in 1914, "it seems
almost as though the cause of democracy would never have got on at all
if now and then it had not had aristocrats to lead it, as ever it had, from
the times of the Gracchi to those of the Mirabeaus and the Lafayettes
and the Jeffersons."[77] Nor is it hard to see why. When Edwin Harrison
Cady reports that "among the many folk definitions of the gentleman
...one of the most intriguing is that [he] can look any man in the world
straight in the eye and tell him to go to hell," he is describing an attitude
inimical to the tyranny of others, whether political or intellectual.[78] The
history of American liberty seeking and liberty defending was, in part, a
history of figures like William Penn, who, as Morison and Commager
say, "never ceased to be Cavalier when he went Quaker, or gentleman
when he became democrat," and who "believed in the traditional
liberties of Englishmen, and intended that they should be respected in
his province....He had been made to feel in his own person the value of
civil liberties, and the aristocrat in him made him fight back when his
rights were infringed."[79] It was the Virginia aristocrats who made
possible the success of the American Revolution: As Edmund Burke
observed, the "people of the southern colonies are much more strongly,
and with an higher and more stubborn spirit, attached to liberty, than
those to the northward...In such a people, the haughtiness of domination combines with the spirit of freedom, fortifies it, and renders it
invincible."[80] It was the aristocrat Thomas Jefferson who believed
unshakeably in people's right to effective power and intellectual liberty,
and who observed apropos of Shay's rebellion in Massachusetts against
unreasonable taxes and voting restrictions, "What country can preserve
its liberties, if its rulers are not warned from time to time that this people
preserve the spirit of resistance?...The tree of liberty must be refreshed
from time to time, with the blood of patriots and tyrants. It is its natural
manure."[81] And Jacksonian democracy had occurred not under a Davy
Crockett backwoodsman but under a politician of, in Arthur Schlesinger, Jr.'s words, "great urbanity and distinction of manner," who

151

during the decade before his election to the presidency led a life "mainly that of a Tennessee gentleman, living on a fine plantation near Nashville."[82] Fenimore Cooper perceptively has one of his New York landowner heroes remark, "Certain I am that all the really manly, independent democrats I have ever known in America have been accused of aristocracy, and this simply because they were disposed...not to let that imperious sovereign, 'the neighborhood,' play the tyrant over them."[83] It is obvious too, that Mark Twain's passion against domination was inseparable from his passion for individual liberty and plenitude, whether displayed by Colonel Grangerford or by those supreme aristocrats, the riverboat pilots.

Moreover, the interrelating of aristocratic and democratic attitudes had been of direct consequence for radicalism in the career of Wendell Phillips, whom Eugene Debs admiringly called "the most perfect aristocrat in the true sense" whom he had ever seen, and whom Thomas Wentworth Higginson remembered comporting himself in antiabolitionist Boston "like some English Jacobite nobleman, carelessly taking snuff and kissing his hand to the crowd, before laying his head upon the block."[84] A Beacon Street aristocrat by birth, and an eloquent defender of hierarchical society as an undergraduate at Harvard, where he had a passion for Scott and G. P. R. James, he went on to become the most impressive of the abolitionists, remarking in the Fifties how "again and again...have I had the opinion, that in the debatable land between Freedom and Slavery, in the thrilling incidents of the escape and sufferings of the fugitive, and the perils of his friends, the future Walter Scott of America would find the 'borderland' of his romances."[85] After the Civil War he defended the Indians and the Irish, attacked the Union Pacific Railroad Company, and said at the time of the Paris Commune, "There is no hope for France but in the reds," calling the Communards "the foremost, the purest and the noblest patriots of France."[86] Debs, who was a twenty-two-year-old grocery clerk when he heard Phillips lecture in the late Seventies, and who got to know him personally, reportedly "never forgot the great orator's withering attacks on monopoly power and unjust labor practices."[87] Henry Demarest Lloyd, later the author of the important protomuckraking attack on the trusts, *Wealth against Commonwealth* (1894), read Phillips's speeches with enthusiasm and considered that his "discovery of the continuity of the abolition movement and the labor movement marks him as the greatest social thinker" of his day.[88]

By now, the nature of the deeper appeal of the Wobblies for the romantic and chivalric young will be clearer, and with it the appeal of the emergent patterns of a new type of radicalism. The new pugnacious radicalism offered an escape from the tyranny of Puritanism and of single-system, neopastoral rationality. It provided a meaningful role for the kind of attitude voiced by Reed in an editorial statement in the *Masses* in 1914: "Standing on the common sidewalk, we intend to lunge at spectres – with a rapier rather than a broad-axe, with frankness rather than innuendo. We intend to be arrogant, impertinent, in bad taste, but not vulgar."[89] As a socialist pointed out in 1913, "capitalism...is essentially Puritan for the worker," and an anti-Puritan style could be a significant feature of an anticapitalist stance.[90] Furthermore, intellectuals could now escape from the dilemmas of Progressive reformism. In *Venture*, Max Eastman's hero reflected apropos of the importance of trying to understand and "feel at one with" working people that "he liked that kind of thing better. It seemed to him more truly aristocratic –more noble."[91] The radical young could fight on behalf of the underdog without having to commit themselves to authoritarianism, in the spirit Scott had described when he spoke of how "the love of personal freedom, and the obligation to maintain and defend it in the persons of others as in their own, was a duty particularly incumbent on those who attained the honour of Chivalry."[92] To fight on behalf of labor as represented by the Wobblies was to desire to see the working class strengthened in its identity and energy, not tamed still further. It was to desire what Maurice Becker represented symbolically in a double-page cartoon in the *Masses* in 1916 entitled "Power," in which a jubilant railway worker fills the whole foreground, his arms flung wide and his right hand clutching a sheet of paper headed "8 hour law," while in the background below him are tiny, scared, fat, indignant capitalists and Congressmen.[93] Instead of aiming to "civilize" and manage the working class, the educated young could come and learn from it.

An exciting redefining of social possibilities was taking place. The Wobblies were extending the tradition of the Holy and Noble Order of the Knights of Labor, which had been open to all workers, believed in local associations and cooperatives, took class conflicts for granted, and was bitterly attacked and ultimately defeated by Samuel Gompers' American Federation of Labor, with its commitment to pure-and-simple paycheck unionism. And in giving the Knights' idealism fresh energy, they drew on other American patterns of working-class self-sufficiency. The so-called common man of the antebellum South, in Cash's words, had been "likely to carry a haughtiness like that of the Spanish peasant underneath his slouch"; Irish unionists like the Molly Maguires, in Louis Adamic's words, were "strong, dynamic, robust fellows, carousers, drinkers, fighters, brawlers"; the Slavs in the Pennsylvania coal-fields, in Michael Novak's words, "amazed the nativist Americans because they were not individualists. They believed in solidarity. They did not admire *laissez faire*, and they made strikes succeed where strikes had not succeeded before. They did not hesitate to...meet the force of sheriff's posse and militia with violent counterforce."[94] It was increasingly possible to see working-class energies and the patterns of working-class culture as morally and intellectually admirable, so that it was reasonable that, as Paul Frederick Brissenden states in his pioneering study of the Wobblies, "the I.W.W. abjures current ethics and morality as *bourgeois*, and therefore inimical to the exploited proletarian for whom a new and approved system of proletarian morality is set forth."[95] The working-class vigor was especially attractive to admirers of romantic and Nietzschean vitalism who despised the YMCA ethos of what the stuffy narrator of *The Late George Apley* approvingly called "the three virtues of Tennyson – faith, hope, and chastity."[96]

Moreover, if the new pattern of robust self-affirmation was splendidly antithetical to the conviction voiced by a nineteenth-century apostle of enlightenment that "all sin consists in selfishness; and all holiness or virtue, in disinterested benevolence,"[97] the working-class energies were also communal and social. Eastman remarked how "wage workers retain that attitude of hospitality which plays so great a part in the moral code of early civilizations – the Homeric virtue."[98] A former Wobbly recalled how "there was far more 'etiquette' on the job than I had observed back east...In the bunkhouse or [hobo] jungle or job there was this considerateness that was rare back east. Individuality and solidarity or sense of community flourished here together."[99] Elizabeth Gurley Flynn remembered how, as a Wobbly organizer, "I traveled alone and was surrounded by men in the IWW halls, where there were only a few women members. Yet I never had a disagreeable experience (outside of getting arrested)."[100] The Wobbly hero of one of Floyd Dell's stories

kept on, organizing the season workers along the coast, assisting in strikes, joining in free-speech fights...He was happy at last. Where else but in the "Wobbly" halls could he hear talk that was not the talk of money and the things money will buy? He had three good friends, Pete the Peg-leg, who knew the poetry of Shelley and Blake by heart; Swede Oscar, a kindly giant out of some heroic fairy-tale; and Little Bill, with a golden tongue for singing, and mocking tongue for speech, who laughed even at the cause he loved. Jasper had always an immense capacity for friendship, and this was, from all accounts, a gay, devil-may-care, epic friendship while it lasted.[101]

Like the Knights of the Round Table and the cowboys out on the range, the Wobbly image was one of cooperation between free and differentiated figures who possessed power themselves and hence could cooperate freely and effectively with others.

Radicalism

As I shall try to show in the next two chapters, this radical spirit had important bearings both on the nature of political violence and on the curiously problematic concept of peace. As before, I shall be pointing to complex reintegrations of chivalric patterns into modern industrial society. I shall also be indicating further paradoxes about the ostensibly rational, pacific, and benign hostility of enlightened persons toward those patterns.

9

Violence and peace (I)

"What are their plans?" asked the Prince.

"They have none," replied Andrews, "except to burn, rob, destroy and murder. They have long lists of the condemned, I am told, including all those here present, and hundreds of thousands besides. They will kill all the women and children of the aristocracy, except the young girls, and these will be reserved for a worse fate."

Ignatius Donnelly, *Caesar's Column* (1891)

To make talk I asked Mr. MacGregor:
"What did the Molly Maguires do?"
He peered at me over the top of his gold glasses.
"Whut did they do? They killed their-r-r bosses and they done r-r-right!" he said and went on reading the Bible.

Mary Heaton Vorse, *A Footnote to Folly* (1935)

"My uniform's my dirty overalls."

Woody Guthrie[1]

A SPIRIT OF REVOLUTION

UP TO A POINT, when it came to violence, the Wobblies were straightforwardly glamorous in the way that the Rough Riders and the White Company were glamorous. They took heroic risks in their free-speech fights, their strikes, their demonstrations. They fought singing, to such tunes as "John Brown's Body," "Marching through Georgia," and "Tramp, Tramp, Tramp, the Boys are Marching," like the militants in the Eighties who had sung, "Storm the fort, you Knights of Labor, / Battle for the Cause." And the new image of the fighting unionist interestingly resembled that of the medieval Japanese labor leaders described by Inazo Nitobe in his book on Bushido: "Staunch fellows were they, every inch of them strong with the strength of massive manhood...at once the spokesmen and the guardians of popular rights...Backed by a vast multitude of rash and impetuous working men, those born 'bosses' formed a formidable check to the rampaging of the two-sworded order" (i.e., the samurai).[2] A major icon in the *Masses* was the nonmacho but firmly self-assertive working-class male, different alike from sporty collegians and from the brutish professional strikebreakers like "Fred the Hell" and "Dum Dum Davitt," with their

156

huge hands and shoulders and tiny heads, who figured in Art Young's cartoon "A Strike-Breaking Agency" in 1915.³

But the Wobblies were not only heroic unionists, they were heroic revolutionists, whose attorney at the trial of 113 Wobblies in 1918 was to demand of the jury, "Do you recognize the right of people to revolt? Do you recognize the idea of revolution as one of the principles of the Declaration of Independence upon which this nation is founded?"⁴ The spokesman for capital in Eastman's *Venture* who said, "This strike in our silk mills in Paterson is not a strike, it's a revolt. It ought to be put down with lead and steel" was, in a sense, seeing things correctly.⁵ In Wobbly terms, as Bill Haywood observed in 1911, "a strike is an incipient revolution";⁶ and if the Wobblies sang "Solidarity Forever," to the tune of "John Brown's Body," they also sang "The Marseillaise" and "The Red Flag," both songs in the first edition of the IWW song book, and encouraged the Paterson strikers to do so. And the respectable public's hostility to the idea of revolution was intense. The *Nation* in its pre-Villard days was voicing a conventional wisdom when it said in 1913,

What is true of Paterson is equally true of many other places in the country. Nor is there anything new about this necessity for the law-abiding citizenship of the country to assert itself. It existed, on a gigantic scale, at the time of the railway troubles of 1877. It rose to extraordinary dimensions during the disorders of 1894 which had their centre at Chicago, and which at one stage seemed to menace the peace and security of the whole country.⁷

When the gentleman-author Frederick Townsend Martin wrote in 1910, "The days of the Terror, the bloody hands, the brutish mob, the wild-eyed, frantic leaders of the hosts that stormed the Bastille, set up the guillotine – so runs the mind of an aristocrat and a plutocrat, reading the *Evening Post* in a rich man's club on upper Fifth Avenue!,"⁸ the fears that he described were not restricted to aristocrats. A sense of the fragility of social order and the propensity of the working classes for violence had been endemic for decades. Hordes of working men had gone on the rampage in 1863 and 1877; innumerable strikes had been, as the *Nation* said about Homestead, "utterly unjustifiable legally, and atrocious morally";⁹ the infamies of assassination practiced by the Molly Maguires in the Pennsylvania coalfields in the Seventies had been continued in the Rocky Mountain labor wars of the Nineties and early 1900s, and in episodes like the dynamiting of the Los Angeles *Times* building by the McNamara brothers in 1910, with its twenty-one deaths. Moreover, the natural propensity of the lower orders toward violence and disorder had been reinforced by imported alien ideologies. The murderous Paris Communards had inaugurated the modern era of large-scale political violence in 1871, and Anarchism, the anarchism of "the deed," had darkened the shores of America as well as Europe in the Haymarket bombing, the attempted assassination of Carnegie's partner Henry Frick, and the successful assassination of President McKinley. As Mencken observed in 1908, "to the average American ...the very name of anarchy causes a shudder, because it invariably conjures up a picture of a land terrorized by low-browed assassins with matted beards, carrying bombs in one hand and mugs of beer in the other."[10] And now there was Syndicalism to cope with. What made everything worse was that America itself had at one time engaged in revolution and had looked sympathetically on what Twain in *A Connecticut Yankee* called "the ever memorable and blessed [French] Revolution, which swept a thousand years of villainy away in one swift tidal wave of blood."[11]

The Wobblies were therefore doubly alarming ideologically. Not only did they invite the attitude displayed at one point in *Stover at Yale* when Stover "vaguely associated the term [Socialist] with dynamite and destruction,"[12] and the deeper fears of social collapse that had been embodied in Ignatius Donnelly's political fantasy *Caesar's Column* (1891), with its echoes of *A Tale of Two Cities*:

Pickpockets, sneak-thieves, confidence-men, burglars, robbers, assassins, the refuse and outpourings of grog-shops and brothels, all are here. And women, too – or creatures that pass for such – having bodies of women and the habits of ruffians; – harpies – all claws and teeth and greed – bold – desperate –shameless –incapable of good. They, too, are here. They dart hither and thither; they swarm – they dance – they howl – they chatter – they quarrel and battle, like carrion-vultures, over the spoils.[13]

As an editorial stated at the time of the Lawrence strike in 1912,

on all sides people are asking: Is this a new thing in the industrial world...? Are we to expect that instead of playing the game respectably, or else frankly breaking out into lawless riot which we know well enough how to deal with, the laborers are to listen to a subtle anarchist philosophy which challenges the fundamental idea of law and order...? We think that our whole current morality as to the sacredness of property and even of life is involved in it.[14]

Given the fact noted by another writer at the time that "syndicalism now comes with a new dialect. There is much mocking of 'reason' and much deification of impulse and feeling," Veblen was quite right when he commented that "the dread word, Syndicalism...has no definable meaning within the constituent principles of the eighteenth century."[15] Even the Socialist Party voted by a large majority in 1912 to expel anyone who "advocates crime, sabotage, or other methods of violence as a weapon of the working class."[16] The anxiety and anger of the better elements about threats to order would intensify when America entered the European war in 1917 and the Wobblies persisted in rejecting the

Violence and peace (I)

claims of the state and refused to be bound by the no-strike policy of the AFL.

The ideological strength that made possible the Wobblies' superb self-confidence in the face of law-and-order intimidation and official Socialist hostility, and the wholehearted support of the Wobblies by the young radicals, involved certain major redefinings of the concept of violence. Not only was the revolutionism of the new radicalism a very different affair from the conventional image of revolution as the general collapse of stable values. Ironically, the actual Wobbly orderliness was as alarming as their reputed disorderliness, because of what it implied about the orderliness of normal nonrevolutionary, non-"ideological," American society.

GENERAL VERSUS TROOPS IN THE ARMY OF INDUSTRY

In a famous passage in "The Moral Equivalent of War," William James, so influential for so many young men at Harvard, had offered in 1910 his quasi-Rooseveltian recipe for making "new energies and hardihoods continue [in peace time] the manliness to which the military mind so faithfully clings." If, said he,

there were, instead of military conscription a conscription of the whole youthful population to form for a certain number of years a part of the army enlisted against Nature, the injustice would tend to be evened out, and numerous other goods to the commonwealth would follow. The military ideals of hardihood and discipline would be wrought into the growing fibre of the people; no-one would remain blind as the luxurious classes now are blind, to man's relations to the globe he lives on, and to the permanently sour and hard foundations of his higher life. To coal and iron mines, to freight trains, to fishing fleets in December, to dish-washing, clothes-washing, and window-washing, to road-building and tunnel-making, to foundries and stoke-holes, and to the frames of sky-scrapers, would our gilded youths be drafted off, according to their choice, to get the childishness knocked out of them, and to come back into society with healthier sympathies and soberer ideas.[17]

But if there was anyone who did not stand in need of conscription in order to learn hardihood, it was the workers themselves, who were already living amid those equivalents of war to which James wished to introduce his gilded youths.

The official view of industry, as I have said, was the rational-pacific one described in 1902 by W. J. Ghent, when he observed sardonically of sermonizing tycoons like Carnegie that "a flattering unction that all lay to their souls is the dictum that success in business is a matter of honesty, intelligence, and energy."[18] The realities were very different. As the muckraker William Hard stated in 1907 in his account of the South Chicago plant of the U.S. Steel Corporation, "Steel is War. When

159

it is finished it brings forth, for the victor, Skibo Castles and Peace Conferences. But while it is in process it is War."[19] And the Beards, working the same metaphor, commented subsequently that the history of the oil industry was

the story of aggressive men, akin in spirit to military captains of the past, working their way up from the ranks, exploiting natural resources without restraint, waging economic war on one another, entering into combinations, making immense fortunes, and then, like successful feudal chieftans or medieval merchants, branching out as patrons of learning, divinity, and charity.[20]

Moreover, if it was true that the great tycoon, as Lord Bryce averred, had needed "gifts for strategical combinations scarcely inferior to those, if not of a great general, yet of a great war minister,"[21] a corollary of the war analogy was that if there were generals and heroic under officers, there were also troops. And during this period, workers in high-risk industries were increasingly perceived both by sympathizers and by themselves in exactly those terms. As Ghent pointed out, "the number of railway employees killed in the year ended June 30, 1893, was 2,727, a number exceeding the Union death roll in every battle of the Civil War except Gettysburg, and within 243 of that record. In the same year the number of wounded (31,279) was...more than double that at Gettysburg."[22] Hard put things more sharply still when he commented of the South Chicago steel plant that "the record of the long battle in the cave of smoke...for the year 1906 would...present 598 killed and wounded men to the consideration of a public which would be appalled by the news of the loss of an equal number of men in a battle in the Philippines."[23]

Furthermore, accidents to the troops, the "army of construction," as the Syndicalist Tom Mann called them in 1913,[24] did not simply happen as the result of acts of God or the workers' own carelessness, as the official business ideology maintained. As Hard pointed out of that representative high-risk industry, the steel business, "the operating men who manage [it] are human beings. They do not wish to commit either murder or suicide. But Steel is War."[25] And in war maximum demands must be made on the troops. The early 1900s increasingly witnessed the attitude voiced by the college president in Robert Herrick's *A Life for a Life* who admired a generator on a tycoon's estate because "it represents efficiency, power without waste! That is the keynote of our highly organized modern civilization."[26] Those were the years of Frederick Winslow Taylor's fervent advocacy of "scientific management," and industrialists and the strong-willed, firm-jawed college men serving them in industry were putting his principles into practice. The result, notoriously, was the time-clock speed-up so hated by workers. Speaking before a Congressional committee in 1918, a

160

Violence and peace (I)

Wobbly recalled, representatively, how "I get [sic] a job in competition with other workers, and speed, efficiency – speed-efficiency, profit-efficiency was the gauge."[27] This quasimartial pattern of intensifying demands on workers contained some profound contradictions.

On the one hand, the pressure towards ever-increasing productivity in high-risk industries, with its accident-causing speed-up of operations, had strong moral overtones. In the armylike collectivities of company towns, set apart by their rhythms and routines from normal urban or rural living, there was a sustained demand for courage and self-sacrifice, for a collective ethos of high-energy risk taking, such as could be found among the "primitive" ethnic groups like the Eastern and Southern Europeans who were being encouraged to immigrate and enter the man-killing industries. And the high-risk industrial processes entailed the creation of cooperative, plantoonlike work gangs possessing special kinds of practical intelligence and skills, who were required to know intimately the actual day-by-day workings of particular processes in this or that mine or mill, and who were thus in a position to judge whether things were really running efficiently or not. But on the other hand, the worker was denied on ideological grounds not only the right but the ability to suggest how things might be run better. He was denied the right to speak of what was happening to his own body – the injuries, the efficiency-diminishing fatigue. He was denied the right to speak similarly on behalf of fellow workers. Even the most articulate and intelligent worker, insofar as he attempted to argue with employers or their agents rather than claw his way ahead in competition with his fellow workers, was by definition someone who did not deserve a respectful hearing – and who, in fact, was made even less of a person by virtue of being defined, *qua* "agitator," as un-American. Implicit in these denials was a cleavage between two classes – the employers and the employed – more absolute and more humiliating to the latter than the class system of Europe, given the American correlation of economic inferiority with defects of character. Furthermore, because in terms of official ideology no class division could exist in America, and because America was preeminently the country in which rational discussion between all individuals was possible, the cleavage ended up being subsumed by a more-than-Southern irrationalism about the superiority and inferiority of various racial "stocks." As Frederic Howe said of the attitude of business to labor, immigrants "can be worked twelve hours a day; by mixing nationalities they can be hindered from organizing; when they are maimed or worn out, others take their place."[28] In other words, employers simultaneously denied workers the right to organize, sneered at them for lacking the organizational abilities that distinguished employers who came from the right kinds of stocks, and claimed a more-than-feudal power over their bodies that resulted in some half a million workers being killed or badly injured each year in the early 1900s.

What the new radicalism in general, and the Wobblies in particular, did was redefine the rules of the game to bring them into line with the actualities. They acted on the perception that historically, as the socialist Gustavus Myers pointed out in his *History of the Great American Fortunes* in 1910,

numberless people [had] sickened and died in the industrial strife and in miserable living quarters; ubiquitous capitalism was a battle-field strewn with countless corpses; but none of the professional expositors of morality, religion or politics gave heed to the wounded or the dead, or to the conditions which produced these hideous and perpetual slaughters of men, women and children ...and the law, the majestic, exalted Law, upheld [the] victors in their possessions by force of courts, police, sheriffs, and by rifles loaded with bullets if necessary.[29]

The Wobblies firmly rejected the conventional distinctions about the term "violence." As the young Wobbly Frank Tannenbaum stated at his trial in 1915 for inciting the poor to occupy New York churches, "a very serious objection against me was that I answered 'Yes' to the statement about bloodshed. Why make all this nonsense about bloodshed? Capital sheds more blood in one year than we would in five. We are being killed every day. We are being killed in the mines, in the buildings, killed everywhere, killed in the battlefield fighting the wars of the capital class."[30] Likewise, the Wobblies and the new radicals emphasized the actual contempt for law displayed by the advocates of order. They sardonically drew attention to the persistent law breaking, the massive chicanery, the wholesale bribery and corruption that had in fact gone into the creation of the great American fortunes. They pointed to the flagrant disregard of labor laws by employers, such as the ignoring of safety regulations that had resulted in the death by fire of a hundred and seventy-five miners in the Speculator copper mine at Butte. They stressed the blatant illegalities in various strike breakings, beginning, in the words of the Wobblies' counsel George F. Vanderveer, "way back in the Coeur d'Alene strike in northern Idaho, where soldiers were employed to put about a thousand men in bull pens, two story affairs, where the excrement from the top story ran down on the men underneath – the most terrible condition imaginable."[31] They brought out how, in John Reed's words in 1913, "There's war in Paterson! But it's a curious kind of war. All the violence is the work of one side – the Mill Owners,"[32] and how big business used the law as a weapon. In a cartoon in the *Masses* in 1915, for example, captioned "During the Prayer," John D. Rockefeller, Jr. whispers gloatingly to his father in a church pew,

Violence and peace (I)

"Well, Pa, we've got John Lawson out of the way!" after the UMW
director of the Ludlow strike had been sentenced to life imprisonment in
a blatantly rigged trial.[33]

The corollary of such perceptions was that when a warlike state
existed between two groups with sharply separate interests, one of
them implacably bent on achieving or maintaining domination, and the
other without any possibility of successful legal action, the latter could
legitimately resort to violence when there was no other way of getting
its rights. The new radicalism rejected the classic no-win situation
defined in a cartoon by Art Young in the *Masses* in 1913 in which a
workingman, pinned down beneath the buttocks of an enormous
uniformed figure holding a rifle and with the initials "U.S." on its belt
buckle, gropes desperately toward a stone to throw, and the caption
reads, "Serene on-looker: (To the Striker) 'Very unfortunate situation,
but whatever you do, don't use force.'"[34] In a cartoon by John Sloan on
the cover of the *Masses* at the time of the Ludlow massacre, a miner
stands in the wrecked miners' camp with a dead child in his left arm and
his dead wife and another child at his feet, and fires at the unseen forces
of "order."[35]

THE USES OF NONVIOLENCE AND CONTROLLED VIOLENCE

But there was a curious paradox here. The IWW had initially been a
breakaway group from the Western Federation of Miners, in which Bill
Haywood had been secretary treasurer, and the labor wars in the
Western mining regions in the Nineties had been ferocious. In Louis
Adamic's words,

almost every month some mine or mill was dynamited. Men were shot dead at
night and in the day time. Pitched battles occurred between members of the
W.F. of M. and non-union men, resulting in hundreds of casualties...
The war reached a sort of climax in the spring of 1899, when the $250,000 mill
of the Bunker Hill Company was destroyed by the miners with dynamite.[36]

Behind the Wobblies, as well, lay the traditions absorbed by Elizabeth
Gurley Flynn during her childhood:

There had been an uprising in each generation in Ireland, and forefathers of
mine were reputed to be in every one of them. The awareness of being Irish
came to us as small children, through plaintive song and heroic story... Before I
was ten I knew of the great heroes – Robert Emmet, Wolfe Tone, Michael Davitt,
Parnell, and O'Donovan Rossa, who was chained hand and foot, like a dog, and
had to eat from a tin plate on the floor of a British prison... We had heard in our
very early childhood of the so-called Molly Maguires, 17 young Irish-American
miners who had been executed in the 1870s in the anthracite area, for trying to
organize a union, and of how they were framed up by a Pinkerton detective.[37]

But what stood out about the Wobblies was their actual moderation in comparison not only with the W.F. of M. and the Fenians, but with "pure and simple" unions like the Steel Workers Union, which between 1905 and 1910 engaged in some 150 dynamitings of buildings and bridges. As Melvyn Dubofsky notes in his history of the IWW, "any careful investigator...soon becomes aware that the organization regularly proclaimed the superiority of passive resistance over the use of dynamite or guns."[38] Even the notorious sabotage that the Wobblies advocated and that became in George F. Vanderveer's words, "the holy terror of the employer,"[39] was primarily a matter of literal-minded rule following and go-slow tactics in the face of "scientific management" and speed-up, rather than of simple destructiveness. As Elizabeth Gurley Flynn said later of her pamphlet *Sabotage* (1915) – and the statement is persuasively corroborated by a recent researcher – "Many of the practices I referred to...were not 'sabotage' at all, but simply old-fashioned working class practices from time immemorial."[40] And the labor writer and Village radical Mary Heaton Vorse recalled of the Lawrence strike that "there was so little actual violence that the government report of the strike, prepared for the Department of Labor, stated that 'Few strikes involving so large a number of employees... have continued so long with so little actual violence or riot.' "[41]

Flynn's postmortem on the Patterson strike was particularly illuminating in this connection. "I contend," she said in 1913, "that there was no use for violence...; that only where violence is necessary shall violence be used. This is not a moral or legal objection but a utilitarian one. I don't say that violence should *not* be used, but where there is no call for it, there is no reason why we should resort to it." Violence, she granted, "is dramatic. It's especially dramatic when you talk about it and don't resort to it. But actual violence is an old-fashioned method of conducting a strike." As she pointed out, "violence may mean just weakness on the part of...workers. Violence occurs in almost every American Federation of Labor strike, because the workers are desperate, because they are losing their strike." She concluded her remarkable analysis by saying,

Before I finish with this question of violence I want to ask you men and women here if you realize that there is a certain responsibility about advocating violence. It's very easy to say, "We will give up our lives on behalf of the workers," but it's another question to ask them to give up their own lives; and men and women who go out as strike agitators should only advocate violence when they are absolutely certain that it is going to do some good other than to spill the blood of the innocent workers on the streets of their cities.[42]

Nevertheless, as Vorse said, "all New England was appalled by Lawrence. It was a new kind of strike."[43] And what especially alarmed and enraged the respectable about the Wobblies was precisely their employment of tactics that could stand up to scrutiny in legal terms. The nonideological violence of the AFL, insofar as it simply replicated the strong-arm violence of employers and was used for simple economic purposes, was in a sense unalarming, being part of a shared language of simple, ruthless economic self-interest. But operations like the Wobblies' free-speech fights and the Lawrence and Paterson strikes, with their peaceful mass picketing and parades and omnipresent singing, not only took place within the limits of the laws, like the industrial sabotage of working to rule, but used the laws themselves and acceptable public principles of morality as weapons. The free-speech fights put the proponents of capitalist law and order in a bind wherein they must either allow the invaders to agitate freely against them on their soap boxes, or else arrest them and have the jails and the court machinery impossibly overloaded. And when Bill Haywood, as a character in Eastman's *Venture*, said half-humorously during the Paterson strike, "I would suggest that we send the men and children away and let the women stay here and win the strike. In my experience one woman is worth two men every time, when it comes to sticking to a fight,"[44] what he was pointing to was more formidable than the simple skull cracking or dynamiting of hired union thugs. The pastoral-heroic orderliness and decency of the Lawrence and Paterson strikes, which Vanderveer called "marvels of order,"[45] were alarmingly different from the traditional image of revolutionism. As Hutchins Hapgood, the free-spirited older brother of *Collier's* Norman Hapgood, wrote at the time about a meeting of 25,000 strikers in Paterson,

there was only one policeman present at this enormous gathering and he had nothing whatever to do. It was not even necessary for him to ask anybody to keep off the carefully taken care of bit of lawn that the lady who loaned her cottage to the strike leaders to speak from cared for. They all stepped carefully over this pathetically green place, as gently as if they were sparing her feelings, as indeed they were.

This considerateness, he commented,

was a symbol of the mood and spirit of these thousands of strikers. Consistently with fighting their industrial battle in which they have been firmly and quietly unyielding, they have shown their patience, feeling for essential right and law, that breathing, deep-seated gentleness which is so marked in the mass of what is called the working class, and which marks them off sharply from the men who are sworn to maintain law and order in this case.[46]

All this not only lent support to, in Flynn's words, "our thesis that force and violence come from the ruling class and not from the people,"[47] it also bore on an important further aspect of the nature of revolution.

In this chapter and in Chapter 10, I have been describing an outlook –essentially a chivalric-martial one – in which justice does not result from people benevolently giving things, including "rights," to others. Implicit in possessing the power to grant is the power to withhold. The agonistic view, in contrast, is that rights are things that are taken, not given, and that they result from people having the necessary strength for effectively taking them. As Max Eastman wrote in 1912, "between revolutionist and reformer there is every difference.... The reformer wishes to procure for the workers their share of the blessings of civilization... The revolutionist wishes the workers to take the blessings of civilization."[48] It is a view in which, as Philip Hallie says in his admirable *The Paradox of Cruelty,* "the opposite of cruelty is not kindness [but] freedom" and ethics are chiefly "a matter of pressures of all sorts used by the powerless against their tormentors. Ethics is the way the weak limit the strong, not simply the way the strong philosophize amongst themselves."[49] The pattern of agonistic peace and justice was observable in the cowboy culture, in which, as in the Arthurian system, men who were armed and prepared to use their arms if necessary worked harmoniously, peaceably, and equitably with one another because none could achieve domination over the rest. It had obtained, too, among those Plains Indians of whom a trader commented in the middle of the nineteenth century that "no man's rule over them is absolute; their government is pure democracy."[50] It had characterized the small-scale clan groupings and allegiances of medieval Ireland. It had been manifested in the antebellum Southern conception of America as a free confederation of independent, power-charged states. And the principles of underdog power and force were sophisticated ones.

The new radicalism was thoroughly militant, and by now there was a tradition wherein political violence was morally acceptable if it was the only way of achieving one's rights. Finley Peter Dunne, for instance, recalled of a couple of Chicago cops that "Jack Shea and Devery hated crimes of violence...But political killings were different. And killings in the unending conflict between Ireland and the British government were acts of war."[51] Hutchins Hapgood reported meeting a convicted dyna-miter who "neither acted nor felt like a criminal. He was in no sense a moral delinquent but a soldier fighting for a cause; that was his state of mind."[52] Even Carnegie proudly remembered how as a boy, back in Dunfermline, "I could have slain king, duke, or lord, and considered their deaths a service to the state and hence an heroic act."[53] But the pattern of acceptable violence in Wobbly thinking was very different from either rioting or political assassination, and important principles were at work in the radical talk of warfare, such as the statement of the defense attorney for Mother Jones and forty-nine miners at a West Virginia trial in 1913 that "the miners accept it as war. If they will resort to violence, their acts will be aimed at a system and not at individuals

Violence and peace (I)

...Their acts will be acts of war, which society should not judge by ordinary rules of law and morality."[54] When an undergroup insists that it is engaged in warfare and that it should be treated as soldiers rather than as criminals, it is not simply claiming the right to commit violence with impunity; it is implicitly invoking the idea of chivalric warfare. Some important corollaries about power relationships are involved.

As Frederick Douglass had pointed out in his autobiography, if a group appeared to accept its powerlessness the natural reaction was to assume that it *deserved* to be without power. The Southern slave, as Bruce Catton observes, had been perceived by many as someone on whom "it was hardly possible to inflict a real injustice, inasmuch as injustice was his natural lot";[55] the half-starved and monstrously exploited Mexican peasants of the Díaz regime were idle, shiftless, characterless, and in need of discipline; so were the broken American Indians. But it was not the mere use of violence that constituted effective force and power, the kind of force and power that produce respect. And this is why the chivalric nature of controlled underdog violence was, and has continued to be, so important.

Implicit in the contempt for underdogs was the belief that they were unworthy of liberty, either because they lacked energy or because their energies, being formless, were ineffectual or indiscriminately destructive. The underdog violence that wins respect demonstrates not only that a group strongly believes in the justice of its cause, but that it does not deserve to be an underdog, because its energies are both powerful and ordered and it can be trusted to manage its own affairs. It also demonstrates that the risk-taking underdog combatants are the spokesmen for, and best embodiments of, their groups, and that the cultural nexus out of which they speak and act is admirable. The unskilled workers of the Lawrence and Paterson strikes, many of them immigrants, showed in their collective self-discipline what working men and women were capable of. So did the Wobbly free-speech fighters who remained calm, nonviolent, and mutually supportive in the face of vigilante brutalities, and the Wobbly organizers like Haywood, Flynn, and Ettor who preserved their composure and sense of humor in the face of the massed forces of law and order. A willingness to follow a chivalric, rule-governed pattern of combat in which the combatant runs risks rather than injure the innocent, and does not sharply separate the values of peace and the values of war, indicates that he is not simply bent on obtaining power and that he indeed cares about justice.

What made the Wobblies' mode of action so potent was that it followed what, in American terms, was the classic pattern of legitimate underdog force. It was the pattern of the official version of the American Revolution, still "a thing of yesterday" in Boston as Wells noted.[56] It was what Americans had admired in a number of other revolutionary enterprises – William Tell's activities in Switzerland; the fight of the Dutch against the Spanish occupiers of the Low Countries as described in John Lothrop Motley's *The Rise of the Dutch Republic*; the struggle of Cuban patriots against Spanish tyranny in the Nineties. It was the pattern of the Good Outlaw – paradigmatically Robin Hood – who was driven into outlawry by the injustices of others and who personified and built up resistance among the oppressed until the unjust authorities were overthrown and a state of justice was restored. It would eventually receive its fullest articulation in the kind of Western, derived from the Johnson County war of 1892 in Wyoming, in which hard-working homesteaders try to make an honest living, a tycoonlike big rancher lusts after imperial domination, his hired bullies and would-be macho son go out to win it for him, his bought sheriff and judge back them up, the good people of the township stay prudently out of harm's way, and the rancher's daughter has a liberal bad conscience about it all.[57] If underdogs in such situations have recourse to violence, it is not because they despise justice and law or desire to destroy the principles and procedures of reason and civilization. They are fighting to rectify situations in which those principles and procedures have ceased to be operative, situations in which not peace and reason but what Carlyle called "Smooth Falsehood" prevail.[58]

This pattern became increasingly visible as the Wobblies goaded the respectable into violence. By taking at face value the official American affirmations about freedom of thought and speech, the Wobblies, like the Knights of Labor before them, were maneuvering the employing class into a position where it must either put up with the subversion of its own authority or else be the first to resort to guns and clubs. And inherent in the Wobbly campaigns was the promise that the forces of law and order would more and more find themselves in the role of the oppressor of something admirable. As Mary Heaton Vorse recalled of the Lawrence strike,

No one could see these singing, disciplined people without being moved by them. A spiritual quality that was felt by everyone showed itself at the strike meetings. Ray Stannard Baker said, "It had a peculiar, tense, vital spirit that I never saw before in a strike."

Something very good was being evolved here. People were thinking in unison. People were acting in unison. Marching together, singing together. Harmony, not disorder, was being established, yet it was a collective harmony. A meeting like this was the antithesis of mob; people coming together to build and create instead of to hate and destroy. What we saw in Lawrence affected us so profoundly that this moment of time in Lawrence changed life for us.[59]

Violence and peace (I)

Those strengths were embodied in the great Paterson pageant in Madison Square Garden that John Reed and other Villagers created in conjunction with the Wobbly leaders. "In two weeks' time," Hutchins Hapgood reported in the *New York Globe,*

this pageant was organized – and yet more than a thousand strikers came to New York, presented in an orderly, systematic, truthful, and moving way the salient features in the history of the great strike. They did it without exaggeration, with gentleness, with a fine mass – not mob – feeling, and in doing it with such instinctively good faith they gave a performance of the utmost importance, not only socially but also artistically.

The art of it was unconscious, and especially lay in the suggestions for the future. People interested in the possibility of a vital and popular art, and in constructive pageantry, would learn much from it. In this way it foreshadowed much more than it realized. Think of using the initiative and the lives of men and women and combining this mass initiative and this phalanx of life into a spectacle![60]

"It was a unique form of proletarian art," Elizabeth Gurley Flynn wrote in her memoirs. "Nothing like it had happened in the American labor movement."[61] By 1914 she was able to announce that the new "method of conducting strikes has proved so successful and so remarkable ...that the United Mine Workers have taken it up, and in Michigan they are holding women's meetings, children's meetings, mass picketings and mass parades, such as never characterized an American Federation of Labor strike before."[62] These techniques would be used in a variety of later strikes, such as the Passaic, New Jersey, textile strike of 1926 and the General Motors sit-down strike at Flint, Michigan, in 1937.

A REVOLUTIONARY VIEW OF REVOLUTIONS

Moreover, when the intelligent young turned their gaze on contemporary revolutions that seemingly demonstrated the full folly and wickedness of revolution, it was possible to discern beneath their agitated surfaces the same fundamental principles at work, making for order. And what John Reed accomplished in his accounts of Mexico in 1913 and Russia in 1917 would have lasting consequences for American radicalism.

In his treatment of Mexico, Reed revived something curiously like the attitude voiced by Charles Mills when he said that "Spanish chivalry awakens the most splendid and romantic associations of the mind."[63] The official view of Mexico prior to the overthrow of Porfirio Díaz's regime in 1910, was that a mass of lazy, drunken, shiftless, quarrelsome peons were being exposed to the discipline of rational and progressive modernization. As the Beards put it, "to the foreigners operating under

169

his beneficences, Díaz was 'the strong man' who knew how to rule Mexico in the only possible way, namely by physical force."[64] And the related view of post-1910 Mexico was that in its simple disorderliness it was a horrendous example of the troubles that Latin America could make for itself when discipline was relaxed. Such countries cried out for the firm hands of Richard Harding Davis's clean-cut soldiers of fortune –or of Woodrow Wilson's marines, who occupied Vera Cruz in 1914. What Reed did in *Insurgent Mexico* (1914) was demonstrate that the revolutionary spirit in Mexico was not mere barbarism or childishness. He showed his readers men who, like the Wobblies, had their own culture and could work out their own destinies, energetic, humorous, festive men possessed of a rough but real sense of justice and able to cooperate effectively, if informally, when cooperation was needed. The personification of these qualities was the 'bandit' Pancho Villa. On the one hand, with his exuberance, his playfulness, his passion for dancing, his "reckless and romantic bravery" that formed "the subject of countless poems," he was the romantic hero of whom Reed reported that "everywhere he was known as The Friend of the Poor. He was the Mexican Robin Hood." On the other, he was not only a very able military leader who, "although he had never heard of the Rules of War, carried with his army the only field hospital of any effectiveness that any Mexican army has ever carried."[65] He also displayed admirable good sense about the business of governing, cut through mystifications, humbug, and mental red tape, and dreamed aloud of dispersing the army once the revolution was won and teaching the peasants and workers how to defend themselves if invaded. Reed's book was all the more important because the revolutionaries were chivalric without being chivalrous in the storybook fashion, and because their order-making strengths were not negated by their occasional savagery.

In Reed's presentation of the Russian Revolution in *Ten Days that Shook the World* (1919), the general configurations that I have been talking about were even more prominent. The final issue of the *Masses* in 1917, whose lead article was a long piece "The Truth about the I.W.W.," had announced on its back cover:

Remember that John Reed is in Petrograd.

He is writing the truth about the Russian Revolution.

His articles will be published exclusively in The Masses.

His story of the first Proletarian Revolution will be an event in the world's literature.

His story of the struggle between Maximalists (I.W.W.?) and Minimalists (A.F. of L.?) will answer the questions every Socialist and every Liberal is asking.

If the Censors permit, we will have his first article in the next number.

Violence and peace (I)

By the time Reed sat down to write the book in New York, he had seen
the reports about Russia in the American press and knew how easy it
was to say, as he noted in an unpublished manuscript, that the Russian
masses "have no sense of Patriotism, Duty, Honor; that they do not
submit to Discipline or appreciate the Privileges of Democracy; that in
short they are Incapable of Self-Government."[66] Like the *Masses'* presentation of the Wobblies, *Ten Days that Shook the World*, with its vivid
particularity, challenged the stereotype of the lower orders as undisciplined, irresponsible, and bloodthirsty. Reed disrupted the stock images
of Red Guards raping, torturing, and butchering, and ignorant peasants
wrecking the machinery of civilized and efficient government. He
showed common soldiers indignantly refusing to shoot unarmed men
and particularly concerned not to endanger women. ("Tired, bloody,
triumphant, the sailors and workers swarmed into the switchboard
room, and finding so many pretty girls, fell back in an embarrassed way
and fumbled with awkward feet. Not a girl was injured, not one
insulted.") He ridiculed the elaborately tiered Czarist bureaucracy, and
showed plain men answering, by word and deed, the accusation that,
lacking intellectuals and expertise, they were unequipped to operate the
social machinery themselves – accusations like, "Red Guards are incapable in handling a complicated business like the railways; as for the
Provisional Government, it has shown itself incapable of holding the
power."

In a number of places, too, he strongly emphasized the pastoral-
heroic nexus of the revolution. Young Red Guards marched under a red
flag with "Peace! Land!" on it. Women marched "with spades, some
with rifles and bandoliers, others wearing the Red Cross on their
arm-bands – the broad, toil-worn women of the slums." At a climactic
moment,

on the steps of Smolny [Institute] about a hundred Workers' and Soldiers'
Deputies were massed, with their banner, dark against the blaze of light,
streaming out between the arches. Like a wave they rushed down, clasping the
peasants in their arms and kissing them; and the procession poured in through
the great door and up the stairs, with a noise like thunder.

The possibility of transcending old structures emerged not only in the
spectacle "in every village, town, city, district and province [of] Soviets
of Workers', Soldiers' and Peasants' Deputies, prepared to assume the
task of local administration," but in the quiet description of an aristocratic colonel cheerfully serving as an executive officer answerable to the
elected regimental committee that had appointed him and that managed
the regiment except when it was in battle.[67]

171

10

Violence and peace (II)

Out of the sly and crafty eyes of many of them leap cupidity, cruelty, insanity, and crime; from their lopsided faces, sloping brows, and misshapen features may be recognized the unmistakable criminal type.

Attorney General A. Mitchell Palmer (1920)

God has marked the American people as His chosen nation to finally lead in the regeneration of the world. This is the divine mission of America, and it holds for us all the profit, all the glory, all the happiness possible to man. We are trustees of the world's progress, guardians of its righteous peace.

Senator Albert J. Beveridge (ca. 1900)

"What do you seriously think," I said, "is the final solution of this problem?" "Kill 'em off – that's all," she answered with equal seriousness.

Max Eastman and wife of Ludlow railroad superintendent (1914)[1]

CHANGING PERCEPTIONS OF WAR AND PEACE

THE NEW CHIVALRIC synthesis in America was all the more effective because it encompassed peace as well as war. In "The Moral Equivalent of War," William James had complained that "our socialistic peace-advocates all believe absolutely in this world's values; and instead of the fear of the Lord and the fear of the enemy, the only fear they reckon with is the fear of poverty if one be lazy." Hence, he said, "the whole atmosphere of present-day utopian literature tastes mawkish and disheartening to people who still keep a sense for life's more bitter flavors." In contrast, as he pointed out,

reflective apologists for war at the present day all take it religiously. It is a sort of sacrament. Its profits are to the vanquished as well as to the victor; and quite apart from any question of profit, it is an absolute good, we are told, for it is human nature at its highest dynamic. Its "horrors" are a cheap price to pay for rescue from the only alternative supposed, of a world of clerks and teachers, of co-education and zo-ophily, of "consumers' leagues" and "associated charities," of industrialism unlimited, and feminism unabashed. No scorn, no hardness, no valor any more![2]

What the new radicalism offered was in fact something very like the broadly appealing "system of morals of civic honor," based on "the

172

ruins of the old morals of military honor," that James had called for as a moral equivalent of traditional warfare.

The radicalism of Wobblies like Haywood and intellectuals like Reed was simultaneously martial and deeply antimilitaristic. When in 1917, after three years of loud calls for "preparedness," America entered the European war, *Collier's* reported that "many men and women are finding that a cause greater than themselves, a cause in which self can be sunk utterly, affords a joy which life had not seemed able to yield"; and Scott Fitzgerald subsequently recalled volunteers "chatter[ing] to each other, like college boys, of war's being the one excuse for, and justification of, the aristocrat, and conjur[ing] up an impossible caste of officers, to be composed, it appeared, chiefly of the more attractive alumni of three or four Eastern colleges."[3] (Reed's Harvard classmate, the aesthete-poet Alan Seeger, had already gone, enlisting in the Foreign Legion and dying in France in 1916.) In contrast, a Wobbly resolution of 1916 stated that "we openly declare ourselves the determined opponents of all nationalistic sectionalism, or patriotism, and to militarism preached and supported by our one enemy, the capitalist class. We condemn all wars."[4] And when America went to war, the Wobblies persisted in pressing the claims of labor by means of strikes, in defiance of clamorous demands for national unity by the press, the government propaganda machine, and super patriots like Gompers. The *Masses*, too, was strongly opposed not only to militarism but to *machismo* or would-be *machismo* in general, whether displayed by the heavily moustached, beer-swilling males gloating in a saloon over the defeat of a women's suffrage bill in Maurice Becker's cartoon "They Ain't Our Equals Yet," or by the narrow-shouldered, stiff-collared, short-haired youth with an empty anxious face in the family parlor, surrounded by six females and his moustached father, singing "None So Dauntless and Free on Land or on Sea."[5] Its suppression by Wilson's government at the end of 1917 was brought about by an acid antirecruiting cartoon.

The radicals' opposition to the war resulted from more than the conviction that it was a capitalist war. By itself that belief would not have been able to sustain so sturdy a resistance, going so clean against the main current, at a time when, as the pacifist Randolph Bourne bitterly observed, "we have had to watch...in this country the same process which so shocked us abroad – the coalescence of the intellectual classes in support of the military programme."[6] A changed perception of the nature of peace was also at work, making it possible for a martial figure like Reed to resist adamantly the call to arms without any sense of self-betrayal.

As I have pointed out, one of the paradoxes of the period was that, as the so-called peace influence grew, discontent with peace likewise grew. William James had expressed that discontent in 1899 when he had gazed skeptically on the Chautauqua Assembly Grounds in New York State, a community in which "sobriety and industry, intelligence and goodness, orderliness and ideality, prosperity and cheerfulness, pervade the air," and that struck him as a "middle-class paradise, without a sin, without a victim, without a blot, without a tear," characterized by a "dead level and quintessence of every mediocrity." He had, he said, returned with relief from "this atrocious harmlessness of all things" to "the big outside worldly wilderness."[7] It had been natural enough for American advocates of universal peace to perceive the essential conflict as one between civilization and barbarism, maturity and immaturity, the benign and nurturing feminine, the hard and destructive masculine. But the kind of peace that James was questioning, and that was questioned by the young radicals who by 1917, as one of them said, "appreciated more than ever" his ideas about "the moral equivalent of war,"[8] was, in fact, deeply duplicitious. Not only was its goodness flat and thin and dull, the goodness of H. G. Wells's garden-city Eloi in *The Time Machine*; it was also dominative and suppressive, both psychologically and politically. It involved what Tocqueville called "that state of administrative somnolence which administrators are in the habit of calling good order and public tranquillity." It continued the process he described when he said, "For half a century Europe has been shaken by many revolutions and counterrevolutions...But in one respect all these movements are alike: they have all undermined or abolished secondary powers... Everywhere it is the state itself which increasingly takes control of the humblest citizen and directs his behavior even in trivial matters."[9]

This kind of peace seeking entailed further paradoxes. It was not fortuitous that antiunion and especially anti-Wobbly activities were so savage. It was not fortuitous that, as the patrician radical Amos Pinchot wrote in the *Masses* in 1917 shortly before America's entry into the war, the "men who are most tireless in telling us that...militarism will be destroyed in Germany, happen to be the same men who are most tireless in booming the spirit of militarism in America, and in urging the United States to get into the war."[10] Nor was it fortuitous that the pacific-minded and progressive Wilson, in the words of Oswald Garrison Villard, engaged in "those bloody and brutal attacks upon Haiti, Santo Domingo, Nicaragua, and Mexico which disgraced [his] Administration,"[11] or that after America entered the war against Germany his government suppressed dissent with unprecedented ruthlessness. The rationalistic, antichivalric, and nonagonistic view of peace that I have been defining led logically to violence, at times massive violence. And

174

conversely, the new radical thinking worked against violence. By virtue of the transpositions of chivalric patterns that I described in Chapters 8 and 9, it permitted a viable passage beyond the crude antithesis of total peace on the one hand and total war, whether literal or metaphorical, on the other, and offered an enriched image of peace that transcended the dichotomies that perturbed writers like James. Because the new synthesis emerged concretely out of the labor wars, I will begin with a further aspect of those wars.

A DOUBLE STANDARD: JUST AND UNJUST VIOLENCE

The central paradox, the paradox of the cartoon by Art Young that I described in Chapter 9, was defined by Samuel Eliot Morison and Henry Steele Commager when they commented that "the use of Pinkerton detectives to protect business property was preserving law and order, but the use of force to protect the job was violence."[12] And what stands out is the amount of law-and-order force that the respectable could stomach without any twinges of moral discomfort. At Lattimer in the Northern Pennsylvania coalfields in 1897, for example, in Michael Novak's words, "a sheriff's posse fired directly into a crowd of men, women, and children, killing nineteen and seriously wounding thirty-nine: twenty-six Poles, five Lithuanians, twenty Slovaks. Naturally the courts found the sheriff and his deputies not guilty."[13] At Ludlow in 1914 the militia fired into the tents where the families of striking miners were sheltering, resulting in the deaths of two women and thirteen children – what Eastman described at the time as "that black orgy ... when a frail fluttering tent city in the meadow, the dwelling place of 120 women and 273 children, was riddled to shreds without a second's warning, and then fired by coal-oil torches... Flags of truce were shot out of hands; women running in the sunlight to rescue their children were whipped back with the hail of a machine gun."[14] At East Youngstown in 1916, as reported in the *Masses*, steel-company guards fired into a crowd of strikers peaceably assembled on Christmas Day, leaving forty men dead or dying. I have already mentioned the violence perpetrated against Wobblies in the West. The attacks by "law-abiding" citizens on union buildings during the Colorado strikes in 1904 were less dramatic, but no less revealing. As Haywood recalled, "the bankers and prominent citizens took part themselves in the riot, played the very devil with everything in the stores, poured coal oil over vast quantities of flour, sugar, meat, and other foodstuffs, smashed the cash registers, the computing scales, and did all the damage they could."[15]

The persisting conviction that armed defenders of peace were nonviolent, that unarmed Wobblies were monsters of violence, and that dead or injured workers and their families simply deserved what they got was due

175

to more than hypocrisy. The intensity of antiunion feeling resulted from more than simple self-interest, the simple selfishness voiced by one of John P. Marquand's proper Bostonians when he told his son that "this talk about the common good is arrant Socialism and nonsense. You and I do not stand for the common good. We stand for a small class."[16] It resulted from more than a simple fear of revolution. Something more complex was needed to produce phenomena such as the assertion in the journal *Coal Age* that it was not the coal operators and militia at Ludlow "who should bear the brunt of our condemnation but these aliens who have brought us a new glimpse of the Middle Ages and have disgraced our orderly civilization by their unwanted crimes."[17] Deeper moral intensities and imperatives were at work, related, as in *A Connecticut Yankee*, to a feared loss of momentum, energy, and power, an interruption of the irresistible, smooth-flowing, forward movement of a power-charged and power-generating civilization.

By a simple extension of rationalist principles, unions were, to use the term applied by President Eliot of Harvard to the closed shop, un-American. The New York banker who announced in 1886 that "the Almighty has made this country for the oppressed of other nations and therefore this is the land of refuge...and the hand of the laboring man should not be raised against it" was almost certainly not being disingenuous, any more than the former abolitionist Henry Ward Beecher was when he declared that "laborers' unions are the worst form of despotism and tyranny in the history of Christendom."[18] Nor was it paradoxical of Carnegie to denounce the Amalgamated Association of Iron and Steel Workers as "feudalism."[19] Unions implicitly rejected the image of American society as a place in which, liberated from the tyranny of fixed categories, individuals negotiated freely with individuals and, if possessing the requisite moral qualities, advanced steadily upwards, to the ultimate benefit of society as a whole. They claimed authority over workers themselves, and sought at times to prevent those who wished to work from doing so.[20] Most importantly, they tried to trammel the free-flowing creative energies of benefit-creating businessmen, not only by demanding contracts that denied the employer's right to be master in his own household, but by making strong moral claims upon employers' compassion in terms of the sufferings of workers and their families. They insisted that employers ought to feel *guilty* about their high-energy figurative warmaking. In his autobiography, Carnegie recalled how, during his boyhood in Dunfermline, "Wallace, of course, was our hero. Everything heroic centered in him";[21] and in conventional terms it was possible for the employer to see himself as being, like Twain's Boss, a heroic fighter on behalf of human liberty. Unions implicitly or explicitly insisted that, on the contrary,

Violence and peace (II)

employers belonged to the oppressor class that celebrators of the American system like Carnegie denounced so hotly.

In this moral struggle, a crucial role was played by the concept of violence. In a technical sense, the use of violence by workers was virtually unavoidable. Any strike would fail if enough workers refused to join in or enough replacements could be hired, and the only way of preventing this was to use force. The frightful implications of this had been spelled out by the *Nation* in the Eighties when it noted that

some friends of "Labor"...are trying to persuade themselves that it is possible in labor troubles to make a distinction between a little intimidation and a great deal – that is, between boycotting and bomb-throwing. But the point is too fine for popular apprehension. There is no difference except one of degree between concerted illegal attempts to injure any citizen in his person, property, or reputation...

When we get outside the law and begin to allow ever so little intimidation or coercion to be practised by either individuals or organizations for purposes of their own, we begin a descent at the bottom of which is anarchy – that is, arson, pillage, and murder, revolvers, rifles, and bombs.[22]

The crucial question was therefore whether there could be preceding actions by employers that justified law breaking, and whether, if workers were to some extent "criminal," employers were as well. And here an interesting set of game rules came into action. Given what Robert H. Wiebe calls "America's traditional separation of the world into two spheres, civilized and barbaric,"[23] and given the identification of the civilized with the rational and the pacific, and the barbaric with the irrational and violent, it was imperative for the employing class to see itself as having wholly clean hands when it came to violence. This was achieved by some interesting psychological maneuvers whereby the working class – or at least militant unionists – were kept in the sphere of the barbaric.

In respectable thinking, violence and criminality had come to be defined in nineteenth-century America essentially in terms of motives and states of mind. Violence was what was done by violent men, men who were unable or unwilling to act according to the principles of universal rationality, and who were characterized by unreason, lawlessness, and pride. Violent men used force rather than reason and enjoyed physical combat and the physical humiliation of others. They belonged, essentially, to the kinds of martial groups – Irish, Indian, "Greaser," Southern, and the rest – that I have discussed in these pages, with their primitive male camaraderie, clannishness, sense of honor, and acceptance of physical violence as a natural mode of behavior. Likewise, crime was essentially something done by criminals, who were also by definition irrational – partly because they were capable of violence, partly

177

because they were lazy, vain, childish, and selfish, and partly because it was patently irrational not to seek money and power inside the normal commercial system where the risks were so much less, given the looseness of the law, the opportunities for manipulating it, and the prevailing conviction that nothing that was legal was immoral. As a writer declared in *McClure's* in 1907, "the criminal is a savage, nothing more nor less. Civilization builds up painfully our definite, orderly rules of life – work, marriage, the constant restraint of the gross and violent impulses of crime. The criminal simply discards these laws and slides back along the way we came up – into license, thieving and violence. He merely lapses back into savagery."[24] Naturally, the criminal was almost certain to come from a chivalric-martial group.

The corollary of these assumptions was that employers were not engaged in activities that were violent, criminal, or cruel. As Morison and Commager say, the sins of business "were impersonal and without evil intent, and consequently produced no sense of guilt."[25] If "badness" was identifiable largely with intentional violence and a desire to hurt, such as in the martial subcultures and the culture of childhood, people who were engaged in activities that were good by definition, and who had no desire to *cause* suffering to particular individuals, were not reprehensible and their actions were not cruel. No one *sought* the dreadful injuries to Chicago meat workers that Upton Sinclair exposed in his novel *The Jungle* in 1905, or wanted the deaths of the 154 workers, mostly young girls, in the New York Triangle Shirtwaist Company fire in 1911. Industrialists were engaged in the rational pursuit of maximum profits, without recourse to soldiers, declarations of war, assaults or other countries. When they happened to break laws, they did not do so out of rebelliousness against rational order. On the contrary, they were simply avoiding certain kinds of unnatural constraints on the pacific benefit-extending maximization of their enterprises. And the invention of the corporation helped to ease individual consciences still further. Hence, by a further corollary, workers were not and could not be the victims of violence or cruelty or criminality. Insofar as industrial accidents occurred, or dwellings were insalubrious, or food insufficient, these were simply part of the natural workings of the industrial process. Workers were free agents, free of the tyranny of aristocracy and the European class system, and every contract entered into was a free one, permitting of indefinite advancement if the worker had the right kind of character. Employers were in no way responsible for those accidents that occurred.

Hence collective agonistic activities by workers were wrong in a variety of ways. The stirred-up hostility to innocent employers was entirely unwarranted. As the young Roosevelt said in 1883, "the worst

foe of the poor man is the labor leader who tries to teach him that he is a
victim of conspiracy and injustice."[26] The notion that there were
mutually hostile classes in America was at odds with the whole
American enterprise. "Characteristically," reports the historian George
F. Mowry, the average Progressive "denounced more vehemently the
philosophic overtones of unionism than its pragmatic economic gains.
He was almost obsessed with the class consciousness implicit in
unionism," and was convinced that, as a character said in a novel in the
Nineties, "the abominable word 'class' could be wiped out of the
English language as it is spoken in America."[27] The creation of martial
organizations was likewise in conflict with the ideal of a pacific America.
"There is nothing ethical about the labor movement," a Progressive
insisted in 1902. "It is simply a war movement, and must be judged by
the analogues of belligerence and not by industrial principles." And
Carnegie had declared a few years earlier that "the gage of battle, or the
duel, is not more senseless, as a means of establishing what is just and
fair, than an industrial strike or lockout."[28] Such procedures interfered
tyrannously with the free bargains being made between employers and
workers, and, as I have said, were likely to take the form of physical
force. In Herbert Croly's words, the unionist "becomes in the interests
of his organization a bad citizen, and at times an inhuman animal, who
is ready to maim or even kill another man." Beyond lay even more
sinister possibilities. As Croly complained, "the militant unionists are
beginning to talk and believe as if they were at war with the existing
social and political order – as if the American political system was as
inimical to their interests as would be that of any European monarchy or
aristocracy."[29]

Thus, on one side lay reason, order, and civilization; on the other,
unreason, lawlessness, and violence. And it was absurd of the Wobblies' attorney George F. Vanderveer to claim that the idea of revolution
was one of the principles upon which the country had been founded.
The American Revolution had not been a mere rebellion in which an
undergroup seized power over its fellows. It had been carried out on
behalf of universal principles and the general interests of mankind. With
those principles once established no further principled revolution was
possible. Any resistance to them was therefore by definition unreasonable, and any resentful subgroup was by definition unreasonable, and
any ideology that encouraged such subgroups was unreasonable.

Accordingly, it was altogether right and proper to preserve order and
oppose criminal violence with force. Employers had the right and duty
to prevent injuries to their property and loyal employees by means of
company guards and Pinkertons. They were entitled to protection by
the police and, if need be, the militia and the army, and to vigorous

support by the courts. They had the right to band together in the interests
of communal order. As the mayor of Paterson reported in *Collier's* in 1902
in "The Reign of Terror in Paterson,"

we have formed a Vigilance Committee. . .composed of business men who have
signified their intention to aid me in ridding the city once and for all of the. . .
group of anarchists which infests this city. Within a short time prison doors will
close upon all the leaders who incited honest workingmen of Paterson to riot, and
all other avowed anarchists will be railroaded out of town in different directions.[30]

A good many such associations of businessmen were formed in the early
years of the new century. As a Pittsburgh employer had put it in the
Nineties, unions "everywhere check production. We are now going to
control our own business, and we are going to do it entirely."[31]

Moreover, by a further ideological twist, it was not just minimal force
against strikes, and strikers, and union organizers that was acceptable.
The vigilantes of the Citizens' Alliance who invaded the offices of the
Victor *Record* in Colorado and "smashed the linotype machine with big
hammers and broke the presses"[32] were acting symbolically. The inevitable metaphors of union smashing and strike breaking were inevitable
because they defined the actual attitudes involved. Unions were meant to
be smashed and stay smashed; agitators were meant to be silenced
permanently; and the more effective the means, the better. Hence strike-
breaking agencies like the Pinkertons had since the sixties been recruiting
and hiring out corps of exactly the kinds of brutally martial types –
"men-at-arms" was how a *Collier's* writer described them in 1910[33] – that
pacific America was committed to doing away with. Hence, also, the
tradition developed that later moved Hemingway to remark that "where
you see gratuitous cruelty most often is in police brutality."[34] And the
legal system itself was used as a weapon, such as when the four innocent
Chicago anarchists were hanged as a moral example after the Haymarket
bombing in the Eighties, or when the philosophical anarchist Robert
MacQueen was sentenced to five years' imprisonment for his role in a
Paterson strike in 1905. As Wells said at the time, "the plain truth is that
no one pretends that [MacQueen] is in jail on his merits; he is in jail as an
example and lesson to any one who proposes to come between master
and immigrant worker in Paterson. He has attacked the system." The
judges in the case to whom he himself had spoken, Wells reported,
acknowledged that MacQueen was being kept in jail "on the score of
public policy. They put it that Paterson is a 'hot-bed' of crime and
violence; and once MacQueen is released, every anarchist in the country
will be emboldened to crime, and so on and so on. . .'What will the
property owners in Paterson say to us if this man is released?' one of the
judges admitted frankly."[35] The ferocious sentences given to Wobblies
like Haywood in 1918, and the massively suppressive Palmer Raids

Violence and peace (II)

carried out against other radicals in 1919–20 under the auspices of Wilson's Quaker-bred Attorney General, were simply part of a long tradition, a tradition that extended well beyond labor conflicts.

AMERICA AS WORLD POLICEMAN: MAKING WAR TO KEEP PEACE

The logic of strike breaking and radical crushing was the same logic that was at work when the pacific Wilson sent the Marines into Latin America and the doughboys into Europe, and that had governed Sherman's march through the South and the ruthlessness of various army groups toward the Indians. It was the logic not of war – or at least of war in the chivalric sense – but of the punishment and prevention of crime. In both antiunionism and America's indignation against the Germany of Wilhelm II, there was a vehement rejection of the notion that two legitimate groups were engaged in legitimate conflict. On the one side were the rational structures of civilized society; on the other disorderly or wicked beings who, like fire-eating antebellum Southerners, marauding Indians, or "medieval" Latin Americans, had chosen to break the social compact and use violence against their fellows. War, viewed in this light, was not what Huizinga calls a "cultural function," a rule-governed activity forming part of the natural spectrum of human experience. As Robert W. Tucker points out in a brilliant monograph, the enlightened view of warfare "implicitly rejects the contention that war can or should be regarded as an institution compatible with some form of order. In this view, the essence of war is that it signifies the breakdown of all order."[36] War was aggressive criminality, an activity analogous to robbery with violence or the brutishness of the barroom brawler. Hence when America, on behalf of reason and civilization, became involved in martial affairs with Spanish or Indian or German aggressors, or with aggressive trade unionists, it was not making war, it was preserving peace. In his first message to Congress in 1902, Roosevelt called wars with "the semi-barbarous peoples" simply "a most regrettable but necessary international police duty which must be performed for the sake of the welfare of mankind."[37] And Wilson's friend and advisor, Colonel Edward House, remarked at the time of the curiously Vietnam-like invasion of Vera Cruz that "if Mexico understood that our motives were unselfish, she should not object to our helping adjust her unruly household."[38] It was police actions that had been undertaken against insurgent Southerners and Indians. It was a police action that was being undertaken against Germany, part of the campaign against what Carnegie had called "international murder, which still passes by the name of war."[39]

Part II Chivalric patterns in industrializing America

But these facts by themselves do not account for the ruthlessness and the moral intensity that I have spoken of. Something else must be noted about the exasperated impatience with resistant "archaic" structures and the desire to break them down completely and permanently. In principle, of course, the patterns of a pacific, industrial society, being derived from fundamental principles of reason and answering to what human beings in their innermost natures essentially were, needed only to be known in order to be gratefully accepted and assented to. In practice, however, some chivalric-martial figures were so gripped by unreason and dominated by false notions of pride that drastic measures were necessary in the interests of permanent peace.

It was here that the identification of war with crime was so important, given that crime, like war, had been conceptually reduced from an agonistic confrontation between groups or individuals pursuing conflicting but rational ends, to a mere bundle of aberrations – foolish or wicked or both – on the part of the insufficiently rational. The agonistic attitude did indeed persist here and there, such as in relations between Irish cops and Irish criminals in the North and between white law-breakers and law enforcers in the South. But in more advanced ideological terms, what lay at the center of American thinking and feeling about the criminal was revealed in the approach to penology that had become widespread in enlightened America during the nineteenth century. Ironically, it was the self-proclaimed country of individualism that went furthest in the attempted crushing of all individuality. When Bill Haywood referred in his memoirs to the "terrible silent system" still enforced at times in American penitentiaries,[40] he was speaking of a key feature of the methodical spirit breaking that began in the 1820s in the New York State penitentiary at Auburn under the appalling Ellam Lynds, was perfected at Sing Sing shortly thereafter, and spread outwards into numerous other states. The logic of that spirit breaking was explicit. In the words of the Auburn prison inspectors in 1823, the prisoners "ought to be deprived of every enjoyment arising from social or kindred feeling and affections; of all knowledge of each other, the world, and their connections with it." In pursuit of this end, the convict under Lynds and his followers was "subjected to a process of calculated humiliation, in which every attempt was made to strip away whatever pride and self-respect he possessed."[41] What was deliberately created at Auburn by the respectable merchant class for the criminals emerging from the unruly working class, among them a substantial number of Irish canal-construction workers and boatmen, was a world in which fee-paying visitors could gaze, as in a zoo, at the mutely laboring prisoners in their grotesquely striped uniforms; a world in which a prisoner's word was never taken and he was permitted no intimations

182

Violence and peace (II)

of respect when talking to officials; a world of lockstep, silence, and merciless automatic floggings for the least infraction of prison regulations. It was a control system more absolute and merciless than anything to be found in the slaveholding South; and some of its techniques would be employed later in the systematic spirit breaking of military stockades and guardhouses described in works like James Jones's *From Here to Eternity* and Kenneth H. Brown's *The Brig*.[42] With a further irony, as Jessica Mitford points out, behind the Auburn system lay the penitentiary of the Philadelphia Quakers, with its system of utter, unrelieved solitary confinement, without sight or sound of any other inmates, whose horrors Dickens reported with such indignation in the Forties in his *American Notes*.[43]

The same determination to break down resistant structures was apparent with respect to war. It manifested itself in Sherman's reiterated assertions that the South had broken the law, that it was proud and willful, and that it must submit and return to obedience, whereupon forgiveness would immediately follow. It manifested itself in the desire of various Northern politicians after the war to imprison figures like Jefferson Davis and Lee as criminals and teach the South a lesson that it would never forget. Similarly, Wilson, when he sought Congressional approval for sending the Marines into Vera Cruz, explained that he was demanding from President Huerta not only a formal apology, but a "new spirit," so that such conduct on the part of the Mexicans would not occur again.[44] And in the exceptionally acute article that I quoted from earlier, Amos Pinchot pointed out how the supporters of intervention in the European war

continue to assure us serenely that the smashing prescription will do the trick. Especially they advise that the war must proceed, so that the Kaiser, the military class, etc., may be thoroughly punished. They want Germany to repent, confess her sin and acknowledge the saving grace of countries with more guns of heavier calibre...They confidently insist also that a nation of seventy million people can be permanently broken and incapacitated for war, as simply and as satisfactorily as we permanently break men and boys in our prisons and incapacitate them for rebellion against society.[45]

Implicit in the peace-making attitudes that I have been describing, moreover, were certain corollaries with respect to how war – peace-making, police-action war – should be waged. As Robert W. Tucker observes, "If the aggressive resort to war is both immoral and illegal, the aggressor as such can no longer be considered as endowed with any rights."[46] And if what is sought is peace and the submission and conversion of the enemy, then to allow a state of criminal violence and disorder to exist longer than necessary would be both foolish and immoral. Hence it was not only logical to wipe out intransigent martial

183

figures if that was the only way to produce permanent peace. It was also logical to discard the conventional chivalric distinction between combatants and noncombatants. If soldiers were supported in their criminal fighting by civilians who stood to benefit from an unrighteous victory, those civilians too were open to will-breaking reprisals. Hence Sherman's march to the sea, so brilliant militarily and producing such lasting hatred, had been perfectly sound morally, as had Phil Sheridan's systematic devastation in the Shenandoah Valley. War, as Sherman put it, "is simply power unrestrained by constitution or compact"; and although he took justifiable pride in the restraint of his troops, the violence of his army against property could logically have extended to persons as well, had that been judged necessary for breaking the will of the South and ending the war. Even as things were, he wrote home in 1865 that "poor North Carolina will have a hard time, for we sweep the country like a swarm of locusts. Thousands of people may perish, but they now realise that war means something else than vainglory and boasting. If Peace ever falls to their lot they will never again invite War."[47] The logic involved would be exhibited more nakedly immediately after the war when Sherman wrote to his Senator brother, apropos of an Indian "massacre" of an army group, that "we must act with vindictive earnestness against the Sioux, even to their extermination, men, women, and children. Nothing else will reach the root of this case." As he remarked a year or two later, "the more we can kill this year, the less will have to be killed the next war."[48] The same logic was at work in the slaughtering of thousands of Filipinos by the American army at the beginning of the century, and the massacring of over three thousand men and women in Haiti in 1915 at the cost of only thirteen Marines.[49]

It was a logic that also invited the use of superweaponry, such as the massive long-range gun with which the Union forces sought to bombard Charleston. In part the development of such weaponry resulted from a "common-sense" resentment of the idea of needlessly sacrificing the lives of one's own soldiers.[50] but beyond that, if one's own system was unquestionably right and that of one's opponents unquestionably wrong, as in the Crusades, then all devices were justified that would bring about the enemy's submission, whether by extermination or by will-breaking terror. Ideologically, the atomic bombs that devastated Hiroshima and Nagasaki belonged with the havoc-wreaking magic swords of Galahad and Ariosto's Amazonian heroines, and the robotic Talus who served as enforcer for Spenser's Artegall in his merciless justice-dealing, and the heavenly technology with which the loyal angels smashed the rebel ones in *Paradise Lost*. The apotheosis of superweaponry in literature was, of course, the holocaust in *A Connecti-*

cut Yankee, in which the anachronistic Arthurian civilization became fair game for the massive technological violence of the civilization-bearing Boss and his handful of young technocrats. As The Boss explained to his "fresh, bright, well-educated, clean-minded young...boys" near the end of the novel,

this campaign is the only one that is going to be fought. It will be brief – the briefest in history. Also the most destructive to life, considered from the standpoint of proportion of casualties to numbers engaged...English knights can be killed but they cannot be conquered...While one of these men remains alive, our task is not finished, the war is not ended. We will kill them all.

Not only did the brief ensuing battle, with its mines, and electrified fences and machine guns leave the chosen fifty-four with 25,000 knights dead around them. The victory climaxed a campaign in which, as the narrator freely conceded, "all England [was] marching against us!" And because there was apparently no way of persuading the country – now in the implacable grip of the Church and unreason – back into the paths of enlightenment, it was natural enough that during the holocaust the hero should have "touched a button" and produced an explosion in which "all our noble civilization-factories went up in the air and disappeared from the earth. It was a pity but it was necessary. We could not afford to let the enemy turn our own weapons against us."[51] So much for pacific reasonableness and the wholesome and practical civilization of the nineteenth century!

THE CHIVALRIC ALTERNATIVE: AGONISTIC WAR AND PEACE

But if, in Michael Novak's words, "the realism of 'enlightenment' creates a windswept vacuum in the soul, into which, finally, only naked power can rush,"[52] these tendencies were being countered by the chivalric patterns and attitudes. They were being countered both in the revived ideals of gentlemanliness and in the thinking of the new radicalism, with its endeavor, in Hutchins Hapgood's words, "to create another ethic, another esthetic, another morality, than those regarded as the ultimate support of the capitalist system."[53] Inherent in the chivalric patterns was the profoundly different view of peace that in Chapter 9 I called the agonistic, a view corroborating Walter Lippmann's statement in 1914 that "it is a commonplace of radicalism that power makes for peace" and that "reason begins when men have enough power to command respect."[54]

As is clear by now, the chivalric view of peace and war, particularly as I tried to define it in Chapters 4 and 5, differed fundamentally from the rationalistic neopastoral one. In terms of the latter, peace and war were absolutely separate conditions, with civilization, order, law, and reason on one side of the divide and barbarism, disorder, criminality, and unreason on the other. I have indicated some of the unfortunate results of that dichotomy. A further consequence, as Robert W. Tucker has pointed out, was the kind of uneasy jockeying in international politics wherein each party professed total pacificity while in fact seeking dominance, and tried to provoke the other into being technically the "aggressor," so that it could unleash the full force of its own military might against the criminal with a clear conscience. Hence, as William James said in 1910, " 'Peace' in military mouths to-day is a synonym for 'war expected.' The word has become a pure provocative...Every up-to-date dictionary should say that 'peace' and 'war' mean the same thing, now *in posse*, now *in actu*."⁵⁵ Moreover, anxieties were increased by the knowledge that if warfare was essentially not a code-governed and legitimate activity, then all that could be predicted of a war in an era of technological changes would be that, like the wars of *A Connecticut Yankee* and H. G. Wells's *The War in the Air* (1908), it would be different from, and more destructive than, any previous war. In the chivalric-martial patterns, in contrast, whether observable in the official rules of knightly warfare or in the warfare of the Plains Indians, war and peace overlapped very differently. The same codes operated in both, so that there was an intelligible spectrum of degrees of violence. And because there was a spectrum and negotiations could take place at all stages, as they could in the elaborate eighteenth-century dueling codes, it was possible for there to be limited confrontations and engagements that did not signify the irrevocable crossing of a moral frontier and from which both parties could withdraw with honor if they chose. Likewise more options became available in peace.

Implicit in the chivalric-martial patterns was the idea of power-charged individuals or groups meeting in certain essential respects as equals and acting according to jointly agreed-upon rules. And the radical years witnessed the growth of an agonistic and pluralistic conception of civic peace, in contrast to the monolithic conceptions of Social Darwinism and Progressivism. As Hutchins Hapgood said, the development was partly implicit, in that no general theory was formulated to describe it. But the outlines of a philosophy of peace were clear in the syndicalism of the Wobblies and the attitudes of the Village young, and were reinforced in other ways. Henry F. May reports, for example, how in those years Harold Laski, "immensely exuberant and brilliant, was spreading at Harvard in the *New Republic* the doctrine of pluralism. Like G. D. H. Cole, the guild socialist, and many others, he was sure that the creative energies of man could best be liberated by a spontaneous network of free associations."⁵⁶ There was a growing implicit perception of the necessity for what Tocqueville called "second-ary powers," and for a structure of power-charged pastoral-heroic groups, sometimes in conflict with each other, sometimes collaborating, but with their own identities and own needs. It was for these reasons that the Wobblies and a number of the *Masses* group could be so resolutely opposed to America's entry into the European war, and to international warfare in general.

The shifts in attitudes were more than merely political, and for that reason they were all the more consequential politically. Implicit in a good deal of what I have been describing was an important shift with respect to the concept of criminality. It was plain that the charming gentlemen crooks of popular fiction were not only governed by coherent codes of their own but were sometimes governed by better ones than technically law-abiding citizens. It was also plain that law-breaking and authority-mocking groups like Robin Hood's band, the Three Mus-keteers, Kipling's Stalky and Co., and the Four Just Men were governed by clear codes and self-imposed limits. And these perceptions carried over to actual subgroups operating outside the borders of "decent" society. Hutchins Hapgood, for example, reported in 1907 how the aim in life of the true tramp, the yegg, was "to escape labor, to be a parasite. He makes a profession of that. It is as dishonourable for him to go against the rules of his profession as it is for a preacher to work in a factory, a lawyer on a farm, or a doctor behind a saloon bar."[57] Lincoln Steffens reported a couple of years later that there was an intelligent judge in the juvenile court in Denver who "made effective use. . .of the 'gang' which the police and all prematurely old reformers seek only to 'break up,' " and who considered that "there's nothing wrong about gangs as such. They are as natural as organizations for men."[58] Subse-quently Louis Adamic would say of the labor racketeers and gangsters whom he knew that

among them I find several who unquestionably are "right guys," men with strict codes of honor and ethics. Their behavior in personal relations, so far as I have been able to determine, is the highest; they are men of their word, and would sooner die than betray a fellow racketeer, friend of enemy, to the police. Their contempt for established authority is boundless; they are self-confessed out-laws, but conscious of their superiority to law and police power.[59]

Furthermore, just as it was becoming clearer that the subculture of crime, with its connections with machine politics, especially Irish politics, was indeed a subculture and not merely a dark region of insensate disorder, so it was becoming clearer that whether an activity was criminal or not could be simply a question of political definition. Romantic novels about the American Revolution, or buccaneering in the Caribbean, or gentleman-adventuring in Europe were full of episodes in which whether someone was a hero or a criminal depended on whose banner he was fighting under and who was doing the judging. The same pattern was apparent for some of the young in the activities of the Wobblies and of groups like the Nihilists of Czarist Russia, who charmed the youthful Floyd Dell with their "combination of student life and military life" and their goal of freedom – "freedom from superstition, from hypocrisy and from tyranny; students and soldiers, they studied, conspired, taught, killed, and endured their punishment, not as individuals but as comrades in a cause greater than themselves."[60]

Moreover, if in radical terms it was perfectly possible for "criminal" groups like the Nihilists to enter peaceably into the just society after it had been achieved, as Robin Hood's band did under good King Richard, the reason was not simply that they had been on the winning side. It was that the right kind of pacific society did not differ sharply from the nonpacific. The fraternal characteristics that I have described in these pages were common to a number of groups and activities that came to mind when people thought of the admirableness of peace and the contrasting hatefulness of large-scale war. They were features, for example, of Mabel Dodge's salon, with its poets, journalists, actors, anarchists, labor leaders, and others; and of the free-form editorial conferences of the *Masses*; and of the Provincetown Players who were started in 1916 by John Reed and George Cram Cook and became, with the Washington Square Players, the prototypical American little-theater group. They were also, of course, features of the IWW and of the organizing of the Paterson pageant. All these activities permitted a free interaction between peers and displayed the "profound affinity between play and order" that Huizinga speaks of.[61] All involved a broad range of personalities, a variety of satisfying roles and functions, an abundance of talk, the give-and-take of humor. All were agonistic; all were reasonable; in all, the sexes met as equals. These values would be operative for a time in the thinking of younger radicals like Joseph Freeman and Michael Gold, for whom the *Masses* group and especially John Reed were inspirational.[62] In the early Twenties Gold, who had joined the Wobblies in 1915, told Upton Sinclair how "I love humor, joy and happy people; I love big groups at play, and friends sitting about a table talking, smoking, and laughing. I love song and athletics and a lot of other things. I wish the world were all play and everybody happy and creative as children. That is Communism; the communism of the future." His Twenties play about the Mexican Revolution ended with the words: "*All* – Viva la fiesta! (the orchestra strikes up and all sing Adelita and dance the jota... Drinking, shouting, singing, laughing, the curtain falls on them, to the shouts of Viva Zapata! Viva México! Viva la Revolución! Viva la Fiesta!)."[63]

Violence and peace (II)

PASTORAL HEROISM AND THE SANE COMMUNITY

There is no mystery, therefore, about how the radical pastoral-heroic pattern that I have been defining worked against war. The enthusiasm of many Americans for the European war resulted not only from servants-of-justice propaganda on the war's behalf but from society's having increasingly demanded warlike energies of people while at the same time narrowing the opportunities for achieving self-respect by way of economic success as America defined success. In contrast, the whole texture of the Wobblies' lives was charged with the pastoral-heroic tensions, and they were busy trying to make them available to others. In the kind of just society that the Wobblies and the *Masses* group were seeking, individuals and groups would have a feeling of plenitude and self-esteem, and a sense of being listened to without condescension. They would be sophisticated in the use of pressure and possess a sophisticated language of negotiation. They would enjoy what Conrad called "that quality of seriousness belonging to every form of open sport where the best man wins under perfectly comprehensible rules,"[64] and the satisfactions of being in a game, in Huizinga's sense, in which gains were always possible because the outcome was not predetermined and the rules rigged. Because their choices could have real consequences, they would be interested, too, in continuing negotiations with others, and rational argument and the making of fine distinctions would become more and not less important. Under such circumstances, to decide at any particular point *not* to use force could be as meaningful and gratifying as using it. The more widespread that these patterns were in society, the less attractive war would be, because it would be less and less able to offer gratifications that were otherwise unobtainable. The more obnoxious, too, would be the kind of destruction or undermining of secondary powers and local autonomy in the name of national unity and efficiency that Wilson's government engaged in. As Charles and Mary Beard note of that government's operations after America entered the war, "never before in history had such a campaign of education been organized; never before had American citizens realized how thoroughly, how irresistibly a modern government could impose its ideas upon the whole nation and, under a barrage of publicity, stifle dissent with declarations, assertions, official versions, and reiteration" – reiteration backed up by a ruthless use of force against dissidents.[65] It was appropriate that it was the militant Wobblies, in contrast to the enlightened Wilson and his cabinet, who opposed the war and supported the kind of true internationalism in which workers were able to pass freely from country to country. Chivalry itself had been international, an order of knights transcending national borders

189

and boundaries, though not seeking to obliterate them, and bound by laws that they themselves had evolved and assented to.

The attitudes, tactics, and structures that I have described were to have an immense influence on American radicalism. And, as with the Arthurian imitations and adaptations, the relationship between ideal images and actual behavior was complex.

Every memory bank produces such images from the Twenties and Thirties in happy abundance—the singing, banner-carrying marches of workers and intellectuals, men, women, children, whites and blacks, linked arm in arm, advancing unarmed upon the guns and clubs of police and militia; the revered, glorious Russian silent movies, turning into flesh and blood the pastoral-heroic patterns of Reed's *Ten Days that Shook the World* and what Joseph Freeman called the "massive black-and-white figures full of muscle, action and an internal spiritual power" of Robert Minor's cartoons;[66] the warm, decent, soil-oriented "people" and heroic, cheerful organizers of novels like Steinbeck's *In Dubious Battle* and *The Grapes of Wrath*; Woody Guthrie and the Almanac Singers singing "This Land Is Your Land"; the heroic struggle of Republican Spain, which, as Malcolm Cowley said, touched persons like himself more deeply than "any other international event since the World War and the Russian Revolution";[67] all the excitement of organizing, meeting, arguing endlessly in creative small-group discussions, comrade to comrade, in the service of a fuller, richer, nobler world to be brought into being. And the Sixties and early Seventies have a similar romantic abundance awaiting the attention of the nostalgia industry, with the sit-ins and demonstrations and marches, the omnipresence of Pete Seeger and Joan Baez and "We Shall Overcome," the general pastoral-heroic configurations noted by a reviewer of Barbara Kopple's documentary *Harlan County, U.S.A.*, about a Kentucky coal strike: "Two elements mark the film particularly. First, the women – wives and mothers and daughters – are powerfully present, marching, picketing, getting jailed and picketing again...Second, there is the music, straightforward lucid songs – 'Which Side Are You On?', 'Oh, Death' and a half-dozen others."[68]

As Robert Warshow noted on reseeing some of the Russian silent classics in 1950, irony comes easily, in view of the subsequently exposed horrors of Stalinism and the related authoritarianism and cold-blooded manipulativeness of the Communist Party of America. It is invited, for instance, when one comes upon the former Wobbly and eventual head of the party, William Z. Foster, assuring the world in 1939 that "Old Russia...has now become a land of song, laughter, culture, hope, and happiness."[69] It is likewise invited when one contemplates the short way with dissenters of that lover of humor, joy, and happy people, Mike

Violence and peace (II)

Gold. And one remembers that the party would also come to be headed by another former Wobbly, Elizabeth Gurley Flynn. But some ironies are nevertheless over-simple.

If the hatefulness of what went wrong in the Thirties is so obvious now, it is partly because in the Sixties the older radical patterns that I have described were once more generating action and understanding. The point is not that the chivalric-martial patterns led naturally to the wrong kind of Communism, any more than they led naturally to Fascism. It is that American Communism in the Thirties, like American radicalism in the Sixties, owed part of its appeal to its offering people the chance to display admirable pastoral-heroic qualities and to work toward a society that would make these qualities available to all. If the Communist Party attracted intellectuals hungry for power in a technological-bureaucratic society of more-than-Progressive rationality, it was also the party of figures like the union organizer Bill Dunne, described by Joseph Freeman:

He was short and stocky, with a tremendous barrel-chest, solid as a rock, and a dark, heavy Irish face. His close-cropped bullet head and thick neck gave him the appearance of great physical power; and his deep, husky voice, pouring out a flood of rhetoric, witty and incisive, revealed a mind that was at once brilliant and fanciful. His whole body, built like a retired prizefighter's, shook with repressed laughter when he told an anecdote.[70]

The heroism of many Communists was real in the same way that the heroism of the Wobblies had been real, and was energized by noble motives – motives that in part continued to be deeply American. As Daniel Aaron says, "Russia had come to symbolise for the radical young intellectuals of 1919 what Italy had symbolised for the young Victorians. It stood for struggle, for joy, for the new day."[71] If their hopes were betrayed, those hopes were none the less noble and generous. Reed's devotion to Communism, a devotion that wore him out and killed him, was a devotion to possibilities that he had seen in the Wobblies and in Mexico and that now seemed realizable on a much larger scale.[72] And other chivalric American writers and artists would be moved by radical attitudes. It is intelligible, for example, that a writer like the Catholic-born Dashiell Hammett, with his Maryland gentlemanliness, his strong sense of honor, and his deeply romantic and chivalric fiction, became a Communist. The nexus of romantic and radical attitudes also obtained in John Steinbeck, on the one hand the author of novels like *In Dubious Battle* and *The Grapes of Wrath*, on the other a lifelong devotee of Malory and an *aficionado* of Mexico, who said of Sidney Lanier's *A Boy's King Arthur* ("the very first book I knew") that "I think my sense of right and wrong, my feeling of noblesse oblige, and any thought I may have against the oppressor and for the oppressed, came from this. . .book."[73]

191

Part II Chivalric patterns in industrializing America

It was apparent for a time in John Ford (born Sean Aloysius O'Feeney), with his Westerns, his IRA-oriented *The Informer*, his pastoral-heroic *Grapes of Wrath*. It has been observable in John Huston, with his private-eye *Maltese Falcon*, his crime-caper *Asphalt Jungle*, his antilucre *Treasure of the Sierra Madre* and antimilitarist *Reflections in a Golden Eye*, his revolutionary-group *We Were Strangers*, his projected filming of B. Traven's quintessential Mexican novel *The Bridge in the Jungle*. And that the idealistic young in general have continued to crave the kinds of syntheses that I have described in these pages has been testified to in their choice of societies to admire.

As Octavio Paz notes in his brilliant study of Mexico, "most revolutions, although they are presented as an invitation to realize certain ideas in the near or not so near future, are founded on an attempt to restore a legal or social order that has been violated by the oppressor."[74] Just as Mexico, with its great cry of "Tierra y Libertad" once embodied the revolutionary tradition on the North American continent, other more or less radical societies have likewise seemed to make it possible to live intensely in the present in ways that continue the energies of the past. Civil War Spain, for example, as defined classically in *For Whom the Bell Tolls*, was a country of pastoral-heroic style and ritual in which a romantic intellectual (fittingly incarnated in the movie by Gary Cooper) could be accepted by aristo-democratic guerillas and become heroically a man of love and war, nourished by the spirit of place and the sane pleasures of the senses, and recapturing some of the *élan* of the American Civil War. Spain permitted you to feel that

you were taking part in a crusade. That was the only word for it, although it was a word that had been so worn and abused that it no longer gave its true meaning...It was a feeling of consecration to a duty towards all of the oppressed of the world...But the best thing was that there was something you could do about this feeling and this necessity too. You could fight.[75]

For a good many people, similarly, Israel in the late Forties and Fifties, epitomized by the *kibbutznik* tilling the soil with a Sten gun slung over his or her shoulder, offered a way of life free both from the business ethos and from success hunting in a cultural bureaucracy; and its strong and literal pastoral heroism (for Walker Percy's Lancelot Lamar the Israelis were "the only Crusaders left in the entire Western world"[76]) linked up with the Biblical past of heroic fighters in a country of milk and honey. Castro's Cuba, likewise born out of combat, had followed the classic Good Outlaw revolutionary pattern during the struggle against Batista and his torturers and had gone on to demonstrate exciting possibilities of power-charged peasant dignity and cooperation that decisively refuted the imperialist view of Latin America. Above all, Mao's China as seen through radical eyes appeared to offer a long-term

Violence and peace (II)

transcendence of constrictive dichotomies. Energized by the memories of over thirty years of heroic warfare and by a continuing sense of enemies to be faced and difficulties overcome, it updated the heroic pastoralism of movies like Eisenstein's *The General Line* and Dovzhenko's *Earth* and enabled the urban and the rural to interpenetrate in a process of mutual enrichment in which workers managed their affairs by collective discussions, bureaucrats were answerable to their clients, and intellectuals engaged periodically in manual labor and did not lose touch with the peasant base of the nation. Behind it stretched a centuries-old culture that valued grace and style and honorableness.

Moreover, *pace* Bertolt Brecht's statement "Unhappy the land that needs heroes,"[77] a consistent attitude informed the admiration aroused by political heroes like the Wobblies in the Wilson years, Sacco and Vanzetti in the Twenties, Dimitrov and La Pasionaria in the Thirties, and Castro and Che, Mao and Chou, Chavez and the Berrigans in the Sixties. Implicit in this admiration was the grateful recognition that there could be a genuinely pastoral-heroic radical personality. "No one," said Ralph Chaplin, "save perhaps Ricardo Flores Magón [the leader of the Mexican Liberal Party] could match Debs for gentleness."[78] Bill Haywood, as recalled by Max Eastman, predicted that proletarian art after the revolution "will be very much kindlier than your art. There will be a social spirit in it. Not so much boasting about personality."[79] Of the martyred Frank Little, "part American Indian, part hard-rock miner, part hobo...all Wobbly," Melvyn Dubofsky comments that "more than any other individual he personified the IWW's rebelliousness and its strange compound of violent rhetoric, pride in physical courage (the *machismo* element), and its seemingly contradictory resort to nonviolent resistance."[80] Robert Minor's biographer and friend remembered that Minor and his wife "made an astonishingly handsome couple, this woman of grace, unassuming beauty and quiet courage whose luminous eyes could light up in gaiety or flash in fire, for she, like Bob, had that incandescent quality that came from sheer joy in being alive, walking under the sun, spending their life for a cause greater than themselves."[81]

There was a familiar shape and feel to such combinations of qualities. In his account of his stay in Russia in the early Twenties, Eastman had described how

a wonderful generation of men and women was born to fulfill this revolution in Russia. You may be traveling in any remote part of that country, and you will see some quiet, strong, exquisite face in your omnibus or your railroad car – a middle-aged man with white, philosophic forehead and soft brown beard, or an elderly woman with sharply arching eyebrows and a stern motherliness about her mouth, or perhaps a middle-aged man, or a younger woman who is still

193

sensuously beautiful, but carries herself as though she had walked up to a cannon – you will enquire, and you will find that they are the "old party workers." Reared in the tradition of the Terrorist movement, a stern and sublime heritage of martyr-faith, taught in infancy to love mankind, and to think without sentimentality, and to be masters of themselves, and to admit death into their company, they learned in youth a new thing – to think practically; and they were tempered in the fires of jail and exile. They became almost a noble order, a selected stock of men and women who could be relied upon to be heroic, like a Knight of the Round Table or the Samurai, but with the patents of their nobility in the future, not the past.[82]

Part III

CHIVALRY AND ETHICS

11

Honor

"Among all these gentlemen, isn't there one man of honor?"

D. W. Griffith, Orphans of the Storm (1921)

"Has Mrs. —— paid that rent yet?"

"No," replied the agent.

"Well, but she must pay it," said the poor old man.

"Mr. Astor," rejoined the agent, "she can't pay it now; she has had misfortunes, and we must give her time."

"No, no," said Astor; "I tell you she can pay it and she will pay it. You don't go the right way to work with her."

Gustavus Myers, History of the Great American
Fortunes (1909)

There is no term in the English language that expresses such concentrated contempt as the word "scab."

William Z. Foster, Pages from a Worker's Life
(1939)[1]

THIS BRINGS ME BACK, for my two concluding chapters, to the question of truth and reason in relation to the chivalric. It is a question raised by what I have said about radicalism, and it might seem to invite a traditional answer. In the perennial conflict between the clerical and the martial, as epitomized in the debate in the *Gorgias* between Socrates and the Nietzschean aristocrat Callicles, the clerisy have figured as the truth seekers and truth tellers, undercutting the irrational imaginings and insistencies of their adversaries. The same undercutting might seem to be called for now. Attractive though the chivalric patterns may be, and even if they may once have made some kind of sense, the proliferating and irreversible complexities of society can presumably no longer be comprehended in such terms. Whatever its limitations, enlightened expertise surely continues to offer the best chance for a society of reasonably distributed benefits, and the most rewarding stance for intelligent persons who do not romantically aspire to become muckraking journalists or maverick radicals. Moreover, it can do so because it appears to be intrinsically in touch with reality in ways that the chivalric attitudes, for all their charm, are not. As I have been intimating throughout these pages, however, the actualities may be somewhat different. Let me recapitulate certain points in the standard intellectual critique of the chivalric.

Part III Chivalry and ethics

REASON OR HONOR

The fundamental struggle, in terms of that critique, is between reason and force, truth and fantasy, justice and arbitrariness. Reasonable persons decide things by talking reasonably together, and if someone has recourse to violence it is because he unreasonably enjoys its gratifications or is too impatient to argue rationally. The life of reason –which is to say systematized reason – consists of an increasing refinement of ways of getting at the truth, particularly in the rational and extended training provided in universities. And the more complex organizations and structures are the most rational, because they correspond closest to the complexities of reason and of the reality that reason uncovers, a complexity embodied in university disciplines. From this point of view, it is not accidental that, in contrast to the inexorable growth of rational bureaucratic structures, the history of the chivalric has been largely a history of failure, and that so many of the images that I have talked about have been images of defeat – Pickett's Virginians advancing in vain against the murderous fire from Cemetery Ridge; Lee surrendering to Grant at Appomattox; Roland and his rear guard perishing at Roncesvalles; Arthur wounded almost to death in his last fight against Mordred; Quixote, broken, returning home to die; Zapata going down before the guns of his ambushers; and the rest. As Damon Runyon remarked, "the race is not always to the swift nor the battle to the strong, but that's the way to bet."[2] The Wobblies, broken by Wilson's *force majeure*, were simply taking their place with all the other defeated chivalric-martial groups like the cowboys of the open range, the Secessionist Southerners, the Cavaliers of the English Civil War, the French chivalry, the knights of Camelot. And attractive as such groups may be, their defeats were merited because of a pattern of unreason that extended deeper than those that I have discussed already, and that centered around the idea of increasing one's prestige by fighting honorably.

When I spoke of agonistic struggles between power-charged groups, and of an agonistic approach to justice in the new radicalism, I was pointing to something fundamental. A recurring feature in the chivalric pattern is the duel, whether the formalized gentlemanly duel, the judicial duel, the duel of chivalric warfare, or the duel of the strike. And on the face of things, the duel is the antithesis of reason-based justice and peace, because the strongest or most skillful combatant is not necessarily the one who is in the right or who is telling the truth. As Huizinga points out,

we moderns cannot conceive justice apart from abstract righteousness... For us, the lawsuit is primarily a dispute about right and wrong; winning and losing take only a second place. Now it is precisely this preoccupation with ethical values that we must abandon if we are to understand archaic justice...It is not so much the abstract question of right and wrong that occupies the archaic mind as the very concrete question of winning or losing...The winning *as such* is, for the archaic mind, proof of truth and rightness.[3]

The concern to win, whether against a fellow knight or a sociopolitical adversary, is liable to entail placing the claims of loyalty and "honor" above the claims of truth and the larger collectivity. When Lancelot defends Guinevere against their mutual enemies, he is obliged to affirm indignantly again and again, on his honor as a knight, that she is innocent of adultery; and in defense of that lie he is ready to challenge all comers – which is to say, to rest his case on his superiority as a fighter. In other traditions as well, the claims of truth have been sacrificed to the claims of honor and loyalty, such as in the systematic lying by underdog Irish, Italians, and Southerners to agents of law and order, and the labor-union detestation of the fink.

Furthermore if honor-oriented persons or groups are not necessarily governed by the claims of universal truth and reason, they are likely to be bound by a set of rules at least as stringent and far less rational. The seeming fundamental absurdity of such handicapping is indicated by that archetypal disillusioned preppy Holden Caulfield in J. D. Salinger's *The Catcher in the Rye* when his old history teacher asks what the headmaster talked about in their farewell chat:

"Oh...well, about Life being a game and all. And how you should play it according to the rules..."
"Life *is* a game, boy. Life *is* a game that one plays according to the rules."...
"Yes, sir. I know it is. I know it."
Game, my ass. Some game. If you get on the side where all the hot-shots are, then it's a game, all right – I'll admit that. But if you get on the *other* side, where there aren't any hot-shots, then what's a game about it? Nothing. No game.[4]

It is as if, where larger social ends are sought, the honor-governed person simultaneously insists that a particular state of affairs is immensely desirable and implicitly denies its importance by refusing to take the steps necessary for its realization, like the French knights who refused to profit from the lie of the land in battle for fear of being accused of not behaving honorably. And he is likely to be playing against persons like Margaret Mitchell's Rhett Butler or the hard-boiled narrator of one of John McPartland's thrillers who remarks of a reform politician, "I could have told him that being a gentleman is sometimes foolish and expensive."[5] Viewed in this light, radicals like the Wobblies were naive in their failure to gauge the strength of the forces opposing them and the powers of the state that could be used against them. They were naive to believe that they could be treated fairly in the courts, let alone by the forces of law and order.

And the handicapping effects of honor are seemingly compounded by certain intellectual problems. When Lillian Hellman observes of honor that "it's all been decided so long ago, when you were very young, all mixed up with your childhood's definition of pride and dignity," the values involved are familiar enough.[6] Walker Percy's Lancelot Lamar speaks of "a stern code, a gentleness toward women and an intolerance of swinishness, a counsel kept, and above all a readiness to act, and act alone if necessary"; Dean Acheson refers to "some well-tested principles of conduct: That it was better to tell the truth than falsehoods; that a half-truth was no truth at all; that duties were older than and as fundamental as rights...; that to perpetuate a harm was always wrong, no matter how many joined in it, but to perpetuate it on a weaker person was particularly detestable";[7] America's archetypal gentleman, the movie Westerner, respects and protects the weak, will not tolerate bullying, keeps his word, does not let down friends and associates, and always meets his obligations. Yet despite Lamar's assertion that "dishonor is sweeter and more mysterious than honor. It holds a secret. There is no secret in honor," things become noticeably blurry in passages like the one in which Faulkner's Bayard Sartoris compares a Civil War episode to "a meeting between two iron knights of the old time, not for martial gain but for principle – honor denied with honor, courage denied with courage – the deed done, not for the end but for the sake of the doing – put to the test and proving nothing save the finality of death and the vanity of all endeavor."[8] There are similar blurs in feverish talk about stains on one's honor that can only be wiped out by killing one's wife, or one's best friend, or an unarmed, terrified old man, or by thrashing a middleaged Senator working peaceably at his desk, or by going to war with a much weaker country. The concept of honor invited Shakespeare's and Corneille's and Calderón's probings and exposings; it invited the famous interrogation by Falstaff:

Honour pricks me on. Yea, but how if honour prick me off when I come on? How then? Can honour set to a leg? No. Or an arm? No. Or take away the grief of a wound? No. Honour hath no skill in surgery then? No. What is honour? A word. What is that word honour? Air. A trim reckoning! Who hath it? He that died a Wednesday. Doth he feel it? No. Doth he hear it? No. 'Tis insensible then? Yea, to the dead. But will it not live with the living? No. Why? Detraction will not suffer it. Therefore I'll none of it. Honour is a mere scutcheon – and so ends my catechism.[9]

The problems of honor are visible in the plight of the duellists of sixteenth-century France and the antebellum South who felt compelled to keep provoking duels for fear of seeming afraid of putting themselves to the test. They are visible in the craving for perfection symbolized by the Grail quest, in which ideals are never realized and there is an omnipresent feeling that, in Hemingway's words, "every damned thing is your own fault if you're any good."[10] Among the results is the spectacle of the honorable man who, because he is too conscious of discrepancies between what he and society ought to be and what they are, retreats into irony, like a legion of courteously alcoholic Southerners, or Nick Carraway entangled in the moral confusions of the East, or those gentlemanly companions of unabashed political power grabbers, Ned Beaumont in Hammett's *The Glass Key* and Jack Burden in Robert Penn Warren's *All the King's Men*. As Hemingway said in *Death in the Afternoon*, "too much honor destroys a man quicker than too much of any other fine quality."[11]

The problems were compounded by developments on the Left. As Vivian Gornick's *The Romance of American Communism* reminds us, the notion of the honorable fighter on the Left – courageous, loyal, self-sacrificing, dedicated to the pursuit of a social Grail – has had a strong continuing influence.[12] But obvious ironies are involved too. To talk about American radical politics is to talk not about pasts that did not exist – as with traditional chivalric nostalgia – but about futures that did not arrive; and there have been grounds for skepticism and irony beyond the normal vulnerability of idealism. It is not simply that the IWW and *Masses* revolution, or the American Communist revolution, or the New Left revolution failed to materialize, and that further romantic Lost Causes have been added to the Lost Cause of the antebellum South. In retrospect, a central strand in the American Left since the Twenties has been the massive and deliberate dishonesty of the best-organized branch of it. What was revealed in the Forties and Fifties was how all the nobility of aspiration, the talk about brotherhood, the yearning voiced by Mike Gold in one of his poems in the Twenties for "a time of revolution and love...A time of workers' joy in boats down a gay golden river,"[13] had become subordinate to the conviction that honesty was a bourgeois luxury and that what mattered was not abstract truthfulness, but a concrete adherence to the "objective" truth of revolutionary socialist principles – which is to say, to the shifting dictates of Stalin's Russia. And just as the great epitomizing image of capitalist falsification in the Twenties was the trial of Sacco and Vanzetti, so the epitomizing image of Communist falsification in the Forties was provided in the trial of Alger Hiss. On the one side there was the handsome, clean-cut, Ivy League *chevalier sans peur et sans reproche*, the man of seeming honor, the man of whom the Secretary of State and fellow gentleman Dean Acheson said, "I do not intend to turn my back on Alger Hiss."[14] On the other there was the shabby, lumpy, neurotic stool pigeon Whittaker Chambers, the turncoat, the failed intellectual –everything that the young would not have wished to take as a role

Part III Chivalry and ethics

model. And it was seemingly the turncoat who told the truth in the case, and the man of honor who lied and went on lying through his teeth with unshakable poise and good manners. Among the consequences of such disclosures were the flight of intellectuals in the Fifties from ideology as something that made for divisiveness and untruth, and the related popularity of irony as a dominant stance. A host of further ironic discrepancies between gleaming ideal images and grubby underlying realities have, of course, become apparent in the revisionist aftermath of the Sixties.

Hence, when one contemplates what Thomas L. Haskell calls "the towering edifice of institutionalized expertise that looms over contemporary society," and the seeming irresistibility of the tendency, in Haskell's words, "for impersonal calculations of least cost and maximum efficiency to enter, and finally dominate, every sphere of life,"[15] it is natural enough to opt for cool-headed professionalism as offering the best chance of survival and mastery. The professional is not naive with respect to the rules of the game. He is not like troops doing battle by the book, such as General Braddock's redcoats or the thick-headed knights of *A Connecticut Yankee*, and being shot to pieces by adversaries who have changed the rules or have recognized that they have changed. The *really* intelligent person is the person who devises strategies for getting beyond the constraints and anomalies of supposedly immutable rules. And even the fact that the idea of the professional has acquired certain unamiable associations has its advantages. As Michael Novak comments, "Americans love professionals, killers especially, ruthless investigators, determined secret agents, anybody who absolutely concentrates on proficiency, undistracted by human involvement."[16] Professionalism has come to stand against the idea of the amateur, construed as someone peculiarly prone to sentimental weaknesses and unwilling to act with the requisite skill and firmness. It has come to stand against "feminine" softness and idealism, and against the notion that one can have all the benefits of peace without any use of force or any hard decision making. Professionals, as Haskell observes, "take...an inordinate pride in the cool self-mastery that enables them to bring their talent and training to bear on challenging problems, thereby advancing themselves and serving society at the same time."[17]

Yet Americans have obstinately, if at times apologetically, persisted in caring about the idea of honor and believing in its civic importance. They have continued to admire courage, to look askance at back stabbing and finking, and to feel that loyalty even in a bad cause is preferable to a world of total Machiavellian opportunism. A good deal of distortion, whether from dog-eat-dog business pressures, or urban combat fatigue, or the theorizings of academic ironists like Marshall

McLuhan, seems to be required before such perceptions can be seriously altered. In the rest of this chapter I shall try to define some of the energies at work in the concept of honor and to suggest that the dichotomies that I have been talking about are false dichotomies.

"THE POWER OF HONOR"

The interest in the idea of honor, as I have said, was particularly keen in the turn-of-the century period. In 1886, Oliver Wendell Holmes observed that "the power of honor to bind men's lives is not less now than it was in the Middle Ages. Now as then it is the breath of our nostrils; it is that for which we live, for which, if need be, we are willing to die."[18] And Henry Seidel Canby said of his youth that "the social code we really lived by was not an 'ought' code, but a code of honor – what an honorable man should feel toward his friend, his wife, his duty."[19] The appeal of the idea of honorableness for romantic youths like Canby and John Reed was in some ways obvious. As Huizinga says, "from the life of childhood right up to the highest achievements of civilization one of the strongest incentives to perfection, both individual and social, is the desire to be praised and honoured for one's excellence."[20] Honorable excellence, when attained, made easier the kind of self-esteem described by the fifteenth-century soldier-author who affirmed that "whoever achieves distinction in arms is thereby ennobled, whatever his rank in life may be. The greatest king may combat the poorest knight, for the armor itself is of such nobility that when the knight has put the helmet on his head he is the equal of anyone in the world."[21] It was a self-esteem that had been earned, not given, as Canby indicated when he remembered how "we all knew that children who belonged to Us had standards of conduct...far more rigorous than the creed of the hated 'micks.' " And when he added that "we had to be polite under stress, and to wear clean underclothes – the outer clothing made no difference," he was pointing to a continuum wherein small things as well as large became charged with significance and every social occasion could "seem a little more than it was." The code of honorableness assimilated from one's private reading as well as from family traditions enriched life in a further way. As Canby said, "you lived in two dimensions, the present and your breeding," rather than in "one dimension of current opinion."[22] If one judged oneself against earlier honorable figures, whether historical or fictional, one could also judge one's immediate family and friends against them too, and have the assistance of a mental court of appeal in one's daily affairs. And if at times one had to condemn this or that failure or failing in oneself, one was only doing what fallible men of honor had done earlier, in Malory and elsewhere, and could retain one's self-respect.[23]

But of course there was more to the idea of honor than that. The concern with honor was particularly significant with respect to the attitudes inculcated in or influential among the governing class, and to the desired emergence of a better type of educated person having social power. William James spoke in 1910 of the growing recognition of the need for "ideals of honor and standards of efficiency."[24] Winston Churchill's Austin Vane in *Mr. Crewe's Career* remarked in the same year that "we cannot have commercial and political stability without commercial and political honor!"[25] And in a discussion of the increasing emphasis on duty, responsibility, tact, and "a measure of urbane self-control," Theodore P. Greene reports that in some ways the new-style heroes described in magazines between 1914 and 1918 "seemed closer to the gentlemanly neo-classic models of 1800 than they did to the forceful, domineering individualists of 1900."[26] The period saw the growth of the attitude voiced recently by Gore Vidal when he suggested that "perhaps our schools should train a proper civil service. Train people who prefer payment in honor rather than in money."[27]

More particularly, honorable professionalism was increasingly seen as offering an alternative to business values and effectively challenging the captains-of-industry image of valor. In *Stover at Yale*, one of the Nineties undergraduate intellectuals complained that:

Twenty years ago we had the idea of the lawyer, of the doctor, of the statesman, of the gentleman, of the man of letters, of the soldier. Now the lawyer is simply a supernumerary enlisting under any banner for pay; the doctor is overshadowed by the specialist with his business development of the possibilities of the rich; we have politicians, and politics are deemed impossible for a gentleman; the gentleman cultured, simple, hospitable, and kind is of the dying generation; the soldier is simply on parade...Everything has conformed to business, everything has been made to pay."[28]

The Progressive period witnessed a renewed confidence that honorable work in professional fields was possible. As a social scientist observed in 1907, "Certainly you may rate the business man by the money he has been able to make under the rules of the game. But the sages of all time agree that the writer, thinker, scholar, clergyman, jurist, officer, administrator, and statesman must not be mere profit seekers, nor may their moral standing depend on their financial rating."[29] The new kind of hero, Greene reports, "might be a government surveyor who had braved the hardships of Alaska," or a medical researcher who was not tempted away from his work by the prospect of earning a huge income as a surgeon.[30] In *The Beautiful and the Damned* F. Scott Fitzgerald noted of Anthony Patch's Harvard contemporaries in the same period that "most of them were in business, it is true, and several were converting the heathen of China or America to a nebulous protestantism; but a few, he found, were working constructively at jobs that were neither sinecures nor routines" – a medical relief doctor in Serbia, a contributor to the *New Democracy* (i.e., *New Republic*), a professor "preaching Marxian doctrines in the classroom."[31]

Moreover, there was a growing feeling that big businessmen and their political agents were not just selfish or crooked but dishonorable. "There is something to be said for government by a great aristocracy," Roosevelt acknowledged in a letter in 1912. "But there is absolutely nothing to be said for government by plutocracy, for government by men very powerful in certain lines and gifted with the money touch; but with ideals which in their essence are merely those of so many glorified pawnbrokers."[32] Finley Peter Dunne's Mr. Dooley, pondering the conduct of George M. Pullman during the railroad strike of 1894, commented: " 'Th' women an' childhern is dyin' iv hunger,' they says. 'Will ye not put out ye'er hand to help thim?' they says. 'Ah, what th' 'ell,' says George. 'What th' 'ell,' he says. 'What th' 'ell, ' he says. 'James,' he says, 'a bottle iv champagne an' a piece iv crambree pie. What th' 'ell, what th' 'ell, what th' 'ell.' "[33] Mother Jones, addressing strikers in Colorado in 1913, told them how during a strike in West Virginia "I called a committee and I said, 'Boys, take this document into the governor's office. . .don't get on your knees. . .and don't say 'Your Honor,' because very few of those fellows. . .know what it is' [laughter]."[34] And the contempt was to continue. The historian James Truslow Adams, for example, the son of Charles Francis Adams, recalled of an unexpected act of generosity by Pierpont Morgan to his father during the financial panic of 1907 that "Morgan alone in that day made such gestures. As contrasted with him, many of the other 'great' bankers, with whom I was occasionally mixed up in episodes as intimately personal as the above, had the souls of pushcart peddlers."[35]

Furthermore, such accusations told. In *A Certain Rich Man*, William Allen White reported of his composite financier, with his "furtive mouth, hard and naked," and "square mean jaw that every cartoonist . . .has emphasized for a dozen years," that around 1902 "Barclay was beginning to feel upon him, night and day, the crushing weight of popular scorn."[36] And at one point in Churchill's *Mr. Crewe's Career* a railroad magnate perceives that the reformist hero "had somehow accomplished the incredible feat of making Hilary Vane [the railroad's lawyer] ashamed – and when such men as Hilary Vane are ashamed, their usefulness is over. Mr. Flint had seen the same thing happen with a certain kind of financiers, one day aggressive, combative, and the next broken, querulous men. Let a man cease to believe in what he is doing, and he loses force."[37] It was not just in fiction that the voiced contempt had consequences. Greene describes a sudden concern around 1902 on the part of magazine biographers to display business heroes who cared about the feelings of the public. Rockefeller was put on the defensive by Tarbell's book and sought to improve his image with the help of a public-relations man. Mark Hanna, according to Frederic Howe, "suffered from newspaper attacks, particularly from the cartoons of Homer Davenport, which portrayed him as a bloated creature covered all over with wriggly dollar-marks. He was not content with the plaudits of his immediate associates; he wanted the approval of the crowd."[38] A similar disquiet would be at work in the curious phenomenon reported more recently by John Kenneth Galbraith about corporate executives: "There is possibly no group of people anywhere in the world who... complain more persistently, plaintively, and even pathologically of the unfairness with which they are treated or of the depths of the misunderstanding to which they are subject."[39]

The potency of the accusation that one is behaving dishonorably is significant. Its force in the turn-of-the-century period is especially noteworthy, given the attitude described by White in *A Certain Rich Man*: "The term honest wealth, which was creeping into respectable periodicals was exceedingly annoying to [Barclay]. For the very presence of the term seemed to indicate that there was such a thing as dishonest wealth, – an obvious absurdity."[40] Let me try to define what the accusation involved.

A chivalric hatred of injustice and unfairness, as I have said, was prominent during the period. As Greene puts it, "almost all the changes in the heroic occupations served to identify the Progressive heroes as the Idols of Justice," heroes who displayed at times what *Everybody's* called "the underlying quality of intense, passionate sadness that is inherent in the character of men who fight to liberate their fellow men."[41] It was the great period of moral indignation—of Twain's cold anger on behalf of the "black" Roxy in *Pudd'nhead Wilson*, Finley Peter Dunne's dry characterization of the Dreyfus case in passages like, " 'Let us pro-ceed,' says th' impartial an' fair-minded judge, 'to th' thrile iv the hyanious monsther Cap Dhry-fuss,' "[42] and both writers' attacks on American brutality in the Philippines, and the national sense of outrage over Germany's invasion of plucky little Belgium. It was the period of a hunger for fair play, a craving to equalize things so that the powerful –the rich, the strong and brutal and ruthless – could not simply beat down the less powerful by *force majeure*. "Golden Rule" Jones pointed out how

the ethical code of business under the competitive system is far below that of such brutal sports as football and prize-fighting, against which there is such an outcry on the part of respectable people...Prize-fighting is guarded by the most carefully prepared, scientific rules to secure to each combatant a fair chance in the battle; but there are no Marquis of Queensbury [sic]...rules to protect the contestants in the daily competition (war) of business.[43]

Roosevelt challenged the trusts in the name of "decent government and fair play" and defined his Square Deal as not only playing fair under the existing rules but amending the rules so as to make for fairer competition.[44] Ida M. Tarbell concluded her exposé of Rockefeller's Standard Oil Company by suggesting that

as for the ethical side, there is no cure but an increasing scorn of unfair play – an increasing sense that a thing won by breaking the rules of the game is not worth the winning. When the business man who fights to secure special privileges, to crowd his competitor off the track by other than fair competitive methods, receives the same summary disdainful ostracism by his fellows that the doctor or lawyer who is "unprofessional," the athlete who abuses the rules, receives, we shall have gone a long way toward making commerce a fit pursuit for our young men.[45]

The relationship between the idea of fair play and the intensity of feeling elicited by *un*fair play was more complex than it might appear. Utility and convenience came into it, of course, such as in the desire of numerous Progressives for a state of business competition in which smaller businessmen would have a chance against the trusts and combines. So too with the yearning for gentlemanliness in business. It would obviously be pleasanter all round if business were conducted in the spirit described by *Collier's* in 1906: "Our navy and our army have, from the beginning, set and maintained unblemished that sportsman's standard in dark and serious days, and that same spirit should rule the nation in its hour of play – that bright, confident courtesy which accepts no unfair advantage [and] instantly accords the odds demanded."[46] Moreover, many Progressives obviously relished the image of themselves and their surrogates as judges and umpires impartially and accurately penalizing unfairness. But such attitudes, or a related desire for a more equitable distribution of social benefits, do not by themselves account for the resentment aroused by certain kinds of conduct. I am thinking here of episodes like the one in Rockefeller's career, described in *Collier's* in 1905, in which he "forced a widow who had inherited from her husband and was successfully carrying on a refining business paying her a clear profit of $25,000 a year, to sell out for $60,000, refusing to let her retain a dollar's interest in the enterprise, and this after he had personally promised her, with tears in his eyes, that she should not be wronged and that she could keep any amount of stock she desired."[47] I am thinking of Frederic Howe's recollection that "liberal laws for the protection of women and children in industry were always discovered to be unconstitutional, while fifty-year grants to street-railways were upheld."[48] I am thinking of the classic situation in

Westerns in which the big rancher, aided by his shyster lawyer, his gunslingers, and his bought sheriff, takes over the land of the homesteader or the homesteader's widow on some legal technicality, and adds insult to injury by blandly suggesting that the victim is the sort of person who easily gets facts wrong and cannot be trusted as a witness.

An interesting set of feelings is involved, particularly when legalistic maneuvers are used. There is, of course, intense empathy with the victims, an appreciation of what it is like to be in a situation in which whatever arguments one uses, one will not be taken seriously and cannot win. But there is also indignation against the victimizer as not simply a bully but a cheat – a conviction that he has violated an agreed-upon code in a way that makes his negating of his victims especially intolerable. The cheat does not simply break or rig the rules; he insists that he is observing them and that he is a man scrupulous about the ways of law and injustice. It was indignation against that sort of behavior that had been aroused by Sherman's march to the sea. In a Southern literary historian's words, "the memory which rankled in the South for generations was that the enemy, while masking himself under pretensions of moral superiority, had dropped the code of civilization and won in a dishonorable manner."[49] As a Southern woman said at the time about the Northern attitude toward the march: "the South has suffered; that they admit in general terms, and add, '*Such is war.*' I desire to call their attention to the fact that such is NOT war, as their own standards declare."[50] If the archetypal Northern perception of the South was of a group of dominators and oppressors, the archetypal Southern perception of the North was of people who were capable of not fighting fair. The cheat in other words plays by a double set of rules, simultaneously claiming benefits for himself and denying them to others. He profits from legality while bending or breaking laws, and from the idea of honorableness while behaving ignobly. He demands the protection of rules – the right to fair treatment in combat, the right to the protection of the law – while insisting on his own right to ignore those rules whenever it suits him.

All these attitudes were at work in the critique of business and businessmen. The large businessman was increasingly perceived as playing by a double set of rules, both when eliminating competitors and when suppressing troublesome workers. This perception was the more consequential in view of what Owen Johnson called "that typical quality so perplexing in the American millionaire of sudden fortune – the childlike eagerness for admiration."[51] Implicit in that eagerness was the belief of businessmen that their occupation was in fact a traditionally honorable one; and the metaphors about robber barons and industrial wars pointed to deeper truths.

In 1854, Charles Sumner had suggested that,

as the feudal chief allocated to himself and his followers the soil, which was the prize of his strong arm, so now the merchant, with a grasp more subtle and reaching, allocates to himself and followers, ranging through multitudinous degrees of dependence, all the spoils of every land triumphantly won by trade. I will not press this parallel too far, but, at this moment, especially in our country, the merchant, more than any other character, stands in the very boots of the feudal chief.[52]

It was not simply hypocrisy that made the New York Stock Exchange, according to a critic in 1905, affirm that "all within our sacred walls is honest and honorable," or that created what David Graham Phillips called the "hypocritical mask of 'Senatorial courtesy.' "[53] Nor was it solely a lust for economic dominance that Max Eastman drew attention to when he said that what existed in the Colorado mining towns was "a state of feudal serfdom. The miners *belong* to the mineowners in the first place, and what follows follows from that."[54] As Oscar Handlin says of the self-made businessmen at the end of the nineteenth century,

they gave their goal various names – order, efficiency, duty – and they described it as God's plan or economic law. But power was what they sought and business was the form in which their society recognized power. They took pleasure when the press referred to them as captains of industry, barons, kings and czars; and Morgan appropriately called the yacht he loved *Corsair*. Zeal for battle led them on, in fascinated absorption with the luck that would test their pluck. They were self-made, not in the sense that they had all risen from nothing, but in the sense that their achievements demonstrated their merit.[55]

"There are few men," said Ida M. Tarbell in 1905, "whatever their practices, who do not instinctively desire to be called honorable and generous, and to be considered gentlemen."[56] Essentially the self-made rich were trying to achieve the honorable stature that merchants had traditionally enjoyed (Charles Sumner had called the merchant the "successor to the chivalrous knight"[57]) and to profit morally from the notion of a benevolent quasifeudal paternalism. Whether they knew it or not, they were attempting to replicate the pattern of late medieval and Renaissance Europe, wherein mercantile and chivalric magnificence intertwined and merchant princes could treat with aristocrats on equal terms because they were partly governed by the same values.[58]

But the corollary of such attitudes was also pointed out by Sumner: "If the merchant be in reality our feudal lord, he must render feudal service; if he be our modern knight, he must do knightly deeds; if he be the baron of our day, let him maintain baronial charity to the humble – aye, sir, and baronial courage, against tyrannical wrong, in whatsoever form it may assume."[59] And the departures of American businessmen from the patterns of honor were becoming increasingly blatant. Given the image of paternalism, the sufferings of women and children were especially eye-catching, not only in the conduct of strike breaking, but in the daily conditions of life and work. The basic inconsistency was underlined in a cartoon by Gibson called "The Army of Work; Dedicated to Employers of Child Labor" that appeared in *Collier's* in 1904 when Mother Jones marched a group of child textile workers from Philadelphia to Roosevelt's summer home at Oyster Bay: In an allegorical procession of persons going to work, the two principal figures were a dour top-hatted, and traditionally goateed employer and a big-eyed, skinny-legged working girl of ten or eleven, the latter gazing wanly out at the reader.[60] Businessmen were likewise inconsistent with respect to the supposedly honorable warfare of business. As the Beards noted, "the armor of mediaeval knights...stood in the halls of captains of industry whose boldest strokes were courageous guesses on the stock market or the employment of Pinkerton detectives against striking workingmen."[61] Not only had the robber barons, as Gustavus Myers pointed out in his *History of the Great American Fortunes*, dodged actual military service during the Civil War, much to their economic advantage; in the conduct of their metaphorical wars they were equally unchivalrous. As Henry Demarest Lloyd observed in *Wealth Against Commonwealth*, "war has been made on poor men, paralytics, boys, cripples, widows, any one who had the 'business that belongs to us,' " with weapons such as the railroad rebate, which "means universal dominion to him who will use it with an iron hand," a weapon "smokeless, noiseless, invisible, of extraordinary range, and the deadliest gun known to commercial warfare."[62] A figure like Rockefeller, as a *Collier's* writer noted, had "never been willing to 'live and let live,' but from the beginning acted on the principle that every competitor must be frozen out, choked out, or clubbed out of his way. [He] has never observed the rules of war, but has resorted to man-traps, explosive bullets, and poisoned wells when open fighting has not served his turn."[63] And Carnegie, who in the mid-Eighties was commending the "honor and loyalty" of labor leaders, had eight years later hidden away on his Scottish estate while his associate Frick smashed the Homestead strike and broke the union, conduct that contributed to the paradox noted in *Collier's* in 1903 that "it would hardly be going too far to say that the man who has given more money for the benefit of the public than any philanthropist of ancient or modern times is one of the most unpopular men in America."[64]

At bottom, the magnates were seen as cheats and frauds who had loaded the dice and stacked the cards in their supposedly heroic and unprotected business venturings. As Charles Francis Adams had observed of the cosseting of railroads by legislatures after the Civil War "every expedient which the mind of man can devise [had] been brought into play to secure to the capitalist the largest possible profit with the least possible risk."[65] Capitalists invited the criticism voiced by a character in William Allen White's *A Certain Rich Man* to the tycoon Barclay: "Why, man, look at yourself – look at yourself – you'd cheat your own mother playing cards with matches for counters – just to win the game."⁶⁶ They invited the contempt of the *Masses* writer who, in a description of a hearing of the Federal Commission on Industrial Relations, noted the contrast between Carnegie, J. P. Morgan, Jr., and the Rockefellers, with "their craft, their cunning, their fox-like evasions and downright mendacity," and "the frankness, sincerity, candor, straightforwardness, the passionate conviction and the forthright expression" of a labor organizer like John Lawson.⁶⁷ Capitalists and their agents were seen as men who lied without compunction whenever the profit motive demanded it. Muckrakers like Lloyd and Tarbell drew attention to their bland prevarications at Congressional hearings into price fixing and rebates; Wells spoke of the "sustained quality of the lying" in the case made against the troublemaker MacQueen by the forces of business law and order in Paterson; Al Smith, seeing a law student at his studies with the presumable aspiration of becoming a company attorney, remarked, "There's a boy learning to take a bribe and call it a fee."⁶⁸ In all these respects the business pattern was at odds with a major element in the chivalric.

The association of truthfulness with the chivalric and martial was old and strong. Bayard's biographer reported that "he was very inexpert at flattery and fawning; he had the greatest possible regard for truth."⁶⁹ The ideal Renaissance gentleman, according to one scholar, "was a man of absolute honesty and integrity. Hence, one of the traditional privileges of the aristocrat had been his right to testify in court without bond and without witnesses."⁷⁰ Francis J. Grund reported how, when Andrew Jackson was sitting for a portrait bust, " 'The *truth*, sir! the whole truth, and nothing but the truth!' exclaimed the general with a stern voice; 'you have no right to represent me otherwise than I am.' "⁷¹ Conversely, in Nietzsche's words, "what is despised is. . . above all the liar: it is the basic faith of all aristocrats that the common people are liars."⁷² Finley Peter Dunne remembered that "of all sins Roosevelt hated lying most," and Roosevelt himself called in 1906 for "the most unsparing exposure of. . . the politician who betrays his trust, of the big businessman who makes or spends his fortune in illegitimate or corrupt ways."⁷³ Johnson's Stover, quizzed about an unpopular decision he gave as a football linesman, rounds on his baffled Lawrenceville schoolmates with, "Why? Because you all, every damn one of you, expected me to *lie!*"⁷⁴ At the bottom of the duel or judicial combat, furthermore, usually lay the fact of someone's word being impugned, an issue coming up again in the special ominousness of the question, "Are you calling me a liar?" As has been said about the South, "even today the suggestion that a man is a liar is an accepted provocation to a blow even more than the suggestion that he is a murderer."[75]

HONOR AND INTEGRITY

It is important to see what is involved in this concern for truth. In terms of the chivalric-martial system, there was no dislike of cunning per se. Warfare could entail a good deal of honorable deception, misdirecting, surprising. As the brilliant Confederate guerrilla leader John S. Mosby said, "I confess my theory of war was severely practical – one not acquired by reading the Waverley novels – but we observed the ethics of the code of war. Strategy is only another name for deception and can be practised by any commander."[76] Lee had been a master of that kind of deception. So, earlier, had Bayard. Certain kinds of deception would be perfectly acceptable in sports as well, at least in American terms, so that one of Frank Merriwell's classmates could note how Merriwell was "full of tricks."[77] In poker playing, that miniaturization of warfare, bluffing and misdirection were part of the game's essence. And Twain's works, especially *Hucklebery Finn* and *Life on the Mississippi*, were full of admiration for successful deceptions and masqueradings, such as the multiple improvisations of Huck, the conning by the King and Duke of the townspeople of Bricksville ("Greenhorns, flatheads!"[78]), and the riverboat card game between professional cheats in which the seeming sucker turned out to be the master cheater. But certain things were unacceptable. Gentlemen did not cheat at cards while playing with fellow gentlemen; officers, as the West Point honor code announced, did not lie, cheat, or steal.[79]

There were, of course, some very practical reasons for that kind of condemnation and for the related emphasis on a man's word. As Newton D. Baker, the then Secretary of War, pointed out in 1921, "men may be inexact or even untruthful in ordinary matters and suffer as a consequence only the disesteem of their associates or the inconvenience of unfavorable litigation; but the inexact or untruthful soldier trifles with the lives of fellow men and with the honor of his government."[80] It was necessary in a battle to be able to trust a fellow soldier's statements about what was going on, and to feel confident that he would trust one's own. It was important to know that one's associates would not lie when under pressure. As Harry Truman said of Dean Acheson, "I sensed immediately that he was a man I could count on in every way. I knew that he would do what had to be done, and I knew that I could count on him to tell me the truth at all times... When you get to be in a position of authority, which I was at that time, that's the most important thing there is. You've got to be able to count on a man's word."[81] It was desirable, moreover, to know that people would have confidence not only in one's promises but in one's threats. In the Bricksville episode in *Huckleberry Finn*, for example, Colonel Sherburn – the gentleman isolated in the frontier town – was able to face down the lynch mob because he was prepared to fight and die if need be and because they knew it; they knew it because he had kept his word earlier and shot Boggs dead in the street. In business matters, too, there were obvious advantages to dealing with men whose word was their bond, in contrast to Machiavellians like the one in White's *A Certain Rich Man*:

"Then you lied to me, sir," snapped Barclay.
"Oh hell, John – come off," sneered Bemis. "Haven't I got a right to lie to you if I want to?"[82]

But it was not only simple practicality that was at stake in such matters or in the felt heinousness of falsifying marine logbooks or cheating in examinations. All such cheating was liable to lead to a situation in which two parties appealed to a third to determine which of them was speaking the truth. And in the solemn face-to-face asseveration of falsehoods in such a situation there was an implicit and disturbing cancellation of social bonds. The collectivity was simply considered unworthy of being told the truth and the perjurer played by a private set of rules. The same applied to cheating at cards, as distinct from being a skillfully deceptive card player. It too broke the communal contract and destroyed the idea of the game itself, or at least the publicly defined game. At times it might involve the creation of a different game, the cheating game, which could be morally acceptable among people with some knowledge of its implicit rules, such as the cheating game in *Life on the Mississippi*. But when done against innocents, it destroyed the social compact and involved a fundamental contempt for others. For the same reason, it was acceptable for Twain's King and Duke to con the playgoers of Bricksville, who prided themselves on their own cunning and were prepared to con in return, but unacceptable for them to try and cheat the three trusting Wilks girls out of their inheritance.

And something else usually went on in cheating, whether at cards or on a larger scale. In one of her novels in this period the British writer E. Nesbit described how her chivalrous children heroes "had a law, unalterable as those of the Medes and Persians, that one had to stand by the results of a toss-up, or a drawing of lots, or any other appeal to chance however much one might happen to dislike the way things were turning out."[83] The cheat, in contrast, refused to abide by the decisions of chance or fate, the deal of the cards, the fall of the dice, after he had declared his readiness to do so; implicit in that refusal was an overestimation of winning and excessive fear of losing. Such attitudes were especially obvious when money was at stake. The logical inference was that what counted for the cheat, above everything, was the financial gain, and that it was simply the amount of money that brought credit in his eyes, not the kind of daring and coolness demanded by playing for high stakes. Hence he appeared both overly self-regarding and, because of his dread of losing, ignoble, like the monarch described in William Gilmore Simms's life of Bayard, who "had the soul of a shopkeeper, rather than a prince – was mean, mercenary and cowardly – audacious when the danger was remote, and impotent when it approached him."[84]

In these attitudes towards honesty there were deeper questions of psychological coherence and stability. Dean Acheson spoke of how "one must live with one's self; and the consequences of living with a decision which one knows has sprung from timidity and cowardice go to the roots of one's life. It is not merely a question of peace of mind, although it is vital; it is a matter of integrity of character."[85] Implicit in the idea of honor was the committing of oneself to a set of rules that one had chosen with a clear understanding of what they entailed. As Huizinga explains "though play as such is outside the range of good and bad, the element of tension imparts to it a certain ethical value in so far as it means a testing of the player's prowess: his courage, tenacity, resources and, last but not least, his spiritual powers – his 'fairness'; because, despite his ardent desire to win, he must still stick to the rules of the game."[86] One does what one commits oneself to, and abides by the outcome of one's chosen rules, in the recognition that merit comes because of the very existence of those rules. When the young Stover realized at one point that a teacher whom he and his schoolmates were trying to trick was putting him on his honor, "it took away all the elements of danger that glorified the conspiracy. It made it easy and, therefore, mean."[87] The same attitude was displayed in *Frank Merriwell at Yale* when one of Frank's antagonists refused to beat him with a trick, telling a classmate that "it is not a square deal, although no referee would call it a foul...That man has entrusted this entire affair to our honor, and if I can't whip him fair I won't whip him at all."[88] The principle of coherence was also at work in the notion of staying loyal to one's associates and of being prepared to value certain commitments above everything else, including staying alive. "The gentleman," Emerson said, "is a man of truth, lord of his own actions, and expressing that lordship in his behavior."[89] And the idea of wholeness and self-determination, so appealing to the young, kept coming in celebrations of honorable chivalric figures. Francis J. Grund called Andrew Jackson "a politician, a soldier, an enthusiast for the rights of the people, and a Christian at the same time," and reported that "he is always a whole; head, heart, and hand – conception, determination, and action – being one and inseparable."[90] A variety of turn-of-the-century figures, among them Tom Johnson, Bill Haywood, and Oliver Wendell Holmes, likewise demonstrated the soundness of Ruth Kelso's suggestion that "integrity comes the nearest perhaps to [honor] as a synonym."[91] Hapgood, for instance, would remember being impressed by "the real marriage there was between Haywood's feeling and his active life. His was not a...split-up personality...His nature was that of a straight line."[92] Conversely, the accusation of having behaved dishonorably pointed to the disturbing possibility of deep self-contradictions in one's psyche, the possibility that one deserved to stand condemned by virtue of the very principles that gave one energy. The bad conscience resulting from a fear of such possible doubleness was obviously at work in some of the more hysterical antilabor violence that I have mentioned.

When looked at more closely, then, the dichotomies and antitheses that I spoke of at the start of this chapter shimmer and blur, especially the putative disjunction of honor and truth. Rightly viewed, the martial and civil overlap, and both are pervaded by the principles of truth and reality. The idea of honorable integrity implies that one's commitments to individuals or groups or principles are pondered ones, and that one has chosen values in which one can take pride and whose implications – including, ultimately, the possibility of violence – one understands, so that there need be no inevitable professional discrepancy between what one says and what one thinks. These interrelationships had been especially plain in that greatest of chivalric wars which did so much to shape the thinking of coevals like Oliver Wendell Holmes and William James, and which has deservedly continued to exercise so strong a fascination.

Far from being mindless and irrational, war had always been informed by intellect, as epitomized in the abstract versions of it in card games and chess, those popular pastimes in medieval castles. Like other games, it involved remembering and predicting, inferring, calculating odds, assessing stakes, bluffing, counterbluffing, bluff calling; and as Clausewitz brilliantly demonstrated in *On War*, its modern practitioners needed powers of analysis and synthesis of a high order. The Civil War had been exceptionally rich in that kind of military greatness – Jackson dominating the Shenandoah Valley, Sherman planning and executing his great march, Lee throughout his long brilliant campaigns, Grant taking Vicksburg and learning, in the words of J. F. C. Fuller, "how to stamp his mind on his operations, turning intellectual conceptions into co-ordinated actions."[93] It had also demonstrated that, as Napoleon observed, "the personality of the general is indispensable, he is the head, he is the all of an army. The Gauls were not conquered by the

Roman legions, but by Caesar."[94] An admiring adversary of Bayard had commented that "he is of that stamp that, had he the greatest dastards upon earth under him, he would make them valiant," and his grieving men-at-arms allegedly declared that though death had "deprived him of life in this world, his renown and glory shall be immortal while that shall endure; for his life has been so exemplary that the memory of it shall survive to all the valiant and virtuous Knights that shall come after him."[95] The Civil War shone with greatness of that sort too; and it involved much more than professional skill in strategy and tactics. What counted was the whole man in his full integrity, just as it had with Bayard, with his courage, his energy, his humor, his courteousness, his sense of justice. And that integrity entailed both intellectual and moral clarity.

Because thought in warfare has more immediate and grave consequences than it does in almost any other area of activity, not only does the commander need to be able to plan resolutely, in full knowledge of the possible human cost; he also has to be confident that his plans will be willingly executed. The Civil War was peculiarly a war in which that willingness had to be *earned*. As a British military observer noted at the time, "the only way in which an officer could acquire influence over the Confederate soldier was by his personal conduct under fire."[96] But the moral authority of generals like Lee and Jackson did not come simply from their great personal courage and resoluteness on the battlefield, or from their military genius. It also came from their manifest purity and disinterestedness, the recognition that their eyes were totally on the winning of the war and the restoration of peace and not on personal advantages or vaporous notions of martial glory, and that any sacrifices that they asked for were asked for because there were no alternatives. The same was true of their Union counterparts, who not only shared the dangers of the men whose lives they were risking and losing, but knew that those men were reading newspapers in which their strategies and tactics were being scrutinized. Sherman reported of his troops in 1864 that "they will march to certain death if I order it, because they know and feel that night and day I labor to the end that not a life shall be lost in vain";[97] and Grant, according to J. F. C. Fuller, could have legitimately said the same of his own planning and preoccupations, even with respect to the dreadful Wilderness campaign. All four generals – and not they alone, of course – displayed what Joyce Cary calls "those simple fundamental qualities which are the elements of all greatness: courage, independence of will, devotion to a cause larger than one's own; a contempt of mean ambition."[98] Moreover, to an unprecedented extent the great commanders on both sides had been obliged to come to terms intellectually with large and problematic moral aspects of the war that they were fighting, such as the slavery issue, the rival claims of States' Rights and of the Union, and the pervasive American resentment of military discipline and military hierarchies. And they were conscious of the obligation not only to convince their opponents that they would persist unshakably until victory had been achieved, but to demonstrate to the world at large, in the behavior of their armies and in their own civility, the strength and validity of the cultural values on whose behalf they were fighting.

Honorableness, in sum, not only enabled the honor-governed individual to see his own life as every bit as charged with meaning, valor, and difficulties overcome as that of the Napoleonic magnate, and furnished him with a secure base from which to criticize the latter. As the Civil War had demonstrated, in practical public terms honor "worked," just as it had worked earlier in the years of the American Revolution and the shaping of the Republic by men like Jefferson, with his complexity, his restlessly analytical intelligence, and his admonition to a favorite nephew, "Never suppose, that in any possible situation, or under any circumstances, it is best for you to do a dishonorable thing, however slightly so it may appear to you."[99]

Rightly apprehended, honor intensified rather than diminished energy and efficiency. As that shrewd observer John William De Forest noted of the archetypal American man of honor, "a Virginian gentleman is popularly supposed to be a combination of laziness and dignity. But this is an error; the type would be considered a marvel of energy in some countries; and...it is capable of amazing activity, audacity, and perseverance. Of all the States which have fought against the Union Virginia has displayed the most formidable military qualities."[100] Honor was perfectly compatible with realism. John S. Mosby, for example, described by Edmund Wilson as "a knight errant in the sense that his audacious successes were in the nature of individual exploits," said in his memoirs that "in one sense the charge that I did not fight fair is true. I fought for success and not for display. There was no man in the Confederate army who had less of the spirit of knight-errantry in him than I did. The combat between Richard and Saladin by the Diamond of the Desert [in *The Talisman*] is a beautiful picture for the imagination to dwell on, but it isn't war, and was no model for me." But he also felt entitled to add that "there is no authenticated act of mine which is not perfectly in accordance with approved military usage. Grant, Sheridan, and Stonewall Jackson had about the same ideas that I had on the subject of war."[101] Honorableness could also display itself without any of the conventional trappings of glamor, as it did in a figure like Grant —shabbily attired, modest of mien, implacable in carrying out his plans, and delicately sparing of the sensibilities of the surrendered foe at

Vicksburg and Appomattox.[102] And behind Grant stood that greatest American embodiment of the chivalric values without the chivalric trappings, of whom Herbert Croly declared in 1910 that "the life of no other American has revealed with anything like the same completeness the peculiar moral promise of genuine democracy."[103] I am referring, of course, to Lincoln, so different from and yet so rightly paired with Lee, with his complex maskings and maneuverings, his miseries, grandeurs, and compassions, his imperturbable courage, his nonvindictiveness towards the foe, his playfulness and flair for debate, his theatrical tale telling and antitheatrical theatrical style, his profound self-education, his deep historical sense of the meaning and potentialities of the Republic.[104]

In this chapter and in earlier ones, I have discussed a wide variety of honorable types and individuals. They include complex, flexible intelligences, capable of deviousness without being Machiavellian, and able to respond imaginatively to the idea of grandeur without opting for a Napoleonic dominativeness.[105] Among them are some of the ablest public men that America has produced. If their roots, and the roots of honor, are partly in romance, especially the romance of childhood, the moral is not that romance is in conflict with reality and needs to be eliminated, but that the sturdiest psyche is one in which connections stay open with the attitudes of childhood, and that those attitudes are fundamentally true to reality – the reality of social relations – and not in conflict with it. Appropriately, one of the master ironists of the turn-of-the-century years had his surrogate in *Man and Superman* confess to having discovered as a boy that "veracity and honour were no longer goody-goody expressions in the mouths of grown-up people, but compelling principles, in myself."[106] And there were further implications here for the life of the mind.

12

Intellect

I recall with a smile and yet with affection your amusing pomp and your martial precision. But you stood erect; and that is a pleasant memory in a world where I have seen many men cringe.

> Walter Hines Page, *The Southerner; a Novel* (1906)

Smooth Falsehood is not Order; it is the general sumtotal of *Dis*order. Order is *Truth*, – each thing standing on the basis that belongs to it: Order and Falsehood cannot subsist together.

> Thomas Carlyle, *On Heroes, Hero-Worship, and the Heroic in History* (1841)

On January 9 [1900] Lieutenant John F. Hall...brought formal charges against his own major:
 ...the said Wilbur S. Metcalf did maliciously, wilfully, and without just cause, shoot and kill an unarmed prisoner of war on his knees before him, begging for life.

> Leon Wolff, *Little Brown Brother* (1961)[1]

HONOR AND PROFESSIONALISM

IN AN ADDRESS at Yale in 1888 on the occasion of his receiving a Doctorate of Laws, Oliver Wendell Holmes said, "I accept it proudly as an accolade, like the little blow upon the shoulder from the sword of a master of war which in ancient days adjudged that a soldier had won his spurs and pledged his life to decline no combat in the future."[2] The glamorizing of the intellect during the late nineteenth and early twentieth centuries – the romanticizing of research, the exaltation of truth seeking, the conviction that trained intelligences ought to have a greater hand in running things – was, of course, partly a celebration of power and potency. The Napoleonic great thinker constructed magnificent new systems after demolishing primitive older ones; the emergent expert stood at the levers of enormous technological powers; vast transformations, such as those celebrated in H. G. Wells's very influential *The World Set Free* (1914), were imminent. But it was a different view of intellectual heroism that inhered in assertions like Holmes's claim that in Law "as well as elsewhere [a man] may drink the bitter cup of heroism, may wear his heart out after the unattainable," or William

James's insistence that "the martial type of character can be bred without war. Strenuous honor and disinterestedness abound elsewhere," or David Graham Phillips's statement about the Woods Hole Marine Biological Laboratory that "its Knights of Science have not reached their goal – their Holy Grail. But under the inspiration of the triple vow of Science for her knights – poverty, self-immolation and obedience to truth – they have had adventures and have made discoveries."[3] Implicit was the idea of truth-seeking professionalism as heroic not because it led to power but because it was honorable. And entailed in this idea were some important corollaries.

The neopastoral conviction that what counted above all was the creation of a rational, pacific, contented, and smooth-running world, and that society needed to be coolly ordered to that end by rational professionals, was subsumed by a particular image of truth and truth seeking. Truth in this view was a permanency. It was like the heavens as they were revealed by astronomers pushing back the darkness of the universe with ever more sophisticated instruments, or like a city buried beneath the sands of the accidental that was being uncovered by archaeologists. And the true nature and configurations of a rational society were likewise being discovered by increasingly sophisticated methods, and with the participation of more and more people. The codified insights and procedures of the social sciences, for example, were becoming available to more and more social workers and being used by them to improve their clients and make society healthy and just. So were the blessings of education, as codified in universities and disseminated methodically by properly trained schoolteachers. And the more professional a person became, the more he or she was governed by objective intelligence, purified of merely personal ambitions and biases. Such a view of the intellectual life and of civic reasonableness was essentially imperial. If it drew partly upon the moral prestige of those daring annexers of whole new territories, the Napoleons of science, it emphasized even more the dignity of the empire of science once it had been established, an empire whose loyal, efficient, disinterested, and modest servants refined its operations and partook of its grandeur. And in certain ways it was curiously duplicitous with respect to the supposed primacy of truth.

A characteristic of certain kinds of dominance, as I have said, was that the dominators need not take the dominated seriously intellectually. There was only one pattern of reasonable truth, of which the dominators were in possession, and all other patterns were beyond the pale of reason and hence of rational argument: The arguments of outsiders were pseudoarguments, and as they grew in intensity and complexity, they became, in an unfavorable sense of the word, ideological, involving entirely unnecessary conflicts. The attitude of the enlightened North toward the unenlightened South before the Civil War, had been paradigmatic. As the hero of Albion W. Tourgée's *A Fool's Errand* put it, "the North and the South are simply convenient names for two distinct, hostile, and irreconsilable ideas, – two civilizations, they are sometimes called, especially at the South. At the North there is somewhat more of an intellectual arrogance; and we are apt to speak of the one as civilization, and of the other as a species of barbarism."[4] Hence the South was not only anachronistic but silly in its attempted resistance to the irresistible forces and currents of progress. In the words of De Forest's exiled Southerner Dr. Ravenel, Southerners were "as ill-informed as Hottentots. They have no more idea of their relative strength as compared to that of the United States than the Root-diggers of the Rocky Mountains. They are doomed to perish by their own ignorance and madness."[5] And immediately after the Civil War, whose outbreak had demonstrated the South's moral inferiority, and whose outcome had proved its organizational inferiority, the Northern attitude was neatly defined by the resentful Southerner who said, "It is urged that the South should...consolidate the peace of the country, and provide against a 'war of ideas'. Now a 'war of ideas' is what the South wants and insists upon perpetrating."[6] What was sought by the reconstructive North was an unconditional acknowledgement by the South of its wrongheadedness and a relinquishment of the right to speak of unfairness at all; the South's duty was to be wholly passive, accepting whatever was done to it by Northerners in the name of justice. The same basic pattern of nonattention would become apparent, as I have said, in other relationships, such as the educating and Americanizing of immigrants and the ameliorative operations of public agencies. Here too, the dominated had no right to object to anything that was done to them in the name of social progress, and the more strongly they objected, or resisted change, the greater was the revealed need for changing them.

Inherent in this pattern was a slackening of intellectual alertness and tension. Not only could a dominator go through the motions of attending but be all the time conscious that the final decision must come down on the side of the benefit-conferring and restructuring overgroup. There were also certain interesting maneuvers with respect to the nature of argument. By definition, the more systematic an organization committed to discovering scientific or social truths became in its drive to maximize benefits, the more efficient would it be. Relatedly, the less desirable would wounding controversy among members of the organization be, not only because it interfered with organizational efficiency, but because it was intellectually at odds with the objectivity of rational cooperation. Because value judgments, as distinct from methodically arrived at and collectively assented to truths, were merely the expression of personal preferences, it would be foolish for someone to commit himself wholeheartedly and passionately to them, especially when discussing matters with colleagues. Hence it was incumbent upon the civilized or would-be civilized person to be tolerant, that is, not given to dogmatic or "ideological" dispute. As a president of Harvard announced at one point in a university context, "You will be courteous to your elders who have explored to the point from which you may advance; and helpful to your juniors who will progress further."[7] Among the results, particularly when such attitudes were demanded of clients, was the fact that, as the political scientist Charles Drekmeier points out, "tolerance protects the realities of power from critical examination insofar as it justifies the avoidance of commitment and of the kind of confrontation which seems to be the only available device for revealing the power base of certain social institutions."[8]

This general view would be reinforced by two others that ostensibly looked like its antithesis. One was the subjectivist-relativist idea – Emersonian, Whitmanesque – of a multiplicity of individual truth perceivers, all perceiving what is true for *them*. Because man was essentially good, each person's truth would in fact, unless some gross distortion intervened, correspond to the larger reality of things; intense disagreements and controversy were therefore needless, foolish, and immoral. This position allowed individuals, particularly in education, to claim simultaneously that there was no such thing as "truth" and that what they themselves said mattered because it was true; it provided magic shields behind which a person could simultaneously insist on the privilege of not being attacked for his own views and dismiss the views of opponents as foolish; it enabled arrogance to masquerade as humility and be all the more offensive on that account. The other and even more duplicitous view was that of corrosive or programmatic irony. With its preoccupation with discrepancies and incongruities, its conviction that scrutiny will always disclose them, its feeling that with the awareness that comes with fuller knowledge all ideals must fail and all actions lose momentum, corrosive irony weakened the will to action, as in figures like Hawthorne's Miles Coverdale in *The Blithedale Romance*, Henry Adams of the later pages of the *Education*, and T.S. Eliot's Prufrock. It was opposed to indignation, to strong feelings of injustice, to a vivid sense of possibilities being ignored and individual or collective energies unrealized, to a refusal to settle for the second or third rate, the compromised, the jaded and defeated. It was inimical to all forms of militancy. As one of Joseph Conrad's characters says, "women, children, and revolutionists hate irony, which is the negation of all saving instincts, of all faith, of all devotion, of all action."[9] But, while helping to cut troublesome idealists down to size, irony could also inflate an ironist's sense of himself as a superior being who saw through to the "real" truth of things, and give an intellectual coloring to the cynicism of power. It was thus admirably suited to men pursuing power inside organizations who thought in terms of ruthless self-advancement, exploitable incongruities, and the foolishness of being locked into any forms of idealism or any naive commitment to notions of truth or loyalty or integrity. Irony as a dominant principle served power – bureaucratic power, imperial power, the power of the large organization.

The contrasting view of truth that I touched on at the outset of this chapter is what might be called the agonistic.

THE HONORABLE INTELLECTUAL

The association of intellectual and knightly honor is an old one. Huizinga reports how

> Long after the Middle Ages a certain equivalence of knighthood and a doctor's degree was generally acknowledged...The two dignities of a knight and of a doctor are conceived as the sacred forms of two superior functions, that of courage and of knowledge. By being knighted the man of action is raised to an ideal level; by taking his doctor's degree the man of knowledge receives a badge of superiority. They are stamped, the one as a hero, the other as a sage.[10]

There are significant overlappings between the two figures. Both, in their ideal aspect, are devoted to the ascetic life. Both possess arduously acquired skills and a large body of knowledge. Both are expected, before receiving their authentication, to have shown endurance, persistance, dedication, a heightened sense of values, the acquisition of a corporate conscience, a contempt for mere money making and comfort. Both are required, in theory at least, to approximate themselves to exemplary figures: In Huizinga's words, "the essence of chivalry is the imitation of the ideal hero, just as the imitation of the ancient sage is the essence of humanism."[11] And like the knight who has committed himself to a quest, or to the service of his lord or of his mistress or of the Faith, the scholar is prepared to affirm that there is nothing higher or more beautiful than the truth to whose service he is dedicated. At the center of both codes is the idea of personal honor, personal integrity, personal trustworthiness and truthfulness, an unswervable personal commitment to a chosen line of action, an unequivocal claim that what one says is true, a willingness to expose oneself to a maximum testing out, an implicit affirmation that, "If I am lying, let me suffer the penalty." Like the knight, the scholar gives his word that his achievements have been arrived at honestly and honorably, without falsification, without short-cuts in the interests of money or prestige, without unacknowledged indebtedness. He implicitly or explicitly calls on his peers to conclude that his chosen route was correct.

Truth seeking for the scholar is a personal, but not merely personal, enterprise, in which honor, risk, and daring continue to be realities. It is agonistic, answering to Oliver Wendell Holmes's conviction that "the final test...is battle in some form – actual war – the crush of Arctic ice – the fight for mastery in the market or the court."[12] The honorable scientist or scholar, *qua* professional, continues to have some of the characteristics of the warrior. He must work with the kind of energy and commitment described by Holmes when he said, "If you want to hit a bird on the wing, you must have all your will in a focus. You must not be thinking about yourself, and, equally, you must not be thinking about your neighbor; you must be living with your eye on that bird. Every achievement is a bird on the wing."[13] He must display the kinds of qualities that Thomas Mann described when he wrote in 1914: "That victorious, war-like principle of today, organisation, is the basic principle, the essence of Art...Endurance, precision, circumspection, boldness, courage in the face of hardship and defeat in the battle with solid matter; contempt for what is known as 'security' in bourgeois life, ...the habit of a dangerous, tense, attentive existence....all these things are both military and artistic."[14]

Truth seeking, in these terms, involves honor, integrity, and commitment. The honorable scholar sets the claims of truth above those of decorum, of deference, of corporate security and comfort, of personal advancement, risking the kinds of sanctions invoked against a figure like Veblen who dared to attack the power of authority, vested interests, and pseudoprofessionalism.[15] He is willing to be accountable to those who are below him in the power system to which he belongs, and over whom he directly or obliquely possesses power. He recognizes that it is disingenuous to simultaneously ask to be honored for the beneficial consequences of one's work and refuse to be blamed when the consequences are harmful, an attitude comparable to that of the industrialist who was in no way responsible for the killings and maimings that happened to the workers in his mills or mines or railroads.[16] He is willing to engage in unmasked, uncondescending, person-to-person encounters, whether with his seniors and peers, or his students, or outsiders. He knows that if reason and the life of the mind are really and not merely nominally estimable, arguments must be allowed to go all the way, without magic shields and without privileged positions and sanctuaries.[17] Huizinga describes how toward the end of the eleventh century

to beat your opponent by reason or the force of the word [became] a sport comparable with the profession of arms...In the Schools of the 12th century the most violent rivalry, going to all the lengths of vilification and slander, reigned supreme...Competition [was] an outstanding feature of the whole development of Scholasticism and the Universities...The whole functioning of the mediaeval University was profoundly agonistic and ludic.[18]

Behind lay the example of Socrates, ready to take on all comers. And in Socrates one had the totally committed intellectual, all of a piece, the man not only of truth but of courage and grace, who was prepared to pay the final penalty for his commitment – on the face of things a counterimage to the heroic figure committed to violence in the service of an idea; in reality, its double. It was courage at once Socratic and heroic that was displayed in Miguel de Unamuno's great reply to the Falangist general invading the university of which he was Rector:

This is the temple of the intellect. And I am its high priest. It is you who profane its sacred precincts. You will win, because you have more than enough brute force. But you will not convince. For to convince you need to persuade. And in order to persuade you would need what you lack: Reason and Right in the struggle. I consider it futile to exhort you to think of Spain. I have done.[19]

It was Huizinga's own courage that resulted in his being imprisoned as a hostage, in his seventies, in the St. Michielsgestad concentration camp.

In professionalism more generally, civil and martial values and attitudes overlap with respect to truth. In both, integrity in a sense precedes truthfulness. That is to say the man of integrity, whether soldier or civilian, seeks and tells the truth because it would be intolerable to his self-respect to do otherwise. And the distinction between martial and nonmartial forms of honor virtually disappears, so that it was perfectly congruous, for example, that Civil War figures like Chamberlain and Lee could pass back and forth between military and academic structures without any fundamental change in values and attitudes. In Ruth Kelso's words, "the only real counterpart" of the knightly code of honor "in modern life, is the professional code of the lawyer, the doctor, and others who have acquired a group consciousness and pride."[20] Embedded in the idea of allegiance to an arduously assimilated professional code is the idea of professional honor and dishonor; from this point of view, military, medical, legal, academic, and other activities are all subbranches of honorable professionalism. They all affirm that there are higher values than monetary ones and have agreed-upon codes of behavior that transcend national and religious borders, with penalties for violations of those codes. In all of them prestige is important, particularly with fellow professionals. They all celebrate what Veblen called the instinct of workmanship and affirm that there are determinable degrees of relative excellence. They all call for consistency and dependability in their practitioners. They all insist that the professional is a truth-*facing* individual who scans the options without self-deception, accepts the way the figurative cards or dice have gone in a particular situation, recognizes that unpleasant things may sometimes have to be done because the other alternatives would all be worse, and is not afraid to reverse a stand when fresh facts come to his attention.

CHIVALRIC PATTERNS AND JUSTICE

These attitudes toward truth and honor bore on the reemergence during the turn-of-the-century period of the idea of the honorable public man and the feeling that, as William James said, "all the qualities of a man acquire dignity when he knows that the service of the collectivity that owns him needs them."[21] The image of the man of honor as a servant of justice had, of course, been a recurring one: Ramón Lull, for instance, asserted that "chivalry is to maintain justice"; and Bayard's biographer recalled that "he never was known to uphold the dearest friend he had upon earth in defiance of equity: the good Gentleman was wont to say, that every Empire, Kingdom, or Province without justice, may be likened to a forest full of robbers."[22] But the chivalric view of justice differed significantly from the rationalistic Progressive one.

In a curious way Progressive and conservative views of justice overlapped. In both, what made a society just was obedience to correct laws, laws that resulted from an irreversible uncovering of the fundamental principles of social order; and in both, the central element in the legal system was the judicial. For conservatives, the judge was the instrument for seeing that the controlled obeyed the laws that forbade them to interfere with the inalienable rights of property. For Progressives, he was the means of ensuring that the benefits of progressive legislation, including improvements in the behavior of businessmen, were fully realized. For each he was the disinterested interpreter of laws whose goal was the creation of law-abiding citizens. If conservatives believed that the correct laws had already been arrived at and constituted a complex and dignified structure that took precedence over individuals (Walter Lippmann referred ironically to "lawyers, like Taft, who see in the courts an intimation of heaven"[23]), Progressives too had confidence in the possibility of such a structure, even if it lay in the future and not in the past. This image of judicial justice giving carried over into the broader business of administration. Higher-level administrators, or legislators acting upon expert professional advice, devised wise new laws and improved imperfect old ones; lower-level administrators interpreted and applied them, likewise judicially.

It was a very different view of law and legal structures that was emerging not only in radical thinking but in the thinking of someone

Intellect

like Holmes, who wrote to a friend in 1911 that "just now I am having one of my periodic wallows in Scott. He also is dear to most people, I suppose – but the older order in which the sword and the gentleman were beliefs, is near enough to me to make this their last voice enchanting in spite of the common sense of commerce."[24] What Holmes and historians like Charles Beard – the muckrakers' "scholarly cousin," as Joseph Freeman called him[25] – perceived was that law-making and legal processes were ineluctably a matter of conflicts between groups with conflicting interests, that the legal structure was fundamentally agonistic and had been so since the inception of the Republic, and that laws were made by power and could be changed by power. Viewed in this light, the masterly maneuverings of Reconstruction-resisting Southerners in the postwar Congress and the successful entry of the power-seeking Irish into the law-making processes in Massachusettes were perfectly legitimate and proper. So were the agonistic activities of trade unions. As Holmes wrote in a dissenting judgment in 1896, "combination on the one side [i.e., that of employers] is patent and powerful. Combination on the other is the necessary and desirable counterpart, if the battle is to be carried out in a fair and equal way." It was also necessary, as he observed in a subsequent judgment, that there be "the equality of position between the parties in which liberty of contract begins."[26] And at the center of the agonistic view of the law and justice, in addition to the agonistic processes of law making, was the courtroom as an agonistic institution.

It is appropriate that the popular American image of the courtroom, the Perry Mason image, is of a place in which attorneys duel with each other under the eyes of a colorless judge and that a muckraker reporting a trial in 1904 should have been moved to describe how, when one of the combatants entered the courtroom and finally let his "eagle eye" rest on his adversary, "the glance was as absolute a challenge and a defiance as ever knights of old exchanged."[27] Law, as Hugh Henry Brackenridge said in his early-nineteenth century novel Modern Chivalry, "is an image of war"[28] – chivalric war – and it relates back, as Huizinga points out, to "the legal proceedings in archaic society: the game of chance, the contest, the verbal battle."[29] In this view, law, justice, and peace are not in opposition to the agonistic – to the duel, the combat, the game – but are inseparable from it. Implicit in the nature of the courtroom perceived in such terms are some of the key principles informing the literal duel, judicial or otherwise. The contending parties are entitled to an honorable combat, a combat before an impartial judge in which, as far as possible, their skills or those of their champions are approximately equal, each side is fully answerable to the other, each is inconvenienced by the process and uncertain as to its outcome, and each will suffer if it

227

loses. And within the bounds of the courtroom the two parties are equal before the law: In Huizinga's words, the courtroom, "whether square or round, is still a magic circle, a play-ground where the customary differences of rank are temporarily abolished."[30] Such conditions make it possible to lose without feeling humiliated, and without animus toward the law. They can obtain whether or not a society is democratic, as they did in those public gardens of Paris in which Louis IX administered justice in his hat of white peacock's feathers.

It is here that one comes back to the broader question of social justice and of the role of intellect in the struggle for a just – or at least less *un*just – society. The same agonistic principles apply where other civil disputes are concerned, whether between scholars with conflicting theories, or the expert and the layman, or the bureaucrat and the client, including the teacher and the taught. When there is a conflict as to who is telling the truth, everyone is entitled to enter a magic circle, before verdict givers who have not made up their minds in advance, and to deal with an opponent of whom full answerability is required, and who is not allowed to hide behind a magic shield, whether of rank or role or alleged expertise, and who will suffer penalties if he is detected lying. The historian John Lukacs was quite right, in one sense, when he asserted that society is "threatened not by the absence of justice," but by "the fantastic prevalence of untruth,"[31] insofar as the justice of which he speaks is the distribution of goods in accordance with this or that blueprint of the good society. But in another sense truth and justice are inseparable, and in the absence of the agonistic patterns that I have described, the ostensibly more just society – a society managed by benevolent bureaucrats and objective "experts" – will not only not feel but will not be just. One of the paradoxes of that medieval society that so enraged Twain was that the peasant could feel that he and the great nobleman were both equally men. This was partly because they would face equally horrendous penalties in the final judgment by the Deity. But partly, too, it was because peasants could observe noblemen engaged in struggles in which they risked their fortunes, their honor, and their lives, and in which, at times, when brought before the bar of justice, they suffered appalling punishments. In the supposedly more rational, egalitarian, and just modern society, on the other hand, the higher someone is in an organization, the freer he is from any ultimate challenges and penalties that link him with the ordinary person; and when the latter deals with bureaucratic structures, he is confronted again and again with figures who are armored against him with magic shields and in whose eyes he is less meaningfully human, in the sense of being answerable to, than they are. Just as the prevalence of untruth among the military diminishes the ability of the military to do those very things on which their claims to distinction rest, so the larger prevalence of untruth means that society will not succeed in achieving even economic justice.

Paradoxically, the idea of honorable behavior and honor-related structures precedes the idea of social justice not only historically but logically. As I pointed out in previous chapters, what Nitobe called "the sense of honour, implying a vivid consciousness of personal dignity and worth," was itself a powerful factor making not only for the aristocrat's defense of his own liberty and a related disposition to defend the liberties of others, but for the kind of agonistic structuring of underdog groups that made possible the equity spoken of by Holmes. All this is as important in a modernized or modernizing society as in any other.

The equating of honorableness with truthfulness has rightly been a major element in the continuing American honoring of honor and the continuing belief in its social indispensability. It informs those media stereotypes that have gone on shaping people's consciousnesses because, despite all the actual departures from them, they embody significant professional ideals – the good doctor who insists on discovering what is really wrong with a patient or a community, regardless of how unwelcome the truth may be; the relentlessly truth-seeking and truth-reporting journalist, undeterred by the power of the big organization or the big name; the fearless attorney, equally resolute when defending an underdog client or attacking corruption on behalf of the public. It displays itself in the instinctive phrasing of certain compliments, like the remark by a lawyer for the Scottsboro Boys that a Southern doctor testifying during their lynchlike trial in the 1930s proved to be "an extraordinarily honorable man, and told the truth."[32] It is apparent in the conviction that the man of honor is willing at any time, anywhere, to answer any challenge honestly – a notion at work, for example, in Gore Vidal's wish that in election campaigns television could "show us the candidates in interviews, debates, *un*controlled encounters in which we can actually see who the candidate really is, answering tough questions, his record up there for all to examine,"[33] and observable earlier when the chivalric Al Smith challenged the Napoleonic Hearst to a public debate about certain accusations being made in his papers, a challenge that Hearst characteristically declined.

And the question of both truth telling and truth seeking comes up with especial force where large organizations are concerned, in ways that bear on the question of justice. More than a cool-blooded concern for imperial efficiency was entailed in the belief that, in Greene's words, "the most important Social Contribution that the New Style hero [circa 1914–18] could make was to prove that a vast organization could be made honest, efficient, and humane."[34] As Teddy Roosevelt said, those fighting for "decent politics" should not only be "disinterested, unselfish, and generous, but also possess the essential manly virtues of energy, of resolution, and of indomitable personal courage."[35] The honorable man in any organization is concerned that specific injustices, whether resulting from his own actions or from those of other members of the organization, must be corrected, and is not afraid of challenging those above him in the organization, or disturbing his peers, or risking injury to his own career in the interests of justice. To ask for this kind of readiness for combat is to ask for something without which any organization, however admirable its professed aims, will become self-serving, morally corrupt, and ultimately tyrannical.

Honor itself makes that readiness easier.

A recurring feature of the idea of honor is commitment to combat on behalf of the more than merely personal, a commitment that may at times take precedence over everything else. "Who is there who would not like to be thought a gentleman?" asked Holmes. "Yet what has that name been built on but the soldiers' choice of honor rather than life? To be a soldier or descended from soldiers, in time of peace to be ready to give one's life rather than to suffer disgrace, that is what the word has meant."[36] Such a vision belongs to a broader tradition of virtue as combat. William James was speaking in that tradition when he said that "the capacity for the strenuous mood probably lies slumbering in every man, but it...needs the wilder passions to arouse it, the big fears, loves, and indignations; or else the deeply penetrating appeal of some one of the higher fidelities, like justice, truth, or freedom."[37] So was Pierre-Joseph Proudhon when he wrote in 1861, "God forbid that I should preach the gentle virtues and joys of peace to my fellow man! I too am a man, and what I like most in man is the bellicose temperament that puts him above all authority and love, as well as above fatalism."[38] The martial rhetoric and songs of the great reforming movements are not peripheral but central: The just society, or entry into the just kingdom, is something that has to be fought for. Describing the hymns of his boyhood, D. H. Lawrence recalled how "men, even Sunday School teachers, still believed in the fight for life and the fun of it.... It was far, far from any militarism or gun-fighting. But it was the battle-cry of a stout soul, and a fine thing too."[39] The anarchist Proudhon affirmed that "before dealings are possible, strife is inevitable; before the peace treaty there is the duel and war. This is true of every moment of existence," and that "true human virtue is not merely negative. It does not simply mean abstaining from everything which law and morality condemn. It consists much more of offering energetic opposition through talent, will and strength of character to people who by their very existence try to blot us out."[40]

The various chivalric-martial syntheses that I have been describing make effective, high-energy combat easier, whether on behalf of so-called traditional or so-called radical principles. Max Lerner pointed toward their moral core when he spoke of "four of the great elements in [Holmes's] thinking: that life is risk, that our fates depend on a throw of the dice, and that law must embody this aleatory quality; that life is battle, and the best meaning of effort comes out under fire; that one must be a good soldier with a 'splendid carelessness for life' in a cause; and that one must have a fighting faith – that to act with enthusiasm is the condition of acting greatly."[41] Holmes himself said finely:

That the joy of life is living, is to put out all one's powers as far as they will go; that the measure of power is obstacles overcome; to ride boldly at what is in front of you...to pray, not for comfort, but for combat; to keep the soldier's faith against the doubts of civil life, more besetting and harder to overcome than all the misgivings of the battle-field...to love glory more than the temptations of wallowing ease...these things we learned from noble enemies in Virginia or Georgia or on the Mssissippi, thirty years ago; these things we believe to be true.[42]

And Steinbeck finely described gallantry as "that quality which, when faced with overwhelming odds, fights on as though it could win and by that very token sometimes does."[43] Moreover, such attitudes, as will be apparent by now, are compatible with a good deal of intellectual sophistication, and are all the stronger on that account. If corrosive irony is the enemy of the chivalric syntheses, those syntheses themselves can accommodate creatively a strong sense of irony. They include a consciousness of ineluctable discrepancies between ideals and actualities. They include an awareness of the variety of ways in which admirable hopes and ambitions can be defeated, and the soldier's knowledge that the accidents of battle and the power of numbers may have at least as much to do as merit in determining the outcome of a conflict. They include an at times amused understanding and enjoyment of role playing and theatrics in the pursuit of worthwhile ends. They include the possibility of a complex intellectual playfulness and sportiveness, as seen in the works of Jorge Luis Borges, that lover of romantic fictions who said in 1967, "I think nowadays, while literary men seem to have neglected their epic duties, the epic has been saved for us, strangely enough, by the Western ...has been saved for the world by of all places, Hollywood."[44] In a number of respects, the word chivalry could have been substituted for the word irony when Proudhon wrote in his *Confessions*: "Irony, you are true liberty! You preserve me from aspirations to gain power, from being a slave to parties, from pedantry in science, from the admiration of the great, from the mystifications of politics, from the fanaticism of reformers, from the superstitions of this vast universe and from self-adoration."[45]

231

And by transcending the simplistic dichotomies that I have discussed in this book, and the simplistic ironic undercuttings, the chivalric values make it easier, too, to carry on after one has lost a literal or figurative battle or campaign or war. They made possible not only the unextinguishable pride of the defeated South but the intellectual adaptations of a Nick Carraway, who, even though the East defeated him, did not pass from the illusionment of Gatsby to Gatsby's kind of disillusionment and deprivation, but instead was able increasingly to make sense of his experiences in all their contradictoriness. They made possible the wry courage of Fitzgerald himself after the collapse of his own Gatsby-like illusions and expectations, and the heroic endurance of a Melville, and the creative perseverance of British writers as different from each other as Conrad, Shaw, Yeats, and Orwell. They have nourished most of the really interesting American writers of this century. All in all, it is not really difficult to understand why Albert Camus – appropriately a particular favorite of American intellectuals – was able to say:

In the conflicts of this century, I have felt close to all obstinate men, particularly to those who have never been able to abandon their faith in honor. I have shared and I continue to share many contemporary hysterias. But I have never been able to make up my mind to spit, as so many have done, on the word "honor" –no doubt because I was and continue to be aware of my human weaknesses and the injustices I have committed, and because I knew and continue to know instinctively that honor, like pity, is the irrational virtue that carries on after justice and reason have become powerless.[46]

Notes

CHAPTER 1. INTRODUCTION: TWAIN AND THE CHIVALRY BUSINESS

1 Mark Twain, *A Connecticut Yankee in King Arthur's Court*, introd. Albert Bigelow Paine, Stormfield Edition of the Writings of Mark Twain (New York: Harper, 1929), p. 10; Stephen Vincent Benét, *John Brown's Body*, introd. Henry Seidel Canby (New York: Rinehart, 1928), p. 168; *National Lampoon* (February 1977), p. 72.

2 Twain, *A Connecticut Yankee*, pp. 387–8, 386, 391, 395, 396, 147.

3 Mark Twain, *Life on the Mississippi*, introd. Albert Bigelow Paine, Stormfield Edition of the Writings of Mark Twain (New York: Harper, 1929), p. 375.

4 Twain, *A Connecticut Yankee*, pp. 272–3.

5 Twain, *Life on the Mississippi*, pp. 6, 375.

6 Mark Twain, *Mark Twain's Notebook*, ed. Albert Bigelow Paine, 2nd ed. (New York: Harper, 1935), p. 198.

7 Twain, *A Connecticut Yankee*, p. 301.

8 Twain, *A Connecticut Yankee*, pp. 233–4.

9 Andrew Carnegie, *Triumphant Democracy: Or Fifty Years' March of the Republic* (New York: Scribner, 1886), p. 498.

10 Edgar Allen Poe, "The Poetic Principle," *The Complete Tales and Poems of Edgar Allen Poe*, introd. Hervey Allen (New York: Modern Library, 1938), p. 906.

11 Joel Barlow, *The Columbiad: A Poem* (London: Richard Phillips, 1809), p. xiv; Carnegie, *Triumphant Democracy*, p. 232.

12 Howard Pyle, *Otto of the Silver Hand* (New York, Scribner, 1940 [1888]), p. 11.

13 On the horrors possible in the slave states, see, for example, Richard O. Curry and Joanna Dunlap Cowden, eds., *Slavery in America: Theodore Weld's American Slavery As It Is* (Itasca, Ill.: Peacock, 1972 [1839]). The editors report that Weld's book was "the most widely read and the most influential abolitionist tract" prior to *Uncle Tom's Cabin* and that "we discovered not only that all of the citations checked (a random sample of approximately 30 percent) were accurate but that Weld used only a fraction of the evidence available to him" (pp. xxii, ix).

14 On American duels and affrays, see, for example, Ben C. Truman's *The Field of Honor: Being a Complete and Comprehensive History of Duelling in All Countries* (New York: Fords, Howard, and Hulbert, 1883) and William Oliver Stevens's *Pistols at Ten Paces: The Story of the Code of Honor in America* (Boston: Houghton Mifflin, 1940). In a footnote in *Life on the Mississippi*, Twain drily quotes a couple of newspaper accounts of murderous affrays as a gloss on a reference to Southern civilization, in a prospectus for a girls'

school, as "the highest type of civilization this continent has seen" (pp. 334–5).

15 *Richmond Enquirer*, quoted in John S. C. Abbott, *South and North: Or, Impressions Received during a Trip to Cuba and the South* (New York: Abbey and Abbott, 1860), pp. 266–7.

16 Joseph B. Cobb, *Mississippi Scenes; or, Sketches of Southern and Western Life, Humorous, Satirical and Descriptive* (Upper Saddle River, N.J.: Literature House, 1971 [1851]), p. 158.

17 W. Gilmore Simms, *The Life of the Chevalier Bayard: the Good Knight, Sans peur et sans reproche* (New York: Harper, 1847), p. 2. On the question of the influence of Scott on the South, see, for example, Hamilton James Eckinrode, "Sir Walter Scott and the South," *North American Review* 206 (October 1917): 595–603; George Harrison Orians, "Sir Walter Scott, Mark Twain, and the Civil War," *South Atlantic Quarterly* 40 (October 1941):342–59; and especially Rollin F. Osterweis, *Romanticism and Nationalism in the Old South* (Baton Rouge: Louisiana State University Press, 1967 [1949]).

Obviously Twain was exaggerating when he complained that "a curious exemplification of the power of a single book for good or harm is shown in the effects wrought by *Don Quixote* and those wrought by *Ivanhoe*. The first swept the world's admiration for the medieval chivalry silliness out of existence; and the other restored it." So too with his suggestion that Scott "had so large a hand in making Southern character, as it existed before the war, that he is in great measure responsible for the war" (*Life on the Mississippi*, pp. 377–8, 376). But one can see why he said what he did and why his academic admirer Eckinrode complained that "beyond doubt Scott gave the South its social ideal, and the South of 1860 might be not inaptly nicknamed Sir Walter Scottland" ("Sir Walter Scott," p. 601). The point is not that other influences were also at work, which of course they were, or that Scott was popular in the North too, which he was, but that when it came to formulating a memorable and easily graspable ideology peculiarly suited to Southern needs, Scott did certain things far better than anyone else. Osterweis abundantly illustrates the kinds of use to which the South put him.

Moreover, the effects of the Scottian poison in the Southern bloodstream – that is, regarded through Twainian eyes – had been strengthened by the numerous writers who were indebted to him. In *Harold* (1848), for example, the Scott–inspired Edward Bulwer Lytton presented his readers with a conflict between noble Saxons and the "superb and matchless chivalry" of the Norman, the latter of whom were men "in whom the brave acknowledge the highest examples of valiant deeds, and the free the manliest assertion of noble thoughts," since the days of the Greeks. In an interesting maneuver he also related both parties back to their common Scandinavian ancestors, with their "thirst for fame and the point of honour," and made it easier for Southerners to identify themselves simultaneously with chivalrous Saxons like Wilfred of Ivanhoe and chivalrous Normans like Richard Lion Heart. (Lytton, *Harold: The Last of the Saxon Kings*, 3rd ed. 2 vols. [Boston: Joseph Knight, n.d.], 1:55,16.) In numerous historical novels, such as *Richelieu* (1829), Scott's friend G. P. R. James furnished his readers with, among other things, what H. G. Wells later recalled affectionately as "the solitary horseman of the classic romances," and reminded them of such phenomena as "that undefinable air, which in all ages, and in every guise, denotes a gentleman, and a distinguished one" (Wells, *The War in the Air* (Harmondsworth, Middlesex: Penguin, 1961 [1908]), p. 66; James, *Richelieu: A Tale of France in the Reign of King Louis XIII* (New York: Burt, n.d.), p.335). In *Crichton* (1837), his most relevant work here, Scott's other chief British imitator in those decades, Harrison Ainsworth, created a noble young sixteenth-century scholar swordsman of Douglas Fairbanks–like grace and agility, of whom one perceptive admirer in the novel exclaims, "This Crichton is a perfect knight of romance, a Bayard as well as a Politian. Was there ever such a combination of qualities?" (Ainsworth, *Crichton* (London: Routledge, n.d.), p.25). Across the Channel, Alexandre Dumas, who had obviously also read Ainsworth and James, had reportedly spent "long sleepless nights thinking of Sir Walter Scott's achievement" before writing *The Three Musketeers* in 1845 and giving romantic chivalric values their greatest boost after Scott. (Dumas, *The Three Musketeers*, introd. Marcel Girard, Everyman's Library (London: Dent, 1966), p. ix.) And in America itself, Scottian patterns were brilliantly transposed into American terms by James Fenimore Cooper, who brought into fiction the knightly frontiersman and the Noble Indian, and who was followed by Southern historical novelists like John Pendleton Kennedy, William Alexander Carruthers ("Ha, Sir Bastard, have at your coward's heart!"), and John Esten Cooke. (Carruthers, *The Cavaliers of Virginia* (New York: Harper, 1834–5) p. 187.) In addition, Scott's learned, intelligent, and far from uncritical "Essay on Chivalry" (1818) had been followed by works like Charles Mills's wickedly attractive *History of Chivalry* (1826), which did more than any other historical study to establish the standard romantic picture of chivalry, and G. P. R. James's *History of Chivalry* (1830), which confidently assured the reader that "the first point required of the aspirants to Chivalry in its earliest state, was certainly a solemn vow, To speak the truth, to succour the helpless and oppressed, and never to turn back from an enemy" (James, *The History of Chivalry* (London: Colburn and Bentley, 1830), p. 12).

18 Twain, *Life on the Mississippi*, p. 368.
19 Twain, *A Connecticut Yankee*, p. 119.
20 Twain, *A Connecticut Yankee*, pp. 102–3.
21 Charles Sumner, *Recent Speeches and Addresses* (Boston: Higgins and Bradley, 1856), p. 595.
22 Emily Wharton Sinkler, in Katharine M. Jones, ed., *The Plantation South*, introd. Robert Selph Henry (Indianapolis: Bobbs-Merrill, 1957), p. 154. In 1859 the Virginian D. R. Hundley said of the ring tournament:
> Placed *vis à vis* to...a Knight of the Past, behold the dwarfish dimensions of our modern Cotton Knight, who ambles daintily forward on the back of a docile gelding, holding a sharpened stick under his arm, and gallantly and gloriously endeavoring to thrust the same through an iron ring, which is suspended by a rope of twine from a horizontal beam! Note well with what a cavalier-like grace the thing is done. How stiffly stands his shirt-collar, how spotless are his patent-leathers, how mildly flaps his lengthened coat tail in the wind, how charmingly glistens his carroty-colored hair underneath his shining beaver! *Plaudite, Romanes, Plaudite, Omnes*! Here is bravery for you, and chivalry, and gallant deeds in arms.... [V]erily Cotton is King of the New Order of Chivalry and the New Order of Chivalry is the Cotton Snob! (D. R. Hundley, *Social*

Relations in Our Southern States (New York: Henry B. Price, 1860; reprinted in facsimile, New York: Arno Press, 1973), p. 175).
A sympathetic recreation of a ring tournament and the skills displayed in it can be found in Allen Tate's historical novel *The Fathers*, introd. Arthur Mizener (Denver: Swallow, 1961 [1938]).

23 An early-warning signal had been the newspaper report of a recent ring tournament in Brooklyn that came to Twain's attention in 1870. His discussion of it at the time included a number of the points that he would make in *A Connecticut Yankee*, as well as reflections upon the incongruousness of pasteboard-clad figures with titles like The Knight of the Secret Sorrow "at the toot of the horn charging fiercely upon a helpless ring hung on a post, and prodding at it intrepidly with their wooden sticks, and by and by skewering it and cavorting back to the judges' stand covered with glory – in Brooklyn." As he himself remarked, "this was doubtless the first appearance of the 'tournament' up here among the rolling-mills and factories, and will probably be the last." But the memory of it had obviously gone on working in him. ("The Tournament in A.D. 1870," *Galaxy* 10 (July 1870): 135–6.) The article is reprinted in *Mark Twain (Samuel Langhorne Clemens): Representative Selections*, ed. and introd. Fred Lewis Pattee (New York: American Book Company, 1935). It is mentioned by Hamlin Hall in his introduction to *A Connecticut Yankee in King Arthur's Court: A Facsimile of the First Edition* (San Francisco: Chandler, 1963). It does not figure in such standard accounts of the novel's genesis as John B. Hoben, "Mark Twain's *A Connecticut Yankee*: A Genetic Study," *American Literature*, 18 (November 1946), pp. 197–218; Howard G. Baetzhold, "The Course of Composition of *A Connecticut Yankee*: A Reinterpretation," *American Literature*, 33 (May 1961), pp. 195–214; Henry Nash Smith, *Mark Twain's Fable of Progress: Political and Economic Ideas in "A Connecticut Yankee"* (New Brunswick, N.J.: Rutgers University Press, 1964) and introduction to *A Connecticut Yankee in King Arthur's Court*, ed. Bernard L. Stein, The Works of Mark Twain, vol. 9 (Berkeley: University of California Press; published for the Iowa Center for Textual Studies, 1979); and Justin Kaplan, introduction to *A Connecticut Yankee in King Arthur's Court* (Harmondsworth, Middlesex: Penguin, 1971).

24 E. S. Brooks, *Chivalric Days: and the Boys and Girls who Helped to Make Them* (New York: Putnam, 1886), p. iii.

25 On Arthurianism in British and American literature, see, for example, Sister Mary Louis Morgan, *Galahad in English Literature* (Washington, D.C.: Catholic University of America, 1932); Nathan Comfort Starr, *King Arthur Today: The Arthurian Legend in English and American Literature, 1901–1953* (Gainesville: University of Florida Press, 1954); and Richard Barber, *King Arthur in Legend and Chivalry* (Ipswich: Boysdell Press, 1973).

26 Henry Seidel Canby, *The Age of Confidence: Life in the Nineties* (New York: Farrar and Rinehart, 1934), p. 190.

27 Canby, *The Age of Confidence*, pp. 199, 191–2. On the history of bestsellerdom, see Frank Luther Mott's *Golden Multitudes: The Story of Best Sellers in the United States* (New York: Macmillan, 1947).

28 Carruthers, *The Cavaliers of Virginia*, p. 4. On the Old South in literature, see Francis Pendleton Gaines, *The Southern Plantation: A Study in the Development and the Accuracy of a Tradition* (New York: Columbia University Press, 1925); Jay B. Hubbell, *The South in American Literature, 1607–1900*

([Durham, N.C.]: Duke University Press, 1954); and William R. Taylor, *Cavalier and Yankee: The Old South and American National Character* (New York: Braziller, 1961).
29 Albion W. Tourgée, quoted in Hubbell, *The South in American Literature*, p. 702.
30 Basil Gildersleeve, *The Creed of the Old South, 1865–1915* (Baltimore: Johns Hopkins Press, 1915), p. 66.
31 Eliza Frances Andrews, *The War-Time Journal of a Georgia Girl, 1864–1865* (New York: Appleton, 1908), p. 289.
32 Art Young, *On My Way: Being the Book of Art Young in Text and Pictures* (New York: Liveright, 1928), p. 229.
33 H. L. Mencken, *Happy Days, 1880–1892* (New York: Knopf, 1940), p. 307.
34 On the evolution and extravagances of American high society, see Dixon Wecter, *The Saga of American Society: A Record of Social Aspiration, 1607–1937*, Ann Arbor Paperbacks (Ann Arbor: University of Michigan Press, 1963 [1941]), and Lucius Beebe, *The Big Spenders* (London: Hutchinson, 1967).
35 Canby, *The Age of Confidence*, p. 198.
36 John P. Marquand, *The Late George Apley: A Novel in the Form of a Memoir* (New York: Modern Library, 1940), p. 196.
37 In this connection see John O. Lyons, *The College Novel in America*, pref. Harry T. Moore (Carbondale: Southern Illinois University Press, 1962).
38 W. J. Ghent, *Our Benevolent Feudalism* (New York: Macmillan, 1902), p. 135. The decade of *A Connecticut Yankee* had been crucially important in these developments. As E. Digby Baltzell explains in an illuminating study of American caste, class, and ethnic prejudice,
> The turning point came in the 1880s, when a number of symbolic events forecast the nature of the American upper class in the twentieth century. Thus, when President Eliot of Harvard built his summer cottage at Northeast Harbor, Maine, in 1881, the exclusive summer resort trend was well under way; the founding of *The* Country Club at Brookline, Massachusetts, in 1882, marked the beginning of the country-club trend; the founding of the Sons of the Revolution, in 1883, symbolized the birth of the genealogical fad and the patrician scramble for old-stock roots; Endicott Peabody's founding of Groton School, in 1884, in order to rear young gentlemen in the tradition of British public schools (and incidentally to protect them from the increasing heterogeneity of the public school system) was an important symbol of both upper-class exclusiveness and patrician Anglophilia; and finally, the Social Register, a convenient index of this new associational aristocracy, was first issued toward the end of this transitional decade in 1887 (the publisher also handled much of the literature of the American Protective Association, which was active in the nativist movement at that time). (*The Protestant Establishment: Aristocracy and Caste in America* (New York: Random House, 1964), p. 113.)
39 Willie Morris, *North toward Home* (Boston: Houghton Mifflin, 1967), p. 126.
40 Rafael Sabatini, *Captain Blood: His Odyssey* (Boston: Houghton Mifflin, 1927 [1922]), p. 121. *Captain Blood* was, of course, the quintessential Good Buccaneer novel, just as Conan Doyle's *Sir Nigel* was the quintessential Young Knight novel.
41 Ernest Hemingway, *The Green Hills of Africa* (London: Jonathan Cape, 1940), p. 162.

42 Oliver Bleeck [Ross Thomas], *Protocol for a Kidnapping* (New York: Pocket Books, 1972), p. 122.
43 Thomas Malory, quoted in John Steinbeck, *A Life in Letters*, ed. Elaine Steinbeck and Robert Wallstein (New York: Viking Press, 1975), p. 794.
44 Allan M. Pitkanen, *Time* (July 12, 1976), p. 1.

CHAPTER 2. VIOLENCE

1 Eliza Frances Andrews, *The War-Time Journal of a Georgia Girl, 1864–1865* (New York: Appleton, 1908), p. 199; Roger Ascham, quoted in William Henry Schofield, *Chivalry in English Literature: Chaucer, Malory, Spenser, and Shakespeare* (Cambridge, Mass.: Harvard University Press, 1912), p. 79; W. H. Auden, "Plains" *Collected Poems*, ed. Edward Mendelson (New York: Random House, 1976), p. 433.
2 Charles Belmont Davis, in Richard Harding Davis, *Adventures and Letters of Richard Harding Davis*, ed. Charles Belmont Davis (New York: Scribner, 1917), p. 4; Owen Johnson, *The Prodigious Hickey* (New York: Baker and Taylor, 1910), p. 249.
3 Booth Tarkington, *Monsieur Beaucaire* (New York: McClure Phillips, 1899), p. 41; Charles Dana Gibson, *The Gibson Girl and Her America; The Best Drawings of Charles Dana Gibson*, sel. Edmund Vincent Gillon, Jr., introd. Henry C. Pity (New York: Dover, 1969), p. 115.
4 F. Scott Fitzgerald, *The Basil and Josephine Stories*, ed. and introd. Jackson R. Bryce and John Kuehl (New York: Scribner, 1973), p. 54.
5 Charles Mills, *The History of Chivalry: Or Knighthood and Its Times*, 2 vols. (Philadelphia: Carey and Lea, 1826), 1:175.
6 E. S. Brooks, *Chivalric Days; and the Boys and Girls who Helped to Make Them* (New York: Putnam, 1886), p. 258.
7 Hamlin Garland, *A Spoil of Office*, introd. Eberhard Alsen (New York: Johnson Reprint Corporation, 1969 [1892]), pp. 380–1.
8 Thomas Osbert Mordaunt, *The Oxford Dictionary of Quotations*, 2nd ed. (London: Oxford University Press, 1953), p. 357; Alexis de Tocqueville, *Democracy in America*, ed. J. P. Mayer, trans. George Lawrence (Garden City, N.Y.: Doubleday Anchor Books, 1969), p. 331.
9 Rafael Sabatini, *Scaramouche: A Romance of the French Revolution* (New York: Grosset and Dunlap, 1949 [1921]), p. 3; W. B. Yeats, "Meditations in Time of Civil War," *Collected Poems*, 2nd. ed. (London: Macmillan, 1950), p. 224.
10 Joseph G. Baldwin, *The Flush Times of Alabama and Mississippi: A Series of Sketches*, introd. William A. Owens (New York: Hill and Wang, 1957 [1853]), pp. 145–6. Baldwin's whole chapter on Prentiss is of great interest, including as it does such passages as:

> He had all those qualities which make us charitable to the character of Prince Hal, as it is painted by Shakespeare, even when our approval is not fully bestowed. Generous as a prince of the royal blood, brave and chivalrous as a knight templar, of a spirit that scorned everything mean, underhanded or servile, he was prodigal to improvidence, instant in resentment, and bitter in his animosities, yet magnanimous to forgive when reparation had been made, or misconstruction explained away. There was no littleness about him. Even towards an avowed enemy he was open and manly, and bore himself with a sort of antique courtesy and knightly hostility, in which self-respect mingled with respect for his

foe, except when contempt was mixed with hatred; then no words can convey any sense of the intensity of his scorn, the depth of his loathing ...It was plain to see whence his boyhood had drawn its romantic inspiration. His imagination was colored and imbued with the light of the shadowy past, and was richly stored with the unreal but life-like creations, which the genius of Shakespeare and Scott had evoked from the ideal world. He had lingered, spell-bound, among the scenes of mediaeval chivalry. His spirit had dwelt, until almost naturalized, in the mystic dream-land they peopled – among paladins, and crusaders, and knights-templars; with Monmouth and Percy – with Bois-Gilbert and Ivanhoe, and the bold McGregor – with the cavaliers of Rupert, and the iron enthusiasts of Fairfax (pp. 144–5, 156).

11 Stephen Vincent Benét, *John Brown's Body*, introd. Henry Seidel Canby (New York: Rinehart, 1928) p. 168.
12 Ernest Hemingway, *Death in the Afternoon* (New York: Scribner, 1932), pp. 505, 58. On Hemingway's early reading, see Leicester Hemingway, "Ernest Hemingway's Boyhood Reading," *Mark Twain Journal* (Spring 1964): 4–5. Apparently Hemingway's mother adored Scott.
13 Richard Harding Davis, *Soldiers of Fortune* (New York: Scribner, 1910 [1897]), p. 291.
14 Alexandre Dumas, *The Three Musketeers*, introd. Marcel Girard, Everyman's Library (London: Dent, 1966), p. 48.
15 Henry Seidel Canby, *The Age of Confidence: Life in the Nineties* (New York: Farrar and Rinehart, 1934), pp. 202–3.
16 Sir Walter Scott, *The Talisman*, preface W. M. Parker, Everyman's Library (London: Dent, 1964 [1825]), pp. 61–2.
17 Richard Harding Davis, *Van Bibber and Others* (New York: Harper, 1892), p. 240.
18 James Branch Cabell, *Chivalry* (New York: Harper, 1909), p. 73.
19 Floyd Dell, *Homecoming: An Autobiography* (New York: Farrar and Rinehart, 1933), p. 20; *Intellectual Vagabondage: An Apology for the Intelligentsia* (New York: Doran, 1926), pp. 161–2.
20 Garland, *A Spoil of Office*, p. 177.
21 Charles Dickens, quoted in Fred Somkin, *Unquiet Eagle: Memory and Desire in the Idea of American Freedom, 1815–1860* (Ithaca: Cornell University Press, 1967), p. 22.
22 John William De Forest, *Miss Ravenel's Conversion from Secession to Loyalty*, ed. and introd. Gordon S. Haight (New York: Rinehart, 1955 [1867]), p. 19; De Forest, quoted in Edmund Wilson, *Patriotic Gore: Studies in the Literature of the American Civil War* (New York: Oxford University Press, 1962), p. 676.
23 Thomas Wentworth Higginson, *Cheerful Yesterdays* (New York: Arno Press and The New York Times, 1968 [1899]), p. 138.
24 Canby, *The Age of Confidence*, p. 204.
25 Canby, *The Age of Confidence*, pp. 193–4.
26 Owen Wister, *Roosevelt: The Story of a Friendship, 1880–1919* (New York: Macmillan, 1929), p. 16; John Reed, "At Thirty," *New Republic* (April 15, 1936), p. 269.
27 Thomas Beer, *The Mauve Decade: American Life at the End of the Nineteenth Century*, introd. Frank Freidel (New York: Vintage Books, 1961), p. 183.
28 John P. Marquand, *H. M. Pulham, Esquire* (Boston: Little, Brown, 1941), p.79.
29 *Newsweek* (January 16, 1978), p. 52.

30 Oscar Handlin, *The Uprooted: The Epic Story of the Great Migrations that Made the American People* (Boston: Little, Brown, 1951), p. 270.
31 Henry Adams, *The Education of Henry Adams*, introd. James Truslow Adams (New York: Modern Library, 1931 [1906]), pp. 57–8.
32 Herbert Languet, quoted in Ruth Kelso, *The Doctrine of the English Gentleman in the Sixteenth Century* (Gloucester, Mass.: Peter Smith, 1964 [1929]), p. 47.
33 Thorstein Veblen, *The Theory of the Leisure Class: An Economic Study of Institutions*, fore. Stuart Chase (New York: Modern Library, 1934 [1899]), pp. 326, 276, 281, 274, 253.
34 Canby, *The Age of Confidence*, pp. 205, 195.
35 Charles A. Beard and Mary R. Beard, *The Rise of American Civilization*, 2 vols. (New York: Macmillan, 1927), 2:372.
36 Poultney Bigelow, "Theodore Roosevelt, President and Sportsman," *Collier's* 29 (May 31,1902), p. 10; Amos Pinchot, "The Courage of the Cripple," in William L. O'Neill, ed., *Echoes of Revolt: The Masses, 1911–1917*, introd. Irving Howe, after. Max Eastman (Chicago: Quadrangle Books, 1966), p. 277.
37 Harry S. Truman, in Merle Miller, *Plain Speaking: An Oral Biography of Harry S. Truman* (New York: Berkley, 1974), p. 118; Henry Fairlie, *The Kennedy Promise: The Politics of Expectation* (London: Eyre Methuen, 1973), p. 242.
38 Theodore Roosevelt, *The Rough Riders* (New York: Putnam, 1900), pp. 26–8.
39 Owen Johnson, *Stover at Yale* (New York: Stokes, 1912), p. 54; Marquand, *H. M. Pulham, Esquire*, p. 13.
40 Donald Hankey, *The Beloved Captain; The Honor of the Brigade; An Englishman Prays* (New York: Dutton, 1917), pp. 7–8.
41 Theodore P. Greene, *America's Heroes: The Changing Models of Success in American Magazines* (New York: Oxford University Press, 1970), p. 119; G. S. Viereck, "The Conqueror," quoted in Sigmund Diamond, *The Reputation of the American Businessman* (Cambridge, Mass.: Harvard University Press, 1955), p. 80.
42 Owen Johnson, *The Sixty-First Second* (New York: Stokes, 1913), pp. 336–7, 155–6.
43 William V. Shannon, *The American Irish*, rev. ed. (New York: Macmillan, 1966), p. 254.
44 Oliver Wendell Holmes, *The Mind and Faith of Justice Holmes: His Speeches, Essays, Letters, and Judicial Opinions*, sel., ed., and introd. Max Lerner (Boston: Little, Brown, 1943), pp. 19–20.
45 H. L. Mencken, *The Philosophy of Friedrich Nietzsche*, 3rd ed. (Fort Washington: Kennikat Press, 1967 [1908, 1913]), pp. 162, 102.
46 Booth Tarkington, quoted in Davis, *Adventures and Letters*, p. 58.
47 H. G. Wells, *The Future in America; A Search after Realities* (London: Chapman and Hall, 1906), p. 342.
48 Davis, *Soldiers of Fortune*, p. 256.
49 Henry James, *The Bostonians*, introd. Irving Howe (New York: Modern Library, 1956 [1886]), p. 198.
50 Theodore Roosevelt, *An Autobiography* (New York: Macmillan, 1913), p. 14.
51 Douglas Branch, *The Cowboy and His Interpreters*, introd. Harry Sinclair Drago (New York: Cooper Square Publications, 1961 [1926]), p. 149. On the three friends and their collective influence, see G. Edward White, *The Eastern Establishment and the Western Experience: The West of Frederic Remington, Theodore Roosevelt, and Owen Wister* (New Haven: Yale University Press, 1968).

52 Owen Wister, quoted in Branch, *The Cowboy and His Interpreters*, p. 194.
53 Francis Pendleton Gaines, *The Southern Plantation: A Study in the Development and the Accuracy of a Tradition* (New York: Columbia University Press, 1925), pp. 2–3.
54 Tocqueville, *Democracy in America*, p. 49.
55 W. H. Mallock, quoted in W. J. Ghent, *Our Benevolent Feudalism* (New York: Macmillan, 1902), p. 134.
56 Finley Peter Dunne, "Mr. Dooley Guesses About Women," *Collier's* 30 (December 6, 1902), p. 10.
57 C. Wright Mills, *The Power Elite* (New York: Oxford University Press, 1959), p. 63.
58 Marquand, *The Late George Apley*, p. 282.
59 Veblen, *The Theory of the Leisure Class*, pp. 257, 273.
60 "Whither Scouting?" *Weekend Magazine* (July 23, 1977), p. 7. A less sympathetic observer remarked that "the Boy Scout movement is an organized, craftily subsidized effort for creating the kill-lust in boys, the love of arms, the desire for the military life, and the brainlessly automatic obedience of soldiers" (George R. Kirkpatrick, "The Boy Scout Movement: To Perpetuate Docility, Stupidity and Brutality," *Masses* (February 1911), p. 17). The original Boy Scout virtues were Honor, Loyalty, Usefulness, Friendliness, Politeness, Kindness to Animals, Obedience, Cheerfulness, Thrift, and Cleanliness.
61 On the pulps, see Tony Goodstone, ed., *The Pulps: Fifty Years of American Pop Culture* (New York: Chelsea House, 1970) and Ron Goulart, *An Informal History of the Pulp Magazines* (New York: Ace Books, 1973).
62 An indictment of the thriller along such lines is provided in William Ruehlmann's *Saint with a Gun: The Unlawful American Private Eye*, fore. Aaron Marc Stein (New York: New York University Press, 1974).
63 Useful information about two of these popular genres is provided in Jeffrey Richards's *Swordsmen of the Screen: From Douglas Fairbanks to Michael York* (London: Routledge and Kegan Paul, 1977) and the long section on "The Cinema of Empire" in his *Visions of Yesterday* (London: Routledge and Kegan Paul, 1973).
64 Ghent, *Our Benevolent Feudalism*, p. 37.
65 Philip Stirling, "The Songs of War," *New Masses* (December 1931), p. 19.
66 Tom Wolfe, "Golden Age," *The New York Times Book Review* (June 4, 1978), p. 45. Wolfe was reviewing Susan E. Meyer's *America's Great Illustrators* (New York: Abrams, 1978), a feast of images.
67 Louis Heren, quoted in Philip French, *Westerns: Aspects of a Movie Genre* (London: Secker and Warburg, in association with the British Film Institute, 1973), p. 123.
68 Henry Kissinger, quoted in Anthony Lewis, "A Matter of Character," *New York Review of Books* (October 27, 1977), p. 10.
69 Lesley Hazleton, "Israel: the Sticking Point," *New York Review of Books* (January 29, 1978), p. 27.
70 Pauline Kael, quoted in *Time* (January 9, 1978), p. 39; John D. MacDonald, *The Brass Cupcake* (Greenwich, Conn.: Fawcett Gold Medal Books, 1950), p. 29.
71 Fairlie, *The Kennedy Promise*, p. 191; Gore Vidal, *Matters of Fact and Fiction: Essays 1973–76* (New York: Random House, 1977), p. 216.
72 W. J. Cash, *The Mind of the South* (New York: Vintage Books, n.d. [1941]), p. 76.

73 Marquand, *The Late George Apley*, p. 242.
74 Rollo May, *Power and Innocence: A Search for the Sources of Violence* (New York: Norton, 1972), p. 178. According to Goulart, the American Legion had evolved out of an idea of the editor of *Adventure*, one of those pulp magazines whose typical contents consisted of "one cowboy, one explorer, one legionaire, one pirate and two or three musketeers" (*An Informal History of the Pulp Magazines*, p. 31).
75 Victor Rosen, *Time* (April 25, 1977), p. 2.
76 Hugh Trevor-Roper, introd. to Andrew Mollo, *A Pictorial History of the SS, 1923–1945* (London: Macdonald and Jane's, 1976), p. 8.
77 See Ignatius Donnelly, *Caesar's Column* (1890), Jack London, *The Iron Heel* (1912), and Sherwood Anderson, *Marching Men* (1917).
78 "Our Own Secret Fascisti," *Nation* (November 15, 1922), p. 514.
79 Ezra Pound, "Sestina: Altaforte," *Collected Shorter Poems*, 2nd. ed. (London: Faber and Faber, 1968), p. 42.
80 Lord Russell of Liverpool, *The Knights of Bushido: The Shocking History of Japanese War Atrocities* (New York: Dutton, 1958).
81 Robert Ardrey, *The Territorial Imperative: A Personal Inquiry into the Animal Origins of Property and Nations* (New York: Atheneum, 1970), p. 234; T. E. Kalem, "Intrepid Soul," *Time* (December 19, 1977), p. 42.

CHAPTER 3. FICTIVENESS

1 Ernest Hemingway, *The Sun Also Rises*, introd. Henry Seidel Canby (New York: Modern Library, 1930 [1926]), p. 36; Margaret Mitchell, *Gone With the Wind* (New York: Macmillan, 1937), p. 287; Barbara W. Tuchman, *A Distant Mirror: The Calamitous 14th Century* (New York: Knopf, 1978), p. xvii.
2 W. J. Cash, *The Mind of the South* (New York: Vintage Books, n.d. [1941]), p. 124.
3 Edwin Arlington Robinson, "Miniver Cheevy," *Collected Poems* (New York: Macmillan, 1937), p. 348.
4 Edwin Arlington Robinson, "Richard Cory," *Collected Poems*, p. 82.
5 William James, "The Moral Equivalent of War," in *The Writings of William James: A Comprehensive Edition*, ed. and introd. John J. McDermott (New York: Modern Library, 1968), p. 663; George Bernard Shaw, *Man and Superman: A Comedy and a Philosophy* (Harmondsworth, Middlesex: Penguin Books, 1975), p. 16.
6 Ernest Hemingway, quoted in R. Z. Sheppard, "The Far Side of Friendship," *Time* (April 3, 1978), p. 89.
7 Walker Percy, *Lancelot* (New York: Farrar, Straus and Giroux, 1977), p. 55.
8 Ernest Hemingway, *A Farewell to Arms* (New York: Scribner, 1969 [1929]), p. 249.
9 Oscar Handlin, *The Americans: A New History of the People of the United States* (Boston: Little, Brown, 1963), p. 362.
10 F. Scott Fitzgerald, "Princeton" (1927), *The Bodley Head Fitzgerald*, 6 vols., rev. ed. (London: The Bodley Head, 1965), 3:317; Michael Gold, quoted in Joseph Freeman, *An American Testament: A Narrative of Rebels and Romantics* (New York: Farrar and Rinehart, 1936), p. 250.
11 W. B. Yeats, "Meru," *Collected Poems*, 2nd. ed. (London: Macmillan, 1950), p. 333.
12 Walker Percy, *The Last Gentleman* (New York: Farrar, Straus and Giroux, 1966), pp. 9–10.

13 John Leonard, "The Literary Scene: Macdonaldizing," *The New York Times* (September 29, 1975), p. 40.
14 William Howard Russell, *My Diary, North and South*, 2 vols. (London: Bradbury and Evans, 1863), 2:166.
15 Anonymous Alabaman, quoted in Rollin F. Osterweis, *Romanticism and Nationalism in the Old South* (Baton Rouge: Louisiana State University Press, 1967 [1949]), p. 79; T. C. De Leon, quoted in Osterweis, p. 101.
16 Thomas Nelson Page, *The Old South: Essays Social and Political* (New York: Scribner, 1911 [1892]), p. 5.
17 James Branch Cabell, *Chivalry* (New York: Harper, 1909), p. vi; Charles Mills, *The History of Chivalry: Of Knighthood and Its Times*, 2 vols. (Philadelphia: Carey and Lea, 1826), 2:5.
18 James Fenimore Cooper, quoted in Edwin Harrison Cady, *The Gentleman in America: A Literary Study in American Culture* (New York: Syracuse University Press, 1949), pp. 130–1.
19 Charles A. Beard and Mary R. Beard, *The American Spirit: A Study of the Idea of Civilization in the United States* (New York: Macmillan, n.d. [1942]), p. 279.
20 Daniel J. Boorstin, *The Americans: The National Experience* (New York: Random House, 1966), p. 466.
21 Frederick Law Olmsted, *The Cotton Kingdom: A Traveller's Observations on Cotton and Slavery in the American Slave States*, ed. and introd. Arthur M. Schlesinger (New York: Knopf, 1953), pp. 554, 416, 476.
22 Basil Gildersleeve, *The Creed of the Old South, 1865–1915* (Baltimore: Johns Hopkins University Press, 1915), p. 11.
23 Louis B. Wright, *The First Gentlemen of Virginia: Intellectual Qualities of the Early Colonial Ruling Class* (San Marino, Calif.: Huntington Library, 1940), pp. 41–2.
24 See, for example, Thomas H. Wertenbaker, *The Shaping of Colonial Virginia* (New York: Russell and Russell, 1958 [1910, 1914, 1922]); Wright, *The First Gentlemen of Virginia*; Virginius Dabney, *Virginia: The New Dominion* (Garden City, N.Y.: Doubleday, 1971); and Clement Eaton, *A History of the Old South: The Emergence of a Reluctant Nation*, 3rd ed. (New York: Macmillan, 1975).
25 Mills, *The History of Chivalry*, 2:201–2; Cabell, *Chivalry*, p. vi.
26 Mills, *The History of Chivalry*, 1:111, 130.
27 The perfect liar, as distinct from the ad hoc improviser, is engaged in an ongoing and elaborate enterprise of fiction making, and can offer his assertions with the aplomb of someone able to meet any challenges with further supportive fictions. The gusto with which Geoffrey writes is of that sort. Of Arthur's great battle with the Romans, for example, we learn how:
The Britons suffered great losses, and would have endured the shame of losing the captives whom they were convoying, if good fortune had not quickly brought the reinforcement of which they were in such need. Guitard, the Duke of the Poitevins, came to hear of the ambush that I have described, and he marched in with three thousand men. Now that they were able to rely upon this help, the Britons won in the end and so managed to take revenge upon their imprudent ambushers for all the slaughter they had caused. However, they lost many of their troops in the first stage of the battle. Indeed, they lost Borellus, the famous leader of the Cenomanni, who was pierced through the throat by his opponent's spear while he was fighting with Evander the King of Syria, and so vomited forth his life with his blood. At the same time they lost four noble

princes: Hyrelgas of Petiron; Maurice Cador of Cahors; Aliduc of Tintagel; and Her, the son of Hider. It would not have been easy to find braver men than these. (Geoffrey of Monmouth, *The History of the Kings of Britain*, trans. and introd. Lewis Thorpe (Harmondsworth, Middlesex: Penguin Books, 1966), pp. 245–6.)

Faced with such circumstantiality, who could possibly disbelieve in Hyrelgas of Petiron, let along Arthur, Guinevere, and the rest? Geoffrey's nearest analogue in literature is Mr. Wormold in Graham Greene's *Our Man in Havana*.

28 Raymond Lincoln Kilgour, *The Decline of Chivalry as Shown in the French Literature of the Late Middle Ages* (Cambridge, Mass.: Harvard University Press, 1937), p. ix.

29 Alfred T. P. Byles, introd. to Ramón Lull, *The Book of the Ordre of Chyvalrie*, trans. and printed by William Caxton, from a French version of Ramón Lull's "Le Libre del Orde de Cauayleria," ed. Alfred T. P. Byles, Early English Text Society, no. 168 (London: Humphrey Milford, Oxford University Press, 1926), p. vii.

30 Honoré Bonet, *The Tree of Battles of Honoré Bonet*, trans. and introd. G. W. Coopland (Cambridge, Mass.: Harvard University Press, 1949 [1387] p. 189.

31 Giraut de Bornelh, quoted in Kilgour, *The Decline of Chivalry*, pp. 5–6.

32 Kilgour, *The Decline of Chivalry*, p. 4.

33 Richard Barber, *The Knight and Chivalry* (London: Longman, 1970), p. 208; M. H. Keen, *The Laws of War in the Late Middle Ages* (London: Routledge and Kegan Paul, 1975), p. 243.

34 Sidney Painter, *French Chivalry: Chivalric Ideas and Practices in Medieval France* (Ithaca: Cornell University Press, 1957 [1940]), p. 88; Gervase Mathew, *The Court of Richard II* (London: John Murray, 1968), p. 125.

35 Barber, *The Knight and Chivalry*, pp. 141, 139.

36 Barber, *The Knight and Chivalry*, p. 208.

37 R. Coltman Clephan, *The Tournament: Its Periods and Phases*, pref. Charles J. ffoulkes (London: Methuen, 1919), pp. 78–80.

38 Barber, *The Knight and Chivalry*, pp. 296–7.

39 On the Eglington tournament in which thirty-five armored participants, among them Louis Napoleon, engaged in various feats of arms before a crowd of over ten thousand, see, for example, Clephan, *The Tournament*, pp. 139–42.

40 Charles Moreau Harger, in William W. Savage, ed., *Cowboy Life: Reconstructing an American Myth* (Norman: University of Oklahoma Press, 1975), p. 100.

41 Joseph G. McCoy, in Savage, *Cowboy Life*, p. 2; Richard Irving Dodge, in Savage, p. 35.

42 Robert R. Dykstra, *The Cattle Towns* (New York: Knopf, 1968), pp. 142–8; Joseph G. Rosa, *The Gunfighter: Man or Myth?* (Norman: University of Oklahoma Press, 1969), p. 124.

43 W. Eugene Hollon, *Frontier Violence: Another Look* (New York: Oxford University Press, 1974), p. 162. Violence did, of course, occur. The Lincoln County War in New Mexico took a good many lives between 1875 and 1881, and in the Graham–Tewkesbury feud in Pleasant Valley, Arizona, in the late Eighties, all the Graham males and all but one of the Tewkesbury males were killed, and a total of twenty-nine persons died (Hollon, *Frontier Violence*, p. 184; Rosa, *The Gunfighter*, p. 25; Hollon, p. 162). Moreover, according to a report submitted to the State Constitutional Convention in

1868, over five hundred killings of whites by whites occurred in Texas during the three years after the Civil War (Hollon, p. 52). The point, however, is that when one is talking about general images of the West and of cowboys, facts and fictions overlap only partially. What appears to have happened is a displacement northwards of images from the southwest, and especially from Texas and its racial conflicts. In the despised and derided Italian Westerns, an interesting further displacement occurred. If the frequent killings over cards, the bloody shootouts in the streets, the armed and mounted gangs terrifying townships, the casual drunken butcherings, the general visual and emotional squalor were not true of the cattle-town West, they were true of parts of the antebellum South. Theodore Weld spoke in 1839 of the *"hundreds* of affrays, murders, assassinations, duels, lynching, assaults" reported in the Louisiana papers during an eighteen-month period around 1838; Richard Harding Davis's mother remembered that in one small town a feud resulted in thirty deaths in six months. (Theodore Weld, *Slavery in America: Theodore Weld's American Slavery As It Is*, ed. and introd. Richard O. Curry and Joanna Dunlap Cowden (Itasca, Ill.: Peacock, 1972 [1839]); Davis, *Bits of Gossip* (Boston: Houghton Mifflin, 1905), pp. 70–83.)

44 Richard Harding Davis, *The West from a Car-Window* (New York: Harper, 1892), p. 143; Dykstra, *The Cattle Towns*, p. 269; Frederic Remington, illustration to Davis, p. 198.

45 On the evolution of the personae of figures like Buffalo Bill Cody and Wild Bill Hickok, see, for example, Kent Ladd Steckmesser's *The Western Hero in History and Legend* (Norman: University of Oklahoma Press, 1965).

46 Mark Twain, *The Adventures of Huckleberry Finn (Tom Sawyer's Comrade)* (London: Zodiac Press, 1963), p. 140.

47 Olmsted, *The Cotton Kingdom*, pp. 453–5.

48 Gilbert Patten, *Frank Merriwell's "Father": An Autobiography by Gilbert Patten ("Burt L. Standish")*, ed. and introd. Harriet Hinsdale (Norman: University of Oklahoma Press, 1964), pp. 21–2.

49 Alexandre Dumas, *The Three Musketeers*, introd. Marcel Girard, Everyman's Library (London: Dent, 1966), p. 3.

50 Johan Huizinga, *Homo Ludens: A Study of the Play-Element in Culture* (Boston: Beacon Press, 1955 [1944]), p. 60.

51 W. J. Cash, *The Mind of the South* (New York: Vintage Books, n.d. [1941]), p. 46.

52 Walter Lippmann, *Drift and Mastery: An Attempt to Diagnose the Current Unrest* (New York: Holt, 1917 [1914]), p. 188; R. Z. Sheppard, "Fifty Years of Total Waugh," *Time* (February 12, 1979), p. 74.

53 Diane Johnson, "Ah, Wilderness!" *New York Review of Books* (March 23, 1978), p. 3. See also Jane Kramer, *The Last Cowboy* (New York: Harper and Row, 1977).

54 Mark Twain, *Life on the Mississippi*, introd. Albert Bigelow Paine, Stormfield Edition of the Writings of Mark Twain (New York: Harper, 1929), p. 443.

55 John P. Marquand, *H. M. Pulham, Esquire* (Boston: Little, Brown, 1941), p. 58.

56 Edmund Wilson, "Galahad," in *Galahad: I Thought of Daisy* (New York: Farrar, Straus and Giroux, 1967), p. 34.

57 Edwin Honig, *Calderón and the Seizures of Honor* (Cambridge, Mass.: Harvard University Press, 1972), pp. 10–11.

58 F. Scott Fitzgerald, *The Beautiful and the Damned* (New York: Scribner, 1950 [1922]), pp. 3, 47.
59 H. G. Wells, *The Future in America: A Search after Realities* (London: Chapman and Hall, 1906), p. 301; Charles A. Beard and Mary R. Beard, *The Rise of American Civilization*, 2 vols. (New York: Macmillan, 1927), 2:759.
60 Hemingway, *The Sun Also Rises*, p. 42.
61 It can be added that the dean of American realism, William Dean Howells, allegedly had "a very early literary passion for *Don Quixote*" (Cady, *The Gentlemen in America*, p.185); that according to Kenneth S. Lynn the realist Frank Norris, as a youth, was obsessed with the medieval; and that Edgar Lee Masters published a couple of Arthurian poems the year after his *Spoon River Anthology*.
62 Robert Warshow, "Movie Chronicle: The Westerner" (1954), in *The Immediate Experience: Movies, Comics, Theatre and Other Aspects of Popular Culture*, introd. Lionel Trilling (New York: Atheneum, 1972), p. 135.
63 Twain, *Life on the Mississippi*, p. 333.
64 Mark Twain, *Personal Recollections of Joan of Arc: by the Sieur Louis de Conte*, 2 vols., pref. Henry Van Dyke, introd. Albert Bigelow Paine, Stormfield Edition of the Writings of Mark Twain (New York: Harper, 1929), 1:xx; 2:203.
65 See in this connection my "In Defence of Culture: *Huckleberry Finn*," *Oxford Review* (Michaelmas 1967), 5:22.
66 Roy Campbell, "The Spanish Dramatists: A Note," in Calderón de la Barca, *The Surgeon of His Honour*, trans. Roy Campbell, introd. Everett W. Hesse (Madison: University of Wisconsin Press, 1960), p. xxix.

CHAPTER 4. FICTIONS AND FORMS

1 Mark Twain, *The Adventures of Huckleberry Finn (Tom Sawyer's Comrade)* (London: Zodiac Press, 1963), pp. 175–6; Charles Marshall, quoted in *The Blue and the Gray: The Story of the Civil War as Told by Participants*, ed. and introd. Henry Steele Commager, 2 vols. (Indianapolis: Bobbs-Merrill, 1950), 2:1139.
2 F. Scott Fitzgerald, *The Great Gatsby* (New York: Scribner, 1925), p. 162.
3 On the pleasures of plantation life, see, for example, Thomas Nelson Page, "Social Life in Old Virginia before the War," in *The Old South: Essays Social and Political* (New York: Scribner, 1911); Ulrich Bonnell Phillips, *Life and Labor in the Old South*, students' ed. (Boston: Little, Brown, 1931), pp. 336–8; and the items by Susan Dabney Smedes, Henry Barnard, Letitia M. Burwell, and I. Jenkins Mikell in Katharine M. Jones, ed., *The Plantation South*, introd. Robert Selph Henry (Indianapolis: Bobbs-Merrill, 1957).
4 Frederick Law Olmsted, *The Cotton Kingdom: A Traveller's Observations on Cotton and Slavery in the American Slave States*, ed. and introd. Arthur M. Schlesinger (New York: Knopf, 1953), p. 620.
5 Twain, *Huckleberry Finn*, pp. 129–30.
6 William Gordon McCabe, quoted in Commager, *The Blue and the Gray*, p. 1126.
7 Gerald W. Johnson, *American Heroes and Hero-Worship* (New York: Harper, 1941), p. 217.
8 Theodore Roosevelt, *An Autobiography* (New York: Macmillan, 1913), p. 133.
9 Edward Everett Dale, *Cow Country*, new ed. (Norman: University of Oklahoma Press, 1965 [1942]), p. 122.
10 W. Eugene Hollon, *Frontier Violence: Another Look* (New York: Oxford University Press, 1974), p. 210.

11 Dale, *Cow Country*, p. 75; Philip Ashton Rollins, *The Cowboy: An Unconventional History of Civilization in the Old-Time Range*, rev. and enl. ed. (New York: Ballantine Books, 1973 [1922, 1936]), p. 66.
12 Theodore Roosevelt, *The Rough Riders* (New York: Putnam, 1900), pp. 77, 48.
13 Dale, *Cow Country*, p. 74.
14 Douglas Southall Freeman, *R. E. Lee: A Biography*, 4 vols. (New York: Scribner, 1940), 1:160.
15 Louis B. Wright, *The First Gentlemen of Virginia: Intellectual Qualities of the Early Colonial Ruling Class* (San Marino, Calif.: Huntington Library, 1940), p. 37.
16 Jeffrey Richards, *Visions of Yesterday* (London: Routledge and Kegan Paul, 1973), p. 64.
17 Ruth Kelso, *The Doctrine of the English Gentleman in the Sixteenth Century* (Gloucester, Mass.: Peter Smith, 1964 [1929]), p. 88; John Henry Cardinal Newman, *The Idea of a University, Defined and Illustrated*, ed. and introd. Martin J. Svaglic (New York: Holt, Rinehart and Winston, 1960), p. 159.
18 Kelso, *The Doctrine of the English Gentleman*, p. 94.
19 Hannah Arendt, *Imperialism*, Harvest Books (New York: Harcourt, Brace and World, 1968), p. 89.
20 *The Death of King Arthur*, trans. and introd. James Cable (Harmondsworth, Middlesex: Penguin Books, 1971), p. 78.
21 Gervase Mathew, *The Court of Richard II* (London: John Murray, 1968), p. 114.
22 Sidney Painter, *French Chivalry: Chivalric Ideas and Practices in Medieval France* (Ithaca: Cornell University Press, 1964 [1940]), pp. 39, 41.
23 Geoffrey Brereton, introd. Jean Froissart, *Chronicles*, sel., trans., and ed. Geoffrey Brereton (Harmondsworth, Middlesex: Penguin Books, 1968), p. 19.
24 Froissart, *Chronicles*, trans. Brereton, pp. 345–6.
25 Johan Huizinga, *The Waning of the Middle Ages: A Study of the Forms of Life, Thought and Art in France and the Netherlands in the XIVth and XVth Centuries* (Garden City, N.Y.: Doubleday Anchor Books, 1959 [1924]), pp. 57, 69.
26 On the influence of Burgundy on Elizabethan England, see Gordon Kipling, *The Triumph of Honour: Burgundian Origins of the Elizabethan Renaissance* (The Hague: Leiden University Press, 1977).
27 Baron Kervyn de Lettenhove, quoted in William Henry Schofield, *Chivalry in English Literature: Chaucer, Malory, Spenser, and Shakespeare* (Cambridge, Mass.: Harvard University Press, 1912), pp. 5–6.
28 Richard Barber, *The Knight and Chivalry* (London: Longman, 1970), p. 102.
29 Walker Percy, *Lancelot* (New York: Farrar, Straus and Giroux, 1977), p. 116.
30 Froissart, *Chronicles*, trans. Brereton, p. 266.
31 Jean Froissart, *Chronicles of England, France, Spain, and the Adjoining Countries, from the Latter Part of the Reign of Edward II to the Coronation of Henry IV*, trans. Thomas Johnes, introd. John Lord (New York: American Book Exchange, 1880), p. 372.
32 Barber, *The Knight and Chivalry*, caption to illustration 15; Chandos Herald, *Life of the Black Prince by the Herald of Sir John Chandos* (ca. 1397), trans., ed., and introd. Mildred K. Pope and Eleanor C. Lodge (Oxford: Clarendon Press, 1910), pp. 148–9.
33 M. H. Keen, *The Laws of War in the Late Middle Ages* (London: Routledge and Kegan Paul, 1975), p. 133, 243.

34 Caxton, Epilogue to Ramón Lull, *The Book of the Ordre of Chyvalrie*, trans. and printed by William Caxton, from a French version of Ramón Lull's "Le Libre del Orde de Cauayleria," ed. Alfred T. P. Byles, Early English Text Society, no. 168 (London: Humphrey Milford, Oxford University Press, 1926), pp. 122–3.

35 Froissart, *Chronicles*, trans. Brereton, pp. 264–5.

36 Jean de Joinville, *The Life of Saint Louis*, in Jean de Joinville and Geoffroy de Villehardouin, *Chronicles of the Crusades*, trans. and introd. M. R. B. Shaw (Harmondsworth, Middlesex: Penguin Books, 1963), pp. 169, 177.

37 The Loyal Servant [Jacques de Mailles], *The Right Joyous and Pleasant History of the Feats, Gests, and Prowesses of the Chevalier Bayard, the Good Knight without Fear and without Reproach*, 2 vols. (London: John Murray, 1825 [1525]), 2:203.

38 Mailles, *The Right Joyous and Pleasant History*, 2:221–2.

39 Mark Twain, *Life on the Mississippi*, introd. Albert Bigelow Paine, Stormfield Edition of the Writings of Mark Twain (New York: Harper, 1929), p. 118.

40 H. L. Mencken, *Happy Days, 1880–1892* (New York: Knopf, 1940), pp. 301–2.

41 Painter, *French Chivalry*, p. 155.

42 *The Death of King Arthur*, trans. and introd. Cable, p. 145.

43 Mathew, *The Court of Richard II*, p. 119.

44 Keen, *The Laws of War*, p. 189.

45 *The Law of Land Warfare*, U. S. Department of the Army Field Manual, No. 27–10 (1956), quoted in *In the Name of America: The Conduct of the War in Vietnam by the Armed Forces of the United States as Shown by Published Reports*, director of research Seymour Milman (New York: Clergy and Laymen Concerned about Vietnam, 1968), p. 47.

46 On the dueling code in its final form, see John Lyle Wilson, *The Code of Honor; or, Rules for the Government of Principals and Seconds in Duelling* (Charleston: James Phinney, 1858 [1838; facsimile ed. 1951]).

47 Robert B. Parker, *Mortal Stakes* (New York: Berkley Medallion Books, 1977), p. 212.

48 Raymond Lincoln Kilgour, *The Decline of Chivalry as Shown in the French Literature of the Late Middle Ages* (Cambridge, Mass.: Harvard University Press, 1937), p. 4.

49 Basil Gildersleeve, *The Creed of the Old South, 1865–1915* (Baltimore: Johns Hopkins Press, 1915), p. 13.

50 Stephen Vincent Benét, *John Brown's Body*, introd. Henry Seidel Canby (New York: Rinehart, 1928), pp. 166, 168. See, in this connection, John W. Thomason's *Jeb Stuart* (New York: Scribner, 1930).

51 On the three-part pattern of chivalry, see Sidney Painter, *French Chivalry: Chivalric Ideas and Practices in Medieval France*, Cornell Paperbacks (Ithaca: Cornell University Press, 1957 [1940]).

52 Julio Caro Baroja, "Honour and Shame: A Historical Account of Several Conflicts," in J. G. Peristiany, ed., *Honour and Shame: The Values of Mediterranean Sociey* (London: Weidenfeldt and Nicolson, 1965), p. 94.

53 Friedrich Nietzsche, *Beyond Good and Evil*, trans. and introd. Marianne Cowan (Chicago: Regnery, 1955), p. 206.
    In Fenimore Cooper's *The Chainbearer*, the narrator remarks (in a passage drawn attention to by Cady in *The Gentleman in America*) that

it is true, there is a connection in manners...between the Christian and the gentleman; but it is in the result, and not in the motive...[The gentleman] is truthful out of self-respect, and not in obedience to the will of God; free with his money, because liberality is an essential feature of his habits, and not in imitation of the self-sacrifice of Christ; superior to scandal and the vices of the busybody, inasmuch as they are low and impair his pride of character, rather than because he has been commanded not to bear false witness against his neighbor. (*The Chainbearer or The Littlepage Manuscripts* (New York: American News, n.d.), pp. 140–1.)

Insofar as it was independent of Christianity, the chivalric ethos did not suffer from one of the obvious disadvantages of the latter in an increasingly secular world. The ideal character types that Christianity held up for emulation all depended for their validation upon an invisible cosmology. A saint was not just someone acting in certain ways, he was someone who believed in a particular cosmology with absolute conviction, so that it was therefore difficult to imitate his behavior if one disbelieved in the cosmology. In the chivalric system, in contrast, the appeal of the behavior of individual figures did not depend upon any metaphysical system. The behavior of those figures, and of others like them, *was* the chivalric system. Significantly, one of the greatest of the works about chivalry is the story of a man who was invulnerable to all the attacks of reason and logic against him. Quixote simply believed unshakably that it was nobler for him to behave in certain ways than in others. And the reader, contemplating the arrogant bureaucrats, journeying Inquisitors, prisoner-herding soldiers, complacently patronizing aristocrats, pastoral-playing lovers, boorish peasants, and prudent protobourgeois men of "good sense," had good cause to share that belief. Quixote, the secular saint of chivalry, was immune to irony.

54 Eugene Manlove Rhodes, quoted in Douglas Branch, *The Cowboy and His Interpreters*, introd. Harry Sinclair Drago (New York: Cooper Square Publications, 1961 [1926]), p. 241.

55 Joseph B. Cobb, *Mississippi Scenes; or, Sketches of Southern and Western Life, Humorous, Satirical and Descriptive* (Upper Saddle River, N.J.: Literature House, 1971 [1851]), p. 177.

56 George Catlin (1841), quoted in Roy Harvey Pearce, *The Savages of America: A Study of the Indian and the Idea of Civilization* (Baltimore: Johns Hopkins Press, 1953), p. 112. In 1889 George Bird Grinnell wrote, "The Indian of Cooper – with his bravery, his endurance, his acuteness, his high qualities of honesty, generosity, courtesy and hospitality – has been laughed at for half a century. Yet every man who has mingled much with the Indians in their homes has known individuals who might have sat for the portraits which Cooper drew of some of his aboriginal heroes" (*Pawnee Hero Stories and Folk-Tales with Notes on the Origin, Customs and Character of the Pawnee People*, introd. Maurice Frink (Lincoln: University of Nebraska Press, 1961), p. 13.

57 Johan Huizinga, *Homo Ludens: A Study of the Play-Element in Culture* (Boston: Beacon Press, 1955 [1944]), p. 102.

58 Alexis de Tocqueville, *Democracy in America*, ed. J. P. Mayer, trans. George Lawrence (Garden City, N.Y.: Doubleday Anchor Books, 1969), p. 570.

59 Paul Bourget, quoted in Henry Steele Commager, ed., *America in Perspective: The United States through Foreign Eyes* (New York: Random House, 1964), pp. 248–9.

60 Twain, *A Connecticut Yankee in King Arthur's Court*, introd. Albert Bigelow Paine, Stormfield Edition of the Writings of Mark Twain (New York: Harper, 1929), p. 32.

61 Commager, *The Blue and the Gray*, pp. xvii–xviii.
62 J. F. C. Fuller, *Grant and Lee: A Study in Personality and Generalship* (London: Eyre and Spottiswoode, 1933), p. 66; William T. Sherman, quoted in Commager, *The Blue and the Gray*, 2:929.
63 Fuller, *Grant and Lee*, pp. 242–3.
64 Horace Porter, quoted in Commager, *The Blue and the Gray*, 2:974–5, 993.
65 Richard Taylor, *Destruction and Reconstruction: Personal Experiences of the Late War* (New York: Appleton, 1879), pp. 149–50.
66 S. H. M. Byers, "Some Personal Recollections of General Sherman," *McClure's* 3 (1894), p. 223.
67 Fuller, *Grant and Lee*, p. 61; B. H. Liddell Hart, *Sherman: The Genius of the Civil War* (London: Ernest Benn, 1930), p. 406.
68 When he embarked on his march to the sea, Sherman, according to his letters, had assumed that it would be accompanied by guerrilla warfare and that the risks run by officers like himself at the hands of sharpshooters would be high. He had not viewed it as a jaunt through a defenseless countryside.
69 J. L. Chamberlain, quoted in Commager, *The Blue and the Gray*, 2:1142–3.
70 Charles Mills, *The History of Chivalry: Of Knighthood and Its Times*, 2 vols. (Philadelphia: Carey and Lea, 1826), 2:210.

CHAPTER 5. THE HEROIC AND THE PASTORAL

1 Huizinga, *Homo Ludens: A Study of the Play-Element in Culture* (Boston: Beacon Press, 1955 [1944]), p. 50; Francis Parkman, *The Oregon Trail* (New York: Doubleday, 1946 [1849]), pp. 11–12.
2 Caxton, Epilogue to Ramón Lull, *The Book of the Ordre of Chyvalrie*, trans. and printed by William Caxton, from a French version of Ramón Lull's "Le Libre del Orde de Cuayleria," ed. Alfred T. P. Byles, Early English Text Society, no. 168 (London: Humphrey Milford, Oxford University Press, 1926), p. 122.
3 Steinbeck, *A Life in Letters*, ed. Elaine Steinbeck and Robert Wallstein (New York: Viking Press, 1975), p. 579. Owen Wister had spelled out some of the connections between the knight and the cowboy in his "The Evolution of the Cow-Puncher," *Harper's* 91 (September 1895), pp. 602–17.
4 The best general English-language monograph on the Western may well be John G. Cawelti's *The Six-Gun Mystique* (Bowling Green: Bowling Green University Popular Press [1971]). On the multifariousness of Westerns, especially since 1950, see also, for example, Philip French, *Westerns: Aspects of a Movie Genre* (London: Secker and Warburg in association with the British Film Institute, 1973). The Western has included among its variations the classic Western (*My Darling Clementine*), the social-conscience Western (*The Oxbow Incident*), the revisionist Western (*Run of the Arrow*), the decline-of-the-West Western (*Ride the High Country*), the domestic Western (*A Man Called Gannon*), the brutalist Western (*Django*), the revisionist-revisionist Western (*The Life and Times of Judge Roy Bean*), the tintype-realist Western (*The Great Northfield Minnesota Raid*), the gently humorous Western (*Rio Bravo*), the scattily humorous Western (*Cat Ballou*), the "camp" Western (*Lonesome Cowboys*), the existentialist Western (*The Shooting*), the surrealist Western (*El Topo*). It has overlapped into other genres with things like the musical Western (*Red Garters*), the caper Western (*The Professionals*), the prison Western (*There was a Crooked Man*), the supernatural Western (*High*

Plains Drifter), and the biblical Western (*Greaser's Palace*). Westerns have enjoyed a creative relationship, going in both directions, with samurai movies, and have assimilated, via the Italian Westerns, some of the Machiavellian ruthlessness of Renaissance Italy. They have been made by a dozen or more countries.

5 Steinbeck, *A Life in Letters*, p. 540.
6 Barber, *The Knight and Chivalry* (London: Longman's, 1970), p. 32.
7 *Sir Gawain and the Green Knight*, trans. Marie Borroff, in M. H. Abrams et al., eds., *The Norton Anthology of English Literature*, 2 vols., rev. ed. (New York: Norton, 1968), 1:264.
8 M. H. Keen, *The Laws of War in the Late Middle Ages* (London: Routledge and Kegan Paul, 1975), p. 20.
9 Sir Thomas Malory, *Le Morte d'Arthur*, 2 vols., introd. Sir John Rhys, Everyman's Library (London: Dent, 1906), 2:151.
10 Charles Mills, *The History of Chivalry: Or Knighthood and Its Times*, 2 vols. (Philadelphia: Carey and Lea, 1826), 2:201.
11 *The Quest of the Holy Grail*, trans. and introd. P. M. Matarosso (Harmondsworth, Middlesex: Penguin Books, 1969), p. 79.
12 Mark Twain, *Personal Recollections of Joan of Arc: by the Sieur Louis de Conte*, 2 vols, pref. Henry Van Dyke, introd. Albert Bigelow Paine, Stormfield Edition of the Writings of Mark Twain (New York: Harper, 1929), 1:191.
13 Lewis Mumford, *The Pentagon of Power* (New York: Harcourt Brace Jovanovich, 1970), p. 290.
14 Quoted in Montagu, Lord of Beaulieu, *More Equal than Others: The Changing Fortunes of the British and European Aristocracies*, fore. Sir Iain Moncreiffe of That Ilk (New York: St. Martin's Press, 1970), p. 61.
15 *Sir Gawain and the Green Knight*, trans. Borroff, p. 222.
16 *The Death of King Arthur*, trans. and introd. James Cable (Harmondsworth, Middlesex: Penguin Books, 1971), p. 175.
17 Sir Walter Scott, "An Essay on Romance" (1824), *Essays on Chivalry, Romance, and the Drama* (Freeport, N.Y.: Books for Libraries Press, 1972 [1834]), p. 193.
18 Gilbert Sheldon, quoted in Mark James Estren, *A History of Underground Comics* (San Francisco: Straight Arrow Books, 1974), p. 192.
19 Richard Barber, *King Arthur in Legend and Chivalry* (Ipswich: Boysdell Press, 1973), p. 83.
20 Sidney Painter, *French Chivalry: Chivalric Ideas and Practices in Medieval France* (Ithaca: Cornell University Press, 1964 [1940]), p. 149.
21 Geoffrey Chaucer, General Prologue to *The Canterbury Tales*, in M. H. Abrams et al., eds., *The Norton Anthology of English Literature*, 2 vols., rev. ed., 1:108–10.
22 Alexandre Dumas, *The Three Musketeers*, introd. Marcel Girard, Everyman's Library (London: Dent, 1966), p. 83.
23 Chrétien de Troyes, *Arthurian Romances*, trans. and introd. W. W. Comfort, Everyman's Library (London: Dent, 1968 [1914]), p. 310.
24 *Sir Gawain and the Green Knight*, trans. Borroff, p. 236.
25 *Sir Gawain and the Green Knight*, trans. Borroff, p. 259.
26 Joseph Pendleton Kennedy, *Swallow Barn, or, A Sojourn in the Old Dominion*, ed. and introd. Jay B. Hubell (New York: Harcourt Brace, 1929 [1832]), p. 190; Mark Twain, *Life on the Mississippi*, introd. Albert Bigelow Paine, Stormfield Edition of the Writings of Mark Twain (New York: Harper, 1929),

p. 374; Edmund Wilson, "Galahad," in *Galahad: I Thought of Daisy* (New York: Farrar, Straus and Giroux, 1967), p. 34.

27 Mills, *The History of Chivalry*, 1:152.

28 Painter, *French Chivalry*, p. 102.

29 Painter, *French Chivalry*, p. 142.

30 There is an interesting moral casualness at times, too, particularly in Marie's Lays. In "Eliduc," for example, a wife says unperturbedly to her husband's mistress who has just awakened from a long trance, "I am very happy that you are alive. Come with me, I will reunite you with your friend"; and in "Milon" an illegitimate son tells his natural father, "By my faith, father, I want to reunite you and my mother. I shall kill the husband she has and let you marry her" (*Les Lais de Marie de France*, translated into modern French by Paul Tuffrau (Paris: L'Edition d'art H. Piazza, n.d.), pp. 150, 121).

31 Chrétien de Troyes, *Arthurian Romances*, p. 213; Malory, *Le Morte d'Arthur*, 1:235.

32 Jean Froissart, *Chronicles of England, France, Spain, and the Adjoining Countries, from the Latter Part of the Reign of Edward II to the Coronation of Henry IV*, trans. Thomas Johnes, introd. John Lord (New York: American Book Exchange, 1880), p. 52.

33 H. L. Mencken, *The Philosophy of Friedrich Nietzsche*, 3rd ed. (Fort Washington: Kennikat Press, 1967 [1908, 1913]), p. 178.

34 Chrétien de Troyes, *Arthurian Romances*, pp. 212, 139. In the account in *The Sun Also Rises* of Pedro Romero in the bull ring, watched by Brett Ashley, Hemingway writes: "Everything of which he could control the locality he did in front of her all that afternoon. Never once did he look up. He made it stronger that way, and did it for himself, too, as well as for her. Because he did not look up to ask if it pleased he did it all for himself inside, and it strengthened him, and yet he did it for her, too. But he did not do it for her at any loss to himself. He gained by it all through the afternoon" (Hemingway, *The Sun Also Rises*, New York: Scribner's, 1926), p. 216.

35 Johan Huizinga, *The Waning of the Middle Ages: A Study of the Forms of Life, Thought and Art in France and the Netherlands in the Fourteenth and Fifteenth Centuries* (Garden City, N.Y.: Doubleday Anchor Books, 1959 [1924]), p. 80.

36 Huizinga, *The Waning of the Middle Ages*, p. 125.

37 The nonpuritanical tolerance and sexual equitableness that I have been describing had an actual sociocultural basis, especially in the south of France, where women enjoyed more power and prestige than in the north. Of the mid-twelfth-century Eleanor of Aquitaine, whom he calls "the most willful and powerful woman of her day" and "by far the fittest...to carry the code of the troubadours into the suspicious north," Michael Foss suggests that "the true infancy of Arthur, Lancelot, all those goodly and fair ladies," was spent in her and her children's courts (Chrétien having written his romances at the court of her daughter, the Countess Marie). (Foss, *Chivalry* (London: Michael Joseph, 1975), p. 107.) The editor of Andreas Capellanus's *The Art of Courtly Love* (introd. and trans. John Jay Parry (New York: Columbia University Press, 1941)) reports that the book "almost certainly" was meant to show conditions at Eleanor's court at Poitiers (Capellanus, p. 21). That court, says Foss, "was a very southern assembly, necessitous knights, landless young squires, a clutch of demoiselles of a marriageable age but as yet unpaired, a bewildering warren of children, adventurers, brawlers, poets, singers, a sporting, litigious, amorous

crew, without the sobriety or nationalism of the north, united chiefly in a...search for pleasure" (Foss, *Chivalry*, p. 107).
38 Malory, *Le Morte d'Arthur*, 1:242.
39 Bertrand de Jouvenel, *Power: The Natural History of Its Growth*, 2nd rev. ed., trans. J. F. Huntington, pref. D. W. Brogan (London: Hutchinson, 1947), pp. 80–1.
40 Huizinga, *The Waning of the Middle Ages*, p. 39.
41 Inazo Nitobe, *Bushido, the Soul of Japan: An Exposition of Japanese Thought*, rev. and enl. ed., introd. William Elliot Griffis (Portland, Vt.: Tuttle, 1969 [1900]), pp. 47–8, 34.
42 Michael Foss, *Chivalry*, p. 68.
43 W. J. Cash, *The Mind of the South* (New York: Vintage Books, n.d. [1941]), p. 32.
44 John William De Forest, *A Union Officer in the Reconstruction*, ed. and introd. James H. Croushore and David Morris Potter (New Haven: Yale University Press, 1948), p. 185; Albion W. Tourgée, *A Fool's Errand*, ed. John Hope Franklin (Cambridge, Mass.: Belknap Press of Harvard University Press, 1961), p. 268.
45 Henry Adams, *The Education of Henry Adams*, introd. James Truslow Adams (New York: Modern Library, 1931 [1906]), p. 246.
46 Henry Seidel Canby, *The Age of Confidence: Life in the Nineties* (New York: Farrar and Rinehart, 1936), p. 28.
47 Walter Hines Page, *The Southerner, a Novel; Being the Autobiography of Nicholas Worth* (New York: Doubleday, Page, 1909), p. 91.
48 De Forest, *A Union Officer*, p. 203.
49 Frances Pendleton Gaines, *The Southern Plantation: A Study in the Development and the Accuracy of a Tradition* (New York: Columbia University Press, 1925), p. 4.
50 Mark Twain, *Life on the Mississippi*, intro. Albert Bigelow Paine, Stormfield Edition of the Writings of Mark Twain (New York, Harper, 1929), p. 370.
51 Cash, *The Mind of the South*, p. 89.
52 William R. Taylor, *Cavalier and Yankee: The Old South and American National Character* (New York: Braziller, 1961), p. 148.
53 Eliza Frances Andrews, *The War-Time Journal of a Georgia Girl 1864–1865* (New York: Appleton, 1908), p. 21.
54 Adams, *The Education of Henry Adams*, p. 384.
55 Canby, *The Age of Confidence*, p. 203.
56 Stephen Vincent Benét, *John Brown's Body*, introd. Henry Seidel Canby (New York: Rinehart, 1928), p. 141.
57 Sarah Morgan, quoted in Edmund Wilson, *Patriotic Gore: Studies in the Literature of the American Civil War* (New York: Oxford University Press, 1962), p. 265. For a scholarly examination of the subject of Southern womanhood, see Anne Firor Scott, *The Southern Lady: From Pedestal to Politics, 1830–1930* (Chicago: University of Chicago Press, 1970), especially Chapters 2 and 4.
58 The pastoral-heroic nexus is also a feature of some of the best American thrillers. John D. MacDonald's Travis McGee books are the most obvious examples, with their protective and luxurious Florida-based houseboat and their emphasis on sea, sun, good food and drink, and the healing powers of affectionate sexuality. But MacDonald, besides taking tips from the American success of the James Bond series, had been codifying features that were

Notes to p. 82

present in other Florida thrillers, such as his own *The Brass Cupcake*, Charles Williams's *Gulf Coast Girl*, and Jonathan Latimer's *The Dead Don't Care*. There are strongly pastoral satisfactions in the works of a number of other thriller writers.

59 Nitobe, *Bushido*, p. 55.
60 Thomas Nelson Page, *The Old South: Essays Social and Political* (New York: Scribner, 1911 [1892]), p. 157.
61 D. R. Hundley, *Social Relations in Our Southern States* (New York: Henry B. Price, 1860; reprinted in facsimile, New York: Arno Press, 1973), pp. 70–1.
62 Alfred Henry Lewis, quoted in William W. Savage, *Cowboy Life: Reconstructing an American Myth* (Norman: University of Oklahoma Press, 1975), p. 157.
63 Philip Ashton Rollins, *The Cowboy: An Unconventional History of Civilization in the Old-Time Range*, rev. and enl. ed. (New York: Ballantine Books, 1973 [1922, 1936]), p. 68.
64 In the traditional enlightened view, hunting was simply killing, and the dreadful consequences of being a hunter-killer were classically defined by Crèvecoeur when he said of American frontiersmen that "the chase renders them ferocious, gloomy, and unsociable; a hunter wants no neighbour, he rather hates them, because he dreads the competition" (J. Hector St. John Crèvecoeur, *Letters from an American Farmer* [Garden City, N.Y.: Doubleday Dolphin Books, n.d.], p. 57). But the relative nonviolence of hunter-gatherers has been noted by a number of investigators, among them Colin M. Turnbull, Elman R. Service, and Stanley Diamond, and was a feature of the new image of the Indians that emerged in the writings of men like George Bird Grinnell, Charles Eastman, and, a little later, Paul Radin. An interesting visual indication of the changing popular perception of Indians is provided in the contrast between Frederic Remington's warrior horsemen from the Nineties and N. C. Wyeth's meditative forest dwellers, circa 1907–1909, in Susan E. Meyer's *America's Great Illustrators* (New York: Abrams, 1978).

The reasons for the relative nonviolence of hunter-gatherers are not obscure. Hunter-gatherer communities can provide the individual with what Edward Sapir calls "a feeling of spiritual mastery" and what Erich Fromm describes as "effectiveness," the feeling of being able to advance "toward a goal without undue hesitation, doubt, or fear" (Sapir, *Selected Writings of Edward Sapir in Language, Culture and Personality*, ed. and introd. David G. Mandelbaum [Berkeley and Los Angeles: University of California Press, 1958], p. 323; Erich Fromm, *The Anatomy of Human Destructiveness* [New York: Holt, Rinehart and Winston, 1973], p. 189). In their hunting, a premium is put upon skills and problem solving; prestige comes unequivocally from performance, as it did in the tournament, and not from accidents of birth, the possession of private sources of wealth, or trickery; and a good deal of sharing and mutual assisting goes on, as well as the enjoyment of what José Ortega y Gasset calls "that basic feeling of risk which is the substance of man" (Ortega y Gasset, quoted in Stanley Diamond, *In Search of the Primitive: A Critique of Civilization*, fore. Eric R. Wolf [New Brunswick, N.J.: Transaction Books, 1974], p. 117). The activities and attitudes of some of the present-day American hunters described in Cleveland Amory's lacerating *Man Kind?* (New York: Dell, 1975) are another matter, of course.

Apropos of the growing emphasis on the pastoral as well as the heroic aspect of the Indians, it should be noted here that in 1895 Grinnell wrote that:

The Indian woman, it is usually thought, is a mere drudge and slave, but, so far as my observations extend, this notion is wholly an erroneous one. . . The place of woman in the tribe was not that of slave or of a beast of burden. . . In many tribes women took part in the councils of the chiefs; in some, women were even the tribal rulers; while in all they received a fair measure of respect and affection from those related to them (Grinnell, *The Story of the Indians,* pref. note by Ripley Hitchcock [New York: Appleton, 1896], pp. 46, 244).

65 The Lorenzian paradox also operated in the appeal of the image of primate communities that had been built up by the end of the Sixties in the writings of C. R. Carpenter, Irven DeVore, S. L. Washburn, Claire and W. M. S. Russell, Jane van Lawick–Goodall, and others. In their accounts the primate communities in their native habitats – free ranging, food gathering, and integrated into their own socially meaningful territories – were very different both from the Rousseauistic image of "natural" man that Sade attacked so forcibly and from Hobbesian, Sadean, and primitive Social Darwinist notions of tooth-and-claw natural ferocity. The admirable features of a number of the described primate communities, such as the relatively small amount of intragroup violence, the relative abstention from serious intergroup violence, the willingness to compromise, and the rareness of dominative pseudosex, were inseparable from the communities' being for the most part fairly highly structured ones. But that structuring, and the shiftings and adjustments going on in it all the time, depended not on so-called brute force but on the kinds of combinations of strength, skill, inventiveness, determination, and courage that both made for effectiveness in combat and lessened the need for combat. Like the gentleman, the primate leaders were prepared to fight if fighting was inescapable. But engaging in combat would simply be the most intense manifestation of the qualities that made them leaders in the first place and gave them the authority to arbitrate the daily life of the group with minimum force. Moreover, those qualities of character permeated the community as a whole. The daily life of the group – its food gathering, socializing, and infant rearing – might wear an enviably innocent pastoral aspect; but in the relationship of the group to an environment in which risks were never entirely absent, the watchful stance of the group leaders was to some extent appropriate to, and partaken of, by all the group.

66 Ernest Hemingway, *Death in the Afternoon* (New York: Scribner, 1932), pp. 113, 127.

CHAPTER 6. QUALITY AND EDUCATION

1 Horatio Alger, *Strive and Succeed: Julius, or The Street Boy Out West; The Store Boy, or The Fortunes of Ben Barclay,* introd. S. N. Behrman (New York: Holt, Rinehart and Winston, 1967), pp. 24–5; Friedrich Nietzsche, *Ecce Homo: Nietzsche's Autobiography,* trans. and introd. Anthony M. Ludovici, Complete Works of Friedrich Nietzsche (New York: Russell and Russell, 1964), p. 23; Mark Sibley Severance, *Hammersmith: His Harvard Days* (Boston: Houghton Mifflin, 1878), p. 522.

2 Henry Seidel Canby, *The Age of Confidence: Life in the Nineties* (New York: Farrar and Rinehart, 1934), p. 192; F. Scott Fitzgerald, *The Great Gatsby* (New York: Scribner, 1925), p. 99.

3 Dashiell Hammett, *The Dain Curse* (New York: Permabooks, 1961), p. 10.

4 Owen Johnson, *The Sixty-First Second* (New York: Stokes, 1913), p. 84.

5 Franklin Giddings, quoted in Robert H. Wiebe, *The Search for Order: 1877–1920*, fore. David Donald (New York: Hill and Wang, 1967), p. 233.
6 Owen Johnson, *Stover at Yale* (New York: Stokes, 1912), pp. 239–40.
7 Richard Hofstadter, *The American Political Tradition and the Men Who Made It* (New York: Knopf, 1957), p. 206.
8 H. G. Wells, *The Future in America: A Search after Realities* (London: Chapman and Hall, 1906), p. 164.
9 William Allen White, *The Autobiography of William Allen White* (New York: Macmillan, 1946), pp. 427, 386.
10 Henry Seidel Canby, *Alma Mater: The Gothic Age of the American College* (New York: Farrar and Rinehart, 1936), pp. 232, 107.
11 Frederick Rudolph, *The American College and University: A History* (New York: Knopf, 1962), p. 388.
12 Canby, *The Age of Confidence*, p. 107.
13 F. Scott Fitzgerald, *The Basil and Josephine Stories*, ed. and introd. Jackson R. Bryce and John Kuehl (New York: Scribner, 1973), p. 147.
14 Canby, *Alma Mater*, p. 235.
15 F. Scott Fitzgerald, *The Beautiful and the Damned* (New York: Scribner, 1950 [1922]), p. 368.
16 Owen Johnson, *The Tennessee Shad* (New York: Burt, 1911), p. 175, 201–2.
17 Fitzgerald, *The Beautiful and the Damned*, p. 5.
18 Fitzgerald, *The Great Gatsby*, p. 7.
19 Thorstein Veblen, *The Higher Learning in America: A Memorandum on the Conduct of Universities by Business Men*, introd. Louis M. Hacker (New York: Hill and Wang, 1957), pp. 87–8.
20 Thorstein Veblen, *The Theory of the Leisure Class: An Economic Study of Institutions*, fore. Stuart Chase (New York: Modern Library, 1934 [1899]), pp. 361–2; W. J. Ghent, *Our Benevolent Feudalism* (New York: Macmillan, 1902), p. 28.
21 Oliver Wendell Holmes, quoted in Richard Hofstadter, *Social Darwinism in American Thought*, rev. ed. (Boston: Beacon Press, 1955), p. 32; Hofstader, *The American Political Tradition*, p. 166.
22 Charles A. Beard and Mary R. Beard, *The American Spirit: A Study of the Idea of Civilization in the United States* (New York: Macmillan, n.d. [1942]), p. 347. For the economic essence of William Graham Sumner, see his *What Social Classes Owe to Each Other* (New York: Arno Press, 1972 [1883]).
23 Andrew Carnegie, *The Gospel of Wealth and Other Timely Essays*, ed. Edward G. Kirkland (Cambridge, Mass.: Belknap Press of Harvard University Press, 1962), p. 173.
24 Ulysses S. Grant, quoted in Edmund Wilson, *Patriotic Gore: Studies in the Literature of the American Civil War* (New York: Oxford University Press, 1962), p. 159.
25 John Stahl Patterson, quoted in Beard and Beard, *The American Spirit*, p. 312; unidentified orator, quoted in Richard Hofstadter, *Anti-Intellectualism in American Life* (New York: Knopf, 1953), p. 239.
26 William Perkins, quoted in W. Eugene Hollon, *Frontier Violence: Another Look* (New York: Oxford University Press, 1974), p. 67.
27 *Topeka Commonwealth*, quoted in Douglas Branch, *The Cowboy and His Interpreters*, introd. Harry Sinclair Drago (New York: Cooper Square Publications, 1961 [1926]), p. 12. Ben C. Truman, *The Field of Honor: Being a Complete and Comprehensive History of Duelling in All Countries* (New York: Fords, Howard, and Hulbert, 1883), pp. 88–9.

Notes to pp. 93–8

28 Charles L. Brace, quoted in *Popular Culture and Industrialism, 1865–1890,* ed. and introd. Henry Nash Smith (New York: New York University Press, 1967), p. 198.
29 Edward Livingstone Youmans, quoted in Hofstadter, *Social Darwinism in America,* p. 47.
30 Wiebe, *The Search for Order,* p. 12.
31 Canby, *Alma Mater,* p. 108; Canby, *The Age of Confidence,* pp. 237, 109–10, 193.
32 Frederic C. Howe, *The Confessions of a Reformer,* introd. John Braeman (Chicago: Quadrangle Books, 1967 [1925]), pp. 14, 17–18.
33 Granville Hicks, *John Reed: The Making of a Revolutionary* (New York: Macmillan, 1936), p. 3.
34 Ralph Waldo Emerson, quoted in Dixon Wecter, *The Hero in America: A Chronicle of Hero-Worship,* Ann Arbor Paperbacks (Ann Arbor: University of Michigan Press, 1963), p. 471.
35 Canby, *The Age of Confidence,* p. 106.
36 J. Hector St. John Crèvecoeur, *Letters from an American Farmer* (Garden City, N.Y.: Doubleday Dolphin Books, n.d. [1782]), p. 17.
37 Alexis de Tocqueville, *Democracy in America,* ed. J. P. Mayer, trans. George Lawrence (Garden City, N.Y.: Doubleday Anchor Books, 1969), pp. 283, 403.
38 Samuel Eliot Morison and Henry Steele Commager, *The Growth of the American Republic,* 2 vols., 4th ed., rev. and enl. (New York: Oxford University Press, 1950), 2:9.
39 Richard D. Mosier, *Making the American Mind: Social and Moral Ideas in the McGuffey Readers* (New York: Russell and Russell, 1965), p. 43; Theodore P. Greene, *America's Heroes: The Changing Models of Success in American Magazines* (New York: Oxford University Press, 1970), p. 119.
40 Johnson, *The Sixty-First Second,* p. 155.
41 Herman Melville, quoted in Robert Jewett, *The Captain America Complex: The Dilemma of Zealous Nationalism* (Philadelphia: Westminster Press, 1973), p. 9.
42 Sir Walter Scott, *Ivanhoe: A Romance,* Everyman's Library (London: Dent, 1906 [1820]), p. 283.
43 James Bryce, *The American Commonwealth,* 2 vols. (London: Macmillan, 1891), 2:530.
44 Andrew Carnegie, *Triumphant Democracy; or Fifty Years' March of the Republic* (New York: Scribner, 1886), pp. 27–8.
45 Lord Raglan, *The Hero: A Study in Tradition, Myth, and Drama* (London: Methuen, 1936), p. 203.
46 Johnson, *The Sixty-First Second,* p. 3.
47 Bryce, *The American Commonwealth,* 2:529–31.
48 Ralph Waldo Emerson, quoted in Greene, *America's Heroes,* p. 110.
49 Alfred Henry Lewis, quoted in Greene, *America's Heroes,* p. 199.
50 Elias Canetti, *Crowds and Power,* trans. Carol Stewart (London: Victor Gollancz, 1962).
51 Carnegie, *Triumphant Democracy,* pp. 205, 301. Twain had prefaced *Life on the Mississippi* with a substantial quotation from *Harper's* about the statistical greatness of the Mississippi.
52 Edwin Lawrence Godkin, *Problems of Modern Democracy: Political and Economic Essays,* ed. and introd. Morton Keller (Cambridge, Mass.: The Belknap Press of Harvard University Press, 1963 [1896]), p. 301.

53 Mark Twain, *Life on the Mississippi*, introd. Albert Bigelow Paine, Stormfield Edition of the Writings of Mark Twain (New York: Harper, 1929), pp. 89–91.
54 John D. Rockefeller, *Random Reminiscences of Men and Events* (New York: Arno Press, 1973 [1909]), p. 152.
55 Howe, *Confessions of a Reformer*, p. 152; H. G. Wells, *The Future in America: A Search after Realities* (London: Chapman and Hall, 1906), p. 138.
56 Grover Cleveland, "The Integrity of American Character," *Harper's* 112 (December 1905), p. 67.
57 Wells, *The Future in America*, p. 134.
58 Carnegie, *The Gospel of Wealth*, p. 83.
59 W. D. Howells, *A Traveller from Altruria* (New York: Harper, 1894), p. 202.
60 *New York Tribune*, quoted in Diamond, *The Reputation of the American Businessman*, p. 83.
61 Henry Adams, *The Education of Henry Adams*, introd. James Truslow Adams (New York: Modern Library, 1931 [1906]), pp. 283, 297.
62 Jay Gould, quoted in Matthew Josephson, *The Robber Barons: The Great American Capitalists, 1861–1901* (New York: Harcourt, Brace, 1934), p. 194.
63 H. L. Mencken, *Happy Days 1880–1892*, (New York: Knopf, 1940), p. 247.
64 Thorstein Veblen, *The Theory of Business Enterprise* (New York: Scribner, 1932 [1904]), pp. 41–2.
65 Howe, *Confessions of a Reformer*, pp. 152, 147.
66 "Editor's Easy Chair," *Harper's*, ca. 1902.
67 Thomas More, *Utopia*, trans. and introd. Paul Turner (Harmondsworth, Middlesex: Penguin Books, 1965), p. 80. The resemblances were presumably not entirely coincidental. Morison and Commager suggest that "the Utopian ideal for America which was in the mind of every important group of English pioneers from Massachusetts to Georgia, takes off from" More's book. (*The Growth of the American Republic*, 1:35.)
68 Carnegie, *The Gospel of Wealth*, p. 57.
69 Andrew Carnegie, *Empire of Business* (Buffalo: Corlis, 1907), p. 4.
70 Carnegie, *The Gospel of Wealth*, p. viii.
71 Carnegie, *The Gospel of Wealth*, pp. 51, 16.
72 Carnegie, *The Gospel of Wealth*, p. viii, and *The Empire of Business*, p. 4. Underlying all this, of course, were other problems implicit in the quantification of worth. A businessman who had worked his income up to, say, $10,000 a year might very well wish to consider himself a good many times worthier than a laborer who earned $500 – and as being entitled to despise him. But this put him in an uncomfortable position with respect to the contempt of someone earning $100,000. And so on upwards. As Ignatius Donnelly pointed out in *Caesar's Column*,
    the man who is worth $100,000 says to himself, "There is Jones; he is worth $500,000; he lives with a display and extravagance I cannot equal. I must increase my fortune to half a million." Jones, on the other hand, is measuring himself against Brown, who has a million. He knows that men cringe lower to Brown than they do to him. He must have a million – half a million is nothing. And Brown feels that he is overshadowed by Smith, with his ten millions (Edmund Boisgilbert [Ignatius Donnelly], *Caesar's Column: A Story of the Twentieth Century* (Toronto: William Bryce, 1890), p. 181).
Because there was no logical limit to how much one could earn, it was always possible to see oneself as having "failed" simply because one was not earning more than one was.

73 H. G. Wells, *Tono-Bungay* (London: Macmillan, 1909), p. 329.
74 Bryce, *The American Commonwealth*, 2:616.
75 David Graham Phillips, *The Reign of Gilt* (New York: Pott, 1905), p. 25.
76 Phillips, *The Reign of Gilt*, p. 31.
77 Lady Jeune, "The American Man: From an Englishwoman's Point of View," *Collier's* 31 (April 25, 1903), p. 17.
78 Herbert Croly, *The Promise of American Life*, ed. and introd. Arthur M. Schlesinger, Jr. (Cambridge, Mass.: Belknap Press of Harvard University Press, 1965 [1909]), pp. 107–8. Cognizance of this problem was taken obliquely in Gibson's very popular wish-fulfillment cartoon series "The Education of Mr. Pipp" (1899), in which a loveable, childlike millionaire and his lumpish wife – endowed by some genetic miracle with a couple of Gibson Girl daughters – visit Europe and become acquainted with the joys of the British aristocracy, society balls, the Derby, golf, the roulette table, and so forth, winding up by marrying off the daughters handsomely, one to a young British aristocrat, the other to the strong-chinned Gibson Man manager of the Pipp Iron Works, appropriately named John Willing.
79 Johnson, *Stover at Yale*, p. 72. On the intimidation of some of the intelligent young by the Horatio Alger view of things, see Kenneth S. Lynn, *The Dream of Success: A Study of the Modern American Imagination* (Boston: Little, Brown, 1955), pp. 173–7.
80 Hannah Arendt, *Imperialism*, Harvest Books (New York: Harcourt, Brace and World, 1968), p. 91.
81 Herbert N. Casson, quoted in Greene, *America's Heroes*, p. 268; Johnson, *The Sixty-First Second*, pp. 3–4.
82 Canby, *Alma Mater*, pp. 228–9.
83 Johnson, *Stover at Yale*, p. 18.
84 Oscar Handlin, *The Americans: A New History of the People of the United States* (Boston: Little, Brown, 1963), p. 255. John Reed said of himself: "Boarding school, I think, meant more to me than anything in my boyhood...The ordered life of the community interested me; I was impressed by its traditional customs and dignities, school patriotism, and the sense of a long settled and established civilization" ("Almost Thirty," *New Republic* 86 (April 15, 1936), p. 270). Changing images of the pleasures of college life can be usefully observed in the line of novels that runs from William T. Washburn's *Fair Harvard: A Story of American College Life* (1869), via Mark Sibley Severance's *Hammersmith: His Harvard Days* (1878) and John Seymour Wood's *College Days; or Harry's Career at Yale* (1894), to *Stover at Yale* (1912) – novels set, respectively, in the Fifties (the first two), the early Seventies, and the early Nineties, and all by alumni. The authors are increasingly conscious of the sequence of "typical" college experiences as *forming* a sequence, and by the time that Stover is sent through the system a good part of the interest comes from the question of how creditably he will do at each stage.
85 Owen Johnson, *The Prodigious Hickey* (New York: Baker and Taylor, 1910), p. 257.
86 Veblen, *The Higher Learning in America*, p. 76.
87 Canby, *Alma Mater*, pp. 119, 37, 41. Another Yale man, George Wilson Pierson, who says that "no more brilliant diagnostic report [than Canby's] can be found" (p. 270) usefully confirms and supplements Canby's account of Yale in the Nineties and early 1900s in Chapters 1 and 2 of his *Yale College:*

An Educational History, 1871–1921 (New Haven: Yale University Press, 1952), a work all the more enlightening because of its genteelly boola-boola tone.

88 Owen Johnson, *The Varmint: A Lawrenceville Story* (Boston: Little, Brown, 1922 [1910]), p. 119.

89 F. Scott Fitzgerald, "Princeton," (1927), *The Bodley Head Fitzgerald*, 6 vols. rev. ed. (London: The Bodley Head, 1965), 3:318.

90 Johnson, *Stover at Yale*, p. 46. Although helmets did not become *de rigueur* until later, a British observer noted with interest in 1898 that

an American football player in full armour resembles a deep-sea diver or a Roman retiarius more than anything else. The dress consists of thickly padded knickerbockers, jersey, canvas jacket, very heavy boots, and very thick stockings. The player then farther protects himself by shin guards, shoulder caps, ankle and knee supporters, and wristbands. The apparatus on his head is fearful and wonderful to behold, including a rubber mouthpiece, a nose-mask, padded ear guards, and a curious headpiece made of steel springs, leather straps, and India rubber (James Fullarton Muirhead, *The Land of Contrasts: A Briton's View of His American Kin* (Montreal: Montreal News, 1898), p.114).

91 Henry Davidson Sheldon, quoted in Rudolph, *The American College*, p. 380.

92 Johnson, *The Varmint*, pp. 239, 232.

93 Robert W. Chambers, "Americans at Play: A Word for Chivalry in Sport," *Collier's* 37 (August 18, 1906), p. 12.

94 Eustace Clavering, "The Fortunes of Football," *Munsey's* 28 (October 1902), p. 72.

95 Johnson, *Stover at Yale*, pp. 79, 113.

96 Chambers, "Americans at Play," p. 12.

97 William V. Shannon, *The American Irish*, rev. ed. (New York: Macmillan, 1966), p. 95. A piquant reminder of the lateness of certain developments is the fact that prior to entering Lawrenceville in the early Nineties, the pugnacious Stover "had never fought a real fight. He had had a few rough-and-tumble skirmishes, but a fight where you stood up and looked a man in the whites of the eyes, a deliberate, planned-out fight, was outside his knowledge" (Johnson, *The Varmint*, p. 110).

98 Johnson, *The Prodigious Hickey*, pp. 143–4; *The Varmint*, p. 390.

99 Burt L. Standish [Gilbert Patten], *Frank Merriwell at Yale* (Philadelphia: McKay, 1903 [1897]), p. 244.

100 Johnson, *Stover at Yale*, p. 232.

101 Patten, *Frank Merriwell at Yale*, p. 10.

102 Johnson, *Stover at Yale*, pp. 139–41.

103 John F. Gregory, quoted in Greene, *America's Heroes*, p. 204. A classic paradigm of the perceived relationship between higher education and efficiency was provided in 1910 in a short story in *Collier's* in which, as described by a working-class young mother who witnessed the events, a group of hyperactive, song-singing, and initially obnoxious college men, led appropriately by a redhead, use their collective energies and imaginative know-how to save the life of a mining engineer (a Yalie beneath his rough exterior) who faces seemingly certain death as the result of a train wreck out West, and finish off with a whip round of the hat to provide an eventual college education for the mother's baby. (John Singleton Moriarty, "Their Higher Kinship: A Transcript of the Mother's Account of Baby's Adventure with the College Men," *Collier's* 6 (December 3, 1910), pp. 21–3, 26.)

104 William James, "On a Certain Blindness in Human Beings" (1899), in *The Writings of William James: A Comprehensive Edition*, ed. and introd. John J. McDermott (New York: Modern Library, 1968), p. 634.
105 Patten, *Frank Merriwell at Yale*, p. 249.
106 Fitzgerald, *The Beautiful and the Damned*, p. 371.
107 Robert Warshow, "Movie Chronicle: The Westerner" (1954), in *The Immediate Experience: Movies, Comics, Theatre and Other Aspects of Popular Culture*, introd. Lionel Trilling (New York: Atheneum, 1972), pp. 140–1.
108 Frederick Orin Bartlett, "Dick Bradford, Gentleman," *Collier's* 33 (August 6, 1904), p. 14. Cf. the statement about the college-educated dropout Jack Duane in Upton Sinclair's *The Jungle* (New York: Vanguard Press, 1926 [1905]) that "he was striking all the time – there was war between him and society. He was a genial freebooter, living off the enemy, without fear or shame. He was not always victorious, but the defeat did not mean annihilation, and need not bend his spirit" (p. 167).
109 Frederick Townsend Martin, *The Passing of the Idle Rich* (Garden City, N.Y.: Doubleday, Page, 1911), pp. 226–7, 229–30.

CHAPTER 7. REFORM

1 J. Hector St. John Crèvecoeur, *Letters from an American Farmer* (Garden City, N.Y.: Doubleday, n.d.), p. 67; Sherwood Anderson, *Marching Men: A Critical Text*, ed. and introd. Ray Lewis White (Cleveland: Press of Case Western Reserve University, 1972), p. 148; Edith Kermit Roosevelt, quoted in William Allen White, *The Autobiography of William Allen White* (New York: Macmillan, 1946), p. 342.
2 Henry Seidel Canby, *Alma Mater: The Gothic Age of the American College* (New York: Farrar and Rinehart, 1936), p. 135.
3 Owen Johnson, *Stover at Yale* (New York: Stokes, 1912), pp. 79, 207–8, 238, 242–3.
4 Johnson, *Stover at Yale*, p. 254.
5 White, *Autobiography*, pp. 325–6.
6 Herbert Croly, *The Promise of American Life*, ed and introd. Arthur M. Schlesinger (Cambridge, Mass.: Belknap Press of Harvard University Press, 1965 [1909]), p. 141.
7 Frederic C. Howe, *Confessions of a Reformer*, introd. John Braeman (Chicago: Quadrangle Books, 1967 [1925]), p. 57.
8 Thomas Benson Foraker, quoted in Theodore P. Greene, *America's Heroes: The Changing Models of Success in American Magazines* (New York: Oxford University Press, 1970), pp. 160–1.
9 White, *Autobiography*, p. 413.
10 Samuel Eliot Morison and Henry Steele Commager, *The Growth of the American Republic*, 2 vols., 4th ed., rev. and enl. (New York: Oxford University Press, 1950), 2:214.
11 William Allen White, quoted in *The American Heritage History of the Confident Years*, by the Editors of *American Heritage* (New York: American Heritage Publishing Co., n.d.), p. 291.
12 Andrew Carnegie, *Triumphant Democracy; or Fifty Years' March of the Republic* (New York: Scribner, 1886), p. 472.
13 Phillips, quoted in Richard Hofstadter, *The American Political Tradition and the Men Who Made It* (New York: Knopf, 1957), p. 150.

14 Edwin Lawrence Godkin, *Unforeseen Tendencies of Democracy* (Boston and New York: Houghton Mifflin, 1898), pp. 225, 213.
15 Carnegie, *Triumphant Democracy*, p. 471.
16 Howe, *Confessions of a Reformer*, p. 5.
17 Carnegie, *Triumphant Democracy*, p. 473.
18 Henry Seidel Canby, *The Age of Confidence: Life in the Nineties* (New York: Farrar and Rinehart, 1936), p. 250.
19 Paul Leicester Ford, *The Honorable Peter Stirling and What People Thought of Him* (New York: Hillary House, 1957 [1894]), p. 304.
20 Unidentified teacher, quoted in John Graham Brooks, *American Syndicalism: The I.W.W.* (New York: Macmillan, 1913), p. 7.
21 Charles Sumner, *Recent Speeches and Addresses* (Boston: Higgins and Bradley, 1856), pp. 505, 508.
22 At the end of the century Thomas Wentworth Higginson, looking back on his expedition into Kansas and Nebraska in the Fifties smuggling arms to the antislavery party there, remembered how "I had some of the strong sensations of a moss-trooper. Never before in my life had I been, distinctively and unequivocally, outside of the world of human law...[My] Sharp's rifle, my revolvers, – or, these failing, my own ingenuity and ready wit, – were all the protection I had. It was a delightful sensation...and there came to mind some thrilling passages from Thornbury's 'Ballads of the Cavaliers and Roundheads' "(*Cheerful Yesterdays* (New York: Arno Press and *The New York Times*, 1968 [1899]), p. 202).
23 Ralph Waldo Emerson, quoted in Edwin Harrison Cady, *The Gentleman in America: A Literary Study in American Culture* (New York: Syracuse University Press, 1949), p. 181.
24 John Lothrop Motley, quoted in Henry Steele Commager, *The Blue and the Gray: The Story of the Civil War as Told by Participants*, ed. and introd. Henry Steele Commager, 2 vols. (Indianapolis: Bobbs-Merrill, 1950), 1:52. Oliver Wendell Holmes himself – the son, that is – commented at the time that "we need all the examples of chivalry to help us bind our rebellious desires to steadfastness in the Christian Crusade of the 19th century" (quoted in Edmund Wilson, *Patriotic Gore: Studies in the Literature of the American Civil War* (New York: Oxford University Press, 1962), p. 748).
25 William Allen White, "What's the Matter with America?: III – The Nation," *Collier's* 38 (December 1, 1906), p. 17.
26 See, in this connection, E. Douglas Branch, *The Sentimental Years: 1836–1860* (New York: Appleton-Century, 1934); C. S. Griffin, *The Ferment of Reform, 1830–1865* (London: Routledge and Kegan Paul, 1969); Richard Hofstadter, *The Age of Reform: From Bryan to F.D.R.* (New York: Knopf, 1958); and John G. Sproat, *"The Best Men": Liberal Reformers in the Gilded Age* (New York: Oxford University Press, 1968). On the development of "feminine" attitudes, see for example Ann Douglas, *The Feminization of American Culture* (New York: Knopf, 1977), Barbara J. Berg, *The Remembered Gate: Origins of American Feminism: The Woman and the City, 1800–1860*, fore. Richard C. Wade (New York: Oxford University Press, 1978), and, more generally, Gordon Rattray Taylor, *The Angel-Makers: A Study in the Psychological Origins of Historical Change* (London: Heinemann, 1958).
27 Edwin Lawrence Godkin, *Problems of Modern Democracy: Political and Economic Essays*, ed. and introd. Morton Keller (Cambridge, Mass.: The Belknap Press of Harvard University Press, 1963 [1896]), p. 282.

28 See Lorin Peterson, *The Day of the Mugwump* (New York: Random House, 1961).
29 White, *Autobiography*, p. 290.
30 Howe, *Confessions of a Reformer*, p. 151.
31 White, *Autobiography*, pp. 349–50.
32 William Allen White, *A Certain Rich Man* (New York: Macmillan, 1909), p. 215.
33 Howe, *Confessions of a Reformer*, p. 146.
34 Mary Heaton Vorse, *A Footnote to Folly: Reminiscences of Mary Heaton Vorse* (New York: Farrar and Rinehart, 1935), p. 29. For fictional celebrations of the pleasures of successful bossism, see Francis Churchill Williams, *J. Devlin–Boss* (Boston: Lothrop, 1901) and Alfred Henry Lewis, *The Boss and How He Came to Rule New York*, introd. Clarence Gohdes (Ridgewood, N.J.: Gregg Press, 1967 [1903]).
35 Editors of the *Century*, quoted in Greene, *America's Heroes*, p. 77.
36 William Allen White, quoted in Greene, *America's Heroes*, p. 131.
37 Charles A. Beard and Mary R. Beard, *The Rise of American Civilization*, 2 vols. (New York: Macmillan, 1927), 2:178, 287.
38 James J. Hill, quoted in James Truslow Adams, *The Epic of America* (Boston: Little, Brown, 1932), p. 348.
39 L. W., "Homestead as Seen by One of Its Workmen," *McClure's* 3 (July 1894), p. 165. The same year also saw the publication in *McClure's* of Hamlin Garland's "Homestead and Its Perilous Trades: Impressions of a Visit," 3 (June), pp. 3–9, and Stephen Crane's "In the Depths of a Coal Mine," 3 (August), pp. 195–209.
40 William Hard, "Making Steel and Killing Men" (1907), in Arthur Weinberg and Lila Weinberg, eds., *The Muckrakers: The Era in Journalism that Moved America to Reform – the Most Significant Magazine Articles of 1902–1912* (New York: Simon and Schuster, 1961), p. 353.
41 C. P. Connolly, "The Story of Montana" (1906), in Weinberg and Weinberg, *The Muckrakers*, p. 105.
42 William Dean Howells, quoted in *The American Heritage History*, p. 236.
43 Frank Norris, quoted in *The American Heritage History*, p. 236.
44 Johnson, *The Sixty-First Second*, p. 218.
45 Winston Churchill, *Mr. Crewe's Career* (New York: Macmillan, 1908), p. 3.
46 Howe, *Confessions of a Reformer*, p. 71.
47 Owen Johnson, *The Sixty-First Second* (New York: Stokes, 1913), p. 261; John P. Marquand, *The Late George Apley: A Novel in the Form of a Memoir* (New York: Modern Library, 1940), p. 149.
48 Churchill, *Mr. Crewe's Career*, p. 264.
49 Howe, *Confessions of a Reformer*, pp. 155, 106.
50 Howe, *Confessions of a Reformer*, pp. 155–6.
51 Norman Hapgood, "Theodore Roosevelt," *Collier's* 34 (January 7, 1905), p. 15.
52 John Reed, in William L. O'Neill, ed., *Echoes of Revolt: The Masses 1911–1917*, introd. Irving Howe, after. Max Eastman (Chicago: Quadrangle Books, 1966), p. 139.
53 Mark Sullivan, quoted in *The American Heritage History*, p. 361.
54 Norman Hapgood, "Theodore Roosevelt," p. 15.
55 White, *Autobiography*, p. 297.
56 White, "What's the Matter with America?" p. 17.

57 Gilbert Patten, *Frank Merriwell at Yale* (Philadelphia: McKay, 1903 [1897]), p. 233.
58 Isaac L. Hunt, quoted in Henry F. Pringle, *Theodore Roosevelt: A Biography* (New York: Harcourt, Brace, 1931), p. 65.
59 Owen Wister, *Roosevelt: The Story of a Friendship, 1880–1919* (New York: Macmillan, 1929), p. 209.
60 Roosevelt, quoted in George F. Mowry, *The Era of Theodore Roosevelt and the Birth of Modern America, 1900–1912*, introd. Henry Steele Commager and Richard Braden Morris (New York: Harper and Row, 1962), p. 220.
61 John P. Marquand, *H. M. Pulham, Esquire* (Boston: Little, Brown, 1941), p. 92.
62 Theodore Roosevelt, *An Autobiography* (New York: Macmillan, 1913), p. 32.
63 Pringle, *Theodore Roosevelt*, p. 97. On the reality of the dangers in the charge up San Juan Hill, see Frank Freidel, *The Splendid Little War* (Boston: Little, Brown, 1958).
64 Carleton Putnam, *Theodore Roosevelt: The Formative Years 1858–1886*, (New York, Scribner, 1958), p. 112.
65 Theodore Roosevelt, quoted in Douglas Branch, *The Cowboy and His Interpreters*, introd. Harry Sinclair Drago (New York: Cooper Square Publications, 1961 [1926]), p. 92.
66 Wister, *Roosevelt*, p. 107.
67 H. G. Wells, *The Future in America: A Search after Realities* (London: Chapman and Hall, 1906), p. 343.
68 White, *Autobiography*, p. 348.
69 Max Eastman, *Venture* (New York: Boni, 1927), p. 45.
70 Wells, *The Future in America*, p. 350.
71 Joseph Bucklin Bishop, quoted in Pringle, *Theodore Roosevelt*, p. 137; White, *Autobiograpy*, p. 348.
72 Pringle, *Theodore Roosevelt*, p. 101.
73 Beard and Beard, *The Rise of American Civilization*, 2:576.
74 Theodore Roosevelt, quoted in Pringle, *Theodore Roosevelt*, pp. 167, 172; Wells, *The Future in America*, pp. 341–2.
75 Theodore Roosevelt, *The Rough Riders* (New York: Putnam, 1900), p. 19.
76 Wister, *Roosevelt*, p. 149.
77 Hofstadter, *The American Political Tradition*, p. 208.
78 Poultney Bigelow, "Theodore Roosevelt, President and Sportsman," *Collier's* 2 (May 31, 1902), p. 10.
79 H. L. Mencken, *Prejudices: Second Series* (New York: Knopf, 1920), p. 134.
80 Theodore Roosevelt, quoted in Charles A. Beard and Mary R. Beard, *The American Spirit: A Study of the Idea of Civilization in the United States* (New York: Macmillan, n.d. [1942]), p. 595.
81 Theodore Roosevelt, quoted in Pringle, *Theodore Roosevelt*, p. 471.
82 Greene, *America's Heroes*, p. 162.
83 White, *Autobiography*, p. 299.
84 F. Scott Fitzgerald, *The Beautiful and the Damned* (New York: Scribner, 1950 [1922]), p. 89.
85 Henry Seidel Canby, *The Age of Confidence: Life in the Nineties* (New York: Farrar and Rinehart, 1934), pp. 29, 41, 44–5. Cf. the Irish-visaged Flip, the tough cigar-smoking kid who keeps muscling in on the elegant dreams of Little Nemo in Winsor McCay's classic comic strip *Little Nemo in Slumberland* (Winsor McCay, *Little Nemo*, 1905, 1906, introd. Woody Gelman, with review by Maurice Sendak (New York, Nostalgia Press, 1976)).

86 Joyce Cary, *A House of Children* (London: Michael Joseph, 1951), p. 134. On the New York gangs, and nineteenth-century New York violence in general, see Herbert Asbury, *The Gangs of New York: An Informal History of the Underworld* (New York: Blue Ribbon Books, 1939 [1928]).

87 William V. Shannon, *The American Irish*, rev. ed. (New York: Macmillan, 1966), p. 246.

88 Shannon, *The American Irish*, p. 144.

89 Shannon, *The American Irish*, p. 144.

90 Greene, *America's Heroes*, pp. 220–1.

91 Shannon, *The American Irish*, p. 393; Howe, *Confessions of a Reformer*, p. 12; Max Eastman, *Heroes I Have Known: Twelve Who Lived Great Lives* (New York: Simon and Schuster, 1942), pp. 69–70; T. S. Eliot, *The Waste Land: A Facsimile and Transcript of the Original Draft*, ed. Valerie Eliot (London: Faber and Faber, 1971), pp. 5, 175.

92 Mark Twain, *The Adventures of Huckleberry Finn (Tom Sawyer's Comrade)* (London: Zodiac Press, 1963), p. 109.

93 F. Scott Fitzgerald, *The Great Gatsby* (New York: Scribner, 1925), p. 2; Hubert Saal, *Newsweek* (October 24, 1977), p. 102.

94 Rafael Sabatini, *Scaramouche: A Romance of the French Revolution* (New York: Grosset and Dunlap, 1949 [1921]), p. 302.

95 Henry Roth, "On Being Blocked and Other Literary Matters: An Interview," *Commentary* (August 1977), p. 33.

96 Shannon, *The American Irish*, p. 393.

97 Shannon, *The American Irish*, p. 231.

98 Shannon, *The American Irish*, p. 36.

99 Frances Perkins, *The Roosevelt I Knew* (New York: Viking Press, 1946), p. 24.

100 Wells, *The Future in America*, pp. 176, 303.

101 Johnson, *Stover at Yale*, p. 240.

102 Johnson, *Stover at Yale*, p. 240.

103 Greene, *America's Heroes*, pp. 259, 264–5.

104 Howe, *Confessions of a Reformer*, pp. 127–8.

105 Brand Whitlock, *Forty Years of It*, introd. Albert J. Knock (New York: Appleton, 1914), p. 113.

106 *Louisville Courier-Journal*, quoted in Mark Twain, *The Letters of Mark Twain*, arr. with comment. Albert Bigelow Paine, The Stormfield Edition of the Writings of Mark Twain (New York: Harper, 1929), 2:703.

107 *McClure's* 20 (March 1903), p. 549.

108 C. C. Regier, *The Era of the Muckrakers* (Gloucester, Mass.: Peter Smith, 1957 [1932]), p. 9.

109 White, *Autobiography*, pp. 429–30; Howe, *Confessions of a Reformer*, p. 113.

110 Howe, *Confessions of a Reformer*, p. 128.

111 Whitlock, *Forty Years of It*, p. 173.

112 Robert Herrick, *A Life for a Life* (New York: Macmillan, 1910), p. 309.

113 Louis Filler, *Crusaders for American Liberalism* (New York: Harcourt Brace, 1939), p. 49; Regier, *The Era of the Muckrakers*, p. 49.

114 *Collier's* 32 (December 19, 1903), p. 4.

115 Churchill, *Mr. Crewe's Career*, p. 261.

116 Charles Dana Gibson, *The Gibson Girl and Her America: The Best Drawings of Charles Dana Gibson*, sel. Edmund Vincent Gillon, Jr., introd. Henry C. Pity (New York: Dover, 1969), p. 105.

117 Henry Demarest Lloyd, *Wealth Against Commonwealth* (New York: Harper, 1894), p. 509.
118 W. J. Cash, *The Mind of the South* (New York: Vintage Books, n.d. [1941]), p. 93.
119 Mencken, *Happy Days*, p. 214.
120 Howe, *Confessions of a Reformer*, p. 26.
121 William Miller, quoted in Jeffrey Richards, *Visions of Yesterday* (London: Routledge and Kegan Paul, 1977), p. 228.
122 White, *Autobiography*, p. 300.
123 Ida M. Tarbell, quoted in Greene, *America's Heroes*, p. 87.
124 Greene, *America's Heroes*, p. 225.
125 Finley Peter Dunne, *Mr. Dooley Remembers: The Informal Memoirs of Finley Peter Dunne* (Boston: Little, Brown, 1963), p. 218.
126 I. F. Stone, quoted in Leonard Downie, Jr., *The New Muckrakers* (New York: New American Library, 1978), p. 201. On the newer muckraking, see Downie and also Carey McWilliams, "The Continuing Tradition of Reform Journalism" in John M. Harrison and Harry H. Stein, eds., *Muckraking: Past, Present, and Future* (University Park: Pennsylvania State University Press, 1973), pp. 118–34.
127 One contribution to keeping alive the idea of the honorable investigator, and to the enthusiasm of the young in heart in the 1960s for the idea of the exposé, was the fictional celebration of heroic investigating in general. Not only did the devil-may-care, hard-drinking, poker-playing, wisecracking reporter figure in a plethora of works like Ben Hecht and Charles MacArthur's *The Front Page*. (A story in *Black Mask* in 1932 opened with the immortal words, "Francis St. Xavier Harrigan – star reporter, deadly gunman, from earlier occupation – lolled at his desk in the *Leader* office and slept dull care away" (Ed Lybeck, "Kick-Back," in Joseph T. Shaw, ed., *The Hard-Boiled Omnibus* (New York: Pocket Books, 1952), p. 251)). The unintimidatable district attorney or lawyer who smells a rat in a case and insists on uncovering it likewise became a stereotype, as did the honest cop. Other important continuities and substitutions occurred in thrillers. Numerous thrillers, whether political or not, have involved pitting individuals against the power structure of a corrupt city and defeating it – works like Dashiell Hammett's *Red Harvest*, Kenneth Millar's *Blue City*, John D. MacDonald's *The Brass Cupcake*, Robert Kyle's *Crooked City*, Ross Thomas's *The Fools in Town Are on Our Side*, and Raymond Chandler's *Farewell My Lovely*, in the last of which the hero makes his perilous way among dishonest cops, professional criminals, and the robber-baron rich. The continuities from investigative reporting are also apparent in the insouciantly risk-taking private eye in general, as distinct from private detectives like S.S. Van Dine's Philo Vance and Rex Stout's Nero Wolfe – men like Hammett's Continental Op and the Hammett-Bogart Sam Spade, the Philip Marlowe (initially Malory) of the half-Irish Chandler, the alcoholic and devil-may-care Bill Crane, Doc Williams, and Tom O'Malley of the Irish-Catholic Jonathan Latimer, the Ben Gates of the Ivy Leagueish Robert Kyle, the fighting-Irish Mike Shane of Brett Halliday, and John D. MacDonald's Travis McGee. For brief introductions to these and other crime-fiction heroes, see Chris Steinbrunner and Otto Penzler, eds., *Encyclopedia of Mystery and Detection* (New York: McGraw-Hill, 1976) and John M. Reilly, ed., *Twentieth-Century Crime and Mystery Writers* (New York: St. Martin's Press, 1980).

Notes to pp. 132–7

128 Theodore H. White, *In Search of History: A Personal Adventure* (New York: Harper and Row, 1978), pp. 524–5.
129 See, for instance, Midge Decter, "Kennedyism," *Commentary* (January 1970), pp. 19–27 and "Kennedyism Again," *Commentary* (December 1978), pp. 23–9; Henry Fairlie, *The Kennedy Promise: The Politics of Expectation* (London: Eyre Methuen, 1973); and Robert Nisbet, *Twilight of Authority* (New York: Oxford University Press, 1975), with its observations like "true White House Royalism...began with John Fitzgerald Kennedy ...And not only did the Kennedys love it, from all we read, but so did an admiring press and entire intellectual class in America" (p. 30).
130 Oscar Handlin, *The Americans: A New History of the People of the United States* (Boston: Little, Brown, 1963), p. 353.
131 Jacqueline Kennedy, quoted in Theodore H. White, *In Search of History*, p. 523 (ellipses sic).
132 Marshall Frady, "The Transformation of Bobby Kennedy," *New York Review of Books* (October 12, 1978), p. 43.
133 Jack Newfield, "The Hurt that Grows with Time," *Village Voice* (August 21, 1978), pp. 27–8.

CHAPTER 8. RADICALISM

1 James Jones, *From Here to Eternity* (New York: Scribner, 1951), p. 640; Vivian Gornick, *The Romance of American Communism* (New York: Basic Books, 1977), p. 180; John Reed, quoted in Mabel Dodge Luhan, *Movers and Shakers*, 4 vols.; *Intimate Memories* (New York: Harcourt, Brace [1936], 3:192.
2 Max Eastman, quoted in Milton Cantor, *Max Eastman* (New York: Twayne, 1970), p. 64. A plausible explanation of the name "Wobbly" is that it derived from the mispronunciation of the initials of the organization by the Chinese proprietor of a restaurant at which some of the members used to meet. "I.W.W." came out as "I Wobble Wobble," and the members characteristically picked up the new term and applied it to themselves.
3 Floyd Dell, *Love in Greenwich Village* (New York: Doran, 1926), p. 17. On Greenwich Village in those days, see, for example, Robert A. Rosenstone, *Romantic Revolutionary: A Biography of John Reed* (New York: Knopf, 1975) and Arthur Frank Wertheim, *The New York Little Renaissance: Iconoclasm, Modernism and Nationalism in American Culture, 1908–1917* (New York: New York University Press, 1976).
4 David Graham Phillips, *The Reign of Gilt* (New York: Pott, 1905), p. 278.
5 H. L. Mencken, *The Philosophy of Friedrich Nietzsche*, 3rd ed. (Fort Washington: Kennikat Press, 1967 [1908, 1913]), pp. 187, 110.
6 Ernest Hemingway, *For Whom the Bell Tolls* (New York: Scribner, 1940), p. 17.
7 W. B. Yeats, "Gods and Fighting Men" (1904), in *Explorations*, sel. Mrs. W. B. Yeats (London: Macmillan, 1962), pp. 20–1.
8 William L. O'Neill, ed. *Echoes of Revolt: The Masses, 1911–1917*, introd. Irving Howe, after. Max Eastman (Chicago: Quadrangle Books, 1966), p. 5.
9 Art Young, *On My Way: Being the Book of Art Young in Text and Pictures* (New York: Liveright, 1928), p. 279; Hutchins Hapgood, *A Victorian in the Modern World*, introd. Robert Allen Shotheim (Seattle: University of Washington Press, 1972 [1939]), p. 313; Max Eastman, *Enjoyment of Living* (New York: Harper,

1948), p. 174, and *Venture*, p. 5. Twain was of course a "shining figure" (Eastman's phrase) for others in this period. Mencken, for instance, called his discovery of *Huckleberry Finn* in 1889 "probably the most stupendous event of my whole life" (*Happy Days, 1880–1892* (New York: Knopf, 1940), p. 162); Whitlock, introduced to Twain by Howells, had "come away with feelings that were no less in intensity I am sure than those with which Moses came down out of Mount Horeb" (*Forty Years of It*, introd. Albert Jay Knock (New York: Appleton, 1914), p. 158; a liberated character in Sherwood Anderson's *Windy McPherson's Son*, introd. Wright Morris (Chicago: University of Chicago Press, 1965), a person "with something lazy and carefree in his every movement and impulse," called Twain "the greatest man in the world" (pp. 5, 52). As to Eastman's early stab at adventuring, the fact that, by his own account, it was partly the play acting of a mother's boy does not undercut the strength of the yearning to make himself over into something more interesting and admirable.

10 Floyd Dell, *Intellectual Vagabondage: An Apology for the Intelligentsia* (New York: Doran, 1926), pp. 180–1, 221, 231.

11 Floyd Dell, *Homecoming: An Autobiography* (New York: Farrar and Rinehart, 1933), pp. 102, 37, 63; Young, *On My Way*, p. 279.

12 Floyd Dell, *Love in Greenwich Village*, p. 27.

13 Max Eastman, *Venture* (New York: Boni, 1927), p. 1; John Reed, "Almost Thirty," *New Republic 86* (April 15, 1936), pp. 268–70. One of Reed's early publications was a pseudomedieval narrative poem in *Poetry*, and among his last works was an unpublished pseudomedieval prose piece "The Ever-Victorious."

14 Walter Lippmann, "Legendary John Reed," *New Republic* (December 26, 1914), p. 15.

15 Lippmann, "Legendary John Reed," p. 15.

16 Daniel Aaron, *Writers on the Left: Episodes in American Literary Communism* (New York: Harcourt, Brace and World, 1961), p. 213. Not surprisingly, Reed has figured in more than one novel and has been the subject of a couple of movies, one of them Mexican.

17 John Reed, quoted in Robert A. Rosenstone, *Romantic Revolutionary: A Biography of John Reed* (New York: Knopf, 1975), p. 124; James Thompson, quoted in Melvyn Dubofsky, *We Shall Be All: A History of the Industrial Workers of the World* (Chicago: Quadrangle Books, 1969), p. 160.

18 Of Haywood, Eastman later wrote that he was

a natural wonder in those days that one would travel miles to see. It is hard for today's reader to imagine what an infernal and awful, underprowling, hate-filled, satanic beast he was in the public mind. One really expected him to smell of sooty smoke and brimstone. He impressed me mainly on that first visit...by his simplicity. He had a Gibraltarlike bearing; he really had majesty as he moved slowly along, planting his feet deliberately, and surrounded by smaller and more jumpy beings. The big coal-black felt hat of the revolutionary agitator – where, I wonder, did that custom come from? – increased his vast size and enhanced his dignity. He had a voice like velvet, nearer the tenor than the bass (Eastman, *Enjoyment of Living* (New York: Harper, 1948), p. 448).

19 Elizabeth Gurley Flynn, *The Rebel Girl, an Autobiography: My First Life (1906–1926)* (New York: International Publishers, 1973), pp. 91–3.

20 Theodore Dreiser, quoted in Flynn, *The Rebel Girl*, p. 65; Mary Heaton Vorse, quoted on dustjacket of *The Rebel Girl*.
21 Benjamin Gitlow, *The Whole of Their Lives: Communism in America – A Personal History and Intimate Portrayal of Its Leaders*, fore. Max Eastman (New York: Scribner, 1948), p. 338.
22 Flynn, *The Rebel Girl*, pp. 88–9, 194.
23 John Dos Passos, *New Masses* (December 1931), p. 14. The episode was alluded to in the lynching of Joe Christmas in Faulkner's *Light in August* and, thus transposed and depoliticized, contributed to the hunting for Christ figures by literary critics in the Fifties.
24 On the Bisbee affair, see, for example, Dubofsky, *We Shall Be All*, and Robert Houston, "Sheriff Harry Rounds Up the Wobblies," *Mother Jones* 1 (December 1976), pp. 43-8.
25 John Graham Brooks, *American Syndicalism: The I.W.W.* (New York: Macmillan, 1913), pp. 92, 21.
26 Floyd Dell, "The Book of the Month," *Masses* (October 1917), p. 29; Nels Anderson, *The Hobo: The Sociology of the Homeless Man*, Phoenix Books (Chicago: University of Chicago Press, 1961 [1923]), pp. xvi–xvii. According to Aaron, the proto-Beat Kenneth Rexroth was a Wobbly in his youth (*Writers on the Left*, pp. 340–1); and Jack Kerouac's *On the Road* was a celebration of Wobbly mobility without Wobbly politics.
27 Eastman, *Venture*, p. 235.
28 Ben Reitman, quoted in Paul Frederick Brissenden, *The I.W.W.: A Study of American Syndicalism*, 2nd ed. (New York: Columbia University Press, 1920), p. 319.
29 Thomas McGrath, *Letters to an Imaginary Friend: Parts I and II* (Chicago: Swallow, 1970), p. 18.
30 Floyd Dell, in O'Neill, *Echoes of Revolt*, p. 18.
31 See, for example Fay M. Blake, *The Strike in the American Novel* (Metuchen, N.J.: Scarecrow Press, 1972). The documentary is *The Wobblies* (1979) by Stewart Bird and Deborah Shaffer.
32 Dell, *Intellectual Vagabondage*, pp. 144–5.
33 Owen Johnson, *The Prodigious Hickey* (New York: Baker and Taylor, 1910), pp. 285–7.
34 William Allen White, *The Autobiography of William Allen White* New York: Macmillan, 1946), p. 319.
35 Frederic C. Howe, *Confessions of a Reformer*, introd. John Braeman (Chicago: Quadrangle Books, 1967 [1925]), p. 8.
36 Henry Adams, *The Education of Henry Adams*, introd. James Truslow Adams (New York: Modern Library, 1931 [1906]), p. 33.
37 May E. Southworth, *Galahad, Knight Errant* (Boston: Gorham Press, 1907), p. 33.
38 William Ellery Channing, quoted in Gilbert Hobbs Barnes, *The Antislavery Impulse, 1830–1844*, new introd. William G. McLoughlin (New York: Harbinger Books, 1964), p. 3.
39 Grover Cleveland, "The Integrity of American Character," *Harper's* 112 (December 1905), p. 69.
40 Robert H. Wiebe, *The Search for Order: 1877–1920*, fore. David Donald (New York: Hill and Wang, 1967), p. 161. In 1914 Walter Lippmann remarked approvingly of the establishment of graduate schools of business administration that "it is obvious that the trusts have created a demand for a new

type of business man – for a man whose motives resemble those of the applied scientist and whose responsibility is that of a public servant" (*Drift and Mastery: An Attempt to Diagnose the Current Unrest* (New York: Holt, 1917 [1914]), p. 63.

41 Wilson, "Galahad," in *Galahad: I Thought of Daisy* (New York: Farrar, Straus and Giroux, 1967), p. 4. In the *National Lampoon*'s splendid parody-pastiche history of the comics one reads how an imaginary strip devoted to a representative White Knight, "Rick Slade, Health Inspector #715," refined upon its artist's "previous attempts to create an unsung urban hero, an incorruptible professional do-gooder, starting with 'Speed Jamison, Building Inspector,' 'Jim Johnson, Housing Project Security Guard,' and 'Day Care Center,' a kind of Grand Hotel treatment of a child care center, with dramatic conflicts between the staff, the parents and the children" (*The Very Large Book of Comical Funnies* (Spring 1976), p. 22).

42 John Erskine, *Galahad: Enough of His Life to Explain His Reputation* (Toronto: McClelland and Stewart, 1926), p. 253.

43 F. Scott Fitzgerald, *This Side of Paradise*, in *The Bodley Head Fitzgerald*, 6 vols., rev. ed. (London: The Bodley Head, 1965), 3:36; *The Beautiful and the Damned* (New York: Scribner, 1950 [1922]), p. 74.

44 Lippmann, *Drift and Mastery*, pp. 320–1. It was Lippmann himself, however, who in the same work made pronouncements such as, "The intelligent men of my generation have the vast opportunity of introducing order and purpose into the business world, of devising administrative methods by which the great resources of the country can be operated on some thought-out plan. They have the whole new field of industrial statesmanship before them" (p. 141).

45 Michael Novak, *The Rise of the Unmeltable Ethnics: Politics and Culture in the Seventies* (New York: Macmillan, 1972), p. 102.

46 *California Weekly*, quoted in George F. Mowry, *The Era of Theodore Roosevelt and the Birth of Modern America, 1900–1912*, introd. Henry Steele Commager and Richard Braden Morris (New York: Harper and Row, 1962), p. 103.

47 George Kibbe Turner, in Arthur Weinberg and Lila Weinberg, eds., *The Muckrakers: The Era in Journalism that Moved America to Reform – The Most Significant Magazine Articles of 1902–1912* (New York: Simon and Schuster, 1961), pp. 393–4.

48 Unidentified Progressive quoted in Oscar Handlin, *The Uprooted: The Epic Story of the Great Migrations that Made the American People* (Boston: Little, Brown, 1951), p. 219.

49 Theodore Roosevelt, quoted in Charles A. Beard and Mary R. Beard, *The Rise of American Civilization*, 2 vols. (New York: Macmillan, 1927), 2:400; Edwin Lawrence Godkin, *Problems of Modern Democracy: Political and Economic Essays*, ed. and introd. Morton Keller (Cambridge, Mass.: The Belknap Press of Harvard University Press, 1963 [1896]), p. 130.

50 Mark Twain, *A Connecticut Yankee in King Arthur's Court*, introd. Albert Bigelow Paine, Stormfield Edition of the Writings of Mark Twain (New York: Harper, 1929), p. 427.

51 Howe, *Confessions of a Reformer*, pp. 113–14; *Collier's* 38 (December 22, 1906), p. 16.

52 Wiebe, *The Search for Order*, p. 170.

53 Paul Leicester Ford, *The Honorable Peter Stirling; and What People Thought of Him* (New York: Hillary House, 1957 [1894]), p. 279.

54 Handlin, *The Uprooted*, pp. 282–3.
55 Joseph Dinneen, quoted in William V. Shannon, *The American Irish*, rev. ed. (New York: Macmillan, 1966), p. 200.
56 W. C. Doane, quoted in Andrew Carnegie, *The Gospel of Wealth; and Other Timely Essays*, ed. Edward G. Kirkland (Cambridge, Mass.: Belknap Press of Harvard University Press, 1962), p. 155.
57 Brand Whitlock, *Forty Years of It*, introd. Albert J. Knock (New York: Appleton, 1914), p. 298.
58 Handlin, *The Uprooted*, p. 278; Fitzgerald, *The Beautiful and the Damned*, p. 268.
59 Handlin, *The Uprooted*, p. 248.
60 Lionel Trilling, introd. Robert Warshow, *The Immediate Experience: Movies, Comics, Theatre and Other Aspects of Popular Culture*, introd. Lionel Trilling (New York: Atheneum, 1972), p. 16. On the dominativeness possible in "progressive" education, see also Richard Hofstadter, *Anti-Intellectualism in American Life* (New York: Knopf, 1963), and Christopher Lasch, "Politics as Social Control," in *The New Radicalism in America (1889–1963): The Intellectual as a Social Type* (New York: Knopf, 1965), pp. 141–80.
61 Peter Cohen, *The Gospel According to the Harvard Business School* (Garden City, N.Y.: Doubleday, 1973), p. 30.
62 Max Weber, *From Max Weber: Essays in Sociology*, trans., ed., and introd. H. H. Gerth and C. Wright Mills (New York: Oxford University Press, 1958), p. 226.
63 Whitlock, *Forty Years of It*, p. 266.
64 Dell, *Intellectual Vagabondage*, pp. 146–7. In 1917 John Dos Passos, just out of Harvard, wrote: "All the thrust and advance and courage in the country now lies in the East Side Jews and in a few of the isolated 'foreigners' whose opinions so shock the New York Times. They're so much more real and alive than we are anyway – I'd like to annihilate these stupid colleges of ours, and all the nice young men, therein, instillers of stodginess – every form of bastard culture, middle class snobbism" (quoted in Aaron, *Writers on the Left*, p. 346). On the appeal of the East Side for young intellectuals, see also Henry F. May, *The End of American Innocence: A Study of the First Years of Our Own Time, 1912–1917* (London: Jonathan Cape, 1959), pp. 282–3.
65 Oscar Handlin, *The Americans: A New History of the People of the United States* (Boston: Little, Brown, 1963), p. 279.
66 William Z. Foster, *Pages from a Worker's Life* (New York: International Publishers, 1939), p. 174.
67 William D. Haywood, *Bill Haywood's Book: The Autobiography of William D. Haywood* (New York: International Publishers, 1929), p. 255.
68 Ralph Chaplin, *Wobbly: The Rough-and-Tumble Story of an American Radical* (Chicago: University of Chicago Press, 1948), p. 176.
69 Elizabeth Gurley Flynn, in Joyce L. Kornbluh, ed., *Rebel Voices: An I.W.W. Anthology* (Ann Arbor: University of Michigan Press, 1965), p. 220.
70 John Graham Brooks, *American Syndicalism: The I.W.W.* (New York: Macmillan, 1913), p. 113.
71 Frederick Douglass, quoted in Philip P. Hallie, *The Paradox of Cruelty* (Middletown, Conn.: Wesleyan University Press, 1969), p. 154.
72 In 1906 Finley Peter Dunne's Mr. Dooley remarked, apropos of the sudden fashionableness of Socialism, "'Twas diff'rent in the goolden days. A gr-rand chance a Socialist had thin. If annybody undherstood him he was kilt be unfuryated wurrukinmen. It was a good thing f'r him that he on'y

spoke German" ("Mr. Dooley Discusses Socialism," *Collier's* 37 (June 2, 1906), p. 17). As late as 1920, however, Dell was commenting that "we only slowly come to learn that what we sometimes contemptuously call 'American' is not American at all; that it is, astonishingly enough, we who are Americans: that Debs and Haywood are as American as Franklin and Lincoln" (quoted in Aaron, *Writers on the Left*, p. 57).

73 Ray Stannard Baker, "Railroads and Popular Unrest," *Collier's* 37 (June 9, 1906), p. 19.

74 Louis Adamic, *Dynamite: The Story of Class Violence in America*, rev. ed. (Gloucester, Mass.: Peter Smith, 1963 [1934]), p. 135.

75 Eastman, *Venture*, p. 349.

76 Cash, *The Mind of the South*, pp. 41, 35.

77 Whitlock, *Forty Years of It*, p. 156.

78 Edwin Harrison Cady, *The Gentleman in America: A Literary Study in American Culture* (New York: Syracuse University Press, 1949), p. 122.

79 Samuel Eliot Morison and Henry Steele Commager, *The Growth of the American Republic*, 2 vols., 4th ed. (New York: Oxford University Press, 1950), 2:76.

80 Edmund Burke, "Speech on Moving His Resolutions for Conciliation with the Colonies" (1775), *Selected Writings and Speeches*, ed. Peter J. Stanlis (Gloucester, Mass.: Peter Smith, 1968), pp. 160–1.

81 Thomas Jefferson, *The Life and Selected Writings of Thomas Jefferson*, ed. and introd. Adrienne Koch and William Peden (New York: Modern Library, 1944), p. 436.

82 Arthur M. Schlesinger, Jr., *The Age of Jackson* (Boston: Little, Brown, 1946), pp. 38, 36.

83 James Fenimore Cooper, quoted in Cady, *The Gentleman in America*, p. 122. For a brilliant analysis of relationships between aristocracy, democracy, and the spirit of liberty, see Bertrand de Jouvenel, *Power: The Natural History of Its Growth*, 2nd rev. ed., trans. J. F. Huntington, pref. D. W. Brogan (London: Hutchinson, 1947), Chapter 17.

84 Eugene V. Debs, quoted in Irving H. Bartlett, *Wendell Phillips: Brahmin Radical* (Boston: Beacon Press, 1961), p. 400; Thomas Wentworth Higginson, quoted in Bartlett, p. 108.

85 Wendell Phillips, in Louis Ruchames, ed., *The Abolitionists: A Collection of Their Writings* (New York: Putnam, 1963), p. 236.

86 Wendell Phillips, quoted in Richard Hofstadter, *The American Political Tradition and the Men Who Made It* (New York: Knopf, 1957), p. 160.

87 Bartlett, *Wendell Phillips*, p. 400.

88 Henry Demarest Lloyd, quoted in Bartlett, *Wendell Phillips*, p. 401.

89 John Reed, quoted in Aaron, *Writers on the Left*, p. 21.

90 Tom Quelch, quoted in Aaron, *Writers on the Left*, p. 20.

91 Eastman, *Venture*, p. 253. In *Sabotage* (1915) Elizabeth Gurley Flynn had written:

> If you place yourself in a position outside of the working class and you presume to dictate to them from some "superior" intellectual plane, what they are to do, they will very soon get rid of you, for you will very soon demonstrate that you are of absolutely no use to them. I believe the mission of the intelligent propagandist is this: we are to see what the workers are doing, and then try to understand why they do it; not tell them its [sic] right or its wrong, but analyze the condition and see if they

do not best understand their need and if, out of the condition, there may not develop a theory that will be of general utility. (*Sabotage: The Conscious Withdrawal of the Workers' Industrial Efficiency* (Cleveland: I.W.W. Publishing Bureau, n.d.), pp. 24–5.)

92 Sir Walter Scott, "An Essay on Chivalry" (1818), *Essays on Chivalry, Romance, and the Drama* (Freeport, N.Y.: Books for Libraries Press, 1972 [1834]), p. 10.
93 *Masses* (November 1916), pp. 12–13.
94 Cash, *The Mind of the South*, p. 43; Adamic, *Dynamite*, pp. 16–17; Novak, *The Rise of the Unmeltable Ethnics*, p. 253.
95 Brissenden, *The I.W.W.*, p. 293.
96 John P. Marquand, *The Late George Apley: A Novel in the Form of a Memoir* (New York: Modern Library, 1940), p. 60.
97 Charles Grandison Finney, quoted in Barnes, *The Antislavery Impulse*, p. 11.
98 Eastman, *Venture*, p. 226.
99 Fred Thompson, quoted in Dubofsky, *We Shall Be All*, p. 25.
100 Flynn, *The Rebel Girl*, pp. 95–6.
101 Dell, *Love in Greenwich Village*, p. 162.

CHAPTER 9. VIOLENCE AND PEACE (I)

1 Edmund Boisgilbert [Ignatius Donnelly], *Caesar's Column: A Story of the Twentieth Century* (Toronto: William Bryce, 1890), pp. 150–1; Mary Heaton Vorse, *A Footnote to Folly: Reminiscences of Mary Heaton Vorse* (New York: Farrar and Rinehart, 1935), p. 322; Woody Guthrie, "My Dirty Overalls."
2 Inazo Nitobe, *Bushido, the Soul of Japan: An Exposition of Japanese Thought*, rev. and enl. ed., introd. William Elliot Griffis (Portland, Vt.: Tuttle, 1969 [1900]), p. 163.
3 *Masses* (August 1915), pp. 12–13.
4 George Vanderveer, quoted in William D. Haywood, *Bill Haywood's Book: The Autobiography of William D. Haywood* (New York: International Publishers, 1929), p. 314.
5 Max Eastman, *Venture* (New York: Boni, 1927), p. 180.
6 William D. Haywood, in Joyce L. Kornbluh, ed., *Rebel Voices: An I.W.W. Anthology* (Ann Arbor: University of Michigan Press, 1965), p. 51.
7 *Nation* (May 22, 1913), p. 515.
8 Frederick Townsend Martin, *The Passing of the Idle Rich* (Garden City, N.Y.: Doubleday, Page, 1911), p. 156.
9 Anon., "The Merits of the Homestead Trouble," *Nation* (July 14, 1892), p. 22.
10 H. L. Mencken, *The Philosophy of Friedrich Nietzsche*, 3rd ed. (Fort Washington: Kennikat Press, 1967 [1908, 1913]), p. 196.
11 Mark Twain, *A Connecticut Yankee in King Arthur's Court*, introd. Albert Bigelow Paine, Stormfield Edition of the Writings of Mark Twain (New York: Harper, 1929), p. 105.
12 Owen Johnson, *Stover at Yale* (New York: Stokes, 1912), p. 151.
13 Donnelly, *Caesar's Column*, pp. 300–1.
14 "After the Battle," *Survey* (1912), quoted in Paul Frederick Brissenden, *The I.W.W.: A Study of American Syndicalism*, 2nd ed. (New York: Columbia University Press, 1920), p. 295.
15 Thorstein Veblen, *The Vested Interests and the Common Man* (New York: Viking Press, 1933 [1919]), pp. 181–2.

16 Quoted in Theodore Draper, *The Roots of American Communism* (New York: Viking Press, 1957), p. 46.
17 William James, "The Moral Equivalent of War," in *The Writings of William James: A Comprehensive Edition*, ed. and introd. John J. McDermott (New York: Modern Library, 1968), pp. 668–9.
18 W. J. Ghent, *Our Benevolent Feudalism* (New York: Macmillan, 1902), p. 29.
19 William Hard, "Making Steel and Killing Men" (1907), in Arthur Weinberg and Lila Weinberg, eds., *The Muckrakers: The Era in Journalism that Moved America to Reform – The Most Significant Magazine Articles of 1902–1912* (New York: Simon and Schuster, 1961), p. 351.
20 Charles A. and Mary R. Beard, *The Rise of American Civilization*, 2 vols. (New York: Macmillan, 1927), 2:177.
21 James Bryce, *The American Commonwealth*, 2 vols. (London: Macmillan, 1891), 2:530.
22 Ghent, *Our Benevolent Feudalism*, p. 100.
23 Hard, "Making Steel and Killing Men," p. 343.
24 "Tom Mann's Address to the Soldiers for Which He Was Imprisoned," *Masses* (January 1913), p. 3.
25 Hard, "Making Steel and Killing Men," in Weinberg and Weinberg, *The Muckrakers*, p. 355.
26 Robert Herrick, *A Life for a Life* (New York: Macmillan, 1910), p. 140.
27 Kornbluh, *Rebel Voices*, p. 62. For the flavor of Taylorism itself, see Frederick Winslow Taylor, *Scientific Management: Comprising Shop Management, The Principles of Scientific Management, Testimony before the Special House Committee*, fore. Harlow S. Person (Westport, Conn.: Greenwood Press, 1972 [1947]).
28 Frederic C. Howe, *The Confessions of a Reformer*, introd. John Braeman (Chicago: Quadrangle Books, 1967 [1925]), pp. 154–5.
29 Gustavus Myers, *History of the Great American Fortunes* (New York: Modern Library, 1936 [1910]), p. 164.
30 Frank Tannenbaum, in William L. O'Neill, ed. *Echoes of Revolt: The Masses, 1911–1917*, introd. Irving Howe, after. Max Eastman (Chicago: Quadrangle Books, 1966), p. 212. See also the statement in *A Connecticut Yankee* apropos the French Revolution:

> There were two "Reigns of Terror," if we would but remember it and consider it; the one wrought murder in hot passion, the other in heartless cold blood; the one lasted mere months, the other had lasted a thousand years; the one inflicted death upon ten thousand persons, the other upon a hundred millions; but our shudders are all for the "horrors" of the minor Terror, the momentary Terror, so to speak; whereas, what is the horror of swift death by the ax compared with lifelong death from hunger, cold, insult, cruelty, and heartbreak? (p. 105).

Twain himself had looked sympathetically on the Knights of Labor.
31 George F. Vanderveer, *Opening Statement of Geo. F. Vanderveer, Counsel for the Defense of One Hundred and One Members of the Industrial Workers of the World in the Case of the U.S.A. vs. Wm. D. Haywood et al* (Chicago: I.W.W. Publishing Bureau, 1918), p. 92.
32 John Reed, quoted in Richard O'Connor and Dale L. Walker, *The Lost Revolutionary: A Biography of John Reed* (New York: Harcourt, Brace and World, 1967), p. 78.
33 Maurice Becker, *Masses* (June 1915), p. 15.

34 Art Young (illustration), *Masses* (February 1913), p. 20.
35 John Sloan (illustration), *Masses* (June 1914), cover.
36 Louis Adamic, *Dynamite: The Story of Class Violence in America*, rev. ed. (Gloucester, Mass.: Peter Smith, 1963 [1934]), pp. 125–6.
37 Flynn, *The Rebel Girl*, pp. 23, 45.
38 Dubofsky, *We Shall Be All*, p. 161.
39 Vanderveer, *Opening Statement*, p. 7.
40 Elizabeth Gurley Flynn, *The Rebel Girl, an Autobiography: My First Life 1906–1926* (New York: International Publishers, 1973), p. 163; Joseph Robert Conlin, *Bread and Roses Too: Studies of the Wobblies*, fore. David A. Shannon (Westport, Conn.: Greenwood Press, 1969).
41 Vorse, *A Footnote to Folly*, p. 6.
42 Elizabeth Gurley Flynn, quoted in Kornbluh, *Rebel Voices*, p. 217–18.
43 Vorse, *A Footnote to Folly*, p. 6.
44 Eastman, *Venture*, p. 259.
45 Vanderveer, *Opening Statement*, p. 78.
46 Hutchins Hapgood, quoted in Mabel Dodge Luhan, *Movers and Shakers*, 4 vols.; *Intimate Memories* (New York: Harcourt, Brace [1936]), 3:203.
47 Elizabeth Gurley Flynn, *13 Communists Speak to the Court: Elizabeth Gurley Flynn and Others* (New York: New Century Publishers [1953]), p. 12.
48 Max Eastman, "Knowledge and Revolution," *Masses* (December 1912), p. 5.
49 Philip P. Hallie, *The Paradox of Cruelty* (Middletown, Conn.: Wesleyan University Press, 1969), pp. 159, 17.
50 Edwin Denig, quoted in Colin Taylor, *The Warriors of the Plains* (London: Hamlyn, 1975), p. 23. In *The Story of the Indian*, George Bird Grinnell reported that:
> In minor matters which pertained to the ordinary affairs of the everyday life of the people, [the chief] acted independently and his orders were obeyed, but grave concerns, such as quarrels between prominent men, relations with neighbouring tribes, the making of war or peace, were discussed in a council of chiefs and prominent men, where each individual was at liberty to express his opinion and to cast his vote. The head chief acted as the presiding officer of such a council, and if he was a strong man his views carried great weight; but unless he could win over to his side a majority of the council he had to yield (Grinnell, *The Story of the Indian*, pref. note by Ripley Hitchcock (New York: Appleton, 1896), pp. 246–7).
51 Finley Peter Dunne, *Mr. Dooley Remembers: The Informal Memoirs of Finley Peter Dunne* (Boston: Little, Brown, 1963), p. 63.
52 Hutchins Hapgood, *A Victorian in the Modern World*, introd. Robert Allen Shotheim (Seattle: University of Washington Press, 1972 [1939]), p. 291.
53 Carnegie, *Autobiography*, p. 10.
54 Adamic, *Dynamite*, p. 261.
55 Bruce Catton, *Never Call Retreat*, The Centennial History of the Civil War, 3 vols. (Garden City, N.Y.: Doubleday, 1965), 3:279.
56 H. G. Wells, *The Future in America: A Search after Realities* (London: Chapman and Hall, 1906), p. 315.
57 In his *History of the Great American Fortunes*, Gustavus Myers remarks how the cattlemen of the Southwest, "in their economic wars with adjacent cattlemen, forced their cowboys to fight and kill the cowboys of their

neighbors and risk being killed themselves; nearly all of those cowboy affrays so romantically described in fiction, arose from nothing more or less than economic disputes between competing rival master cattlemen" (p. 571). The big Western "wars" – e.g., in Lincoln County, New Mexico (1875–81), Pleasant Valley, Arizona (in the late 1880s), and Johnson County, Wyoming (in the early 1890s) – were essentially replications of the larger wars of industry, with a related displacement of blame to the innate unruliness and pugnacity of the work force.

58 Thomas Carlyle, *On Heroes, Hero-Worship, and the Heroic in History: Six Lectures, Reprinted, with Emendations and Additions*, 2nd ed. (London: Chapman and Hall, 1842), p. 237.

59 Vorse, *A Footnote to Folly*, pp. 13–14.

60 Hapgood, *A Victorian in the Modern World*, p. 351.

61 Flynn, *The Rebel Girl*, p. 168.

62 Elizabeth Gurley Flynn, in Kornbluh, *Rebel Voices*, pp. 219–20.

63 Charles Mills, *The History of Chivalry: Or Knighthood and Its Times*, 2 vols. (Philadelphia: Carey and Lea, 1826), 2:136.

64 Beard and Beard, *The Rise of American Civilization*, 2:518. On the kinds of "discipline" to which the Mexican peons were submitted, see John Kenneth Turner's horrifying *Barbarous Mexico*, 4th ed. (Chicago: Kerr, 1914 [1910]).

65 John Reed, *Insurgent Mexico*, pref. Renata Leduc (New York: International Publishers, 1969 [1914]), pp. 118, 144.

66 John Reed, quoted in Robert A. Rosenstone, *Romantic Revolutionary: A Biography of John Reed* (New York: Knopf, 1975), p. 279.

67 John Reed, *Ten Days that Shook the World*, introd. V. I. Lenin (New York: International Publishers, 1919), pp. 197, 200, 183, 230, 310, xii.

CHAPTER 10. VIOLENCE AND PEACE (II)

1 A. Mitchell Palmer, quoted in Robert K. Murray, *Red Scare: A Study in National Hysteria, 1919–1920* (Minneapolis: University of Minnesota Press, 1955), p. 219; Senator Albert J. Beveridge, quoted in Editors of Time-Life Books, *1900–1910*, vol. 1 of *This Fabulous Century* (New York: Time, 1969), p. 30; Max Eastman, in William L. O'Neill, ed., *Echoes of Revolt: The Masses, 1911–1917*, introd. Irving Howe, after. Max Eastman (Chicago: Quadrangle Books, 1966), p. 157.

2 William James, "The Moral Equivalent of War," *The Writings of William James: A Comprehensive Edition*, ed. and introd. John J. McDermott (New York: Modern Library, 1968), pp. 668, 667, 664, 668.

3 *Collier's*, quoted in Theodore P. Greene, *America's Heroes: The Changing Models of Success in American Magazines* (New York: Oxford University Press, 1970), p. 304; F. Scott Fitzgerald, *The Beautiful and the Damned* (New York: Scribner, 1950 [1922]), p. 307.

4 William D. Haywood, *Bill Haywood's Book: The Autobiography of William D. Haywood* (New York: International Publishers, 1929), p. 294.

5 Maurice Becker, *Masses* (January 1917), in O'Neill, *Echoes of Revolt*, p. 197; Cornelia Barns, *Masses* (December 1914), p. 21. The *Masses*, the most visually erotic of serious American journals prior to the Sixties, was vigorously and good-humoredly profeminist. John Sloan's cartoon sequence "The Real Adam and Eve," for example, portrays a huge benign Eve holding a tiny, capering Adam by the hand and bending down a tree branch

so that he can reach the apple: caption, "He Won't Be Happy 'Til He Gets It' " (March 1913, p. 9).

6 Randolph Bourne, "The War and the Intellectuals," *Seven Arts* (June 1917), p. 138. As Robert E. Nisbet comments in *The Twilight of Authority*, "To this day I think few people, even American historians, have an adequate conception of what took place in the intellectual class, and between the intellectual class and the American public, from 1917 to about 1920. With but the rarest of exceptions, *trahison des clercs* was the rule of the day" (New York: Oxford University Press, 1975), p. 179.
7 William James, "What Makes a Life Significant," *Writings*, pp. 646–7.
8 Joseph Freeman, *An American Testament: A Narrative of Rebels and Romantics* (New York: Farrar and Rinehart, 1936), p. 127.
9 Alexis de Tocqueville, *Democracy in America*, ed. J. P. Mayer, trans. George Lawrence (Garden City, N.Y.: Doubleday Anchor Books, 1969), pp. 91, 680. On the drive toward leveling and domination, see Bertrand de Jouvenel's *Power: The Natural History of Its Growth*, 2nd rev. ed., trans. J. F. Huntington, pref. D. W. Brogan (London: Hutchinson, 1947) and Nisbet's *The Twilight of Authority*, particularly Chapter 4, "The New Science of Despotism."
10 Amos Pinchot, quoted in O'Neill, *Echoes of Revolt*, p. 281.
11 Oswald Garrison Villard, *Fighting Years: Memoirs of a Liberal Editor* (New York: Harcourt Brace, 1939), p. 294.
12 Samuel Eliot Morison and Henry Steele Commager, quoted in Leon Wolff, *Lockout: The Story of the Homestead Strike of 1892: A Study of Violence, Unionism, and the Carnegie Steel Empire* (New York: Harper and Row, 1965), p. 4.
13 Michael Novak, *The Rise of the Unmeltable Ethnics: Politics and Culture in the Seventies* (New York: Macmillan, 1972), p. 254.
14 Max Eastman, quoted in O'Neill, *Echoes of Revolt*, p. 150.
15 Haywood, *Bill Haywood's Book*, p. 166.
16 John P. Marquand, *The Late George Apley: A Novel in the Form of a Memoir* (New York: Modern Library, 1940), p. 149.
17 George S. McGovern and Leonard F. Guttridge, *The Great Coalfield War* (Boston: Houghton Mifflin, 1972), p. 272.
18 Henry Clews, quoted in Samuel Eliot Morison and Henry Steele Commager, *The Growth of the American Republic*, 2 vols., 4th ed., rev. and enl. (New York: Oxford University Press, 1950), 2:142–53; Henry Ward Beecher, quoted in Matthew Josephson, *The Robber Barons: The Great American Capitalists: 1861–1901* (New York: Harcourt, Brace, 1934), pp. 364–5.
19 Andrew Carnegie, quoted in Jonathan Hughes, *The Vital Few: American Economic Progress and Its Protagonists* (Boston: Houghton Mifflin, 1966), p. 246.
20 At the time of the Homestead strike the *Nation* reiterated the fundamental social principle that "every human being is entitled to pursue happiness in his own way, subject only to such limitations as experience has shown to be indispensable to the maintenance of this right for all. This is the spirit which breathes in our Declaration of Independence, this is the principle which is formulated and applied in our Bill of Rights and in our Constitution" ("Warring Protectionists at Homestead," *Nation* (July 21, 1892), p. 41). It also reminded its readers that

    riotous workmen...have no right to exercise any compulsion in obtaining from their employers such remuneration for their labor as they desire, or in preventing other workmen from taking their places....Trade unions are laudable institutions in so far as they assist their members in obtaining the fair market value of their labor, but they become mischievous when they are employed in depriving capitalists of the use of their property, or in depriving workmen who are outside of the unions of their inalienable right to support themselves by laboring for whoever wishes to hire them (p. 41).

21 Andrew Carnegie, *Autobioraphy of Andrew Carnegie*, ed. John C. Van Dyke (Boston: Houghton Mifflin, 1924), p. 16.
22 *Nation* (May 13, 1886), pp. 391–2.
23 Robert H. Wiebe, *The Search for Order: 1877–1920*, fore. David Donald (New York: Hill and Wang, 1967), p. 278.
24 George Kibbe Turner, in Arthur Weinberg and Lila Weinberg, eds., *The Muckrakers: The Era in Journalism that Moved America to Reform – The Most Significant Magazine Articles of 1902–1912* (New York: Simon and Schuster, 1961), p. 390.
25 Morison and Commager, *The Growth of the American Republic*, 2:359.
26 Theodore Roosevelt, quoted in Putnam, *Theodore Roosevelt*, p. 292.
27 Harold Frederic, quoted in George F. Mowry, *The Era of Theodore Roosevelt and the Birth of Modern America, 1900–1912*, introd. Henry Steele Commager and Richard Braden Morris (New York: Harper and Row, 1962), p. 101.
28 *Outlook*, quoted in Mowry, *The Era of Theodore Roosevelt*, p. 100; Andrew Carnegie, *The Gospel of Wealth; and other Timely Essays*, ed. Edward G. Kirkland (Cambridge, Mass.: Belknap Press of Harvard University Press, 1962), p. 94.
29 Herbert Croly, *The Promise of American Life*, ed. and introd. Arthur M. Schlesinger, Jr. (Cambridge, Mass.: Belknap Press of Harvard University Press, 1965 [1909]), p. 128.
30 John Hinchcliffe, "The Reign of Terror in Paterson," *Collier's* 29 (July 5, 1902), p. 24.
31 Unidentified employer, quoted in John Graham Brooks, *American Syndicalism: The I.W.W.* (New York: Macmillan, 1913), p. 13.
32 Haywood, *Bill Haywood's Book*, p. 166.
33 John H. Craige, "The Professional Strike-Breaker," *Collier's* 46 (December 3, 1910), p. 32.
34 Ernest Hemingway, *Death in the Afternoon* (New York: Scribner, 1932), p. 187.
35 H. G. Wells, *The Future in America: A Search after Realities* (London: Chapman and Hall, 1906), pp. 247, 245.
36 Robert W. Tucker, *The Just War: A Study in Contemporary American Doctrine* (Baltimore: Johns Hopkins Press, 1960), p. 82.
37 Theodore Roosevelt, quoted in Mowry, *The Era of Theodore Roosevelt*, p. 144.
38 Edward House, quoted in Robert Quirk, *An Affair of Honor: Woodrow Wilson and the Occupation of Vera Cruz* (New York: Norton, 1967), p. 77.
39 Andrew Carnegie, *Triumphant Democracy; or Fifty Years' March of the Republic* (New York: Scribner, 1886), p. 384.
40 Haywood, *Bill Haywood's Book*, p. 337.
41 W. David Lewis, *From Newgate to Dannemora: The Rise of the Penitentiary in New York, 1796–1848* (Ithaca: Cornell University Press, 1965), pp. 69, 91.
42 Oswald Garrison Villard remarks of the period of the Palmer Raids, 1919–20, that "much has occurred under Adolf Hitler which could be paralleled by official misconduct in this country during this period. One could [almost] believe that the dictators were patterning after us" (*Fighting Years*, p. 465). Faced with such things as the Auburn horrors, the genocide

in the Philippines, the violence against Wobblies during the West Coast free-speech fights, the cattle cars of Bisbee, and "the authenticated cases of torture, sadism, and crime, committed by agents of the Department of Justice" during the Palmer Raids, which according to Villard "would take several chapters to recite" (p. 465), it is difficult to resist the impression that borrowings and adaptations indeed occurred.

43 On the American prison system in general, see the superb *Kind and Usual Punishment: The Prison Business* (New York: Knopf, 1973) by the muckraking radical daughter of Lord Redesdale, Jessica Mitford.

44 Woodrow Wilson, in Quirk, *An Affair of Honor*, p. 75.

45 Amos Pinchot, quoted in O'Neill, *Echoes of Revolt*, p. 279.

46 Tucker, *The Just War*, p. 82.

47 William T. Sherman, quoted in Bruce Catton, *Never Call Retreat*, The Centennial History of the Civil War, 3 vols. (Garden City, N.Y.: Doubleday, 1965), 3:370; William Tecumseh Sherman, *Home Letters of General Sherman*, ed. M. A. De Wolfe Howe (New York: Scribner, 1909), pp. 341–2. What makes Sherman the most interesting, or at least the most complex, general of the Civil War is, of course, the coexistence in him of two radically different attitudes to warfare – the chivalric and the peace-action one. See B. H. Liddell Hart, *Sherman: The Genius of the Civil War* (London: Ernest Benn, 1930), pp. 2, 3–18, 438–43.

48 William T. Sherman, quoted in Ralph K. Andrist, *The Long March: The Last Days of the Plains Indians* (New York: Macmillan, 1964), p. 124, 154.

49 Leon Wolff, *Little Brown Brother: America's Forgotten Bid for Empire which Cost 250,000 Lives* (London: Longmans, 1961); Villard, *Fighting Years*, p. 483.

50 In *The American Character* (New York: Alfred A. Knopf, 1950 [1944]), D. W. Brogan admirably defines a certain kind of intense American resentment of having to become involved in warfare at all.

51 Mark Twain, *A Connecticut Yankee in King Arthur's Court*, introd. Albert Bigelow Paine, Stormfield Edition of the Writings of Mark Twain (New York: Harper, 1929), pp. 428, 435, 430, 432.

52 Novak, *The Rise of the Unmeltable Ethnics*, p. 48.

53 Hutchins Hapgood, *A Victorian in the Modern World*, introd. Robert Allen Shotheim (Seattle: University of Washington Press, 1972 [1939]), p. 206.

54 Walter Lippmann, *Drift and Mastery: An Attempt to Diagnose the Current Unrest* (New York: Holt, 1917 [1914]), pp. 90, 86.

55 James, "The Moral Equivalent of War," *Writings*, p. 663.

56 Henry F. May, *The End of American Innocence: A Study of the First Years of Our Own Time, 1912–1917* (London: Jonathan Cape, 1959), p. 231.

57 Hutchins Hapgood, *The Spirit of Labor* (New York: Duffield, 1907), p. 45.

58 Lincoln Steffens, quoted in Christopher Lasch, *The New Radicalism in America (1889–1963): The Intellectual as a Social Type* (New York: Knopf, 1965), p. 154.

59 Louis Adamic, *Dynamite: The Story of Class Violence in America*, rev. ed. (Gloucester, Mass.: Peter Smith, 1963 [1934]), pp. 367–8.

60 Floyd Dell, *Homecoming: An Autobiography* (New York: Farrar and Rinehart, 1933), p. 63.

61 Johan Huizinga, *Homo Ludens: A Study of the Play-Element in Culture* (Boston: Beacon Press, 1955 [1944]), p. 10.

62 Mike Gold (b.1894), who said later that the *Masses* "became my guide and teacher, as it was to a whole generation of youth," and remembered of Reed that "thousands of American workers and young people worshipped that

279

tall, swaggering westerner, with his big, luminous green eyes, his broad shoulders and capacity for love, poetry and adventure," had followed Reed in spending time in Mexico, and Freeman recalled that in the early Twenties Gold "affected dirty shirts, a big, black, uncleaned Stetson with the brim of a sombrero; smoked stinking, twisted, Italian three-cent cigars, and spat frequently and vigorously on the floor.... These 'proletarian' props were as much a costume as the bohemian's sideburns and opera cape." By his own account Gold, during his process of self-education before coming upon the *Masses*, "also devoured the romantic junk found in the public libraries – everything and anything" (Michael Gold, "The Masses Tradition," *Masses and Mainstream* 4 (August 1951), pp. 46, 52, 46; Freeman, *American Testament*, p. 257). For Freeman himself (b. 1897), who had immigrated at the age of seven, Reed's life, together with that of the "Texas giant" Robert Minor, seemed "a model for middle-class intellectuals who went over to the proletariat." In his account of his own growing up, he describes how, after a boyhood in which "Happy Hooligan and Buster Brown marched across [my imagination] with Jean Valjean and d'Artagnan," and one of his friends was "that wonderful American thing I was trying to understand, a good sport," and Philip Sidney was a literary hero ("combining action with poetry") he went on to Columbia, where students did papers on "*Il Cortegiano*, Sir Philip Sidney's sonnets and the chivalrous characteristics of men," and where on one occasion he "wrote about Don Quixote not as a comic figure but as a rebel dashing himself against the unjust world, a Spanish Shelley with lance instead of lyre." At Columbia "four streams of my life converged... literature, echoes of adolescent Zionism, American radical thought and memories of wobbly romance" (pp. 301–3, 57, 21, 374, 85, 119, 104).

63 Michael Gold, quoted in Daniel Aaron, *Writers on the Left: Episodes in American Literary Communism* (New York: Harcourt, Brace and World, 1961), p. 99; Gold, "La Fiesta: a Comedy of the Mexican Revolution in Three Acts," Manuscript in Library of Congress, ca. 1925.

64 Joseph Conrad, *The Secret Agent*, Collected Edition of the Works of Joseph Conrad (London: Dent, 1947), p. 97.

65 Charles A. Beard and Mary R. Beard, *The Rise of American Civilization*, 2 vols. (New York: Macmillan, 1927), 2:640. It was Wilson who allowed his Attorney General to run riot against "subversives"; Wilson during whose presidency conscientious objectors were tortured; Wilson whose government imprisoned the ailing Eugene Debs for opposing the war and who refused to pardon him at the end of it; Wilson of whom Floyd Dell reports that, "fantastically enough, we had private advices from people who talked with [him] that he was grimly determined to have The Masses editors sent to prison" (*Homecoming*, p. 326), with the result that they were tried for a second time after the first prosecution of them for sedition failed. Of Wilson, Mr. Clean himself, Nisbet remarks that "his hatred of those who opposed him in however small a degree was religious in intensity." He also comments that "I believe it no exaggeration to say that the West's first real experience with totalitarianism – political absolutism extended into every possible area of culture and society, education, religion, industry, the arts, local community and family included, with a kind of terror always waiting in the wings – came

with the American war state under Woodrow Wilson" (*The Twilight of Authority* (New York: Oxford University Press, 1975), p. 183).
66 Freeman, *An American Testament*, p. 304.
67 Malcolm Cowley, quoted in Aaron, *Writers on the Left*, p. 343.
68 Stanley Kaufmann, *New Republic* (February 12, 1977), p. 18.
69 Foster, *Pages from a Worker's Life*, pp. 313.
70 Freeman, *An American Testament*, pp. 293–4.
71 Aaron, *Writers on the Left*, p. 63.
72 It seems plain from Robert A. Rosenstone's account in *Romantic Revolutionary: A Biography of John Reed* (New York: Knopf, 1975) of Reed's career from 1917 until his death in 1920, including his part in founding the breakaway Communist Labor party of America and his fights on behalf of democratic procedures at the Second Congress of the Communist International, that had he lived he would increasingly have opposed the authoritarianism of Moscow Communism, like the Wobblies and his maverick boyhood mentor Colonel Charles Erskine Scott Wood (on whom see, in this connection, Aaron, *Writers on the Left*, pp. 394–5). As Arthur Koestler says, "the rebel always has a touch of the Quixotic; the revolutionary is a bureaucrat of Utopia" (quoted in Aaron, *Writers on the Left*, p. 218). In that sense, Reed was a natural rebel.
73 John Steinbeck, *A Life in Letters*, ed. Elaine Steinbeck and Robert Wallstein (New York: Viking Press, 1975), p. 540; John Steinbeck, *The Acts of King Arthur and His Noble Knights: From the Winchester MSS. of Thomas Malory and Other Sources*, ed. Chase Horton (New York: Farrar, Straus and Giroux, 1976), p.xii.
74 Octavio Paz, *The Labyrinth of Solitude: Life and Thought in Mexico*, trans. Lysander Kemp (New York: Grove Press, 1961), pp. 142–4.
75 Ernest Hemingway, *For Whom the Bell Tolls* (New York: Scribner, 1940), p. 235.
76 Walker Percy, *Lancelot* (New York: Farrar, Straus and Giroux, 1977), p. 178.
77 Bertolt Brecht, *Leben des Galilei*, sc. 13, Gesammelte Werke, in 20 Bänden, Stücke 3 (Frankfurt am Main: Suhrkamp Verlag, 1968), p. 1329.
78 Ralph Chaplin, *Wobbly: The Rough-and-Tumble Story of an American Radical* (Chicago: University of Chicago Press, 1948), p. 342.
79 Max Eastman, quoted in Aaron, *Writers on the Left*, p. 16.
80 Melvyn Dubofsky, *We Shall Be All: A History of the Industrial Workers of the World* (Chicago: Quadrangle Books, 1969), p. 186.
81 Joseph North, *Robert Minor, Artist and Crusader: An Informal Biography* (New York: International Publishers, 1956), pp. 152–3.
82 Max Eastman, quoted in Edmund Wilson, *To the Finland Station: A Study in the Writing and Acting of History* (Garden City, N.Y.: Doubleday Anchor Books, 1953 [1940]), pp. 454–5.

CHAPTER 11. HONOR

1 D. W. Griffith, title in *Orphans of the Storm* (1921); Gustavus Myers, *History of the Great American Fortunes* (New York: Modern Library, 1936), p. 147; William Z. Foster, *Pages from a Worker's Life* (New York: International Publishers, 1939), p. 211.
2 Damon Runyon, quoted in *Time* (February 26, 1979), p. 17.
3 Johan Huizinga, *Homo Ludens: A Study of the Play-Element in Culture* (Boston: Beacon Press, 1955 [1944]), pp. 78–81.

4 J. D. Salinger, *The Catcher in the Rye* (New York: New American Library, 1953), p. 12. For a recent unenchanted view of preppies by an ex-preppie, see Nelson W. Aldrich, Jr., "Preppies: The Last Upper Class?" *Harper's* (January 1979), pp. 56–60. It is nicely complemented by Al Laney's appreciative, illustrated *Prep Schools: Profiles of More than Fifty American Schools* (Garden City, N.Y.: Doubleday, 1961).

5 John McPartland, *The Face of Evil* (New York: Gold Medal Books, 1954), p. 33.

6 Lillian Hellmann, quoted in Murray Kempton, "Witnesses," *New York Review of Books* (June 10, 1967), p. 22.

7 Walker Percy, *Lancelot* (New York: Farrar, Straus and Giroux, 1977), p. 157; Dean Acheson, quoted in Merle Miller, *Plain Speaking: An Oral Biography of Harry S. Truman* (New York: Berkley, 1974), p. 239.

8 Percy, *Lancelot*, p. 213; William Faulkner, *The Unvanquished* (New York: Random House, 1934), p.111.

9 William Shakespeare, *The First Part of King Henry the Fourth*, IV, i, 130–140, ed. George Lyman Kittredge (Boston: Ginn, 1940), p. 88.

10 Ernest Hemingway, *The Green Hills of Africa* (London: Jonathan Cape, 1934), p. 271. The overstrain resulting from a quasimystical absolutism whereby one is either wholly honorable or else is utterly destitute of honor – an absolutism that destroyed Othello, for example – apparently skewed the West Point honor system. According to K. Bruce Galloway and Robert Bowie Johnson, Jr., it "tolerates no mistakes, no matter how small. In the realm of West Point ethics, one is not allowed to learn from error. An error is a mortal sin." As they point out, "the absolute nature of the system makes it difficult for graduates to differentiate between insignificant moral problems and those of great moment" (*West Point: America's Power Fraternity*, fore. Anthony B. Herbert (New York: Simon and Schuster, 1973).

11 Ernest Hemingway, *Death in the Afternoon* (New York: Scribner,1932), p. 258.

12 Vivian Gornick, *The Romance of American Communism* (New York: Basic Books, 1977).

13 Michael Gold, "The Girl by the River," *New Masses* 1 (August 1926), p. 20.

14 Dean Acheson, quoted in Miller, *Plain Speaking*, p. 383.

15 Thomas L. Haskell, "Power to the Experts," *New York Review of Books* (October 13, 1977), pp. 31–2.

16 Michael Novak, *Choosing Our King: Powerful Symbols in American Politics* (New York: Macmillan, 1974), pp. 211–12.

17 Haskell, "Power to the Experts," p. 28.

18 Oliver Wendell Holmes, *The Mind and Faith of Justice Holmes: His Speeches, Essays, Letters, and Judicial Opinions*, sel., ed., and introd., Max Lerner (Boston: Little, Brown, 1943), p. 33.

19 Henry Seidel Canby, *The Age of Confidence: Life in the Nineties* (New York: Farrar and Rinehart, 1934), p. 196.

20 Huizinga, *Homo Ludens*, p. 63.

21 Jean de Bueil, as summarized by Raymond Lincoln Kilgour, *The Decline of Chivalry as Shown in the French Literature of the Late Middle Ages* (Cambridge, Mass.: Harvard University Press, 1937), p. 331.

22 Canby, *The Age of Confidence*, pp. 40, 20–1.

23 Robert Nisbet remarks that "in Burke's day...the idea of a [political] dishonor too great to be borne was a familiar one; resignation was what was expected of any public servant whose honor had been tarnished, in whatever

degree, by his own acts or by those of his trusted aides" (*The Twilight of Authority* (New York: Oxford University Press, 1975), p. 50). In accepting the rules of the game and the fall of the dice and assenting to such a punishment as right and proper, a man of honor could retain moral control over his destiny and remain honorable.

24 William James, "The Moral Equivalent of War," in *The Writings of William James: A Comprehensive Edition*, ed. and introd. John J. McDermott (New York: Modern Library, 1968), p. 670.

25 Winston Churchill, *Mr. Crewe's Career* (New York: Macmillan, 1908), pp. 477–8.

26 Theodore P. Greene, *America's Heroes: The Changing Models of Success in American Magazines* (New York: Oxford University Press, 1970), p. 324.

27 Gore Vidal, *Matters of Fact and Fiction: Essays 1973–1976* (New York: Random House, 1977), p. 278.

28 Owen Johnson, *Stover at Yale* (New York: Stokes, 1912), pp. 238–9.

29 Edward A. Ross, quoted in Greene, *America's Heroes*, pp. 255–6.

30 Greene, *America's Heroes*, p. 256.

31 F. Scott Fitzgerald, *The Beautiful and the Damned* (New York: Scribner, 1950 [1922]), p. 285.

32 Theodore Roosevelt, quoted in Charles A. Beard and Mary R. Beard, *The Rise of American Civilization*, 2 vols. (New York: Macmillan, 1927), 2:426.

33 Finley Peter Dunne, quoted in *The American Heritage History*, p. 289.

34 Mother Jones, quoted in George S. McGovern and Leonard F. Guttridge, *The Great Coalfield War* (Boston: Houghton Mifflin, 1972), p. 101.

35 James Truslow Adams, *The Epic of America* (Boston: Little, Brown, 1932), p. 346.

36 White, *A Certain Rich Man*, p. 326.

37 Churchill, *Mr. Crewe's Career*, pp. 376–7.

38 Frederic C. Howe, *Confessions of a Reformer*, introd. John Braeman (Chicago: Quadrangle Books, 1967 [1925]), p. 150.

39 John Kenneth Galbraith, "The Refined and the Crude," *New York Review of Books* (February 3, 1977), p. 6.

40 William Allen White, *A Certain Rich Man* (New York: Macmillan, 1909), pp. 326–7.

41 Greene, *America's Heroes*, pp. 276, 262.

42 Finley Peter Dunne, *Mr. Dooley Remembers: The Informal Memoirs of Finley Peter Dunne* (Boston: Little, Brown, 1963), p. 181.

43 Samuel M. Jones, *The New Right: A Plea for Fair Play through a More Just Social Order*, introd. N. O. Nelson (New York: Eastern Book Concern, 1899), p. 60.

44 Theodore Roosevelt, quoted in Charles A. Beard and Mary R. Beard, *The Rise of American Civilization*, 2 vols. (New York: Macmillan, 1927), 2:423.

45 Ida M. Tarbell, *The History of the Standard Oil Company*, 2 vols. (New York: Macmillan, 1925 [1904]), 2:292.

46 Chambers, "Americans at Play," p. 13.

47 Samuel E. Moffett, "Why Mr. Rockefeller is Disliked," *Collier's* 35 (May 6, 1905), p. 15.

48 Howe, *Confessions of a Reformer*, p. 170.

49 Richard M. Weaver, *The Southern Tradition at Bay: A History of Postbellum Thought*, ed. George Core and M. E. Bradford, pref. Donald Davidson (New Rochelle: Arlington House, 1968), pp. 67–8.

50 Cornelia Philips Spencer, *The Last Ninety Days of the War in North Carolina* (New York: Watchman, 1866), p. 70.
51 Owen Johnson, *The Sixty-First Second* (New York: Stokes, 1913), p. 270.
52 Charles Sumner, *Recent Speeches and Addresses* (Boston: Higgins and Bradley, 1856), p. 419.
53 Thomas W. Lawson, in Arthur Weinberg and Lila Weinberg, eds., *The Muckrakers: The Era in Journalism that Moved America to Reform – the Most Significant Magazine Articles of 1902–1912* (New York: Simon and Schuster, 1961), p. 287; Phillips, in Weinberg and Weinberg, p. 75.
54 Max Eastman, in William L. O'Neill, ed., *Echoes of Revolt: The Masses, 1911–1917*, introd. Irving Howe, after. Max Eastman (Chicago: Quadrangle Books, 1966), p. 155.
55 Oscar Handlin, *The Americans: A New History of the People of the United States* (Boston: Little, Brown, 1963), p. 277.
56 Ida M. Tarbell, "Commercial Machiavellianism," *McClure's* 26 (March 1906), p. 459.
57 Sumner, *Recent Speeches*, p. 448.
58 In *The Knight of the Grip: Being a Series of Dissertations on His Conditions, Character and Conduct as They Appear to an Ordinary Chap Who Has Studied Him* (New York: David Williams [1900]), Thomas Joseph Carey celebrated "the modern knight errant," the traveling salesman, with such comments as, "The essence of gentlemanliness lies not in the manner, but in the activating spirit behind it, and I have found in these exponents of everyday manliness a considerateness and a fine courtesy that are indices of the innate breeding that marks the highest type of American manhood" (p. 163). The articles composing the book had appeared in the principal journal of the iron and steel industry, the *Iron Age*. In one of the issues containing them, Andrew Carnegie was reproved in an editorial for having been "more than any man the type of the untiring, incalculable exponent of unrestrained competition which the younger generation of business men and manufacturers may admire but do not care to imitate" ("Andrew Carnegie's Retirement" (May 11, 1899), p. 16).
59 Sumner, *Recent Speeches*, pp. 419–20.
60 "Going to Work; Dedicated to the Employers of Children," in Charles Dana Gibson, *The Gibson Girl and Her America: The Best Drawings of Charles Dana Gibson*, sel. Edmund Vincent Gillon, Jr., introd. Henry C. Pity (New York: Dover, 1969), p. 126.
61 Beard and Beard, *The Rise of American Civilization*, 2:386.
62 Henry Demarest Lloyd, *Wealth Against Commonwealth* (New York: Harper, 1894), pp. 427, 474.
63 Moffett, "Why Mr. Rockefeller is Disliked," p. 15.
64 *Collier's* 30 (March 14, 1903), p. 4.
65 Charles Francis Adams, quoted in Beard and Beard, *The Rise of American Civilization*, 2:203.
66 White, *A Certain Rich Man*, p. 285.
67 Inez Haynes Gilmore, in O'Neill, *Echoes of Revolt*, p. 163.
68 H. G. Wells, *The Future in America: A Search After Realities* (London: Chapman and Hall, 1906), p. 247; A. Smith, quoted in William V. Shannon, *The American Irish*, rev. ed. (New York: Macmillan, 1966), p. 163. In 1906 Tarbell wrote: "It is not only cruelty which is necessary in modern businesses. It is lying. Follow the testimony in the great insurance investi-

gations of the past fall and compare it with the investigations of other years, and perjury sticks out at every corner, perjury so obvious in many cases that it is laughable. Follow the testimony of the leader of the great oil trust – that of many railroad men. When it is necessary they lie" ("Commercial Machiavellianism," p. 458).

69 Jacques de Mailles, *The Right Joyous and Pleasant History of the Feats, Gests, and Prowesses of the Chevalier Bayard, the Good Knight without Fear and without Reproach*, 2 vols. (London: John Murray, 1825 [1525]), 2:234–5.

70 Curtis Brown Watson, *Shakespeare and the Renaissance Concept of Honor* (Princeton: Princeton University Press, 1966), p. 97.

71 Francis J. Grund, *Aristocracy in America: From the Sketch-Book of a German Nobleman*, introd. George E. Probst (Gloucester, Mass.: Peter Smith, 1968 [1839]).

72 Friedrich Nietzsche, *Beyond Good and Evil*, trans. and introd. Marianne Cowan (Chicago: Regnery, 1955), p. 203.

73 Dunne, *Mr. Dooley Remembers*, p. 198; Theodore Roosevelt, in Weinberg and Weinberg, *The Muckrakers*, p. 60.

74 Owen Johnson, *The Varmint: A Lawrenceville Story* (Boston: Little, Brown, 1922 [1910]), p. 252.

75 Watson, *Shakespeare and the Renaissance Concept of Honor*, p. 135.

76 John S. Mosby, quoted in Edmund Wilson, *Patriotic Gore: Studies in the Literature of the American Civil War* (New York: Oxford University Press, 1962), p. 311. The subject of chivalric "realism" is interestingly explored by three of the best American thriller writers – Dashiell Hammett, Ross Thomas, and above all Donald Hamilton, whose intelligent and impressive oeuvre includes spy fiction, crime fiction, and Westerns, and whose interest in the subject, and in American adaptations of chivalric values in general, presumably partly stems from his first-hand acquaintance with aristocratic attitudes. See also the estimable thrillers of British writers like Simon Harvester and Geoffrey Household.

77 Burt L. Standish [Gilbert Patten], *Frank Merriwell at Yale* (Philadelphia: McKay, 1903 [1897]), p. 198.

78 Mark Twain, *The Adventures of Huckleberry Finn (Tom Sawyer's Comrade)* (London: Zodiac Press, 1963), p. 181.

79 A melancholy irony about the flagrant Army lying during the Vietnam War was how alien to the martial ethos it really was. This dishonorable unprofessionalism in fact formed part of a larger pattern, namely the increasing bureaucratization of the military and the attempt to turn quality back into quantity. The military, especially in the Pentagon, had become more and more permeated by the attitudes of business corporations – the desire for organizational growth, for financial increase, for ever more sophisticated and prestigious equipment. The disingenuousness and flattery that made it easier to rise inside a bureaucratized system were reinforced by the civilian demand for a cost-free win that would not necessitate "sacrificing" American lives and that could be achieved through smashing the enemy by technological might. These attitudes led to the pressure on the fighting Army for quantification – for body counts, for progress charts, for reassuring statistics about the amount of ammunition discharged at the enemy – and to the related necessity to cover up failures and crimes in the interests of good public-relations images. Hence an army captain could recall that "we did not have a single major fire-fight that

month, and we had a legitimate body-count of three, but I was told to report 50, and I did." Hence another one could recall that "General – – – amassed an unsurpassed record of body count and it was based on lies. And everybody in the unit knew it" (quoted in Galloway and Johnson, *West Point*, pp. 100–1). The West Point feeling that what counted primarily was loyalty to one's fellow officers and the "team" was strengthened by the more hysterical polemics of the antiwar movement, in which what was conveyed was not that this particular war was unnecessary, mismanaged, and in its larger aspects immoral, but that war itself was immoral and that it was unnecessary for Americans to be involved in wars at all. It was natural to close ranks against civilians in the face of the implication that being a soldier at all was discreditable.

80 Newton D. Baker, quoted in Galloway and Johnson, *West Point*, p. 101.
81 Harry S. Truman, quoted in Miller, *Plain Speaking*, p. 373.
82 White, *A Certain Rich Man*, p. 379.
83 E. Nesbit, *The Phoenix and the Carpet* (Harmondsworth, Middlesex: Penguin Books, 1959 [1904]), p. 13.
84 W. Gilmore Simms, *The Life of the Chevalier Bayard: The Good Knight, Sans peur et sans reproche* (New York: Harper, 1847), p. 147.
85 Dean Acheson, quoted in Miller, *Plain Speaking*, p. 386.
86 Huizinga, *Homo Ludens*, p. 11.
87 Johnson, *The Varmint*, p. 386.
88 Patten, *Frank Merriwell at Yale*, p. 194.
89 Ralph Waldo Emerson, quoted in Edwin Harrison Cady, *The Gentleman in America: A Literary Study in American Culture* (New York: Syracuse University Press, 1949), p. 163.
90 Grund, *Aristocracy in America*, p. 291.
91 Ruth Kelso, *The Doctrine of the English Gentleman in the Sixteenth Century* (Gloucester, Mass.: Peter Smith, 1964 [1929]), p. 104.
92 Hutchins Hapgood, *A Victorian in the Modern World*, introd. Robert Allen Shotheim (Seattle: University of Washington Press, 1972 [1939]), p. 301.
93 J. F. C. Fuller, *Grant and Lee: A Study in Personality and Generalship* (London: Eyre and Spottiswoode, 1933), p. 244.
94 Napoleon, quoted in Fuller, *Grant and Lee*, p. 282.
95 Mailles, *The Right Joyous and Pleasant History*, 2:202, 224.
96 Colonel Grenfell, quoted in Fuller, *Grant and Lee*, p. 121.
97 William Tecumseh Sherman, *Home Letters of General Sherman*, ed. M. A. DeWolfe Howe (New York: Scribner, 1909), p. 321.
98 Joyce Cary, *A House of Children* (London: Michael Joseph, 1951), p. 170.
99 Thomas Jefferson, *The Life and Selected Writings of Thomas Jefferson*, ed. and introd. Adrienne Koch and William Peden (New York: Modern Library, 1944), p. 373.
100 John William De Forest, *Miss Ravenel's Conversion from Secession to Loyalty*, ed. and introd. Gordon S. Haight (New York: Rinehart, 1955 [1867]), p. 149.
101 Wilson, *Patriotic Gore*, p. 312; John S. Mosby, *Mosby's War Reminiscencs and Stuart's Cavalry Campaigns* (New York: Dodd, Mead, 1887), pp. 80–1.
102 Plainclothes American honorableness was also displayed later by Harry Truman. In conventional romantic terms, he was, of course, all "wrong": He looked wrong, he dressed wrong, his origins were wrong; he had been, like Grant, whom he admired, an unsuccessful small businessman; he had been associated with a political machine; he had an unpicturesque wife

whom he deferred to as The Boss. But he was as ready as Grant to act firmly regardless of public opinion, and employed limited force successfully in Berlin and Korea, and was unafraid of the large adversary, whether Stalin, Douglas MacArthur, the Republican Party in the quintessential underdog campaign, or American big business. Of the latter, he remarked in Congress in 1937 that "no one ever considers the Carnegie libraries steeped in the blood of the Homestead steel workers, but they are. We do not remember that the Rockefeller Foundation is founded on the dead miners of the Colorado Fuel Company and a dozen other performances" (quoted in Miller, *Plain Speaking*, p. 152). He was loyal to associates, whether the members of Battery D or the Virginian gentleman George Marshall and the New England gentleman Dean Acheson, both of whom reciprocated his esteem and the latter of whom dedicated his political memoirs to him as "the Captain with the mighty heart." He was unconcerned with acquiring personal wealth, did not lust after personal power, and used the trappings of the presidency with great restraint. He felt strongly for the underdog, and had an old-fashioned reverence for women. When he affirmed and acted on the principle that "The buck stops here," the integrity that enabled him to do so and to be one of the great American presidents was a complex one that derived in part from his unusually extensive reading, especially in history. According to Acheson, Lee was "his hero" (Dean Acheson, *Present at the Creation: My Years in the State Department* (New York: Norton, 1969), p. 730).

103 Herbert Croly, *The Promise of American Life*, ed. and introd. Arthur M. Schlesinger, Jr. (Cambridge, Mass.: Belknap Press of Harvard University Press, 1965 [1909]), p. 89.

104 It is presumably relevant here that Lincoln's parents were Virginians.

105 In an excellent article, Robert Conquest says of Lee: "He challenges flatly and unanswerably certain personal and public standards which have come to be accepted (or talked about as if they were accepted) in the last few years. He was a 'gentleman' in every sense, including those now most reprobated – and yet no amateur but a supreme professional expert. He was heroically combative, fighting past the point of desperation with brilliant aggressiveness – and yet he was never bitter and always considerate. Above all, he was a man of power and command totally without personal ambition – democracy's answer to the conventional 'great man.' " ("Robert E. Lee: A Morality for Moderns?" *Encounter* 44 (June 1975), p. 49.)

106 George Bernard Shaw, *Man and Superman: A Comedy and a Philosophy* (Harmondsworth, Middlesex: Penguin Books, 1975), p. 73.

CHAPTER 12. INTELLECT

1 Walter Hines Page, *The Southerner: A Novel; Being the Autobiography of Nicholas Worth* (New York: Doubleday, Page, 1909), p. 57; Thomas Carlyle, *On Heroes, Hero-Worship, and the Heroic in History: Six Lectures, Reprinted, with Emendations and Additions*, 2nd ed. (London: Chapman and Hall, 1842), p. 237; Leon Wolff, *Little Brown Brother: America's Forgotten Bid for Empire which Cost 250,000 Lives* (London: Longmans, 1961), pp. 305–6.

2 Holmes, *The Mind and Faith of Justice Holmes: His Speeches, Essays, Letters, and Judicial Opinions*, sel., ed., and introd. Max Lerner (Boston: Little, Brown, 1943), p. 33.

3 Holmes, *The Mind and Faith of Justice Holmes*, p. 31; William James, "The Moral Equivalent of War," in *The Writings of William James: A Comprehensive Edition*, ed. and introd. John J. McDermott (New York: Modern Library, 1968), p. 669; David Graham Phillips, *The Reign of Gilt* (New York: Pott, 1905), p. 102.

4 Albion W. Tourgée, *A Fool's Errand*, ed. John Hope Franklin (Cambridge, Mass,: Belknap Press of Harvard University Press, 1961), p. 381.

5 John William De Forest, *Miss Ravenel's Conversion from Secession to Loyalty*, ed. and introd. Gordon S. Haight (New York: Rinehart, 1955 [1867]), p. 3.

6 Edward A. Pollard, *The Lost Cause: A New Southern History of the War of the Confederates* (New York: Treat, 1866), p. 750.

7 Lawrence Lowell, quoted in Gary Wills, *Nixon Agonistes: The Crisis of the Self-Made Man* (Boston: Houghton Mifflin, 1970), pp. 335–6.

8 Charles Drekmeier, "Knowledge as Virtue, Knowledge as Power," in Nevitt Sanford, Craig Comstock, et al., eds., *Sanctions for Evil: Sources of Social Destructiveness* (Boston: Beacon Press, 1971), p. 231.

9 Joseph Conrad, *Under Western Eyes*, The Works of Joseph Conrad (Edinburgh and London: John Grant, 1925), p. 279.

10 Johan Huizinga, *The Waning of the Middle Ages: A Study of the Forms of Life, Thought and Art in France and the Netherlands in the XIVth and XVth Centuries* (Garden City, N.Y.: Doubleday Anchor Books, 1959 [1924]), pp. 66–7.

11 Huizinga, *The Waning of the Middle Ages*, p. 39.

12 Holmes, *The Mind and Faith of Justice Holmes*, p. 39.

13 Oliver Wendell Holmes, quoted in Merle Miller, *Plain Speaking: An Oral Biography of Harry S. Truman* (New York: Berkley, 1974), p. 373.

14 Thomas Mann, quoted in Alastair Hamilton, *The Appeal of Fascism: A Study of Intellectuals and Fascism* (London: Anthony Blond, 1971), p. 96.

15 It is worth noting here that shortly after his marriage in the Eighties, Veblen had translated the *Laxdaela Saga*, described by two recent translators as "essentially a romantic work; romantic in style, romantic in taste, romantic in theme, culminating in that most enduring and timeless of human relationships in story-telling, the love-triangle" (*Laxdaela Saga*, trans. and introd. Magnus Magnusson and Hermann Palsson (Harmondsworth, Middlesex: Penguin Books, 1969), p. 9).

16 Jerome Ravetz reported in 1971 that "some scientific communities maintain their independence and integrity by astonishingly direct means. In Japan, physicists who associate themselves with the Japan Defense Agency are ostracized by the Japanese Physical Society, not being permitted to present papers at its conferences" (*Scientific Knowledge and Its Social Problems* (Oxford: Clarendon Press, 1971), p. 421).

17 Interestingly, the figure of Yvor Winters, who displayed a fiercer integrity and a prouder sense of the dignity of letters than any other American critic, has been largely ignored by American academic admirers of the heroic in art because of his "ill–mannered" disrespect for magic shields. It was Winters, too, who got into trouble at his own university in the early 1930s for his successful efforts on behalf of an innocent man condemned to death in part because of "expert" testimony by members of the prestigious Stanford medical school. He wrote of the trial that it displayed
   The villainy of pride in scholarship,
   The villainy of cold impartial hate,
   The brutal quiet of the lying lip,

The brutal power, judicial and sedate,...
Outrage and anarchy in formal mien.
("To a Woman on Her Defense of Her Brother Unjustly Convicted of Murder.")

18 Johan Huizinga, *Homo Ludens: A Study of the Play-Element in Culture* (Boston: Beacon Press, 1955 [1944]), pp. 155–6.
19 Unamuno, quoted in Erich Fromm, *The Anatomy of Human Destructiveness* (New York: Holt, Rinehart and Winston, 1973), p. 331.
20 Ruth Kelso, *The Doctrine of the English Gentleman in the Sixteenth Century* (Gloucester, Mass.: Peter Smith, 1964 [1929]), p. 96.
21 James, "The Moral Equivalent of War," *Writings*, p. 667.
22 Ramón Lull, *The Book of the Ordre of Chyvalrie*, trans. and printed by William Caxton from a French version of Ramón Lull's "Le Libre del Orde de Cauayleria," ed. Alfred T. P. Byles, Early English Text Society, no. 168 (London: Humphrey Milford, Oxford University Press, 1926), p. 77; Jacques de Mailles, *The Right Joyous and Pleasant History of the Feats, Gests, and Prowesses of the Chevalier Bayard, the Good Knight without Fear and without Reproach*, 2 vols. (London: John Murray, 1825 [1525]), 2:237.
23 Walter Lippmann, *Drift and Mastery: An Attempt to Diagnose the Current Unrest* (New York: Holt, 1917 [1914], p. 185.
24 Oliver Wendell Holmes, quoted in Edmund Wilson, *Patriotic Gore: Studies in the Literature of the American Civil War* (New York: Oxford University Press, 1962), p. 747.
25 Joseph Freeman, *An American Testament: A Narrative of Rebels and Romantics* (New York: Farrar and Rinehart, 1936), p. 106.
26 Holmes, *The Mind and Faith of Justice Holmes*, pp. 115–16, 155.
27 Thomas W. Lawson, in Arthur Weinberg and Lila Weinberg, eds., *The Muckrakers: The Era in Journalism that Moved America to Reform – the Most Significant Magazine Articles of 1902–1912* (New York: Simon and Schuster, 1961), p. 277.
28 Hugh Henry Brackenridge, *Modern Chivalry*, ed. and introd. Claude M. Newlin (New York: Hafner, 1962), p. 365.
29 Huizinga, *Homo Ludens*, p. 84.
30 Huizinga, *Homo Ludens*, p. 77.
31 John Lukacs, *The Passing of the Modern Age* (New York: Harper and Row, 1970), p. 166.
32 Elias Schwartzkopf, Canadian Broadcasting Corporation program, July 17, 1977.
33 Gore Vidal, *Matters of Fact and Fiction: Essays 1973–76* (New York: Random House, 1977), p. 282.
34 Theodore P. Greene, *America's Heroes: The Changing Models of Success in American Magazines* (New York: Oxford University Press, 1970), p. 321.
35 Theodore Roosevelt, quoted in Greene's *America's Heroes*, pp. 258–9.
36 Holmes, *The Mind and Faith of Justice Holmes*, p. 20.
37 James, "The Moral Philosopher and the Moral Life," *Writings*, p. 627.
38 Pierre-Joseph Proudhon, *Selected Writings of Pierre-Joseph Proudhon*, ed. and introd. Stewart Edwards, trans. Elizabeth Fraser (London: Macmillan, 1970), p. 210.
39 D. H. Lawrence, "Hymns in a Man's Life," *Phoenix II: Uncollected, Unpublished and Other Prose Works by D. H. Lawrence*, coll., ed., and introd. Warren Roberts and Harry T. Moore (London: Heinemann, 1968), pp. 600–1.

40 Proudhon, *Selected Writings*, p. 205. All this can hold true, of course, of the valiant pacifist, as distinct from the sort of person who identifies peace with quiet and believes that bringing about peace is simply a matter of finding the right psychological buttons to push. According to Rollo May, an American Quaker reviewing Franz Fanon's *The Wretched of the Earth* suggested that in fact the term "nonviolence" could be substituted throughout it for the word "violence." As May points out, "Fanon is talking of human dignity, the birth and growth of conscience, integrity of relationships" (Rollo May, *Power and Innocence: A Search for the Sources of Violence* (New York: Norton, 1972), p. 193).

41 Max Lerner, introd. Holmes, *The Mind and Faith of Justice Holmes*, p. 5.

42 Holmes, *The Mind and Faith of Justice Holmes*, pp. 23–4.

43 John Steinbeck, *A Life in Letters*, ed. Elaine Steinbeck and Robert Wallstein (New York: Viking Press, 1975), p. 793.

44 Jorge Luis Borges, quoted in Philip French, *Westerns: Aspects of a Movie Genre* (London: Secker and Warburg, in association with the British Film Institute, 1973), p. 6.

45 Proudhon, *Selected Writings*, p. 264.

46 Albert Camus, quoted in Curtis Brown Watson, *Shakespeare and the Renaissance Concept of Honor* (Westport, Conn.: Greenwood, 1976 [1960]), p. 12.

Index

Index

Braddock, Edward, 202
Brady, James B. ("Diamond Jim"), 96
Brecht, Bertolt, 193
Bridge in the Jungle, The (Traven), 192
Brig, The (Brown), 183
Brissenden, Paul Frederick, 154
Brooks, E. S., 16
Brooks, John Graham, 149–50
Brooks, Preston, 6
Brown, John, 139
Brown, Kenneth H., 183
Bryce, Lord, 95, 96, 101, 113, 142, 160
Buchan, John, 29, 30
Buchanan, Daisy, 34, 48
Buchanan, Tom, 90, 98, 105
Bumppo, Natty, 33
Burden, Jack, 201
Burgess, John William, 91
Burke, Edmund, 151
Burroughs, Edgar Rice, 25
Bushido, 156
Butler, Benjamin F., 65
Butler, Rhett, 34, 199
Butler, Samuel, 45

Cabell, James Branch, 19, 35, 36
Caesar's Column (Donnelly), 156, 158, 258n–9n
Cagney, James, 125
Calderón de la Barca, Pedro, 200
Calhoun, John C., 7, 111
Cambridge University, 90
Camelot, 13, 29, 37, 38, 67, 123, 133, 198
Campbell, Roy, 46
Camus, Albert, 34, 232
Canby, Henry Seidel, 9–10, 11, 18, 20, 22, 78, 81, 87, 89, 90, 93–4, 103, 104, 107–8, 110, 113, 124, 203, 259n–60n
Canetti, Elias, 97
Canterbury Tales, The (Chaucer), 39
Canyon, Steve, 12
Capellanus, Andreas, 76
Captain Blood, 28
Carlyle, Thomas, 14, 168, 219
Carnegie, Andrew, 5–6, 11, 91–2, 95–102, 112, 113, 114, 115, 116–17, 123, 158, 166, 176, 179, 181, 210, 211, 258n–9n, 284n
Carraway, Nick, 48, 126, 201, 232
Carroll, Lewis, 44
Carruthers, William Alexander, 10, 235n
Carter, Nick, 27, 33, 137
Cary, Joyce, 125, 216
Cash, W. J., 30, 32, 43, 46, 78, 79, 130, 151, 153
Caskoden, Edwin, 46
Castiglione, Baldassare, 53
Castro, Fidel, 192, 193

Catcher in the Rye, The (Salinger), 199
Catch-22 (Heller), 34
Catholicism, Catholic Church, 63–4, 70, 134, 144, 147
Catlin, George, 62
Catton, Bruce, 167
Cavaliers of Virginia, The (Carruthers), 10
Caxton, William, 38, 54, 56, 68
Certain Rich Man, A (White), 115, 205, 206, 210–11, 213
Cervantes, Miguel de, 44, 46
Chamberlain, J. L., 66, 225
Chambers, Robert W., 20
Chambers, Whittaker, 201–2
Chandler, Raymond, 12, 33, 45, 266n
Chandos, Sir John, 56
Channing, William Ellery, 142
Chaplin, Charles, 12
Chaplin, Ralph, 139, 140, 149, 193
Charles, Nick, 12
Chaucer, Geoffrey, 44, 61, 73
Chavez, Cesar, 193
Cheevy, Miniver, 32–3
Chicago Exposition (1893), 145
China, 192–3
Chivalric Days: and the Boys and Girls who Helped to Make Them (Brooks), 9
Chivalry (Cabell), 19
Chou En-lai, 193
Chrétien de Troyes, 37, 38, 39, 55, 67, 73, 75, 76, 252n
Chronicles (Froissart), 7, 38, 52
Churchill, Winston, 9, 117, 127, 204, 205
CIA (Central Intelligence Agency), 29–30
Citizens' Alliance, 180
Civil War, U.S., 17, 19, 20, 26, 30, 32, 35, 42–4, 50, 51, 58, 64–6, 78, 80, 81, 82, 92, 94, 100, 103, 112, 113, 114, 125, 151, 192, 208, 210, 215–16, 217, 221, 225, 262n
Clausewitz, Karl von, 215
Clay, Henry, 111
Cleveland, Grover, 98, 118, 142–3
Cligés (Chrétien), 76
Coal Age, 176
Code of Bushido, The (Nitobe), 63
Cody, William (Buffalo Bill), 41
Cohan, George M., 28, 126
Cole, G. D. H., 186
Collier, Robert J., 125, 131
Collier's, 105, 119, 123, 125, 129, 130, 131, 136, 145, 173, 180, 207, 210
Colman, Ronald, 12
Commager, Henry Steele, 64, 94, 112, 151, 175, 178
Communism, Communists, 188, 191, 201, 281n
Communist Party of America, 190

Index

Index

Falstaff, Sir John, 200
Farewell to Arms, A (Hemingway), 33
Farrell, James T., 24
Fascism, 191
Faulkner, William, 33, 34, 45, 200, 269n
Finn, Huck, 6, 41, 49, 58, 60, 104, 126, 212
Fitzgerald, F. Scott, 15, 19, 33, 45, 64, 89, 90,
    104, 105, 107, 108, 124, 125, 143, 147,
    173, 204–5, 232
Fitzhugh, George, 7
Flynn, Elizabeth Gurley, 139, 149, 163, 164,
    165, 167, 169, 191, 272n–3n
Flynn, Errol, 12, 46
Foix, Count of, 56
Fool's Errand, A (Tourgée), 221
Footnote to Folly, A (Vorse), 156
Ford, John, 191–2
Ford, Paul Leicester, 113, 144, 145–6
Foreign Legion, 28, 173
For Whom the Bell Tolls (Hemingway), 137,
    192
Foss, Michael, 77
Foster, William Z., 149, 190, 197
Four Just Men, 28, 187
Franklin, Sidney, 17
Frank Merriwell at Yale (Patten), 214
Freeman, Joseph, 188, 190, 191, 227
French Revolution, 95, 158, 274n
Frick, Henry, 158, 210
Froissart, Jean, 7, 9, 38, 44, 52, 53–4, 54–5, 56,
    76
From Here to Eternity (Jones), 136, 141, 183
Fuller, J. F. C., 215, 216

Galahad (Erskine), 143
"Galahad" (Wilson), 44, 74, 143, 270n
Galahad, Sir, 4, 43, 44, 61, 71, 73, 138, 142,
    184, 270n
Galbraith, John Kenneth, 206
Gardner, Ava, 12
Garland, Hamlin, 16, 19, 263n
Gates, John W. ("Bet-a-Million"), 96
Gatsby, Jay, 34, 48, 87, 125, 126, 133, 232
Gawain, Sir, 42, 55, 61, 69–77, 134, 143
Geddes, Patrick, 145
General Line, The, 193
Georgics (Virgil), 92
Ghent, W. J., 11, 26, 28, 90, 159, 160
Gibson, Charles Dana, 11, 15, 24, 28, 88,
    108, 130, 210, 259n
Gildersleeve, Basil S., 10, 36, 61
Giovannitti, Arturo, 139–40
Glass Key, The (Hammett), 201
Godkin, E. L., 91, 98, 112, 114, 115, 130, 144
Gold, Michael, 34, 188, 190–1, 279n–8on
Gompers, Samuel, 149, 153, 173

Gone with the Wind (Mitchell), 32
Gordon, Caroline, 81
Gorgias (Plato), 197
Gornick, Vivian, 136, 201
Gould, Jay, 99, 107
Grail, Holy, 43, 44, 69, 71, 200–1
Grangerford, Colonel, 46, 49, 82, 152
Grant, Ulysses S., 42, 65, 82, 91–2, 95, 198,
    215, 216, 217–18, 286n–7n
Grapes of Wrath, The (Steinbeck), 190, 191;
    film, 192
Great Gatsby, The (Fitzgerald), 48, 98, 108
Greene, Theodore P., 23, 124, 128, 131, 204,
    205–6, 229
Green Knight, 69
Greenwich Village, 136–8, 148
Grey, Zane, 40
Greystoke, Lord (Tarzan), 12, 25
Griffith, D. W., 197
Grinnell, George Bird, 62, 275n
Grund, Francis J., 26, 80, 211, 214–15
Du Guesclin, Bertrand, 57
Guevara, Ernesto (Ché), 193
Guinevere, Queen, 59, 61, 69–77, 138, 199
Gunga Din, 28
Guthrie, Woodie, 140, 156, 190

Haggard, Sir Henry Rider, 24
Haiti massacre (1915), 184
"Hallelujah I'm a Bum" (Hill), 140
Hallie, Philip, 166
Hamilton, Donald, 41, 45
Hamlet (Shakespeare), 73
Hammer, Mike, 28
Hammersmith: His Harvard Days (Severance),
    87
Hammett, Dashiell, 12, 28, 33, 45, 87–8, 141,
    191, 266n, 285n
Handlin, Oscar, 21, 33, 103, 133–4, 146, 147,
    149, 209
Hanna, Mark, 98, 100, 113, 115–16, 206
Hannay, Richard, 30
Hapgood, Hutchins, 165, 166, 169, 185, 186,
    187, 215
Hapgood, Norman, 119, 131–2
Hard, William, 159–60
Hardy, Oliver, 12, 68
Harlan County, U.S.A., 190
Harper's Magazine, 10, 100, 130
Harriman, Edward H., 120
Harvard University, 20, 107, 131, 132, 138
Haskell, Thomas L., 202
Hawkwoode, Sir John, 56
Hawthorne, Nathaniel, 9, 34, 48, 222
Hayden, Tom, 135
Haymarket Square riot (1886), 158, 180

Index

Haywood, William D. (Big Bill), 139, 140, 149, 157, 163, 165, 167, 173, 175, 180–1, 182, 193, 215, 268n, 272n
Hearst, William Randolph, 44, 131, 229
Heller, Joseph, 34
Hellman, Lillian, 200
Hemingway, Ernest, 12, 17, 20, 28, 32, 33, 41, 45, 48, 83, 137, 180, 201, 252n
Henry, Patrick, 139
Henry V, King of England, 9, 56
Hentoff, Nat, 132
Henty, G. A., 137
Hepburn, Katharine, 12
Herrick, Robert, 129, 160
Hickok, James Butler (Wild Bill), 64
Higginson, Thomas Wentworth, 19, 152, 262n
High Noon, 41
Hightower, Gail, 33
Hill, James J., 116
Hill, Joe, 139–40
Hiroshima, Japan, 184
Hiss, Alger, 201
History of Chivalry (Mills), 16
History of the Great American Fortunes (Myers), 162, 197, 210
History of the Kings of Britain (Geoffrey of Monmouth), 37
Hitler, Adolf, 30–1
H. M. Pulham, Esquire (Marquand), 44
Hofstadter, Richard, 88, 91, 123
Holmes, Oliver Wendell, 24, 45, 91, 113, 123, 203, 215, 219–20, 224, 226–7, 229, 230, 231, 262n
Homer, 20
Homer, Winslow, 92
Homestead strike (1892), 157, 210, 277n–8n
Homo Ludens (Huizinga), 67
Honourable Peter Stirling, The (Ford), 113
Hope, Anthony, 131
House, Edward, 181
Howe, Frederic C., 93, 98, 100, 115–16, 118, 126, 127, 128, 130, 142, 145, 161, 206, 207
Howe, Irving, 137
Howell, William Dean, 99, 117
Huckleberry Finn (Twain), 4, 8, 46–7, 48, 49, 58, 64, 94, 212, 213, 268n
Hudson River school of painting, 92
Huizinga, Johan, 43, 44, 54, 58, 60, 63, 67, 76, 77, 181, 188, 189, 198–9, 203, 214, 223, 224–5, 227–8
Humphrey, Hubert H., 134
Hundley, D. R., 82
Hundred Years' War, 39, 42, 53, 57
Hungerford, James, 10
Huston, John, 72, 192

Idylls of the King (Tennyson), 9, 43
I. F. Stone's Weekly, 132
Indian Boyhood (Eastman), 62
Indians, 62, 100, 109, 166, 167, 184, 186, 249n, 254n–5n, 275n
In Dubious Battle (Steinbeck), 190, 191
Industrial Worker, 140
Informer, The, 191–2
Ingersoll, Ralph, 132
Insurgent Mexico (Reed), 170
Irish Americans, 124–7
Irving, Washington, 9, 36, 65
Israel, 192
Ivanhoe, 56, 106, 238n–9n
Ivanhoe (Scott), 7, 36, 40, 80, 95, 234n
Ivy League, 89–91, 201
IWW (Industrial Workers of the World): *see* Wobblies

Jackson, Andrew, 22, 119, 120, 211, 214
Jackson, Stonewall, 82, 215, 216, 217
James, G. P. R., 7, 10, 152, 234n–5n
James, Henry, 25, 45
James, William, 24, 33, 45, 74, 108, 159, 172–3, 174, 175, 186, 215, 219–20, 226, 230
Japan, 31, 63, 77, 288n
Jefferson, Thomas, 151, 217
Jenkins, Micah, 23
Joan of Arc, 38, 70
Joe Hill, 41
John Brown's Body (Benét), 3
Johnes, Thomas, 7
Johns Hopkins University, 142
Johnson, Diane, 43
Johnson, Lyndon B., 29, 135
Johnson, Owen, 11, 15, 23–4, 88, 89, 90, 95, 102–3, 105, 110–11, 117, 141, 208, 211, 260n
Johnson, Tom, 128–9
Johnson County war, 41, 168
Johnston, Joseph E., 65
Joinville, Jean de, 7, 56–7
Jones, James, 136, 141, 183
Jones, Mother, 139, 166–7, 205, 210
Jones, R. P., 23
Jones, Samuel M. ("Golden Rule"), 206–7
Jordan, Robert, 137
Josephson, Matthew, 132
Jouvenel, Betrand de, 77
Jungle, The (Sinclair), 178, 261n
Jungle Books (Kipling), 25

Kael, Pauline, 29
Kay, Sir, 40, 71, 73
Kaye, Danny, 12

Index

Index

Mailles, Jacques de, 39, 57
Malory, Thomas, 9, 15, 36, 37, 53, 61, 67–8, 75, 77, 138, 191, 203
Maltese Falcon, 192
Man and Superman (Shaw), 218
Mann, Thomas, 160, 224
Manny, Sir Walter, 56, 69
Mao Tse-tung, 192, 193
Marching Men (Anderson), 110
Marie de France, 75, 252n
Mark, King of Cornwall, 71
Marlowe, Philip, 12, 266n
Marquand, John P., 11, 20, 23, 27, 30, 44, 120, 176
Marryat, Frederick, 65
Marshall, Charles, 48
Marshall, William, 39
Martin, Frederick Townsend, 157
Masses, 136–8, 140, 141, 153, 156–7, 162–3, 170–1, 173, 174, 175, 187, 188, 189, 201, 211, 276n–7n, 279n–81n
May, Henry F., 186
May, Rollo, 30, 290n
Melville, Herman, 34, 48, 95, 232
Mencken, H. L., 10–11, 24, 34, 45, 58, 76, 99, 123, 130, 137, 158, 268n
Merlin, 3
Merlin (Robinson), 45
Merriwell, Frank, 11, 27, 33, 42, 89, 106, 119–20, 125, 137, 212, 214
Mexican Revolution, 169–70, 188
Mexican War, 22
Mexico, Mexicans, 167, 169–70, 181, 191, 192
Middle Ages, 7, 36–40, 55, 59, 77, 176, 203, 223
Mills, Charles, 7, 16, 35, 36–7, 66, 70, 74–5, 169, 235n
Mills, C. Wright, 26–7, 103
Milner, Lord, 29
Mind of the South, The (Cash), 46
Minor, Robert, 193
Mitchell, Margaret, 32, 34, 199
Mitford, Jessica, 183
Mix, Tom, 33
Modern Chivalry (Brackenridge), 227
Molly Maguires, 153, 156, 163
Monmouth, Geoffrey of, 37, 67, 238n–9n, 243n–4n
Monsieur Beaucaire (Tarkington), 10, 15
"Moral Equivalent of War, The" (James), 159, 172
Mordaunt, Thomas Osbert, 16–17
More, Sir Thomas, 100
Morgan, J. Pierpont, 23, 98, 99, 115–16, 117, 119, 120, 123, 128, 205, 211
Morison, Samuel Eliot, 94, 112, 151, 175, 178

Morris, William, 14, 68
Morte d'Arthur, Le (Malory), 15, 38, 67–8
Mosby, John S., 64, 212, 217
Moses, Robert, 145
Motley, John Lothrop, 113, 168
Mowry, George F., 179
Mr. Crewe's Career (Churchill), 117–18, 127, 130, 204, 205
Mugwumps, 114–15, 119–20, 144, 146
Mumford, Lewis, 70–1
Munsey's, 27, 102
Mussolini, Benito, 30, 31
Myers, Gustavus, 162, 197, 210, 275n

Nader, Ralph, 132
Napoleon, 23, 30, 94–6, 129, 215–16
Nast, Thomas B., 130
Nation, 31, 91, 114, 132, 157, 177, 277n–8n
National Geographic, 147
Nesbit, E., 213
Newbolt, Sir Henry, 23, 41
New Deal, 134
New England, 142, 164
Newfield, Jack, 132, 134–5
New Frontier, 29
Newman, Cardinal John H., 52
New Masses, 28
New Republic, 132, 147, 186, 205
Newsweek, 20, 126
New York Times, 34, 130
Nietzsche, Friedrich, 24, 31, 62, 76, 137, 211
Nihilism, Nihilists, 138, 188
Nisbet, Robert E., 277n, 280n–1n
Nitobe, Inazo, 63, 77, 82, 156
Nixon, Richard M., 135
Normans, 7, 34, 234n–5n
Norris, Frank, 117
Novak, Michael, 143–4, 153, 173, 202

O'Connor, Flannery, 81
Odyssey (Homer), 77
Ojibway Indians, 62
O'Keefe, Chevalier, 124
Old Dominion, The (James), 10
Old Indian Days (Eastman), 62
Old Plantation, The (Hungerford), 10
Olmsted, Frederick Law, 35, 41, 49
Once and Future King, The (White), 37
O'Neill, Bucky, 50–1, 122
On Germany (Tacitus), 61
On Heroes, Hero-Worship, and the Heroic in History (Carlyle), 219
On War (Clausewitz), 215
Orders of Chivalry, The (Lull), 61
Oregon Trail, The (Parkman), 67
Orphans of the Storm, 197
Orwell, George, 34, 232

297

Index

Index

Index

Index

Wilson, Edmund, 44, 74, 132, 143, 217

Wilson, Woodrow, 113, 136, 140, 142, 143, 147, 170, 173, 174, 181, 183, 189, 193, 198, 280n–1n

Wingate, Mary Lou, 81

Winning of the West, The (Roosevelt), 62

Winters, Yvor, 288n–9n

Winterset, Duke of, 15

Wister, Owen, 12, 20, 25, 33, 35, 40, 41, 62, 82, 120, 121, 123

Wobblies (Industrial Workers of the World), 136, 139–41, 148–50, 153, 154, 159–62, 163–5, 168, 170–1, 173–5, 179, 180, 186–91, 193, 198, 199, 201, 267n, 279n, 281n

Wolfe, Tom, 28

Wolff, Leon, 219

World Set Free, The (Wells), 219

World War I, 29, 30, 41, 158, 173, 174, 183, 187, 189, 190

World War II, 28, 31

Wright, Louis B., 52, 63

Yale University, 33, 89, 92, 104, 106, 107, 132, 259n–6on

Yeats, William Butler, 34, 137, 232

YMCA (Young Men's Christian Association), 64, 147, 154

Young, Art, 10, 138, 157, 163, 175

"Young Goodman Brown" (Hawthorne), 34

Zapata, Emiliano, 198

Zorro, 12